Converging Alternatives

SUNY series in Israeli Studies

Russell Stone, editor

Converging Alternatives

*The Bund and the Zionist
Labor Movement, 1897–1985*

Yosef Gorny

State University of New York Press

Published by
State University of New York Press, Albany

© 2006 State University of New York

For information, address State University of New York Press,
194 Washington Avenue, Suite 305, Albany, NY 12210-2384

Production by Judith Block
Marketing by Michael Campochiaro

Library of Congress Cataloging-in-Publication Data

Gorny, Yosef.
    Converging alternatives : the Bund and the Zionist Labor Movement,
1897–1985 / Yosef Gorny.
            p. cm. — (SUNY series in Israeli studies)
    Includes bibliographical references and index.
    ISBN 0-7914-6659-0 (hardcover : alk. paper) —ISBN 0-7914-6660-4
(pbk. : alk. paper)
    1. Allgemeyner Idisher arbayòterbund in Liòta, Poylen un Rusland.   2. Labor
Zionism—Europe, Eastern—History.   3. Jews—Europe, Eastern—Politics and
government—20th century.   4. Jewish socialists—Europe, Eastern—History.
I. Title. II. Series.
    HD6305.J3G67 2005
    331.6'3924004—dc22
    ISBN-13 978-0-7914-6659-9 (hardcover : alk. paper)
    ISBN-13 978-0-7914-6660-5 (pbk. : alk.paper)
                                                        2005007684

10 9 8 7 6 5 4 3 2 1

To Geulah, my wife and companion,
the one without alternative.

Our movement in Palestine is a revolt movement. Jewish history has known many revolt movements. If we consider only the past century—the Jewish Enlightenment. . . . There was a second revolt movement, Hibbat Tsiyyon. There was a third revolt movement, the world Jewish labor movement, the Bund, which rebelled against the downtroddenness of the Jews, their fear of the gentiles, the depressed state of the Jewish artisan and worker, who was the first to hoist the banner of war for equal rights and organization of the worker and the collective, and active war to organize Jews' lives. There was one more large revolt movement, political Zionism. . . . However, no revolt movement was as profound as the revolt movement that the Jewish worker in Palestine set in motion. All the aforementioned revolts took place, more or less, in the public cognitive field only, in the field of public life; they had no bearing on personal life and on the foundations of people's lives. Now a new movement has come into being in Jewish history, the revolt of the Hebrew worker, who rebels not only against Exile, but also against the Zionism and Socialism that were prevalent in the Jewish street, and has raised the banner of change of the most fundamental values in personal life, in being.

—David Ben-Gurion, "Breaching the Siege,"
(lecture at the Socialist Youth Council,
1928, Tel Aviv), *Mishmarot*, Tel Aviv:
1935.

CONTENTS

PREFACE

The time: May 1, 1999.
The place: Park Avenue, New York, aglitter with the profusion of
lights that denote a thriving capitalist market economy.
The building: a community center of the Central Reform synagogue.
The congregation: about two hundred veterans of the Bund and some fifty
impassioned young people who consider themselves the successors of the
veterans' heritage.

On the *bima* is a Bundist who survived the Holocaust, amassed wealth, and became an important philanthropist. He speaks in spicy Yiddish about the all-embracing Jewish universalistic mission of the Bund. In the background, a choir warbles melodies of personalities from the past who believed wholeheartedly in the Jewish socialist revolution. The melodies bring sad memories over the creased faces of many of the participants, but here and there one observes a smile of satisfaction for the role that they played in a world that once had a meaning that surpassed them.

Amidst the singing, a sudden thought crosses my mind: these melodies also belong to another movement, a different one, one that prosecuted a severe dispute with the Bund, and one that met a different historical fate—the Zionist Labor Movement in Eretz Israel (Palestine). Although the lyrics are different, the musical tones were a vehicle for modern Jewry's most powerful yearnings to change the situation and the national and social status of the Jewish people. This movement, which spearheaded the effort to create an alternative Jewish society to that in eastern Europe—the society in which the Bund was so active and in whose existence it so believed—has also expired. It stepped off the historical stage not because of the disaster that befell the Jewish people but for a much different reason: it headed the struggle that led the Jewish people to the greatest national political accomplishment since the exile began, the establishment of a Jewish state. Just the same, the funeral bells toll for the Zionist Labor Movement, too.

Nevertheless, the melancholy at that occasion carried a special symbolism. What a paradoxical occasion it was: Bundist May Day rally held at a bastion of capitalist wealth and in a synagogue, albeit a Reform one. After all, among all the modern Jewish movements, religious and secular, that were tragically pummeled by anti-Semitism and the Holocaust, the Bund was the most tragic. Agudath Israel, as a modern Orthodox movement, lost millions of believers but managed to rebuild itself as a dynamic Orthodoxy in the West and in Israel. The new heterodox religious movements—the Reform and the Conservative—whose belief in progress and liberalism was buffeted by murderous anti-Semitism, established a new religious culture in the West. Zionism, which was unable to save even a part of the European Jewish masses, established a Jewish state, where a new national society is developing in lieu of the eastern European one, which has become extinct. Unlike them all, the Bund was left with no achievements save historical memory. The sorrowful occasion in New York demonstrated this symbolically. However, there was also something encouraging about it: that group of several dozen enthusiastic young people, including the grandchildren of several famous personalities in the Polish and the American Bund, who believe in the resurrection of Yiddish culture. Thus, like their intellectual forebears, they again clutch the coattails of Jewish Utopianism, but with one fundamental difference. Their predecessors were an elite that addressed its message to a people living in its culture. They, in contrast, are an elite attempting to create a culture on behalf of a people whose collective existence is increasingly dubious. Nevertheless, both in spite and because of their Utopianism, these very people are the successors to the Jewish rebels in the modern era, those who stood up to fight against all odds, those vanguards of national resurrection in the Diaspora and the national enterprise in Eretz Israel. It is to these few scattered grandchildren, in Israel and the Diaspora, that this book is dedicated.

ACKNOWLEDGMENTS

Creating this book was not a single-handed effort; institutions and friends have a part in it. That is the reason I am grateful, first of all, to the following institutions: Tel Aviv University, which enabled me to devote a sabbatical year for this research; YIVO archives in New York, and its efficient staff; New York University and especially to Professor David Engel, for his services as a visiting professor; the Medem Library in Paris and its staff for their helpful assistance; the Labor Movement Archive in Beit Berl for their kind help; The Abraham and Edita Spiegel Chair for the financial support; and State University of New York Press and its editors for their accurate and patient editing work.

Personally, I owe thanks to my friend, Zvi Zameret, for his good advice, to Naftali Greenwood for his excellent translations, and to Leo Greenbaum of the YIVO Institute and Rabbi Jerry Schwartzbard from the Jewish Theological Seminary for their friendly assistance.

To all of the organizations and individuals mentioned, I express my deepest gratitude.

INTRODUCTION

The Bund Party and the Zionist Labor Movement were two different—
clashing and rival—versions of the idea of Jewish national revival in modern society. This study does not aim to examine the history of each version
on its own merits; a series of important researchers have already done this
in comprehensive studies. Its purpose is to contrast the two in regard to a
main point in their national perspective: the attitude toward the Jewish nation at large or, as to use the term conventionally used in the public political
debate of the time, *Klal Yisrael*.

The term Klal Yisrael is the modern political twin of an ancient concept in Jewish tradition, *'Am Yisrael* (the Jewish people). It is used in the
public discourse to furnish 'Am Yisrael, an entity that threatens to disintegrate or fragment in modern society, with a conceptual political framework.
In view of the widening rift between religious and nonreligious Jews, the
growing chasm between Jews immersed in different national cultures
among themselves and between themselves and the masses who maintain
the particularistic Jewish culture, and the rise in discord among different
worldviews in Jewish public life—the concept of Klal Yisrael is invoked to
strengthen national commonality in two respects. One is the principled
claim that, despite manifestations of difference and fragmentation in culture, civil status, religious faith, and so forth, the Jews are one nation or
people. Second, in practical political terms, it attempts to unite all ideological streams and affiliations under one umbrella for struggle to secure or
protect the civil rights of Jews in their countries of dispersion. Therefore,
the concept has become a cornerstone and a symbolic marker not only in
the overall national creed, but also a slogan for political action of various
organizations at the national and international levels.

Neither movement subjected the very concept of Klal Yisrael, with all
its historical meanings in the conceptual and political senses, to systematic
debate. However, the concept lurked in the background of their public

thought as changes in time and place caused to acquire and shed intellectual and political form. Thus, one may attribute to the Bund, upon its inception in Russia, the concept of the "proletarian Klal," even though the Bund itself did not coin this ideological phrase, which served as an alternative to the Klal Yisrael concept, which, in their opinion, was blatantly bourgeois. Later on, in interwar Poland, the Bund actually adopted a populist view of Klal Yisrael, that is, the impoverished Jewish masses, and thence to all of Jewry, foremost eastern European Jewry, which suffered from the ravages of anti-Semitism. Finally, after the Holocaust, the Bund came around to the doctrine of a "world Klal Yisrael" as the bearer of Yiddish culture.

The Zionist Labor Movement made similar transitions at the same periods in time: from the "halutsic (pioneering) Klal," which engaged in actualization on behalf of the national Klal, to the "popular Zionist Klal" in the 1930s, and thence, after the attainment of statehood, to the "world Jewish Klal" affiliated with the State of Israel.

In both movements, the concept underwent a process of contraction-to-expansion change in its view of the national scope. In both, the Klal shifted from proletarian-halutsic to pan-Jewish, albeit, of course, in different magnitudes, contents, and times.

This comparative study sets out from the premise that the Klal Yisrael perception, in its principled and political senses, was not simple in either movement and contained substantive internal contradictions. This is because the revolutionary class avant-garde beliefs of the Bund, and the halutsic fulfillment perspectives of the Labor Movement inevitably created a buffer between the movements and the Klal Yisrael, the Jewish people at large. The Bund erected the buffer by viewing class differentiation and struggle as the last word in all affairs; the Labor Movement did so through its all-inclusive "negation of the Diaspora." This ostensible paradox seemingly points to an ideational proximity or symbolic similarity amidst bitter and uncompromising political debate. This matter deserves special attention. The basis for our comparison of the two movements is not confined to the problem discussed thus far; it had much broader conceptual, historical, and cultural meaning.

In the first of these senses—the conceptual—the study takes up two worldviews that sensed the crucial historical role of the working class not only in the social domain, but also in the national sphere as well. Due to the peculiar conditions of Jewish existence, this role set both movements apart, in several senses, from the general Socialist labor movements in Europe. Therefore, there was a large degree of misunderstanding, disagreement, and even severe conceptual and political collision between the general movements and the leaderships of these parties with respect to the national definition of the

Jewish working class. Of concern here was not only the famous dispute between the Bund and the Russian Socialist Democratic Party under Lenin and Georgy Valentinovich Plekhanov concerning the Bund's entitlement to autonomous status, but also disagreement with most Social Democratic leaders at the anti-communist organization of Labor parties' (1919–1939) Second International, to which both movements belonged. The Zionist Labor Movement also followed a serpentine course in its relations with social democratic parties, especially the British Labour Party in regard to Jewish national rights in Palestine.[1]

In the second sense—the historical one—the two movements made several parallel stops on their path of development and amassing of political power. In 1901–1906, as the Bund fashioned its national platform and struggled with Russian Social Democrats to assert it, and as the Bund appeared in the Jewish street as an active, organized entity in self defense, the Second Aliya (1904–1914), eventually a landmark in the development of the Zionist movement, began to create the Labor movement in Palestine.

After World War I, in 1920, the dispute between the Polish Bund and the Comintern concerning the conditions for joining the latter was resolved. The Bund rejected the famous twenty-one conditions that added up to the gradual liquidation of the Bund as a Socialist Party representing the Jewish proletariat. The 21 points were the unconditional demands in order to join the Comintern. The majority of the Bund leaders could not, categorically, accept two major demands: to rename itself as a communist party, and to expel all the non-communist (right-wing) members, especially among its leaders. After a caustic internal debate, the Bund set out on its own Socialist-Marxist-nationalist path. Concurrently, the Histadrut, the General Federation of Jewish Labor in Palestine, was established as a national Jewish organization that would become the political power base of the working class in the Yishuv, the organized Jewish community in Palestine.

In the 1930s, and especially in the second half of that decade, the Bund, by virtue of its organization and its radical politics in struggle against anti-Semitism, became the party that won the greatest proportional popular support in municipal and *kehilla* (Jewish community administration) elections in large and medium Polish cities. Concurrently, the Zionist Labor Movement, owing to its organizational prowess and halutsic Zionist activism, became the leading political player in the Zionist movement. As the Bund spearheaded the struggle against anti-Semitic Polish nationalism, the Zionist Labor Movement spearheaded the Jews' national struggle with the Arabs for Palestine.

Comparison of the respective movements' political strength at this time points to several similarities in electoral achievements and political organization under the twin umbrellas of party and trade unions. In the

1939 municipal elections in Poland, the Bund attained a prodigious 38 percent of the vote on a countrywide average. The Zionist candidate lists, in contrast, combined to attract 36 percent of voters and Agudath Israel and others received 26 percent.[2] The same year, in elections for the *Asefat ha-Nivharim* (Assembly of Representatives) in Palestine, the Labor Palestine list received 42 percent of votes cast and the XXI Zionist Congress 44 percent.[3] Another similarity is in the number of "hard core" party members. In Poland, the Bund had about seven thousand dues-paying members. On the eve of the war, the party's political successes caused this population to swell to twenty thousand. At the time, there were seven thousand to eight thousand persons in training programs for emigration to Palestine in Poland. Even though the Zionist Movement was engulfed in crisis in the late 1930s, He-Haluts still had fifty thousand registered members.[4] In Palestine in the early 1940s, Mapai had some twenty thousand members, as did the Bund in Poland.[5]

The Bund's political power base was the constellation of trade unions that it controlled, whereas that of the Zionist Labor Movement was Federation of Jewish Labor in Palestine (the Histadrut). On the eve of World War II in Poland, about ninety thousand workers and artisans belonged to Jewish trade unions; about half of them were members of unions headed by the Bund. In Palestine, the Histadrut had amassed a membership of one hundred twenty thousand by that time.

These figures demonstrate beyond doubt that at times of national distress and political uncertainty, better-organized groups that can demonstrate to the public resolve in pursuing their ideological and political line and that can implement it in various ways have an advantage. The political ascendancy of the Bund in Poland and the Zionist Labor Movement in Palestine proves it.

After World War II and the disaster of the Holocaust, the Bund followed its historical rivals' lead and, at the Brussels convention in 1947, established a world coordinating organization for Bund parties, similar to the "World Alliance" that the Po'aley Tsiyyon parties had created forty years earlier. By that time, however, the Bund had already undergone its postmortem and Po'aley Tsiyyon had begun to die off. In the cultural sense, these were two eastern European phenomena that had a "Polu-intelligentsia" leadership—to adopt Jonathan Frankel's expression[6]—infused with the spirit of ethical collectivism and powered by fierce revolutionary drives that had been typical of the "Russian intelligentsia" since the middle of the nineteenth century.[7]

The shared ethos of the two rival groups, the Bund and the Zionist Labor Movement, was manifested in the willingness of the individual to sacrifice him/herself for the collective, in revolutionary underground halut-sism or self-actualization through labor in Palestine, and in personal valor. Therefore, the role played by Hirsch Lekert in the Bund mythology was played by Yosef Trumpeldor in the Zionist Labor Movement mythology. Members of both groups cherished the national honor of the Jewish masses. From this standpoint, both were extreme "negators of exile" at the level of ethical values—one liquidating the Diaspora by leaving it, the other liqui-dating it by staying there, or, in the telling expression of the post-Holocaust Bund leader, Emanuel Szerer, "to live in exile without the exile soul."[8] As a consequence of this sense of rebelliousness, they condemned the Jewish policy of *shtadlanut* (securing of Jewish interests by interceding with Gen-tile authorities) and advocated assertive national activism in politics and self-defense. Both movements aimed to transform Jewish "dust-man" into a normal nation (*der tseshtoybter yidisher statsie makhn a yidishe natsie*), to adopt the expression of the Bundist author Y. Y. Trunk. Both movements sanctified remembrance of the Warsaw ghetto uprising, which, to them, was not only a valorous war against the Germans, but also a manifestation of the straightening of the Jewish spine against the national condition of "dust-men." Therefore, they described the uprising with the same symbols and in the same style. Both organizations also shared a myth of founding fathers—the "Vilna Dynasty" of the Bund, as they defined it, and Second Aliya for the Zionist Labor Movement.

Both movements' "negation of the Diaspora" stemmed not only from real economic, social, and political factors, but also from Utopian tendencies that were an inseparable part of their leaders' personalities. The leaders' Utopianism was manifested above all in belief in the possibility of funda-mental social change in the Jews' political stature and ways of life, a change that would eliminate most hardships that enveloped the individual Jew. The respective paths to a solution were the establishment of a Socialist society or the construction of a national society on Socialist foundations in Palestine. This Utopianism, however imaginative, was not the product of the leaders' in-tellects. Instead, it acquired its logic and derived its strength from reality. After all, "negation of the Diaspora" in the present was also a revolution on behalf of a different future, in which the hardships and contradictions of the present would be absent. Before going any further, however, we should dis-tinguish between two types of Utopian inclinations—"realistic Utopianism" and "Utopian realism." The former emphasizes Utopia, the latter realism. The former concept, paradoxically, is Marxist. It stems from the consciousness, which evolved into an article of faith, that objective social development would bring the perfect, contradiction-free society into being. In the latter concept, in contrast, the emphasis is on realism, and Utopia serves as an auxiliary device only—a device that guides and corrects, but does not determine, the actions of the movement. Thus, the Bundists spent over fifty years, from the establishment of the party to the Holocaust, as "dogmatic optimists," whereas the leaders of the Zionist Labor Movement were "pragmatic optimists." As such, their judgment was flexible enough to allow them to tailor their attitudes to changing historical conditions without losing sight of their goal.

The Bund also had a Utopian trait that the other Socialist movements lacked. It was manifested in the cycle of self-imposed withdrawal—"isolation" or "separatism" (as contemporaries called it)—in which the Bund immersed itself. This cycle was delimited by the absolutist ideological principles in which Bundists believed. Thus, in the name of "proletarian democracy" the Bund clashed with the Communist Party and severely criticized the Bolshevik regime in the Soviet Union. In pursuit of its aim to establish a "social national autonomy," it worked itself into a rupture with the Russian Social Democratic party before World War I and tumbled into strange relations with the Polish PPS in the interwar period. The Bund's radical Marxist outlook left it isolated at the Second International. By upholding its class and secular viewpoint consistently, it chose to be isolated among the Jews. To keep its antinationalist doctrine unsullied, it ruled out any cooperation with Zionism. In all these respects, the Bund placed itself in a state of "Utopian disengagement"—somewhat akin to Tommaso Campanella's "city of the sun," surrounded by walls, the Utopia island in Thomas More's book of that name, or even, paradoxically, religious communes in the United States. Even assuming that this "separatism" must have had political and even personal motives, the Bund flew the flag of belligerent isolation. And we know how flags have influenced the course of history.

The Zionist Labor Movement, in contrast to the Bund, established a base for the entire Jewish people in Palestine. Thus, despite its elitist particularism, this movement did not ensnare itself in isolation. On the contrary: it positioned itself at the forefront of the broadest Jewish organization in existence, the Zionist movement.

Both movements also had the pretension of bearing a unique idea in the international labor movement, as members of the Second International between the world wars. The Zionists in Palestine advocated constructive Socialism as the ideal Socialist model; the Bund depicted national multiculturalism as a material part of the future Socialist society. In this respect, practically speaking, they presented the international labor movement with two Jewish approaches that maintained the particularistic Jewish national identity and disagreed about the ideal national vision.

* * *

The discussion of the Klal Yisrael issue in this book spans three periods in the history of the Bund and the Zionist Labor Movement. The first runs from the beginning of the twentieth century until the end of World War I and the Bolshevik Revolution, on the one hand, and the Balfour Declaration, on the other hand. The second period extends from the early 1920s to the beginning of World War II in 1939. Finally, the era following the war, the Holocaust, and the establishment of the State of Israel, up to the 1980s is discussed.

There is a substantive difference between the first two periods in the political and state realities in which the movements were immersed. The Russian Bund was an underground organization during the Tsarist era—with all the implications of this status for its political culture—that quickly "self-liquidated" under the new Soviet regime. In contrast, the Polish Bund operated as a legal party within the framework of the formal democratic regime of the Polish republic. The political freedom deprived the Bund leaders in Poland of the romantic halo that had ringed the heads of the underground Bund leaders in Russia. Notably, these personalities, notwithstanding the legend that has grown up around them—men such as Arkady Kremer, Vladimir Kossovski, Noah Portnoy, and Beinish Mikhalevich—and despite the great respect that the Polish Bund accorded to them, did not, for various reasons, attain leading positions in the Polish party. Therefore, they either retired from politics, like Kremer, or became pundits and honorary presidents of the party.

Similarly, the Zionist Labor Movement, like all Zionist movement institutions, operated semi-legally during the Second Aliya, in the Ottoman era. In contrast, in the second period, after the Balfour Declaration, it became a recognized part of the Zionist Movement and had a status given it by international institutions. Although it also had an underground dimension—the Hagana—that entity existed with the British authorities' tacit consent. In other words, both movements operated concurrently within the formal framework of a democratic regime. However, there was one basic internal difference: Second Aliya people such as Berl Katznelson, David Ben-Gurion, Yitzhak Tabenkin, and Yosef Sprinzak were not crowded out of the leadership by their Third Aliya successors. On the contrary: these "mythological" personalities, unlike those of the Bund, became the movement leaders.

Political and national imbalance, fated by historical developments, stood in the last phase of both movements' history. The Bund survived with its idea intact but without status and without Jewish masses in eastern Europe. The Zionist Labor Movement, in contrast, stood at the helm of a Jewish nation-state that came into being largely to its credit and that, in its policy during the mass immigration era, fulfilled the principle of Klal Yisrael at the sovereign level. The Bund's only recourse was to vacillate in its attitude toward the Zionist Movement and exit the stage of history. Was the decline of the Bund also related to vagueness in the party's attitude toward Klal Yisrael? That is the question that this study will attempt to answer.

This problem leads to another question, occasioned by the adjectives affixed to the two movements' names. The concepts of "Russian Bund" and "Polish Bund," like that of the "Zionist Labor Movement in Palestine," are not mere geographical definitions; they are also concepts that have value and cultural content. From the standpoint of each, the location was foremost a homeland, not a place of residence. The question is to what extent each movement's homeland ethos dictated the course of its history, especially in respect to the last two mentioned—the "Polish Bund" and the "Zionist Labor Movement." After all, it was each movement's polar "negation of the Diaspora" that guided its attitude toward the location, influenced its political efforts and aspirations, and affected its organizational and constructive actions—which, in turn, ultimately determined its historical fate.

As stated above, this study is unique relative to its predecessors because it focuses on one dimension, the national outlook of the Bund and the Zionist Labor Movement—the perception of Klal Yisrael—as construed in view of historical changes during the eighty years since the Bund phrased its national program and from the onset of the Second Aliya to the consolidation of the State of Israel and the 1980s.

The Klal Yisrael concept, in the context of concern in this study, brings several questions to the fore. The first pertains to its limits. In other words, how severely did the Labor Movement ideology downscale the concept to a "Zionist Klal" and how severely did the Bund ideology confine it to a "proletarian Klal?" The second question, flowing from the first, is whether each movement's attitude toward the Jewish Klal was a matter of a grand principle or of practical politics. This leads to the third question: did the proletarian culture of the Bund, on the one hand, and the halutsic culture of the Zionist Labor Movement on the other hand, not trap the movements in a cycle of isolation or value separatism that limited their political sphere of influence? Did this sphere remain constant and intact, or did historical changes over the years breach it? The fourth question pertains to the synthesis that each movement created—of *nationalism* and Socialism in one case, of *Socialism* and *nationalism* in the other—and the focal issue, the weight of the national interest in this synthesis. In other words, may the national principle have defeated the class interest in both cases?

These questions lend this book its name, *Converging Alternatives*. In both movements—their consciousness, their reality, and their collective class experience, imbued with historical mission—one may discern both trends without noticing any clear distinction between them in essence and in time. The trend "from class to people," as Ben-Gurion expressed it in the past, was political in nature: it aimed to attract petty bourgeoisie elements. The Bund evinced a similar tendency at the very same time. However, the trend "from people to class" reflected the socio-ideological aim of molding the Jewish masses into the form of a class, be it a revolutionary-halutsic class that would build a new Jewish society in Palestine or a proletarian revolutionary class that would struggle for the social and national emancipation of the Jews in their countries of residence. Both tendencies had the coercive elements that typify all elite groups that wish to make sacrifices *on behalf* of the people but not *with* the people. The strength of these groups, in fact, was manifested in the distance they created between themselves and the masses and in the formation of a quasi–monastic isolation around themselves. This paradigm was typical of the underground Russian Bund, the hard core of party members in Poland, and even the rump community of post-Holocaust Bundists. The same may be said about the halutsic youth movements, collective settlement, and the Palmah in Palestine.

Although the values and concepts of the second trend, "from class to people," were identical to those of the first, this trend, as stated, sought to reform society amidst rapprochement with the masses and to avail itself of the masses for the attainment of its social and national goals. Both the Bund and the Zionist Labor Movement transformed this intention into a course of political action in the early 1930s, and both trends interrelated meaningfully with the ideology and politics of Klal Yisrael. How far did the two movements advance along the path that led them from the "from people to class" trend to that of "from class to people?" This question may be rephrased: at what point did one movement stop, and toward what destination did the other continue to advance? This is the main question of concern in this study. In the Bund's ninety year history (1897–1985), the focal point of debate on the nationalism issue shifted from circle to circle, and each circle was distinct in the nature of the historical juncture in its history. The first circle belongs to the Russian era, the second to the Polish era, and the third to the American era. The debate was primarily *ideological* in the first of these periods, *political* in the second, and *intellectual* in the third. At the first period, Bundists spoke on behalf of a class that had national attributes. In the second, the impoverished Jewish masses were added. In the third, the party spoke for the few

surviving Jews who still adhered to the Yiddish culture. In view of this
historical development, the question is whether the Bund's rapprochement
with the Jewish people was prompted by exogenous events only, such as
the upturn in anti-Semitism in Russia, political changes in Poland, and, finally, the Holocaust, or was it also an internal development that the
Bund's national conception made inevitable? This question will preoc-
cupy us throughout this study. Obviously one cannot ask such a question
with respect to the Zionist Labor Movement, since that movement
defined itself ab initio as a vanguard force of self-actualizers who were
preparing the national base for Klal Yisrael, even if the idea was to serve
not all Jewish masses but only some. Even so, the national principle included and embraced all Jewish classes, but in this movement, too, one
may discern phases of transition from extreme pioneering elitism to more
popular outlooks that made compromises with social and political reality.

The discussion thus far indicates that this study is interested mainly in
the two movements' political ideology and ideological politics in regard to
the Klal Yisrael question. The distinction between "political ideology" and
"ideological politics" is not a dialectic that wishes to emphasize the same
point but a statement: in the course of history, both movements alternately
overemphasized ideology and politics without severing the strong relationship between the two. After all, in social movements led by relatively small
entities of elitist pioneering nature, ideologies play an important if not a
decisive guiding role in the social and political process.

The essential pairing of ideology and politics in two movements that
acted in history to change the course of history created the intellectual pattern that I term "public thought." Public thought is composed of ideological
principles and political pragmatism that are publicly manifested to persuade
the public to mobilize for a certain goal. Unlike intellectual thought divorced from public action, it is the thinking of people who operate in the
public political sphere. At issue, then, at the personal and public levels, are
not intellectuals who reside outside the political organization as critics and
prophets of doom but exactly the opposite: those positioned within the
organization who voice their criticism from within.

Both types, critics from the outside and as shapers from the inside,
fall within the definition of intellectuals mobilized in the service of a
cause. Thus, each type has a role to play in the process of social change.
From this standpoint, in both entities, the Bund and the Zionist Labor
Movement, the "inside" intellectuals were the agents of the Russian intelligentsia of the late nineteenth and the twentieth centuries.

Even if, following Jonathan Frankel, we term both groups a "Polu-
intelligentsia," and even though most of their activity took place in the polit-

ical sphere, ideology was of decisive importance because one cannot describe their political culture if one overlooks its ideological basis, and because their political idealism could not exist without being set within a comprehensive conceptual framework. The dialectic development that led these and similar Socialist movements from ideology to politics and thence to bureaucracy seems inevitable in the historical process, but this does not diminish the importance, if not the crucialness, of ideology, which shaped the "public thought" as part of the overall "public discourse" at that time. Otherwise, one could neither understand nor explain the choice that these young people made, as Jews, between pioneering in Palestine and revolutionary activism in their places of residence. This is in addition to their choice not to leave the "Jewish Klal" by dedicating themselves to revolutionary political action in non-Jewish social movements or by attempting, at the personal level, to assimilate into the culture of their surrounding societies.

In both movements, the confrontation with these options formed and sharpened special trends of thought within the general Socialist movement. Perhaps for this reason, the Zionist Labor Movement, which undertook an exceptional task in the setting of world Socialism, had more original thinkers than the Bund had. None of the Bundist intellectuals attained the philosophical level and originality of Nachman Syrkin, Dov Ber Borochov, A. D. Gordon, and Berl Katznelson. Even Vladimir Medem, who for nearly twenty years attempted to furnish the Bund with its own national doctrine, did not attain their caliber in the intellectual debate.

However, one may not ignore the fact that the Bund and the Zionist Labor Movement were, in the main, practical sociopolitical movements. Each was a vessel, so to speak, that held a political party, a trade union, an education system, and youth movements. The practical complexion of the Zionist Labor Movement was more salient in that it spearheaded the constructive enterprise of building a labor economy. Here it should be emphasized that the practical nature of both movements also had ideological significance, since each movement constituted a palpable, profound, and far-reaching reflection of the national and social revolutionary process that was unfolding on the Jewish scene. However, due to the very magnitude of the revolution, the way both movements understood the concept of Klal Yisrael which was rife with vagueness, confusion, and at times contradictions—as the chapters of this study will show. Still, we will not portray the movements as equal in this regard. On the contrary: the Labor Movement's perception of Klal Yisrael, however problematic, was an inseparable part of the comprehensive Zionist national worldview from beginning to end. The perception of the Bund, mainly focused at the class level, created a buffer between this movement and the Jewish people at large.

Here the general question arises about the sense of reality among groups of revolutionaries, who use the present as a springboard to the future. How, in relative terms, do such groups understand reality and how do they connect reality with ideology and politics? This question is especially pertinent in regard to the twentieth century, in both its lengthy sense, a hundred-year span, and its shorter sense, between World War I and the toppling of the Berlin Wall. However one views it, it was one of the most dramatic centuries in human history generally and Jewish history particularly. Even before World War II, the Holocaust, and the establishment of the State of Israel, the Jews' situation underwent more sweeping changes than that of any other contemporaneous people. Furthermore, one needs no profound historical and sociological insights to realize that the establishment of the great Jewish center in the United States, the creation of a national focal point in Palestine, the salient change in the status of Russian Jewry under the new Soviet regime, and the upturn in nationalism and anti-Semitism in Central Europe and, especially, in Poland portended a new era in Jewish history. After World War II, as a result of the Holocaust and pursuant to the establishment of the State of Israel, the global Jewish reality changed in ways that were even more transformative.

This study, then, probes these two movements' sense of time, in two respects: a *segmented* sense, corresponding to the movements' eras of historical development, and an *inclusive* sense, from a twofold comprehensive perspective—a historical vision that looks ahead to future developments and a historical reckoning that attempts to evaluate what has already happened. This perspective clearly relates to the Utopian tendencies in both movements. The question is whether one of the movements had a more realistic grasp of present time and a firmer vision of the future, or whether both perspectives converged inseparably in each movement.

In a nutshell, one may understand the characteristics of the Bund and the Zionist Labor Movement and their status in modern Jewish history only within the framework of the revolutionary pattern of public behavior that Frankel termed "the new Jewish politics." This pattern originated in the response to the pogroms against Russian Jews in 1882, continued in 1903–1905, and, in my opinion, persists to this very day, more than a hundred years on. The "newness" of this pattern, as against the "oldness" of its forerunner, is captured in the transition from a politics of a paternalistic approach *for* Jews to the new politics *of* the Jews. It is pronouncedly a politics of autoemancipation, an ideologically multifarious politics that not only has different if not clashing national goals, but also one common denominator: the principle of the Jews' entitlement to general recognition as a people in the global family of peoples. The voice of this new politics, which emerged from Russia in the late nineteenth century and reverberated in the West on the eve of World War I, continued to speak during the interwar period with the international political war on anti-Semitism. The establishment of the World Jewish Congress in 1936 may serve as an example.

After the Holocaust, Jewish politics was reflected in the struggle of *Klal Yisrael*—the Jewish people at large—for the establishment of Jewish statehood and, in the 1960s and 1970s, according to its policy, Diaspora Jewry's joint campaign with the Government of Israel on behalf of Soviet Jewry. The political support that Israel has received from Diaspora Jewry from the day it was established is also part of this politics.

The Bund and the Zionist Labor Movement made an important and, at times, a decisive contribution to the shaping of the new Jewish politics. They created the ethos of Jewish self-defense; they spearheaded the national struggles against anti-Semitism and Arab nationalism; they created a basis of fighting political power in Poland and Palestine, respectively, and they transformed the Jews from a collective that survived to a people that struggles for its national rights.

Consequently, this study of the Bund and the Zionist Labor Movement is not a parallel to Jonathan Frankel's study of the period between the end of the nineteenth century and World War I. It probes the twists and turns of national thinking that have lasted for nearly a century and in five spheres of political culture: Tsarist Russia, the Zionist Yishuv in Palestine, national Poland, the free and democratic United States, and the Jewish State of Israel. Thus, the study focuses on continuity and change in this outlook as one era segues into another. Obviously, a study that spans the twentieth century could not have been written had it not been preceded by important historical studies that touch upon it directly and indirectly. Therefore, these studies are cited at the appropriate locations. I am deeply appreciative of all of them, including those written by my personal teachers and friends.

Finally, this researcher owes his readers a confession: he is not absolutely objective in his attitude toward the subject. Assuming that there is no historian who lacks a worldview, be it concealed or revealed, I believe that precisely in "sensitive" issues such as these, which carry an emotional load that the passage of time has not lightened—a load that has been passed on directly and indirectly from generation to generation—the historian must tell the reader where he stands. The preface to this book should leave no doubt that I am not neutral in the ideological dispute between Bundism and Zionism. However, my Weltanschauung, which vindicates Zionism in respect to the future of the Jewish people in the historical process, neither diminishes my appreciation of the Bund as a Jewish national political party, nor belittles its social and political attitudes at various junctures in its history. Furthermore, I admit to a "weakness" for Utopian idealists even when, in their zealotry and the monodimensional nature of their worldview, they often cause damage. Such personalities were not lacking in the Zionist Labor Movement as well. Indeed, that zealotry was welcome in its time; in its absence, neither movement would have affected the course of Jewish history. Precisely because that passion was gladly received back then, one should ask how far and to what point in time it extends. Therefore, the determining aspect of the historical influence of the Bund and the Labor Movement was the ability and willingness to bridle ideological zealotry and find ways to adjust to the "decrees" of historical development.

This approach prompted me to distinguish between a pair of concepts, "illusion" and "disillusion," that recurs in all chapters of this study and emphasizes the difference in the historical fate of the two movements. Illusion denotes false hope or a belief in the unattainable; disillusion is the disappointment that occurs when hopes fail to materialize fully. This is not to say that hopes of illusion and disillusion were never realistic at any point in time. However, both the Bundists and the Labor Zionists were too myopic to understand the contradiction between historical processes and Utopian yearnings. To emphasize and elucidate this point, however, I must return to the dichotomy I sketched above: "realistic Utopianism" versus "Utopian realism." The former, rooted in the Marxist worldview, reflects the belief that, in the course of history, objective social development will resolve most existing social contradictions. Thus, the Utopian end sanctifies the political means. The Bund, throughout its history, was one of the most pronounced examples of this way of thinking. The latter outlook, in contrast, is supremely practical because it is set in historical reality. From its standpoint, Utopia is not an alternative to social and political reality but a corrective option only. Therefore, the historical fate of the Bund was determined by dogmatic principles and that of the Labor Movement by pragmatic approaches. In other words, one may say that the Bund had a political ideology in which praxis, of course, had some pragmatic elements, whereas the Zionist Labor Movement was powered by a constructive ideology in which political pragmatism was a built-in fundamental. The distinction is between one movement that stresses ideology and another that focuses on the act itself, which takes place within an ideological framework.

This distinction leads me to a paradoxical reflection. Although both movements expressed modern Jewish culture, they also had postmodern elements to which they were oblivious. I refer to their rejection of the "grand narrative" of Marxism and liberalism in respect to Jewish nationhood and their adherence to the principle of multiculturalism in civil nation-states. However, the Zionist revolution generally, and that of the Zionist Labor Movement specifically, against the antinational "grand narrative" concerning the Jews was more radical in its existential essence and, therefore, more meaningful in the sense of historical importance.

These matters are by no means the evaluation of a researcher who has a particular worldview and observes events from a distance of time. Contemporaries of the era at issue in this study were well aware of the nature of their movements and repeatedly preached the tenets of their beliefs to their movement or party flock. In Bund circles, the ideological principle was always stressed as the supreme value in all political steps toward the goal. In the Labor Movement, in contrast, ideology was described as a mere "compass"—to use Berl Katznelson's term—that points toward the goal but does not determine how to get there. I hope to convince the reader that my argument is historically justified and valid and that I have neither wronged nor overvalued either of them.

CHAPTER 1

BETWEEN CLASS AND NATION
The Bund in Russia, 1897–1917

Only the dead become fossils. Living people adjust themselves to the demands of life. The point of departure remains the old one; the conclusions can be new.

—Vladimir Medem, 1916

The twenty-year history of the Bund in Russia—1897–1917—may be divided into two ten-year subperiods. In the first, 1897–1906, the Bund coalesced both organizationally and politically as an autonomous entity within the general Russian Social Democratic (SD) movement. At the end of this subperiod, in the 1905 Revolution, it reached the pinnacle of its power in the Jewish street, both in membership—about thirty thousand in its own estimation—and as a political player in Jewish public life that struggled for civil rights as an active participant in self-defense groups wherever Jews faced pogroms. Although the ideological foundations of the Bund's national outlook were laid at that time, its final goal was not determined, as we will see.

The second subperiod began after the failure of the 1905 Revolution and lasted from 1907 to the October Revolution in 1917. The Bund lost strength during this time and, like other revolutionary and liberal movements, its membership declined severely. It took the Bund four years, until 1910, to begin to recover. It was then of all times, in the midst of the trough, that the Bund started not only to exhibit a clear and unequivocal inclination in its existential national outlook, but also to choose the directions in which its political and cultural action would head.

The process of the Bund's gradual ascent in the Jewish popular national cultural reality in Russia and, especially, in Lithuania, is well known.[1] The Bund evolved from an intelligentsia circle to a labor circle; from ideological and intellectual "propaganda" to "agitation" in the form of information and education for groups of workers and artisans culled from the simple, poorly educated classes; from Yiddish as a language of communication with the Jewish proletariat to Yiddish as a manifestation of national culture; from "circles" into a political party in 1897; from an autonomous organizational status within the Russian SD Party to the idea of Jewish national and cultural autonomy in Russia. Underlying this political and ideological evolution, which shifted the Bund from an "international" Socialist outlook to a "national" proletarian awareness, was the issue of the Jewish people as a worldwide historical phenomenon and a problem of ideological principle—matters that could not be ignored intellectually or politically.

In the sphere of ideology, the national definition of the proletariat made it necessary to explain where the Jewish people belonged vis-à-vis the population at large. Within a short time, due to the advent of Herzl and the passion that "political Zionism" evoked when the Jewish masses first encountered it, the Bund faced active political competition that forced it to explain where it stood on the national question. Importantly, the danger flowing from Zionism first arose in the Hibbat Tsiyyon era, even before the first Zionist Congress in Basel. The premier issue of *Der Idisher Arbayter*, published in Switzerland, gave evidence to this by devoting an editorial to the matter. "Capitalism has fragmented the Jewish people [*der idishen natsion*] into two hostile classes, workers and capitalists."[2] However, once Herzl came on the scene, as stated, some Bund intellectuals understood that this mechanistic bisection of the national organism into two warring classes failed to respond to the national yearnings of the Jewish masses. This is what prompted Joseph (Dzhan) Mill, the editor of the journal, to contact Hayyim Zhitlovsky,[3] who was not a member of the Bund, and propose a public debate over what differentiated the Bund from Zionism. Zhitlovsky honored the request by publishing a four-article series under the title "Zionism or Socialism?"[4]

It was Zhitlovsky (1865–1943) of all people—the ideological itinerant troubadour of Jewish ultramodernism, a man who switched worldviews but never abandoned his belief in Jewish nationhood, an intellectual who was never bound by doctrinaire thinking—who got to the root of the national problem from the Socialist perspective and predicted the development that the Bund would experience decades later.

The four articles, written in the spirit of conventional Bund views, dealt mainly with an attempt to debunk the basic premises of the Zionist idea. Zhitlovsky defines Zionism as a movement of the Jewish bourgeoisie and assertes that, from the class perspective, Socialism and Zionism are irreconcilable. What is worse, Zionism is misleading the Jewish masses with its Utopian dreams and, for this reason, is the greatest enemy of the Jewish people. Furthermore, Zhitlovsky, following the classic Bund line, strongly doubts the existence of a world Jewish nation, in which both the Zionists and Dubnow believed. After all, he reasoned, a Jewish worker in New York or Vilna has more in common with a non-Jewish worker than with the Jewish bourgeoisie in his place of residence.[5] However, Zhitlovsky did not stop at this juncture of total dismissal of Klal Yisrael. Unlike the Bundists, he did not rule out ab initio the possibility that a world of Jewish people might come into being in a future world Socialist society. In fact, he upheld the right of the Jews, like all other peoples, to exist as nations within that society. In his opinion, Jewish Socialists who stay in touch with their origins love their people no less, if not more, than Zionists who ceaselessly trumpet this sentiment in public. The eastern European Jewish proletariat has much deeper and stronger Jewish roots, he asserted, than Zionist leaders such as Theodor Herzl and Max Nordau, who came from the world of the assimilationists. As A. Littwak, a grassroots Bund leader, would argue later on, Zhitlovsky stressed the loyal Jewish Socialists' emotional connection to their people. Following this premise, Zhitlovsky expressed the hope that Jewish workers in all countries would establish a world Jewish proletarian Bund that would safeguard and struggle for the interests of all of Jewry while participating in the surrounding peoples' struggle for freedom and equality. Such a Bund, in Zhitlovsky's opinion, should establish a world-embracing set of Yiddish-speaking Jewish cultural institutions. This would make Jews the world over proud of their people and culture. His practical conclusion was to establish an international proletarian Jewish secretariat, *Ayn internatsionalen idishen arbayter sekretariat* [italics in the original].[6]

Thus, Zhitlovsky proposed an alternative of sorts to the Zionist creed— a proletarian Klal Yisrael instead of a national one. By so doing, he expressed a prophecy that the Bund would attempt to fulfill fifty years later, under different and tragic conditions for the Jewish people and for him personally, after World War II and the Holocaust.

Zhitlovsky's last-mentioned remarks attracted a response from the editorial board, which expressed doubt that the Yiddish "jargon" could develop into a language of culture and creative endeavor as other peoples' languages had. Only future social developments could answer this question. Notably, however, even the editors did not rule out, theoretically, the existence of a proletarian Jewish Klal on a worldwide cultural basis. They were simply less confident than Zhitlovsky about the possibility of bringing this about. In this sense, in fact, they assumed that national existence depended not only on material factors, but also on spiritual ones as well. Furthermore, they believed that physical national existence hinged more on the cultural and spiritual factor in the case of world Jewry than among any other people.

At the initiative of John (Dzhan) Mill, Zhitlovsky's article was published in advance of the third Bund convention, held in 1899 in Kovno. At the convention, Mill himself fought for a resolution stressing the need to furnish Jewish workers with national rights so that they could defend their proletarian interests. Mill's opponents preferred to struggle for Jews' civil rights and believed that a demand for national rights would fragment and, thereby, vitiate the political struggle. In the typical Bundist manner, the debates over this issue ended with a compromise: a resolution to struggle for civil rights first and to refer the national question to broad debate in party circles.[7]

Two different clusters of basic views stood out in this debate, which lasted for more than three years. One cluster regarded Yiddish speakers and them alone, as opposed to French, English, or German speakers, as the Jewish nation.[8] In regard to those who spoke Yiddish and practiced the Yiddish culture, this group assumed that the success of their Socialist struggle would depend on expanding the common denominator of the folk classes—the natural carriers of the indigenous national culture. Socialism, in turn, should assure the unobstructed development of this culture by removing all obstacles and impediments.[9]

In the opinion of members of the second cluster, the Jews are not a nation but an origin group that has "a certain attitude" about its origin (*a shtammeinheit, a shtammgenossenshaft*). A common historical fate strengthens people's affiliation with an origin group so powerfully that it is sometimes stronger than the national sentiment. Sixteenth-century German Protestants, for example, felt closer to French Huguenots than to German Catholics. In the changing historical reality, there is no hope that the Jews will again be a nation, since they have neither a shared language nor, as stated, any likelihood of acquiring one. Therefore, the Jews have no issue of national policy or assimilation to worry about, and in this regard Jewish social democracy has neither principles nor interests. However, it does have a special interest, if not a special mission, in disseminating progressive Western enlightenment among the Jewish proletarian masses.[10]

The intellectual debate surrounding the national issue was accompanied by a penetrating political debate within the Bund itself and between it and the Russian SD Party, under the leadership of Lenin and Plekhanov, on the one hand, and Dubnowian and Zionist Jewish nationalism, on the other hand. In terms of balance of forces, the Bund maintained a delicate equilibrium between "nationalists" and "internationalists." Accordingly, at the third, fourth, and fifth party conventions, the debate on this issue led not to unequivocal resolutions but to compromise formulae between the two outlooks.

The Bundist debate on the national problem took place at two levels: political and ideational. The first concerned the status of the Bund within the Russian SD Party. The Bund advocated a federative party structure, in which each national party would have an autonomous status as the sole representative of its national proletariat. The leaders of the Russian SD Party objected to this, touching off a political struggle that led to the Bund's succession from the party in 1903 and its hesitant return in 1906.[11] This struggle, pronouncedly organizational in nature, had nothing to do with the Klal Yisrael issue. The ethnic identity of working-class Bund members sufficed to justify a certain form of internal organizational autonomy within the general party, much as that enjoyed by other ethnic groups.

At the ideological level, however, the idea of establishing national–cultural autonomy, proclaimed by the Bund in 1901, pertained to the Klal Yisrael question in both the principled and the political senses. After all, its validity applied to all Jews. The Bund limited this autonomy to cultural matters and took care not to expand its powers to the community-organization sphere, as Simon Dubnow and, later, the Zionists advocated, because the expansionary national significance of such a demand clashed with the concept of the class division of society. The Bund "nationalists" kept this danger in mind and therefore, paradoxically with respect to those who adhered to a Marxist materialist worldview, placed growing emphasis on the Yiddish language and culture as the basis of Jewish nationhood as that of an exterritorial people.

The intellectual formula of national autonomy was phrased at that convention, as we know. This formula, based on a compromise between "nationalists" and "internationalists" in the party, was not meant to be fulfilled as a political platform. It states: "The convention asserts that a state such as Russia, composed of many different nationalities, is fated to become a federation of nationalities with *full* national autonomy [emphasis mine] for each of these peoples, irrespective of the territory that it settles."[12]

In the course of the debate at that convention, one of the "nationalists" stated:

> Let us be consistent. If we recognize every nation's right to freedom and national autonomy, and if we consider Jewry a nation, then the Bund, which protects the interests of the Jewish proletariat in particular—must *by necessity* [emphasis mine] champion Jewish national autonomy and must not in any way content itself with a demand for equality in civil and political rights, as has been the case thus far.[13]

The inclusion of these remarks in a resolution favoring *full* autonomy and asserting the *necessity* of espousing it expressed the identity of the proletariat interest and the national interest. The entire vision was geared, of course, to a future that would follow the historical episode of class warfare. Even so, however, the "nationalist" Bundists affirmed the existence of a Jewish nation.

Two years later, in 1903, V. Kossovski clashed verbal swords with the leaders of *Iskra* over the latter's vehement opposition to giving the Bund the status of representative of the Jewish proletariat throughout Russia. He stated vigorously that the Bund existed, in and of itself, for the sake of the Jewish proletariat and maintained relations with the general Socialist Party because it considered the latter not a Russian-national (*Rusishe*) party but a Russian-country (*Ruslandishe*) one.

Basing himself on these premises, Kossovski explained that the Bund would not settle for autonomous status within the Russian SD Party. Such a status corresponded to the view of the *Iskra* leadership, which agreed to give the Bund the right to organize on a regional but not on a national basis. In contrast, to organize the proletariat of an entire nation, a federative form of organization was the most suitable.[14] This leaves no doubt that, in the minds of the "nationalist" Bundists, there was a Jewish nation in eastern Europe. Just as the working class represented the genuine future national interests of all "normal" that is, territorial, nationalities, so it was with the Jewish nation, even though the Jews were exceptional in this respect. The *Iskra* leaders' opposition to national recognition of the Jewish proletariat, and its result—the devaluation of the Bund's political status—prompted the "nationalists" in the party to put together and strengthen their Socialist national outlook en bloc. Thus, it was not by chance that the clashing "internationalist" and "nationalist" views escalated into an internecine confrontation at an encounter of Bund leaders in Zurich in 1903, in preparation for the second convention of the Russian SD Party.

The outlook of the "internationalists" was fueled by a social analysis and a universalistic ideology. In their estimation, the objective process of the development of capitalism in Russia would gradually destroy the civic and economic barriers between Jews and non-Jews until the former fully integrated into society at large. This explains their staunch opposition to the idea of national autonomy, which, they believed, carried the taint of Dubnowian national ideology, and, with its subjectivity, clashed with the objective process of integration. Worse still, it had elements of Zionist nationalism. Furthermore, the "internationalists" doubted whether, a particularistic Jewish culture was at all possible in the absence of a material basis for the existence of a Jewish nation. Boris Frumkin, a leading internationalist, argued vehemently that Jewish nationhood cannot exist in the

Diaspora and that those who disagree flirt with Zionism. Therefore, there is no Jewish national problem (*Yidishe natsionale frage*) but only a "problem of Jews" (*nor a yidn frage*), since Jews are strangers everywhere amidst cultures that reciprocate by estranging themselves from them. It is this foreignness that animates the psychology from which the Klal Yisrael ideology stems. Therefore, for the very reason of the abnormality of Jewish existence, that is, the absence of Jewish territory, one should be wary about cultivating a psychologically based nationalism, one influenced by the national ideology of the Polish PPS and the Zionists. This ideology did influence the nationalists, as they did not deny. In Frumkin's judgment, the Bund should represent only the interests of the Jewish proletariat. As such, it is a national organization and no more, and the entire issue of *full* national autonomy is none of its concern but rather that of the Zionist nationalists.[15]

Frumkin's remarks reflect the crux of the internationalist worldview, which sheds additional light on the outlook of the nationalists—those who, in their opinion, could not deliberately (or inadvertently) circumvent the Klal Yisrael question that beset the Bund from the beginning of the century—at the fourth convention, held in 1901—to the middle of the century, after the Holocaust.

Vladimir Kossovski, who formulated the Bund's national creed in the course of his struggle with the *Iskra* leaders,[16] was one of the main rivals of the internationalists in this sphere, too. To oppose them, he cited three rationales. The first, the universalistic, was the national platform of the Austrian Social Democratic Party, which recognized the national majority's right to territorial autonomy in part of the state and added, as a corrective and complementary measure, personal autonomy for national groups that lacked a territorial majority. This rule, of course, applied especially to the Jews. The second rationale was social. Kossovski, unlike his comrades, argued that the development of capitalism not only sharpened class warfare, but also forged peoples into national units. This was happening in Russia as well, where the Jewish question would not vanish any time soon. As evidence, he noted that even though Jews were emigrating to countries overseas, foremost the United States, their numbers in Russia were not declining. The third rationale was political. Kossovski admitted that the Zionist idea, which had gripped masses of Jews in eastern Europe, presented the Bund with a sticky challenge. Instead of dismissing the allure of Zionism as an artificial and transitory phenomenon, Kossovski argued that Zionism expressed the national spirit and aspirations of the Jewish masses and that, therefore, they were the soil in which Zionism grew.[17] Thus, the Bund must not ignore the national problem of these Jewish masses and leave the search for its solution to the Zionists only. With this in mind, he and others of similar conviction inferred that until the Jewish national issue found a political solution, it should be tackled by developing the Yiddish national culture of the Jewish masses. In other words, the culture to be fostered was that of the masses and not necessarily that of the organized proletariat, as Kossovski's disputants believed. Kossovski's rivals pointed to the intrinsic riskiness of his approach, which might steer the Bund toward Dubnow's national philosophy, an ideological Klal Yisrael, and even Zionist nationalism. Kossovski was undeterred by this accusation. In his opinion, the demand to encourage popular national culture among the Jewish liberal bourgeoisie did not in itself rule out the very idea, especially when national autonomy might be attained by mobilizing social forces from the progressive bourgeoisie for a political struggle that the Bund would lead. Hearing this, Kossovski's aforementioned rival, Frumkin, charged that his outlook was Zionistic (*Vladimirs kuk is a tsiyoynistishe*).[18]

Mark Lieber (Michael Goldman), who shared Kossovski's national beliefs, added a theoretical dimension to this question. Basing himself on discussions at the Second International, he elucidated the difference between a nation-state and a nation—arguing that the two are not always absolutely identical. A nation is a cultural and psychological unity (*a kulturel-psikhologishe aynhayt*). As such, a nation is a complete entity, even though from the political standpoint it may be dispersed across different states, as in the cases of the Armenians and, especially, the Poles. Once the dis-identity of nation and state was recognized, various nations that had not asserted their national and cultural identity as a major value now embarked on a national awakening. Consequently, for all peoples, it is the national proletariat that should solve its people's national problem. In this respect, the Jews are no exception.[19]

In this context, it is noteworthy that the convention of the Russian SD Party, held in Brussels and London that year immediately after the Bund convention, Lieber led the struggle against the *Iskra* people, including L. Martov (Yuly Osipovich Tsederbaum), one of the Menshevik leaders, who was not one of them. In the draft resolutions that he presented to the convention concerning the Bund, Martov defined the Jews as a "race." Liber opposed this vehemently and insisted, unsuccessfully, that they be defined as a "nation" (*natsie*).[20]

Intellectual hairsplitting aside, Lieber's remarks indirectly but very importantly touched upon the issue discussed here, that of Klal Yisrael. After all, Lieber spoke explicitly of a Jewish nation—a cultural and psychological unity—dispersed among different states. However, it should be emphasized that in terms of Klal Yisrael, this was a silver lining within a cloud. Lieber concerned himself with a cultural and psychological integrity or unity and not a historical one, such as that in which Dubnow and the Zionists believed. This, of course, is an overture to the grand question: who among the Jews belongs to this nation? We explore this matter below.

The stance of the nationalists cannot be fully understood without the personal, emotional dimension—that sense of a Jewish folk-home that which A. Littwak described in his memoirs,[21] or of home-nostalgia, to use Vladimir Medem's famous expression.[22] In the debate itself, Tsvia Horovitch articulated this feeling by defining the ambition for national autonomy as a liberation from the sense of enslavement that typified the assimilationist Jewish intellectuals who ruled out the existence of a Jewish nation. It is the Bund's duty to liberate itself from this slavish psychology and ideology (*knekhtishkayt*). She lauded the natural sense of Jewish nationhood, which requires neither inquiries nor justifications because, after all, it exists.[23]

This was Vladimir Medem's first participation in the national debate, for which he would be the Bund's main ideologue for the next twenty years or so. Thus, we devote a special place to his national thought at a later stage in this chapter.

The end of this dispute was typical of political party life in the Bund. Usually the leadership managed to settle disagreements by phrasing an ambiguous compromise resolution, as had happened at the fourth convention in regard to the very same issue. This time, however, that stratagem did not work. The dispute was both principled and political. The "national" majority at the convention was afraid to resolve the issue before the convention of the Russian SD Party, which, as stated, took place that year in Brussels and London. Therefore, it preferred not to bring the question of national autonomy to a vote. This being the case, the Bund delegation could present a united front on the issue of the party's autonomous status within the SD Party. When its demand was turned down, of course, the refusal prompted the Bund to secede from the SD Party.[24]

The secession of the Bund—both wings, the "national" and the "international"—from the general Russian SD Party at the London convention attests to the uniqueness of the Bund, which managed to maintain its unity in spite of its internal differences of principle. The Bund remained outside the SD Party for nearly three years. In 1906, it returned "home" after a compromise of sorts between most of its leadership and the heads of *Iskra*, prompted by pressure from rank and file members who wished to break out of their isolation and affiliate with the general Socialist Party of Russia—especially after the failure of the revolution in 1905 left the Bund severely weakened.[25]

The Bund's return to the Russian Socialist Party, although largely formal—since the Bund remained politically separate—distanced the party from the political Klal Yisrael. This occurred, of all times, after the Bund in 1905 had stationed itself at the forefront of defenders of "self-defense" postures against anti-Jewish pogroms. From the political standpoint, however, the Bund refused to participate with the other Jewish parties in the Association for the Attainment of Total Equality for Jews in Russia. This resulted in a series of furious anti-Bund articles by Simon Dubnow, one of the mentors of the association.[26]

The title of Dubnow's first article in the series, "Slavery in Revolution," speaks for itself. It excoriated Jewish socialists who aligned themselves with assimilators into general Socialist parties, such as the Russian SD or the Polish PPS, and self-proclaimed carriers of Jewish national consciousness, such as the Bund and even the Zionist Po'aley Tsiyyon. However, as stated, Dubnow was concerned chiefly with the Bund and attempted to expose the party's true "national face." He accused the Bund of several sins of principle against the all-embracing national concept of Klal Yisrael. The Bund's national program in regard to cultural autonomy, he argued, was severely narrow because it limited itself solely to a demand for recognition of Yiddish and a search for a way to promote it. The Bund ignored and even opposed the broad, inclusive organizational and cultural grasp of cultural autonomy that should provide the entire nation with a permanent framework for the cultivation of its culture, the shaping of its new national image, and a barrier against the menace of assimilation. This, Dubnow wrote, is because the Bund, according to its class ideological outlook, considers itself a representative of the interest of only part of the Jewish people. Therefore, it has no inclusive national interest and is unwilling to participate in the struggle for Jewish national continuity. Consequently, Dubnow maintained angrily, Bundists' loyalties accreted to "one nation" only, the "proletarian" one. If so, they were fragmenting the Jewish nation ab initio—not inadvertently but deliberately and consciously. By so doing, instead of a politics that reflects the general national interest, the Bund dragged segments of the Jewish people into a class politics that devastated national unity. When normal peoples that have a permanent national territorial base practice this kind of class politics, the harm that might result cannot endanger the nation's integrity as such. However, when a non-territorial people, dispersed across many countries, engages in this form of political behavior, it engenders a severe risk of fragmentation and disintegration.

The anomaly of Jewish national existence traces to the lack of national territory, Dubnow wrote. He admitted that normal phenomena such as class struggle exist within this anomaly, provided that the class struggle not contradict and clash with the national politics, as the Bund was doing.

In contrast to the Bund, even the Diaspora-negating Zionists, Dubnow stressed, participated in the struggle for the rights of Jewry at large in Russia. Thus, when all is said and done, the upholding of the class principle among Russian Jewish society, even though this society is composed mainly of an impoverished petty bourgeoisie, is also a manifestation of the Jewish anomaly. However, unlike the defenders of Klal Yisrael, exponents of the class worldview threatened Jewish national continuity, in which, for him, the Klal Yisrael framework provided a surrogate for the absence of national territory.[27]

Dubnow repeated this argument with greater emphasis and passion in his response to the poet An-Ski, who was not a member of the Bund even though the party adopted his poem, "The Oath," as its anthem. An-Ski, disputing Dubnow, argued that among other peoples class struggle does not undermine national unity. In fact, it aims to create unity in the long-term historical process. In response, Dubnow ruled on principled and historical grounds that a national policy that integrates the interests of all national strata is totally at odds with the Marxist-style class philosophy. By so stating, Dubnow transformed the Jews' anomalous state into a categorical worldview of sorts that should dictate the particular national policy of the Jewish people.

This being the case, Dubnow sought to base Jewish nationhood in the Diaspora (as he termed it) on the subjective wish for national unity—a wish that, when implemented through a comprehensive autonomous community organization, would provide a substitute for the territorial setting that "normal" peoples have. This explains why the class-struggle ideology was dangerous for the Jews, since it undermined the subjective wish for Klal Yisrael.

Notably, Dubnow was so angry with the Bundists for their "slavish" attitude toward Socialism at large and their "treasonous" posture toward Jewish peoplehood that he did not even see fit to respond directly to a series of rebuttal articles that they published in the Vilna newspaper *Der Verker* in 1906.

The article was signed by B. Babsky. No one knew who this was, but since V. Kossovski and V. Medem were the editors of the Vilna newspaper that year, they must have assented to its contents, at the very least.[28] It is more likely that Kossovski wrote the article. The author, whoever he was, traced Dubnow's assault on the Bund to its refusal to join the association that the Jewish national parties had formed to struggle together for Jewish civil and national rights in Russia. In the spirit of remarks by the Bund nationalists, the writer agreed with Dubnow that the Jews at large (*gantsn idishn folk*) were severely encumbered by their inferior civil status. By implication,

however, by liberating itself the Jewish proletariat would also liberate the entire Jewish people. (*Az befreyendig zikh, befrayt der proletariat di gantse
natsion zayne.*) This attitude—verging on an indirect "national caretaker"
role of sorts—does not, according to the author, constitute a retreat from the
Bund's original classic posture as a piously Marxist Party, a posture that divided the nation into warring classes. It does the opposite, the author insisted, stressing that the class division was a universal phenomenon that
typified all progressive nations that were experiencing modernization
through the medium of capitalist economics. However, the Bund participated in the Jewish national front in an indirect manner only, by struggling
for the rights of the working class, and this very factor made its ideological
attitude toward Klal Yisrael increasingly complex. After all, the entire argument thus far implies that the Bund rejected the Klal Yisrael idea as a political framework but not as a national-cultural one. The remaining question,
then, is how far this framework should extend in the global, pan-Jewish context. From the political standpoint, the Bund ruled out the establishment of a
united Jewish front lest this set a precedent for similar nationally based organizational initiatives in Russia—initiatives that would fragment and vitiate the political struggle of the progressive forces in that country[29]—in
addition to the Zionist nationalist "scheme" that, according to the authors,
lurked behind the plan.

Thus far, the position was clear. However, what about the nurturing of
the national culture? What set the Bund apart, in this respect, from the Jewish
liberal bourgeoisie? After all, the identity of class interest and genuine national interest has already been stated explicitly. Lest the borders between
"class" and "national" interests be blurred, one of the intellectuals hurriedly
marked them with a series of "negative commandments."[30] The Bund for-
swore expressions such as "national consciousness," "national revival," and
"national efflorescence"; it recognized culture as an existing phenomenon. It
presumed that the more politically conscious the proletariat became, the
stronger the national culture would be. Following its neutralistic formulation,
however, if it transpires that the historical process was weakening this culture,
the Bund would allow the process to play itself out without resistance.

In this sense, there was no room for either an in-between solution or a
compromise between the liberal nationalists and the Bund. The liberal nationalists aspired to unite the people into a single bloc— *"Am tsuzamensh-
lisn tsu ayn lebn, tsu di zelbe natsionale shtrebungn un tsu glaykhe
natsionale idealn."* In contrast, the Bund wished to separate these two
classes totally—*"Mir shteln far unz—abtayln dem proletariat fun der
burzhwazi"*—and to educate workers to take a sober view toward the social
processes that set the Jewish nation apart.

The conclusion to draw from the whole debate over Dubnow's articles is that the Bund, at this phase, did not keep politics, ideology, and culture separate. However, the intellectual leadership of the party understood that things were not so simple and that the question of Socialism and nationalism needed elucidation. It was Vladimir Medem (1879–1923) who devoted his entire political and intellectual life to this question. His intellectual outpouring attested to the Bund's internal vacillations on this issue and to the changes that occurred in Medem's views during a twenty-year period. Below, then, we devote a central and special subchapter to Medem.

"VLADIMIR MEDEM—THE LEGEND OF THE JEWISH LABOR MOVEMENT"

Vladimir Medem was born in Minsk in 1879 and died in New York in 1923. His comrades and admirers engraved the following words on his tombstone: "Vladimir Medem—the legend of the Jewish labor movement." What did Medem accomplish that earned him this accolade, which eluded his comrades in the Bund leadership even if their contribution to the party matched or even surpassed his? Medem did not belong to the "Vilna dynasty," as the Bund's founding fathers were called. He was not a charismatic organizer like Arkady Kremer, an underground hero such as Yekutiel (Noah) Portnoy, or a pioneer in phrasing the national-autonomy idea. In the last-mentioned respect, Vladimir Kossovski preceded him. He never founded a Bund "Committee Abroad," as John (Dzhan) Mill did. He was neither a prolific pundit like Rafael Abramovitz, A. Littwak, and Beinish Mikhalevich, nor a polemicist who challenged *Iskra* leaders intrepidly, like Mark Lieber. He was not an authoratative political leader like Henryk Erlich or Wiktor Alter. Medem joined the Bund in 1901, after the party worked out its ideological line on the national issue at its fourth convention, earlier that year, and after the Bund had solidified its position as a proletarian party and an underground organization of Jewish workers.

If so, whence did Medem derive his spell? Generally speaking, one may say that it originated in . . . his differentness! Moshe Mishkinsky believed, correctly, that "The source of the legendary halo that formed around Medem was his origin from far on the outside, and not necessarily his being a 'repenter,' the sort of person whom people treat with some ambivalence, as we know."[31]

Medem was born to a wealthy, high-class assimilated family that gradually exchanged its Jewish religion for the Lutheran faith. Medem himself was baptized into the Provoslav Church at birth. Although he had been Christian as a child—something he never concealed or denied—he was not an ordinary "repenter" for two reasons. First, he never dissociated himself from the cultural and aesthetic values that he had imbibed as a boy. Second, he had no unequivocal explanation for his gradual return to Jewry and Judaism—a process that began with a strong interest in the Bible, continued with rapprochement with Jewish students at the University of Kiev, and ended with his enlistment in the Bund. When a comrade asked him in 1906 to explain the significance of his move, he replied that he had no intellectual explanation save this: "I wanted very badly to come home." What is more, he returned to this home as an unswervable romanticist in his attitude toward his people, whom he chose, and toward his past, from which he could not disengage.

Due to his romantic sentiment, Medem was enamored with the grassroots echelon of the Jewish people even before he became an active member of the Bund. In his student days, he retained the memory of a Sabbath eve outing with a good friend named Teomin. As the two strolled through the Jewish quarter of Minsk, he instigated a lengthy conversation about the Jews

> in the poor and remote alleys with their small houses. That Sabbath eve lives on in my memory. The silent and empty streets, with the Sabbath candles glowing in the small houses. . . . I felt in my heart *a romantic bonding* with the gray Jewish past, a warm and intimate psychic encounter that exists only vis-à-vis one's most intimate matters, vis-à-vis your own past. . . .[32]

This feeling also had its reverse: Medem's profound attachment to Russian culture and his aesthetic disgust with the outer image of Jewish life.

In 1906, after he returned from several years of exile in Switzerland and became publisher of the Bund newspaper in Vilna, Medem visited his relatives in Moscow. The following excerpt of his writings from Moscow is worth presenting verbatim:

> I came to Moscow. A totally different world. A Russian city, Moscow, and the people there are real Russians who speak Russian worthy of the name. How lovely the tones of this language are! It is altogether unlike the distorted, wretched Russian spoken in "our northwestern districts". . . . People speak in other tones that do not resemble the Jews' tones. Ninety percent of our Jews speak in bad, stammering, weak voices that lack flash and tone. The Russian voice, in contrast, is a loud, full-throated voice. . . . I must admit, however, that after spending a few weeks there, I felt a pro-

found inner nostalgia for the twisted, dirty alleys of Vilna and the unwashed, impoverished Jews of Vilna. *I wanted very badly to come home.*[33]

If so, notably, Medem had that sense of aesthetic negation-of-the-Diaspora that beset many Zionists of his generation whom he had encountered in Bern, Switzerland. One of them was Chaim Weizmann; Medem made friends with him and his fiancée.[34] Despite their irreconcilable ideological differences, both rejected the Jewish existential reality in eastern Europe on cultural grounds. Weizmann was five years older than Medem. In 1895, after a stay in Berlin, Weizmann wrote to his friend Leo Motzkin,

> After having lived in Berlin, I found Pinsk so repugnant and repulsive that I find it uncomfortable, if not unpleasant, to share my writings with you, my dear friend. There is nothing and no one here; instead of a city—a tremendous pile of trash. . . . masses of Jews milling and scurrying in the streets of our town, their faces worried and pained. But they do it all unknowingly, as if they were drunk.[35]

Furthermore, although an anti-Zionist and an ultra-Diasporist, Medem was impressed by the persona of Theodor Herzl due to his aesthetic penchant. He saw Herzl at the Zionist Congress in Basel in 1903, during the "Uganda debate," and described him, unflatteringly, as a person who had a hypnotic affect on the masses of delegates. However, he continued, "Truth to tell, Herzl knew how one should comport oneself in public. His stride was regal, proud, quiet, and his face gave off an uncommon aura." After Herzl died, Medem wrote: "Herzl never enchanted me as a public functionary. I always considered his 'policies' juvenile . . . but his very image was impressive. I mean his physical image." Therefore, when he was informed about Herzl's death, "I felt a sort of disappointment. An odd idea passed through me: could it be that a person with such a beautiful face would die? I cannot understand how I got caught up in this weird idea. But that was my mood."[36] This is probably one of the most authentic testimonies to Herzl's hypnotic, charismatic force.

Medem's aestheticism flowed from his high-mindedness as a person, a friend, and a political rival—a high-mindedness that included a thirst for sanctity. Medem revealed this trait with a silence that expressed a special attitude toward people, a pietism of sorts, as he defined it, that, in his mind, reflected man's prosaic attitude toward the sacred and his love and concern for others. This quality, man's true need, was lacking in the ordinary Jew.

Sanctity, after all, resides in life and in the human soul, "and everyone must have his own 'holy of holies'" that one should enter, as one would enter a church, "with quiet steps, downcast eyes, and sealed lips."

The Jew, however, does not behave that way, Medem ruled. He shouts, in glee or in grief. Even when he asks God for a favor, he engages Him in vociferous litigation as if the Almighty were his peer, and attempts to strike deals with his God if not to mislead Him. Even in the cemetery he continues to bargain with Him. Medem wrote these remarks in 1919 in the memory of his friend, the author Jacob Dineson, whom he considered the bearer of a mission in "sanctity" and "tenderness" (*haylikayt* and *aydlkayt*).[37]

It was this dialectic and ambivalent attitude toward the Jews—romantic attraction and cultural rejection—that determined and shaped Medem's Jewish national outlook from its onset in the early twentieth century. He never rid himself of it totally, even though it underwent changes, as he frankly admitted, in the 1920s.[38]

Medem was the Bund's systematic spokesman on the national question. For eighteen years—from 1904, when his essay, "Social Democracy and the National Question," was published, to shortly before his death in 1923— Medem published several works that aimed to shape the party's national worldview. The basic premises in this creed and the changes that it underwent pertain to the years 1904–1916. Medem himself viewed matters thus in 1917, when he produced a collection of his articles on the national issue while he was living in independent Poland.[39] The articles, originally written in Russian, were translated into Yiddish. Only five of them are important: "Social Democracy and the National Question" (1906); "Nationalism or Neutralism" (1910); "The World Jewish Nation" (1911); "Deep in Life"; and "Again, 'Ourselves and Our Nationalism'" (1916). All in all, it is a rather meager corpus of theoretical literature in view of the gravity of the issue that the Bund had tackled—defining the Jews as an extraterritorial nation and determining the working class's attitude toward it, both in intra-Jewish relations and in the essence of relations between the Bund and the Russian Socialist Party. Notably, however, Medem wrote the first of these articles—"Social Democracy and the National Question"—two years before the Austrian social democratic leader, Otto Bauer, published his famous and very influential book under the same title.[40] Medem was quite proud to have preceded Bauer, the great mentor of social democracy, in both the idea and its dissemination. It showed that an issue of minor importance in general Socialist thinking was central to Jewish Socialism in both its Zionist and its Bundist versions. Notably, Dov Ber Borochov's original writings on the national issue and the role of the Jewish proletariat in it—"On the Question of Zion and Territory"(1905) and "Our Platform" (1906)—appeared concurrently with Medem's writings and predated Bauer's book. Although Medem's writings did not refer to Borochov's articles, the "national awakening" that Herzl had instigated among the Jewish masses (as even Bund leaders admitted) presented the Bund with a problem, as its leaders attested, and motivated it to explain its stance on the national issue. If we recall the foregoing discussion, we may note that Medem was not the first to subject the question of the Bund and the national issue to systematic debate. In 1902, in the aftermath of the fourth convention of the Bund— a year before he participated in his first debate on this topic—a pamphlet entitled "On the Question of National Cultural Autonomy and the Building of the Russian Social Democratic Party on a Federative Basis," was published under the Bund imprimatur.[41]

The essay, although written by Vladimir Kossovski, was painstakingly shaped by the party's central committee to avoid unnecessary polemics with the *Iskra* people.[42] Therefore, before we discuss the debate on this issue in the general Russian party at its convention in London in 1903, we should set forth Kossovski's main arguments.

The title of the pamphlet speaks for itself and sufficed to attract the general opposition of Plekhanov, Lenin, and Martov, who considered a federative structure inappropriate. To counter their views, Kossovski based his arguments on the premise—from which the Bund in Russia and Poland would not stray until World War II and its aftermath—that a Socialist Party must not disregard the masses' deeply rooted national sentiments and aspirations. In view of the proliferation of nations that have clashing interests and aspirations, the party should implement a policy that seeks to ordain compromises among them. In other words, recognition of national multiculturalism should, in the political sense, be based on a federative arrangement. As Kossovski attested—reliably, by all accounts—he was asked to rediscuss the issue after the schismatic convention in London in 1903, but he refused to do so for two reasons. First, his aforementioned pamphlet left no doubt about his stance. Second, in the meantime a new concept, "neutralism," had appeared in the national debate. He disapproved of this notion but did not wish to foment further unnecessary discord in the party. The father of the neutralism concept was Vladimir Medem, who played an active role at the fifth Bund convention, where the national question was debated. This is why the central committee tasked Medem with writing the article.

Before he wrote the essay "Social Democracy and the National Question," Medem participated in the debate over this question at the fifth Bund convention, which, as stated, took place in June 1903 in Zurich.[43] In this debate, between the champions of national autonomy, headed by Kossovski, and those who frowned on this idea for various reasons, Medem adopted an in-between stance of sorts—either due to modesty, being one of the youngest and newest members of the Bund circle, or because he had not yet formed a cohesive attitude toward this question. Evidently for the same reason, as a disappointed Kossovski hints, Medem did not play an important role in the debate with the *Iskra* people, as he had been expected to do, at the famous London convention that followed the Bund convention in Zurich. Be this as it may, in Zurich Medem laid the foundations for his "neutralistic" approach toward the national issue, which he phrased in his aforementioned essay about a year later, in 1904, and attempted to explain and amend for more than ten years.

In that debate, Medem credited the "neutral" approach toward nationalism to the social democrats. Neutralism, he explained, denoted the very opposite of the absence of an approach. It was the social democratic stance, he said, to recognize the entitlement of every social collective and to solve the national problem in any way it deemed acceptable. In Medem's opinion, this solution is attainable in three ways: nationalism, assimilation, and social democracy. The first two paths—clashing ones—flow from the objective developmental process of modern capitalistic society. Although they lead to contrasting goals—assimilation and nationalism, respectively, both of which attempt to alter an existing situation, one by forging national identity and the other by nullifying it—in this sense, according to Medem, they are not neutral on the national question. Social democracy, in contrast, is objective in its approach to the nationalism phenomenon. In social democracy, national affiliation is unimportant per se but does take account of the diverse needs of separate social groups. By recognizing this, social democracy accepts social development whether it seeks to assimilate or to move toward national determination, and it has no preference for either trend. However, the objective social neutralism of social democracy should not be construed as political negativism, since the SD Party plays a positive role in defending every nation from enslavement that strives to bring about its assimilation by violent and artificial means.[44]

By implication, since the Jewish masses still lived within an entrenched traditional religious culture that had been enduring for thousands of years, the SD Party should seek on their behalf a cultural-political solution that would let them continue to maintain this way of life as long as they wish to maintain it. Thus, although Medem did not say so explicitly, assimilation, if unimposed and generated by an objective social process, is not illegitimate. Nor did Medem state that assimilation is desirable or preferable to the aspiration for a culturally based national self-determination.

At this stage, Medem gives us the impression of a person still groping to find his way in the maze of psychological, cultural, and political meanings of the national question, particularly in its Jewish context. Thus, he found it convenient at first to lean on a strong brace, the social democratic theory. A year later, however, when he sat down to express his thoughts systematically and in writing, he shifted his point of departure from the universalistic to the Jewish-particularistic. He did so for two reasons that he stressed at the beginning of his work. First, the world social democratic movement did not concern itself greatly with the national issue and, therefore, had not developed a specific national Socialist theory. (Importantly, he wrote in this vein before Otto Bauer published his aforementioned book.) Second—and, from his standpoint, more important—among the Jews, unlike other peoples that gave national consciousness centrality, assimilation was on the ascent.[45] Medem rejected conscious ideological and cultural assimilationism because it reflected the aim of uprooting a historical folk culture, modifying traditional ways of life artificially, and subjecting the collective past to sweeping repudiation. Concurrently, however, Medem rejected national ideology that defines the nation, in the main, as a spiritual and historical unity based on psychological solidarity, as in the thinking of the French historian Joseph-Ernest Renan and the Jewish historian Simon Dubnow. Especially infuriating to Medem was the concept of national solidarity, which disregards and repudiates the class struggle that takes place in every society and nation. Therefore, he categorically opposed the national political principle that animated the arguments of both Dubnow and the Zionists.

In contrast to them, Medem considered the national problem an inseparable part of the class outlook that flowed from objective rivalry between the bourgeois and proletarian classes of territorial and exterritorial peoples. However, Medem and his comrades could not conceive of a national struggle between proletarian classes. Therefore, they—paradoxically, as devout Marxists—judged the national problem to be a cultural and psychological issue, such as that manifested in the class struggle of the Jewish proletariat among Jews and in society at large. Marxism sanctions the cultural dimension of this class struggle, in Medem's opinion, because every culture has a universalistic basis and a particularistic superstructure. Does this mean that the Bund considers the national differentiation historically and socially permanent? Certainly not, Medem replied, since "we are not nationalists." Does it signify the opposite—that Bundists reject nationalism outright? Absolutely not: "We are not assimilationists." Each socionational development has a class struggle that is particular to it. The outcome of the national struggle— assimilation or national coalescence—will be a result of "a blind process, over which we have no control."[46]

In Medem's opinion, the nationalists and the assimilationists err by transforming possible results into goals. In other words, if history decrees that the Jews must assimilate into the peoples among whom they live, the Bund, for its part, will make no effort to arrest the process: *"We will not intervene in this; we are neutral."* Although the Bund rejects assimilation as a goal, it does so because it opposes making assimilation a goal but not because of principled objection to assimilation as such. Assimilation must occur only through a developmental process. In other words, "We are not against assimilation but against the aim to assimilate, against assimilation as a goal."[47] If historical development prompts the Jews to reinforce and develop their national culture, the Bund will not oppose this either, because "We do not rule out the national nature of a culture but oppose nationalist policy." In sum, the Bund is neutral on every issue that typifies the bourgeoisie in one way or another. In this respect, neither nationalism nor assimilationism has any bearing on the Jewish working class.

From the political standpoint, Medem, pursuant to Austria's social democracy, distinguishes between two methods of nationally based determination. One is statehood, which, in its essence, is a nation's political self-determination within specific borders. The second is the right of ethnic groups to develop their national particularism on a cultural basis in multinational states.

In Medem's opinion, cultural autonomy is the only credible social democratic manifestation of national self-determination in multinational states. Apart from the issue of culture, the "national Klal" has ceased to exist and has merged into the general interest of the multinational state. In any case, Medem stressed, national autonomy is the most significant manifestation of national self-determination in a state or a given territory within the state. Medem did not oppose nationhood based on territory but nationhood based *solely* on territory. Furthermore, Medem considered territorialism an incorrect and even false basis for self-determination. This is because historical development, while destroying or lowering many national barriers, has not extirpated the wish of collectives that have a cultural national tradition to continue sustaining that tradition in the present and in the future. Therefore, the popular collective national cultural heritage can still stand up to capitalism, which in essence promotes integration among peoples and assimilation of individuals. It is true that in this sense, the comprehensive idea of national autonomism in its three dimensions—state, territory, and personal—can impede a capitalist development that may uproot entrenched cultures. However, Medem re-expressed the right of a collective to self-determination: not as a territory but rather as a nation, "the combination of all individuals who belong to a historical-cultural group, irrespective of its commanding a demographic majority in a given territory."[48] This phrasing, coupled with political demands for equal civil rights for Jews and full recognition of Yiddish as a language of the state, is the national platform of the Bund.

However, in contrast to the party's clearly articulated political demands, the definition of a nation as a partnership of individuals who are bound to each other by a historical-culture tradition left some residual confusion at the theoretical level. The question here is thus: if so, what is the difference between this outlook and Dubnow's? Even if we assume, like Medem and unlike Dubnow, that the future Jewish nation will be not a Klal Yisrael but a "proletariat Yisrael," the national relationship between its various segments, dispersed in different countries, will be based on the cultural historical tradition. Admittedly, Medem, unlike Dubnow, assumed on the basis of the "neutralist" outlook that the Jewish nation, like other nations, might vanish at some future time. Even so, however, there was no principled difference between the two in terms of vindicating nationhood within the existing historical process, for which no time limits can be set. Furthermore, the two were also politically indistinguishable; both sought the establishment of national-cultural autonomy, official status for the Yiddish language, and equal civil rights for Jews in the Russian state. This, in Medem's mind, is what created an internal contradiction between the future national "neutralism" and the present national "dynamism" in the political and the cultural respects.

National neutralism, even as a prognosis, discomfited the Bund nationalists—the group headed by Vladimir Kossovski. In obituary remarks for Medem twenty years after the pamphlet came out, Kossovski explained that the party's official endorsement of neutralism had been nothing but a "false" thought and a political ruse of sorts to prevent internal schism and exacerbation of the struggle with the *Iskra* people in the Russian Social Democratic Party. As for the issue as such, the theory was of no practical importance in the political and ideological life of the Bund.[49]

Did Medem, too, consider the neutralist theory a political subterfuge from its outset? If not, did he attempt to back away from it in subsequent years, or did he retain something of it until the end of his days? We will pursue these questions as this chapter continues.

Four years after he published his first work, Medem wrote an article with a title that speaks for itself: "Nationalism or 'Neutralism.'"[50] Implicit in the article from start to finish is the idea that Medem had been continually criticized for defining matters that way. He admits that the concept has not been particularly successful and that he would replace it if a better one could be found. The main thing from his standpoint, however, was not the name but the content behind it. This is the thrust of the article. The debate over the national issue, in his opinion, forces the party to answer two questions—one of *prognosis,* pertaining to the future of the Jewish people, and one of *ideology,* aiming to express the national goal in the here and now. In regard to the first question, Medem repeats his opposition to the prognoses of both the "assimilationists" and the "nationalists." The future that both outlooks expect hinges totally on historical development, even if their predictions are firmly rooted in reality in one way or another. Accordingly, the Bund faces a different question. The Jewish nation exists and its national consciousness is on the ascent. Thus, the issue is not one of prognosis but of a social fact that requires an ideological viewpoint.

The party, Medem stated, should view this phenomenon favorably without erasing the question mark that hovers over the survivability of Jewish nationhood in the distant future. Medem stressed that even Otto Bauer, "the assimilator" as he called him, and persons of like mind had to admit that the Jews were experiencing a national awakening on their way to total assimilation.[51]

This situation is accompanied by a psychological doubt: since assimilation may ultimately win the day, is the national endeavor futile? Medem countered this doubt by clinging to his original formula: staunch opposition to forced assimilation and acquiescence in volitional assimilation (*fraye asimilatsie*). However, his dialectical method of thinking led him immediately to ask: What does "volitional" assimilation mean? In his opinion, even if the masses are not directly pressured to assimilate but are denied government assistance for the development of their national culture by establishing national schools, or if their national language is not freely recognized—indirect repression to bring about assimilation is being applied. Capitalist governance, which by its very nature destroys, erodes, or commingles groups of people that have national historical traditions by making them into "scattered dust" (*tsushtoybt un tsushotn*), should also be considered indirect repression. The question that Medem asks here is whether this inexorable process can be fought in view of the assimilative economic process of ascendant capitalism. After all, the entire nation, and not only marginal groups within it, is involved in and susceptible to this process. In that case, Medem asks, why struggle at all? For the idea? Can one base oneself on the notion that both Dubnow and Ahad Ha'am called "the national will" (*natsionaler viln*)? Medem did not deny the existence of the "national will" but argued that this will flows from, instead of clashing with, the social reality and its requirements. In other words, if reality were to change in such a way as to obviate the existence of nations, the Jewish national will would not be able to obstruct the Jews' assimilation. By the same token, if this situation does not exist, one should stop asking, Hamlet-like, "To be or not to be."[52] Medem denied that this stance denotes national fatalism. In fact, he asserted, it inspires positive national activism in the political and cultural respects. Medem was aware that the Bund's national activity seemed to be moving the party closer to nationalist circles in the Jewish bourgeoisie. Therefore, he hurriedly stressed the substantive difference that, he said, separated them. In his opinion, the Bund's outlook rested on a firm foundation and employed criteria in assessing correct and incorrect conduct in respect to the national issue. Sometimes the Bund cooperated with the "nationalists" and sometimes followed its own counsel. Either way, however, it never lost sight of the abyss between itself, as a proletarian party, and the organs of the nationalist Jewish bourgeoisie.

This article is undoubtedly an updated interpretation, of sorts, of its predecessor, written three years earlier. Basically, Medem had not changed his mind about neither affirming nor rejecting nationalism at the level of principle. Everything, in his opinion, depends on future social development. In two respects, however, the latter article has something new to say. First, it stresses that forced assimilation occurs not only due to deliberate policy, but also due to the process of capitalism, which causes historical societies to disintegrate. By explicit implication, the political struggle for cultural autonomy is part of the anticapitalist struggle of Western social democracy, especially the Austrian version, which recognizes the right of peoples to national cultural self-determination. Second, Medem is newly aware that the struggle for national-cultural autonomy draws the Bund closer to the views of Jewish liberal circles, for which Simon Dubnow was considered the main communicator. For this reason, Medem states that this rapprochement is transitory and partial and that, basically, the two paths are essentially separate. He was right. Liberal nationalism affirmed the principle of nationhood as an everlasting phenomenon; Medem presumed that it might be also temporary. The temporary and partial rapprochement between Medem's and Dubnow's national outlooks, and the distance of principle and substance that separated them, were manifested about a year later in an article concerning the main bone of contention: "The World Jewish Nation."[53] This article is novel because it constitutes the only intellectual attempt in the intellectual and ideological world of the Bund, and in Bund history up to World War II, to explore the question of whether there is a world Jewish people. According to Professor Hersch Liebman (Pesach Liebman Hersch), a demographer who belonged to the leading intellectual circles in the Bund, the Bund as a practitioner of applied politics never pondered this question deeply and systematically. Indeed, the Bund's set of pundits did not respond to Medem's article in this regard, in contrast to their behavior in regard to the "neutralism" article. Even C. S. Kazdan, who thirty-six years later, in a pamphlet devoted to the fiftieth anniversary of the Bund in 1947, tried to rehabilitate Medem's national outlook in respect to neutralism, did not address himself to this article.[54]

In terms of Medem's national beliefs, the article is important because it discusses the third dimension of the Jewish national problem. The first is *recognition* of the existence of a Jewish working class; the second is *familiarity* with the Jewish masses. The third is *vacillation* about whether the Jews are a "world people"—a long-repressed matter that rose in full fury after the Holocaust.

The article begins with a sarcastic remark by rivals of the Bund who countered his arguments by accusing the Bund of believing that Jewish peoplehood ended at the borders of Russia, that is, that other countries have adherents of the Mosaic faith or citizens of Jewish origin, but not a Jewish people.

At the beginning of the article, Medem crafts an intellectual definition of the nation. From his standpoint, the concept of "cultural community" (*kulturgemaynshaft*) is too broad and vague. After all, various national entities may fall within the ambit of one culture. However, even if we accept the cultural-community definition of nationhood—Medem asked himself—may we then consider the Jews a world people? His answer: "Absolutely not" (*Beshum oyfn nisht*)—because Jews in the Pale of Settlement have no cultural partnership whatsoever with Jews in France, Germany, England, or Bulgaria. In other words, there is a crisscross cultural divide, between eastern and western Europe and between Ashkenazi and Sephardi Jewry, and therefore those collectivities are not related in any real sense. Without shared cultural life, there is no particular peoplehood.[55]

Medem does admit to a possible counterclaim: that in other peoples, too, that is, the Russians or the Germans, the upper and lower classes do not share a singular culture. In their case, however, Medem replied, the paltry culture that the lower classes possess is wholly national. Within the Jews, things are utterly different. Western European Jews have no indigenous Jewish culture of their own; their culture is that of the nation amidst which they live. A Jew in the West speaks neither Yiddish nor Hebrew. He considers himself an inseparable part of the French or German national collective. Even if he does not forget his origin and even if he is willing to help Jews elsewhere when in trouble, the cultural gap between them remains.[56] From this point of departure, Medem contested Simon Dubnow head-on. On what, he asked, are the consciousness and feeling that hold the Jewish nation together based? He doubted that one could predicate a collective national feeling solely on a shared historical past. In Medem's opinion, the existence of a Jewish nation in the past does not mean that, in view of historical developments and changes, such a nation still exists. Then, paraphrasing Descartes, he described Dubnow's outlook ironically: "I was, therefore I am."[57]

Furthermore, Medem argued, one cannot base a national consciousness on historical memory only, as Renan and, following him, Dubnow believed. A shared national consciousness is generated by life in common, under real historical conditions, and it changes as these conditions change. The Jews' real social and political conditions have changed radically indeed. Therefore, there is a sociocultural gap not only between western and eastern European Jews, but also, since Poland was partitioned among three powers (Russia, Prussia, and Austria), among Polish Jews. Jews in Congress Poland were different from Jews in Galicia. Therefore, at the dawn of the twentieth century, even though "one cannot identify several Jewish nations" (*etlikhe yudishe natsies*), one can no longer speak of a united Jewish nation (*aynhaytlikher yudisher natsie*). This is because slowly but steadily, for more than two hundred years since the advent of rationalism in Western civilization, "the historical process unfolding before our eyes"[58] has been destroying the religious framework that has given the Jews, dispersed around the globe, the consciousness and sense of being a single collective.

In sum, Medem repeats his traditional stance, and that of the Bund, against assimilation and against nationalism. Since he cannot ignore the collective national sentiments that the dispersed Jews still maintain, he admits that some things still bind the Jews together. However, to deal with these matters jointly and successfully, it is first necessary to *dispose* of the excess weight (*gevikhtn*) that burdens the Jewish reality. Since belief in the cause of building a world Jewish nation disturbs even those Jewish nationalists who are not Socialists, it must be stamped out altogether. Paradoxically, Medem argues sarcastically, the obesity of the national Klal Yisrael idea is not dragging the nation downward, toward the ground of reality, but lifting and propelling toward the firmament of the abstract and vague historical past.

In contrast, the original, living Jewish culture, that is, the Yiddish, not the Hebrew, can and should be developed, on a global basis, as a cooperative cultural venture of the Jewish collectivities that originated in the Yiddish culture, for as long as they wish to sustain that culture. This cooperation, however, Medem stresses, must not be identified with the idea of a world Jewish people, which changes the picture totally.[59] The very idea of a world people—a Klal Yisrael—inserts mutually exclusive elements into the cultural framework, such as Hebrew versus Yiddish, religious faith versus a secular national Weltanschauung, folk Yiddishist culture versus elitist Hebrew culture, and so forth. Anything of that nature may actually accent the real contradiction that exists between the national unity idea and the Yiddishist folk culture of the Jewish masses, especially in eastern Europe. By so arguing, Medem created an unbridgeable dichotomy of a national culture that does not exist and a folk culture that does (*natsionaln un folkishn*). Thus, Medem retreated from neutralism by asserting the importance of the

Jewish national feeling at large, especially in eastern Europe, and was even willing to accept the cultivation of this culture on a global basis. However, he categorically rejected the national idea of a "world people" as argued by Dubnow and, especially, by Zionism.

Does this actually point to a change in Medem's outlook? Indirectly, Medem definitely devalued his argument—even if the question of his having done so directly is not discussed—by extending the incidence of national cultural "activism" to Jewish collectivities in eastern Europe outside Tsarist Russia. By so doing, he invested the national culture with meaning that transcends daily folk existence within a specific, defined social reality and transformed it into a bridge between the various segments of Jewry of eastern European origin. Thus, he strengthened the spiritual dimension of national identity by elevating it over various existential realities such as the Russian and the American.

However, Medem remained true to his basic premise, the foundation stone of neutralism: the conviction that economic and social development would eventually determine everything. Furthermore, in the matter of a "world people," it was no longer necessary to wait for the prognostic process to unfold; after all, even then anyone could see that the widening divide among Jewry's diverse segments was leading to national fragmentation. The sociohistorical process proved that several societies of Jewish origin were coming into being. Practically, perhaps, this means that the process of Jewish disintegration was but a preparatory—an objective— phase that would lead to the Jews' disappearance as a world nation at some indeterminate future time.

Five years later, after the beginning of World War I, this expansion of cultural validity to a domain outside the particularistic social reality of eastern European Jewry prompted Medem to modify the "neutralism" doctrine substantially in the intellectual sense. Sofia Erlich—the staunch Marxist, daughter of Simon Dubnow, and wife of the future Bund leader in Poland, Henryk Erlich—attributed this change to Medem's encounter with the Jewish masses in Poland.[60] While this mechanistic social perspective contains some truth, it obviously disregards the organic ideational process that Medem had developed in the decade preceding World War I. There is no doubt, however, that five years after he debated the meaning of the Jews' existence as a world people, Medem took another step forward in developing his "neutralism" concept and adjusting it to existing and changing reality.

In a six-article series, published in 1916 under the pregnant title "Deeper in Life" (*Tifer in lebn*),[61] Medem describes the development of his national outlook as a collective Bundist phenomenon from 1901 to that time. Without retreating from his first premise—that the fate of peoples, especially the Jews, hinges on the development of "historical forces" (*historishe kreftn*)—he invests those forces with special meaning. His description of the development of the neutralistic view offers nothing new apart from one important point. Writing about the historical forces that change and determine the fate of nations, he stresses that the people is one of these forces and, therefore, the fate of the nation depends on the actions of the people.[62] On the basis of this activistic premise, Medem distinguishes between the "old neutralism" (*alter neutralism*) and the other neutralism, the new, that has developed as its outgrowth. The erstwhile neutralism, valid until 1905, called for total multicultural freedom within a framework of Jewish cultural autonomy. Thus, only if groups of Jewish activists wished to maintain a school system that did not use the national language would they be allowed to do so, and so forth. However, Medem continues, what was logical ten years ago no longer passes the test of current reality, because political consciousness has spread and become more deeply entrenched among the Jewish masses. This change has shifted the national question from the field of an essentially intellectual debate to the applied domain of practical and clashing political demands, such as recognition of the national language (Russian, Polish, Yiddish), national schools, and so forth. These practical issues, in Medem's opinion, entail prior decisions of principle in advance of the struggle over what political path to follow. In this new reality, the Bund, as a political and social party, cannot avoid the fray on the basis of the "old neutralism" argument. Just as the Bund has adopted an active stance on the issue of class struggle, so should it in the national struggle, because the two are related. For this reason, the decision should not be left to objective or neutral historical forces.[63]

Medem explains that the transformation of neutralism from passivism to national activism for inroads in popular life (*tifer in lebn arayn*) corresponds to the transformation of the Bund from an underground organization to a mass political movement. This transition has made abstract intellectual issues into practical daily problems, and "in this manner we have moved deeper into life" (*Mit dem dazign veg zenen mir gegangen alts tifer in lebn arayn*).[64]

Medem summarized his "new neutralism" outlook, if one may thus define the change that occurred in his understanding of the national issue, in an article titled "Again, Ourselves and Our Nationalism."[65] His purpose in writing it was to justify the party's active involvement in political struggle for the organization and shaping of Jewish national-cultural life by advocating the abandonment of the old theory of total separation of class and national interests. Indeed, he believed that, despite the class differences, class interest and national interest should not be totally separated.[66] Thus, concern for the nation at large should be a trait of the working class, too, and not the Jewish nationalists only. The Bund, as a political party, no longer floats in the mist of abstract theories but strides on the ground of reality. This being the case, when realities change, so do the party's views on class interest versus national interest. This, the class outlook, is, in Medem's opinion, a litmus test of sorts with which one may assess developments and make policy accordingly. However, even if the old litmus test (*der altn probirshtayn*) is not abandoned, it should be borne in mind that the principled class approach is merely a point of departure and by no means a rubber stamp (*shtempl*) in debating political and social issues. After all, people are the ones who adjust to reality. Therefore, although the point of departure is admittedly old, its fulfillment can be new.[67] At the end of World War I, this perspective prompted Medem to create a synthesis of sorts between the "internationalist" and the nationalist prognoses. In 1918, in view of the Versailles Treaty, Medem expressed the belief that the establishment of new nationally based states was a stopgap solution only. The social process, in his opinion, would by necessity lead to the creation of large supranational political and economic units. This objective trend would invest the cultural autonomy, the function of which would be to protect the specific nation within the multinational state, with particular importance.[68]

Medem implemented this creed in his activity in independent Poland in 1917–1920, after which he left for the United States. During those years, he devoted himself mainly to the party's Yiddish Jewish-education enterprise. Another factor in this was his disillusionment with what was happening in the party, that is, the internecine struggle between the left wing, which labored to bring the Bund into the Third International—an act that would quickly destroy the party's independence—and the mainstream, which, to preserve the Bund's independence, refused to accept the Comintern's conditions. Medem, a traditional anti-Bolshevik and an uncompromising rival of Lenin, inveighed vehemently against the Comintern—a form of behavior that left him isolated in the party.

Politically isolated from his comrades, Medem worked actively to bring the Bund into the Congress for Yiddish Culture. By rejecting this initiative, too, the party exacerbated his isolation. Ultimately, however, there is no doubt that Medem's activity for the creation of a broad organizational framework that would encourage national culture subsequently formed the basis on which the Bund, Po'aley Tsiyyon Left, and various Yiddishist groups built the CYSHO school system.[69]

Yiddish language and culture, in Medem's opinion, were more than matters of intellectual attitude and ideology; they were manifestations of the Jewish masses' nationhood and national interest. Language also became a very urgent problem in the new democratic regime in independent Poland. Therefore, he demanded that at the present time, an era so different from its recent predecessor, when the political situation was different—the class interest of the Jewish workers should give rise to a struggle for the overarching national task, for the Yiddish language, in conjunction with other progressive national forces.[70] At that time, the party turned a deaf ear to his urgings.

These views of Medem's, expressed in 1916–1918, also translated into political terms from his standpoint. In 1916, while in Warsaw, he was invited to take part in a conference of Jewish public figures, intellectuals, and journalists in that city. At the conference, the question of the struggle for Jewish national autonomy was debated. Medem took the occasion to express a political view that was far-reaching relative to the Bundist ideological tradition and relative to his own ideological and political development. He spoke vehemently about the need to establish an autonomous national framework of Klal Yisrael and stressed that, under the existing circumstances, the Jews must be in charge of their own affairs. Then he added a sentence pregnant with significance: "I say this knowing that the Bund will lose the elections to the Hasidim. *That's always better than controlling a Polish municipal council*" [emphasis mine].[71] As I will show in chapter 3, in 1919 a dispute erupted between Medem and Wiktor Alter in this matter—the importance of national autonomy in the era following World War I.

Medem's views were carried on, directly or indirectly, in the resolutions of the Russian Bund on the national autonomy question the party's tenth convention (April 1–6, 1917), after the February 1917 revolution. At this gathering, the Bund expressed a favorable view toward participating "*in a pan-Jewish convention* convened on the basis of a *general* franchise . . . of *all* citizens . . . who *affiliate themselves* with the Jewish nation—because it regards this as an instrumentality for the attainment of national-cultural autonomy" [emphasis mine].[72] Therefore, the Bund placed the interests of the nation at large over sectional interests that were clashed in substantive ways: between the working class and the bourgeoisie, between the Zionist and the Bundist ideologies, between the nonreligious and the religious, and between Yiddish-speaking Jews and those who had adopted Russian as their vernacular.

Pursuant to this resolution, the Bund agreed, after internal vacillations and external disagreements, to participate in elections for the general convention of Russian Jews.[73] Although these elections took place in January 1918, the convention was not held because the Bolsheviks assumed power in December 1917. Medem put his outlook into practice in independent Poland between 1917 and 1920, when he left for the United States. During those years, he devoted himself mainly to the Yiddish-language Jewish education enterprise. He had an additional reason for spending his time this way: disillusionment with the wranglings of two forces within the party. The left flank of the Bund strove to bring the party into the Third International, which would result in the Bund's imminent self-liquidation, whereas the mainstream, wishing to keep an autonomous Bund in existence, rejected some of the Comintern's terms. Medem, a traditional anti-Bolshevik and an uncompromising rival of Lenin's, came out passionately against the Comintern, which isolated him within the party.

Politically sequestered from his comrades, Medem sponsored a motion to enlist the Bund in the Congress for Yiddish Culture. The party rejected this initiative, too, thus aggravating his isolation. Ultimately, however, there is no doubt that Medem's activities for the creation of a broad organizational framework that would foster national culture helped to lay the foundations of the CYSHO school system, a cooperative venture of the Bund, Po'aley Tsiyyon Left, and various Yiddishist circles.[74]

For Medem, the Yiddish language and its culture reflected the Jewish national essence and the authentic interest of the Jewish masses, as opposed to an intellectual posture or a question of ideology. Language was also an urgent, pressing problem in the new democratic regime of independent Poland. Therefore, he insisted that at the present time, a time so different from the recent past, in which the political situation was different, Jewish workers should act on their class interest by struggling for the overall national mission, that is, the Yiddish language, in concert with other progressive national forces. At the time, his was the only voice in the party that expressed such a demand.

Outside the party, however, one person could observe Medem's struggle with both satisfaction and sorrow: the historian Simon Dubnow, sire of the national autonomy idea. After all, as I show in chapter 3, Medem was the last fighter for pan-Jewish national-cultural autonomy at that point in time, shortly before his departure from Poland.

Thus, Medem "came in from the cold" and died outside his eastern European home—in the United States.[75] Might this symbolism be indicative of Medem's national outlook? I would answer in the affirmative. The high-minded Medem was an outsider and so he remained; Medem the Jew wished to become one with his people. His Jewishness was not natural but intellectual and emotional. As an intellectual of the Marxist persuasion, he could not repudiate the "prognostic neutralism" doctrine, which flowed from the very theory of social and historical development. However, the passion that brought him back to Jewry and his folk roots stood in a sort of dialectic contrast to his intellectualism. In the tension between the two—intellect and passion—the latter won out. Medem became the great champion of the Yiddish language and an indefatigable fighter for its national and political status. In this struggle, as an exponent of the prognostic view, he was willing to accommodate the assimilationists who had abandoned Yiddish in favor of Polish and with the ultranationalists who repudiated it in favor of Hebrew. However, he zealously fought against the in-between solution of a Yiddish-Hebrew diglossia and those who favored it.[76] In this matter, he brooked no compromise. Yiddish was the people, and Medem, after all, had returned to his people. In his uncompromising struggle for Yiddish, he made himself into a counterweight of sorts to the possibility of a neutralistic prognosis in the future. To his fellow Bundists, Medem was important not only as a national theoretician and a warm, charming person but also as a national "repenter." For them—people whose national beliefs prompted them to divorce from their ideological surroundings—Medem became an emblem of the correctness of the path and, therefore, the legend of the Jewish labor movement.

In this sense, Medem resembled Zionist personalities on the fringes of the Jewish national sphere who, for various reasons, penetrated its core, gave it its shape, or left their imprint on it. Such personalities were Theodor Herzl, Max Nordau, Yosef Trumpeldor, and the poetess Rachel. This may explain Medem's unexplained sympathy for the persona of Herzl.

SUMMATION

Summing up the Russian chapter in the history of the Bund from the perspective of the Klal Yisrael concept, the question is whether the Klal Yisrael principle have any status in the development of the party's national thinking? I would answer in the affirmative. By examining how the "cultural autonomy" concept evolved during the 1901–1917 period, we see how complex and serpentine the party's exertions on this issue were. Ber Borochov, of all people, noticed these vacillations at the very beginning of the century, and he pointed out the Bund's weakness on the national question. This weakness, he said, was manifested in "[the party's] inability to determine a clear source for it, one way or another"—either to regard nationalism as a reactionary phenomenon and a Utopian outlook or to admit that national rights were among the specific needs of the Jewish masses. For this reason, Borochov concluded, "Bundist rationales on the national question always stop in the middle and always leave something expressed halfway—half-assimilationist and half-national."[77]

Another question is this: in 1917, pursuant to the February revolution in Russia, did the Bund really pull into the Klal Yisrael "station" in its attitude toward the organization and powers of Jewish national autonomy? This question is unanswerable because it was not put to the practical political test; the October Revolution elevated the Bolshevik Party to power, and the Bolsheviks, by ruling out Jewish nationalism, forced the Bund to dissolve within two years.

Nevertheless, it is hard to resist a speculative thought in regard to the political reality and the ideological spirit of the Russian Bund. If we assume that a liberal democratic regime would have taken shape in Russia after the February revolution, and that the constitution of this regime would have endowed minorities with self-determination in the form of national-cultural autonomy, would the Bund have continued to favor the idea of Dubnow-style comprehensive Jewish autonomy in the Russian state, as it did, after much vacillation, at the pan-Russian convention in 1917? Although this question is totally ahistorical, one may, I believe, answer it in the affirmative. After all, this chapter has shown how firmly, continually, and stubbornly the Bund adhered to the pairing of its national outlook and its class awareness, even though, according to its dialectic outlook, a national autonomy that wields powers that extend beyond the cultural domain might serve as an arena for social and class struggle. History developed in the opposite direction, of course. The Bolshevik Revolution dashed the Bund's hopes in all senses. Therefore, the question we ask here is shifted to the second era in the history and the Bund and to its second setting, independent interwar Poland.

CHAPTER 2

BETWEEN ERETZ ISRAEL AND THE DIASPORA
The Second Aliya, 1904–1914

Exile is like a chronic illness. . . . It is a perpetual game between the
power of extinction and the power of survival, neither of which can tip
the scales. It is a global drama that never ends.

—A. Heshin, 1914

INTRODUCTION

In the Zionist Labor Movement during the Second Aliya era, the Klal Yisrael
question was discussed in three different arenas, in each of which the movement attempted to deal with the internal structural contrasts of the Jewish
people. The first of these arenas was the Eretz Israel–Diaspora relationship;
its gist was reflected in the well-known concept "negation of the Diaspora."
The second arena was the cultural struggle over the use of Hebrew as the
vernacular in Eretz Israel. The third was the ramified and contradiction-
riddled social encounter between two groups of Jewish proletarians—those
of eastern European origin and those from Yemen—in the *moshavot* (Zionist farming settlements; sing. *moshava*) in Palestine.

Thus, paradoxically, the Labor Movement's affiliation with Klal Yisrael, a matter of ab initio principle from its standpoint, created between the
movement and the Klal a set of contrasts and frictions at various political
and cultural levels—the "New Yishuv" in Palestine, the Zionist Organization, and the World Socialist Union of Jewish Workers—Po'aley Tsiyyon,
in which Socialist Zionist parties in various countries sat together. To explore the ideational, political, and emotional aspects of this tension and to
probe the issues of concern in this chapter, it is first necessary to elucidate
several basic concepts.

The first, the term "Second Aliya," has two meanings—broad and narrow. The broad meaning includes everyone who settled in Palestine in
1904–1914: Zionist and Orthodox Jews from eastern Europe and Yemenite

Jews, irrespective of which Yishuv they joined, the Old or the New. The narrow meaning relates to the minority of young, unmarried *olim* who laid the foundations for the Zionist Labor Movement in Palestine. Although they accomplished little in the practical sense, they set revolutionary precedents by pointing the national development of the Jewish and Zionist Yishuv in a new direction. Therefore, henceforth our reference to the Second Aliya, capitalized and containing the definite article, refers to them. Notably, notwithstanding its inclusive name, the Second Aliya was not homogeneous but ideologically diverse and politically fragmented. In both respects, it was made up of three organized political and ideological entities: the non-Socialist Hapo'el ha-Tsa'ir federation, the Socialist Po'aley Tsiyyon Party; and a nonpartisan group in which both of the aforementioned were represented.

The second concept is the "Siamese" pairing of two Hebrew words, *gola* and *galut*. Although the minute difference between them in Zionist thinking is often blurred, it deserves emphasis for the purposes of our discussion. Gola refers to political and social exile; galut is a psychological and spiritual phenomenon that flows from gola but is not totally related to it, since one may have a sense of galut even in Eretz Israel. This distinction is crucial in understanding the Eretz Israel–Diaspora relationship in Zionist thinking generally and in regard to the Zionist Labor Movement particularly, because this movement, theoretically and practically, espoused a "Palestinocentric" policy that placed pragmatic endeavor in Palestine at the forefront of the national reality. Herzl and his successors, for example, negated the Diaspora as gola and believed that the relocation to Palestine of millions of Jews from the great centers in Europe would liquidate it in the quantitative sense. Ahad Ha'am, in contrast, negated galut as a value phenomenon that threatened national and spiritual Jewishness but did not believe in liquidating the gola. Paradoxically, for him the negation of galut, the exilic state of mind, was meant to sustain gola, the Diaspora. Indeed, the very point of establishing a "spiritual center" of qualitative and social nature in Palestine was to sustain Jewish nationhood in dispersion. It is true that Second Aliya people rejected the principle of gola, exile, in its Herzlian rendering. Concurrently, however, due to their worldview, they were concerned that mass emigration to Palestine might inundate their pioneering enterprise due to its magnitude. Therefore, they chose the Ahad Ha'am outlook at the practical level but dressed it in methods that Ahad Ha'am could not accept. Instead of his paragonic spiritual and social center, they sought to build a labor society of an almost Utopian complexion, a contrast to both gola and galut, as a basis for the construction of the new Jewish-Hebrew nation. Consequently, the focal point that brings Klal Yisrael together should be a Palestinocentric effort informed by a doctrine of "negation of galut."

Here we should reemphasize the difference between the "negation of galut" concept, rejection of the exilic state of mind, as espoused by the Zionist Labor Movement, and the meaning of the term that I ascribe to the Bund—even though the Bund held the concept in contempt due to its Zionist origin and nature. Both movements engraved rebellion against galut on their standard, but in clashing ways. The Bund rejected galut in its class and national struggle; the Labor Movement ruled out in its national pioneering actions. Paradoxically, the Bund's class radicalism gradually prompted the Bund to reach out to the impoverished Jewish masses, whereas the halutsic radicalism of the Labor Movement, due to its elitist nature and its doctrine of practical fulfillment, distanced the movement from them. Contrarily but for the very same reasons, the Bund distanced itself from Klal Yisrael in the national and political senses whereas the Labor Movement, regarding itself as a national vanguard, increasingly integrated itself into the Klal, motivated from its first steps in Palestine by the desire and the will to become the national leadership or at least to influence this leadership significantly. Therefore, the myth and ethos of the Bund, in its political education of the "new Jew," became in the Labor Movement an ethos and a myth in shaping the "new Hebrew" amidst a reality of life that offered an alternative to the Diasporic one.

Furthermore, in contrast to the Bund's ideological ethos, which was linked foremost with the political reality of social democracy at large, the basic ideological beliefs of the Labor Movement rested entirely in the sphere of the Jewish national and political reality. At that time, due to the political weakness of the Labor Movement, the movement's beliefs were important mainly in the domain of personal and public national action: aliya (emigration to Eretz Israel), development of Jewish labor and defense, cooperative settlement, and the entrenchment of the Hebrew language. Even though little was accomplished in these fields, the actions taken set revolutionary precedents.

Because the Labor Movement followed this path, which the contemporaries termed "constructivist," it always had to interact regularly with the various organizations of the political Klal Yisrael: the Zionist Labor Movement in eastern and Central Europe for political assistance, the Zionist Organization for financial aid, and the public institutions and settlement committees in Palestine in matters of "Hebrew labor," "Hebrew defense," and, in particular, anything involving labor settlement in cooperative agricultural localities. Thus, while the Bund took a consistent ab initio "separatist" stance vis-à-vis Klal Yisrael, the Labor Movement, for practical and ideological reasons, adopted an "integrationist" position at its own initiative, even as it stressed the value difference between itself and the rest of the "Zionist Klal."

NEGATION OF GALUT—REPUDIATING THE EXILIC STATE OF MIND

Among factions in the Second Aliya aggregate, the most consistent and uncompromising negator of galut was Ha-po'el ha-Tsa'ir, which rebelled even against the "labor in the present" policy in Diaspora countries, which the Zionist Movement adopted, theoretically and practically, after the Helsingfors convention in 1906.

In a broadsheet issued in 1908, after the "Young Turks" revolution, Ha-po'el ha-Tsa'ir urged young Jews to abandon their "barren and purposeless" Sisyphean exertions in exile and "make aliya."[1]

Among the intellectuals who contributed articles to the party journal, *Ha-po'el ha-Tsa'ir,* the editor of the journal, Yosef Aharonowitz, was the most extreme negator of galut of them all. For Aharonowitz, galut was a comprehensive moral concept that carried more than territorial meaning. Therefore, he said, galut was dominant even in Eretz Israel, as the farmers in the New Yishuv and, especially, in the "colonies," preferred non-Jewish (Arab) labor over Jewish labor. He regarded this as the exilic trait of submission to realities.[2] Following A. D. Gordon, Aharonowitz defined Diaspora Jewry as "a parasite despite itself," its moral human image warped by its exilic state. For this reason, "the eternal human ideals of the Jewish prophets have, admittedly, become a matter of concern to the Gentiles but are not the property of our people."[3] These extreme remarks, which if lifted out of their ideological and psychological context would be redolent of anti-Semitism, were written as counterpoints to statements by Ahad Ha'am in his article "The Bottom Line,"[4] which contemptuously dismiss the struggle of the young Second Aliya pioneers to "conquer" Hebrew labor and establish cooperative settlements. In Aharonowitz's opinion, Ahad Ha'am's "spiritual center" outlook was merely another version of the exilic spirit that sought ways to sustain the state of exile. "Therefore," Aharonowitz countered, "the renaissance is a rebellion against galut life, an escape from both the old and the modern settings and from lives of nebulousness, and a return to the field and to natural life. Anyone who steers us away from this path is *a prophet of galut* and not a *prophet of renaissance.*" Thus, Aharonowitz, in contrast to Ahad-Ha'am's dry intellectualism—the heritage of those generations of exilic thinking—offers vitality and passion by stating that "Eretz Israel will be redeemed not by the mind and book but by the heart and the hands."[5] Aharonowitz had no doubt that the Diaspora was fated to end in one way only—spiritual and national extinction. Everyone who hopes to revive secular Yiddish culture in the Diaspora ought to be told so explicitly, he prescribed, however cruel that may be, because the objective reality of assimilation is pushing the nation toward collective perdition by destroying every will and action "that have the qualities of national renaissance" and encouraging "all enterprises that spell galut and national death."[6]

The author Ya'akov Rabinowitz, a member of Ha-po'el ha-Tsa'ir, sustained Aharonowitz's trend of thought in "negation of galut." However, he expanded on it with respect to differences and similarities between galut and the New Yishuv in Palestine, which he considered the opposite of galut even if there were no assurances that the hopes placed in it would actually come to pass. Indeed, Rabinowitz admitted that "Seventy to 100 percent [of Jews] in Eretz Israel are still Diaspora Jews, and their exilic mentality is the worst and lowliest." The people he had in mind were those of the antimodern, *haredi* (ultra-Orthodox) Old Yishuv who lived on charity, as the Zionists and, especially the Second Aliya Zionists alleged. However, he did not withhold his caustic remarks from the New Yishuv as well: "I also know all the ailments of the 'new' Yishuv, a parasitic and speculative Yishuv that progressively strangles the very same fresh forces that the Diaspora is sending it." Just the same, in contrast to the Diaspora, "[The New Yishuv] has a positive facet. Some forces are being strangled but others are blossoming. There is something to like here; one cannot negate it totally. Here lies our advantage."[7] Thus, the illusion-free national hope, the opposite of the exilic thinking of Zionists of the Ahad Ha'am persuasion and of the Yiddishist and Dubnowist non-Zionists, resides here, in Eretz Israel.

Three personalities who were not card-carrying party members—the philosopher A. D. Gordon, the "old man" of the Second Aliya; Y. H. Brenner, the agonized and agonizing author who belonged to the same group; and Berl Katznelson, the future "rebbe" of the Zionist Labor Movement—gave the concept of galut and its negation greater breadth and depth.

Katznelson was struck with the sense of galut, the Diaspora state of mind, the moment he debarked in Palestine and during his first visit to Petah Tiqva. In a lecture to his young students some thirty years later, he recalled the trauma of his encounter with galut in Palestine:

> I immediately tumbled *not into galut but into something more horrible—enslavement to Jews who are not Jews at all.* . . . Everyone wants to profit from you, to sell you something. I could have accepted the toil and the way of life lovingly, but this was something I could not accept from—Eretz Israel.[8]

A. D. Gordon, in his spiritualist-national philosophy and personal way of life, was the most extreme and consistent "negator of galut" of all. He conditioned the Jewish spiritual and moral national renaissance on a return to Eretz Israel as the nation's historical home, to the Jewish people's nature—amidst which the nation would cure itself of the illnesses of exile—and to working the land, this being the path to the health of the new and moral Jew who, by means of his way of life, would create a "nation of man."

Yosef Hayyim Brenner's negation of galut was much more complex and contradictory. Brenner negated exile in both the moral and the aesthetic senses. He had experienced the pain of the cowardice of a father who had fled from the terror of pogromists, so humiliated as to be ludicrous,[9] and he despised what he termed the cheap ugliness of the Jews in the streets of Whitechapel, London. However, Brenner also decried the galut that existed in Eretz Israel and outdid his Second Aliya contemporaries in so doing. He ruthlessly exposed the illegitimate exilic traits of these proletarians, too. Unlike Gordon, who projected his beliefs by means of his special image, way of living, and teachings, Brenner so strongly reflected an extreme "Zionist despair" that he made it into a creed of sorts. Therefore, he personified concurrently the drive to abandon Eretz Israel and the strength to stay there, brutal criticism of the workers and allegiance to their enterprise, radical negation of the Diaspora and inability to divorce himself from it. Thus, Brenner, who had despaired of the comprehensive Zionist solution, came around to an acquiescence in Klal Yisrael, as expressed below by a hero in his novella, *From Here, From There,* published in 1911, the crisis year of the Second Aliya. Turning Ahad Haʿam's doctrine on its head, he argued that

> What we need isn't a false "center" that will link all the diasporas to it but rather the consolidation of each and every Jewish collective in accordance with its way and mutual influence. Indeed, give us, O land of Russia, tough-minded Jews who know how to devote themselves to the sanctification of their lives; [give us, O] land of Galicia, goodhearted Jews who value every lofty aspiration; [give us, O] America, multitalented Jews who have clear goals; [give us, O] Eretz Israel, Jews who have the sense of homeland and who love working the soil. May they all come together and influence each other. Then, you'll see, our strength will last. (*Writings,* vol. 1, Tel Aviv: Devir, 1964, p. 372)

Brenner reached this Dubnowistic conclusion not because he affirmed the Diaspora but because he concurrently negated and, for lack of choice, acquiesced in it—all of which because his Zionist perspective was so extreme as to cross into despair. In 1906, three years before he settled in Palestine, he had placed his definition of a Zionist in the mouth of one of the heroes of his play, *Beyond the Borders:*

To be a Zionist, you should first be a person who understands the sorrow of a nation and a tragedy of a nation. A sincere, clear-thinking person who also believes in the possibility of the impossible and has limitless strength to work for it and to walk without a path. There are no such people in our midst, aren't there, none, none! I know the value of the masses generally, but what does one gain from this? a rabble of Jewish gypsies. (act 2, scene 15)

Despite or perhaps because of this, Brenner settled in Eretz Israel in 1909. Indeed, this was a special Brennerian dialectic—from absolute negation of the Diaspora to acquiescence in the special existence of each of the diasporas.

Po'aley Tsiyyon, the political rival of Ha-po'el ha-Tsa'ir, brought an equally radical if not more radical approach to the "negation of the Diaspora" (galut). However, the leaders of this party, David Ben-Gurion, Ya'akov Zerubavel, and Yizhak Ben-Zvi, unlike Aharonowitz and Katznelson, distinguished explicitly between gola (the Diaspora) and Eretz Israel. They stressed the national uniqueness of the Jewish community in Eretz Israel and soft-pedaled its "Diasporic" nature. From their standpoint, the Yishuv was the front line in the Jewish people's war for national renaissance, and such a war demanded self-sacrifice and personal valor.

In 1907, while in the Galilee, Ben-Gurion heard from his father that visitors from Palestine were painting a bleak view of life there. Ben-Gurion responded sorrowfully: "I'm not afraid that they will truly besmirch the country with these stories. The mummified Jews who have already sunk up to their necks *in the bogs of the Diaspora* will not wake up even if they hear that in Eretz Israel gold coins roll around in the streets." However, he was convinced that "The proud, fighting *new Jew* will neither panic nor turn back even if these new [biblical] spies are telling the truth."[10] Ben-Gurion also termed these visitors cowards who had fled the "battlefield." Jacob Zerubavel, defending the Ha-shomer organization against those who criticized it for allegedly behaving rashly toward the Arabs and harming the Yishuv, responded similarly. He distinguished between two clashing paths that the Jewish people was taking: the Diasporist accommodationist path, always willing to compromise with reality at the cost of national pride; and the path of revolt against the Diaspora, occasioned by yearnings for redemption as epitomized by Ha-shomer.[11] Yizhak Ben-Zvi encapsulated the war front trend of thought by stating that the "Diasporist" character had castrated the Jew of the "whole spirit of heroism and courage related to love of homeland,"[12] which he would derive from natural devotion to his country. Therefore, in the absence of the homeland, the Jews as a collective lack the political prowess, the military heroism, and the wisdom of legislators. All they retain in their "Diasporist" lives is the cunning to adjust swiftly and cleverly to changing environmental conditions. Ben-Zvi admitted that one could also find occasional indications of national awakening and personal valor in exile, as evinced among members of the Bund, for example, but these could not cure the Jewish people of its national illness—exile.

Ben-Zvi's friend and teacher, Dov Ber Borochov, defined galutic existence in pungent and telling terms. In his opinion,

> In the Diaspora the Jewish people is unique; as individuals, Jews are so gifted, agile, tenacious, flexible, and versatile in their the personal war for existence. And there is no people in the world like the Jewish people, so weak and feckless, so sycophantic and unstable in its war for national fortification. *Uncommon strength of the individual and unparalleled weakness of the aggregate* [italics in the original]—this is one of the contradictions of the Jewish people in dispersion.[13]

After the Balfour Declaration came out, negation of the Diaspora prompted Ben-Gurion to perform a far-reaching historical assessment—one that is still timely—about Jewish history. In his article "The Redemption," published in Yiddish in the United States, he states that the Declaration is not only politically important but also sweepingly significant in the historical sense.

> Since our last national disaster, the quashing of the Bar-Kokhba revolt, we have had "histories" of persecutions and discrimination by force of law, Inquisition, and pogroms; of supreme devotion and martyrdom; [and] of towering scholars, but we have no longer had Jewish history, because the history of a people is only that which creates a people as a whole, as a political unit, [a people] that undergoes ordeals and engages in joint creative endeavor, not what happens to individuals or groups of that people. For the past 1,800 years, our people has not had an existence as a national whole. We have been expunged from the world history that is comprised of the history of peoples.[14]

In terms of the principled aspect of the Klal Yisrael idea, Ben-Gurion drew a distinction between a national entity and national history. In this respect, the galutic anomaly lies in the existence of a Jewish Klal that lacks collective history due to its territorial dispersion, lack of political autonomy, and conditions of social enslavement and religious pressure. The interesting thing is that Ben-Gurion is unwilling to consider this special Jewish reality a trait of collective national history. Only normal peoples—those who dwell in their own country and on their own soil—have a common history. Herein lies the uniqueness of the Zionist thinking, which Ben-Gurion typically expresses in extreme terms. While the Bund and the Dubnowists also aspired to re-insert the Jewish people, in greater or smaller part, into the cycle of history, the Zionists hinged this on the Jews' return to their historical national territory.

Ostensibly, Ben-Gurion's outlook on Jewish collective existence over the generations somewhat resembles that of the Bund. Both agree that a "world people" does not have a common history, and both asserted a connection between national history and a specific territory, such as eastern European Jewry from the standpoint of the Bund. However, the basic and decisive difference between them is that Ben-Gurion, notwithstanding his claim that the Jews lacked a single history such as that of a normal territorial people, recognized ab initio that there is a Jewish national entity despite its anomalous way of existing, whereas the Bund continued to waver on this question. However, his remarks undoubtedly express doubt about the historiosophy of Graetz and, especially, of Dubnow, concerning a single and singular Jewish history—of a "world people" in both of senses of the Hebrew expression 'am 'olam, which includes time and space. Thus, notwithstanding everything he said, Ben-Gurion remains in the throes of a slightly mystical trend of thought as the vision of the Jewish national "resurrection of the dead" is played out before his very eyes.

Disparagement of the exilic way was a common chord for most writers in the newspaper *Ha'Ahdut,* but not for among all. The author Aharon Reuveni, Yizhak Ben-Zvi's brother, responded to writings in *Ha-po'el ha-Tsa'ir*[15] in his article, "Trivialities and Inaccuracies, Too,"[16] and noted the immense vitality that Diaspora displayed in economic affairs, natural increase, and intellectual endeavor. While inveighing against materialism, he regarded the Jewish immigrant masses' ability to adjust to the United States and other immigration countries as important evidence of the great vitality of the Diaspora:

> This talent in physical and intellectual adjustment, social growth, and economic and cultural progress—are they indications of dilution, degeneration, and extinction? Or should we acknowledge the abiding strength of the vital force even when it reveals itself in a special way and [admit that] the Jewish people

is still far from devaluation and bankruptcy, and the process of exhaustion and extinction has not yet begun and its reserves of vitality are steadily growing and gaining in richness?[16]

The pundit Alexander Heshin also urged readers not to disregard the Diaspora's great struggles for its physical existence and the preservation of its national image.[17]

As stated, however, this was the minority view. The majority negated the Diaspora on grounds similar to those expressed by Ha-po'el ha-Tsa'ir and did so no less acidly. In view of the pessimistic diagnosis of the Diaspora's condition and the bleak prognosis resulting from it, it was necessary to devise an alternative that would respond to and solve its problems. A Socialist-labor Eretz Israel seemed to be such an alternative, of course. However, the Diaspora would not liquidate itself by force of rhetoric and Eretz Israel would not be built overnight. Obviously, the two would coexist for quite some time. If so, on what basis would they interrelate?—that was the question Po'aley Tsiyyon had to ask itself on both sides of the sea. The problem was especially severe for the party in Palestine because of its members' ambivalence toward the Diaspora. They negated it, as stated, but could not overlook the organizational, ideological, and emotional connections that bound them to it.

From this standpoint, Borochov's thinking underwent an interesting development. At the outset of his Zionist career, Eretz Israel occupied the forefront of his thinking and all his aspirations. Thus, in his 1905 essay, "On the Question of Zion and Territory," he wrote, "Eretz Israel is the only *desired* territory, for Eretz Israel is the only *possible* territory, for Eretz Israel is the only territory *destined* for us, for Eretz Israel will be conquered *gradually*, by force of the historical imperative!" [Italics in the original].[18]

Loyalty to Eretz Israel on the one hand, and the awareness of the gradual nature of the conquest process on the other hand—a "stichic" process in Marxist terms—prompted Borochov to strike a balance between Eretz Israel and the Diaspora. A year later, in 1906, in his fundamental work, "Our Platform," Borochov explained that the Jewish proletariats in the Diaspora and in Palestine were struggling for the same goal.

> The rules of the stichic process are such that the freer and more privileged our lives are *here*, the more easily we will be able to aspire to freedom *there*; the more abundant freedom is *there*, the more effectively will the entitlements acquired *here* be guaranteed. It is in our interest to enhance life *here*, for two reasons: because we live here, in exile, and because our doing so facili-

tates the acquisition of entitlements there, in Eretz Israel, to which the stichic process is gradually shifting the center of gravity in our lives. It is also in our interest to enhance life there for two reasons: because the stichic process is shifting the center of gravity in our lives there, and because strengthening our positions there has the effect of guaranteeing our rights here. It is this that reflects the relationship—a stichic relationship, not an artificial one—between the interests and the struggle here and there. *The better things are here, the better they will be there, too,* and vice versa. (B. Borochov, "Our Platform," *Writings*, Vol. I, p. 153 (Hebrew ed.), 1955)

Thus, the national importance of the two settings remains in balance as long as the stichic process of the ingathering in Eretz Israel continues. The historical trend, however, is a shift of the center of gravity in Jewish life to Eretz Israel. Thus, the equilibrium will be undermined in the distant future.

Borochov's Zionist tactics, although not his basic outlook, changed in 1909. This was reflected in his resignation from the Zionist Congress,[19] his attempt to establish an "immigration congress" even as he belittled the immediate importance of Aliya,[20] and his attempt to reach out to the Bund in the realization that the changes in his views would facilitate some degree of cooperation. In a debate over these three issues at the convention of the Russian party (Vienna, 1909), Borochov shifted the focal point of concern from the quest for the right balance between the Diaspora and Eretz Israel toward the Jewish proletariat and its problems. "The basic problem of the Jewish proletariat is the unity of the Jewish workers," Borochov contended at the convention. In his opinion, the Bund was no longer so sure about the perpetuity of exile and, in contrast, "although we [Po'aley Tsiyyon] once derided Diaspora life and everything intrinsic to it, we have now learned *to hold it in higher esteem.*" "For what purpose do we wish to create unity?" he asked rhetorically. "Not to strengthen territorialism but to unify Socialism in the Jewish street."[21] Responding to Ben-Zvi's polemic attack on Po'aley Tsiyyon-Russia for its decision to withdraw from the Congress, Borochov stated: "We are a party not only for Eretz Israel but also for the Jewish proletariat, and anything pertaining to it should attract our attention."[22] This, however, is too cautious an answer; it does not reflect the genuine turnaround that had occurred in Borochov's sensitivities. A quest for ways to cooperate with a belligerent anti-Zionist party such as the Bund, for the reasons Borochov cited, meant treating the state of Jewish workers in the Diaspora as the main problem and relegating Palestine-related problems to a second tier. Either way, the aforementioned equilibrium did not hold.

Borochov's political tilt toward the Bund, in the belief that changes in the Bund's thinking had created an opportunity for collaboration between the Jewish class perspective of the Bund and the pan-Jewish proletarian outlook of Po'aley Tsiyyon, was not requited by the Bund. Therefore, Borochov resumed his anti-Bundist polemics. In 1913, he published an acrid critique of Vladimir Medem's recent series of articles on the national question.[23] Borochov related to Medem's national outlook contemptuously and termed it "one of the most parlor-roomy prattlings among the Jewish Socialists," because Medem had dared *"to deny the existence of a single world Jewish nation."* Borochov railed against Medem's views on the process of Jewish disintegration that, Medem said, was leading to the possibility of several Jewish peoples in the future: eastern European, western European, American, and Afro-Asian. According to Borochov, despite the differences among the various segments of Jewry, "it is *the same national organism."* This led him to an unequivocal conclusion: "I call any form of fragmentation of the living, organic fabric of history and reality a *national nihilism"* [Italics in the original]. These remarks, pertaining to the fragmentation of history, may also have been aimed at Ben-Gurion's historiosophic worldview.

In opposition to Medem and the Bund, Borochov crafted a totally different rule in regard to the Klal Yisrael outlook: "We"—Po'aley Tsiyyon—"state as an a priori premise that Jewry is a collective body, *a uniform organism with continuity in time and space,* [even as we admit that its] organic connection is flawed and, in several senses, also defective, but in no way disengaged or imaginary."

For Po'aley Tsiyyon and Ha-po'el ha-Tsa'ir, the ideological debate about Jewish unity was paradoxical in nature. One may say that both Ha-po'el ha-Tsa'ir and Berl Katznelson viewed the unity as centering on aspects that they considered negative in both the Diaspora and Eretz Israel, whereas most Po'aley Tsiyyon ideologues in Palestine distinguished between the two locations. Ultimately, Borochov, shortly before his death in 1917, proved that he, too, had been caught up in the Palestinocentric passion by stating, in a speech at the Po'aley Tsiyyon convention in Kiev, that the working class in Eretz Israel, which was fulfilling the cooperative socioeconomic method in rural settlement, was the communicator of the national message to the Jewish people.[24] This did not occur in regard to the two parties' positions on the organizational questions on the agenda: establishing a joint fund for workers in Palestine from donations by Jewish workers abroad (KPAI, pr. "Kappai") and the Hebrew-language issue.

The key issue for both parties was the development of a national labor society in Palestine. However, this shared goal, of all things, led to disagreements between them. Ha-po'el ha-Tsa'ir based its Palestinocentric concept on disengagement from the Diaspora, whereas for the very same reason Po'aley Tsiyyon inveighed against any attempt at such a disengagement because, in both parties' thinking, the development of the Yishuv depended on the Diaspora's vast reserves of people and resources. An interesting and instructive debate on this issue occurred at the Po'aley Yehuda convention on Shavuot 1911 (June 2) for the purpose of discussing the Po'aley Tsiyyon proposal to establish KPAI as a way to support labor enterprises, with funding raised from workers in the Diaspora. The proposal was very strongly opposed, not only by the Ha-po'el ha-Tsa'ir delegates, but also by the nonpartisans. The opponents expressed two rationales: first, they regarded the fund as a "labor" version of traditional Jewish philanthropy. Thus, they rejected any support from the Diaspora and proposed that they go it alone in all respects. The second problem, as the Ha-po'el ha-Tsa'ir delegates emphasized in particular, was the class nature of the fund.[25] In his keynote address on the matter, Izhak Ben-Zvi explained that the fund was not meant to be philanthropic in nature. By donating their money, Jewish workers in the Diaspora would be giving charity (tsedaqa) not to workers in Palestine but to themselves. Since Jewish workers had no future except in Eretz Israel, a contribution that strengthened and reinforced the working class in Palestine was tantamount to strengthening the future basis on they would stand one day.[26]

By expressing himself this way, Ben-Zvi adhered to the approach that Borochov had articulated in his essay, "Our Platform." In contrast, the opponents argued that the money for the fund should come solely from local workers and categorically rejected contributions from counterparts abroad.[27]

Those in favor accused the opponents of hypocrisy—after all, workers availed themselves of national institutions that obtained their funding from Diaspora Jews. In response, the opponents contended that a distinction should be made between a general national institution, which should support workers due to their national mission, and an institution to be founded at the workers' direct initiative. Such an institution, they said, should reflect the unique value position of the labor movement in Palestine. By implication, the opponents, unlike the proponents (Po'aley Tsiyyon), underestimated the importance of organizational relations between workers in Palestine and in the Diaspora. The debate was adjourned with no clear outcome.

The main problem debated—the method of fundraising—resurfaced at the second convention of Po'aley Yehuda, held in Petah Tiqva in December 1913. Izhak Ben-Zvi and Jacob Zerubavel repeated their view that workers in both Jewish centers would have to interrelate in both the present and the future. The resolution adopted by the second convention represented a victory for Po'aley Tsiyyon: "The second convention acknowledges the necessity of a joint fund for the workers of Eretz Israel and those in the Diaspora who have an interest in labor in Eretz Israel, in order to meet their mutual needs. The fund should be under the sole care of a general nonpartisan federation of labor in Eretz Israel."[28] This resolution, adopted by a slender majority (13:12), was a victory for the Po'aley Tsiyyon approach because it emphasized *partnership* between labor in Eretz Israel and that in the Diaspora without compromising the autonomy of Eretz Israel in maintaining the fund.

The debate reignited the old controversy between Po'aley Tsiyyon and Ha-po'el ha-Tsa'ir. The Po'aley Tsiyyon delegates accused their counterparts of "Bundist" leanings: just as the Bund repudiated Jewish national unity and, perforce, the Jewish working class, so did Po'aley Tsiyyon advocate the construction of a buffer between workers in the two venues.[29] Ha-po'el ha-Tsa'ir was also accused of having adopted a condescending "chosen-people" attitude. In contrast, the need for collaboration was explained: "Our historic labor has been cleansed of territorial borders. Here *the shared exile* stands out, the shared wish *to be redeemed* awakens, shared needs are discovered—and in front of us is only one ladder, *planted in the Diaspora,* its top climbs to redemption—our people's creative forces ascend and descend on it."

Po'aley Tsiyyon's unwillingness or inability to bring about political disengagement from the Diaspora also found expression in the cultural field. In 1914, Dr. Hayyim Zhitlovsky visited Palestine for a series of lectures for workers. The students at Herzliya Gymnasium and associates of this institution launched a fierce offensive against his intention to lecture in Yiddish, and matters escalated until a protest demonstration was held in front of the lecturer's home. Responding in *Ha'Ahdut,* Alexander Heshin furiously accused the anti-Yiddishists of harboring separatist tendencies that wished to divorce Eretz Israel from the Diaspora due to contempt for and hatred of the latter. He also charged them with harboring aristocratic emotions "that would do the [Jewish] people and even more so the Hebrew language a severe disservice by widening the abyss that separates the Hebrew language from the masses and by making Hebrew the possession of 'aristocrats" and a 'select few.'"

Most seriously, Heshin accused the anti-Yiddishists of intending to impair Jewish historical continuity and undermine Jewish national unity by applying a historiosophy that skips from the Second Temple period to the onset of the New Yishuv, dismissing the two millennia between these events. *"They are making such a neck-breaking leap, from the destruction of the Second Temple to the construction of Rishon Lezion,* in total disregard of the lengthy period between them. They're slamming the gate on the many eras in our national lives that had contents of their own, and are deleting the thing that is called a people from the Book of Life. The [Jewish] people, in its tens of thousands and its millions, they're dismissing the whole thing with one terrible word, 'galut'" [emphasis mine].[30] Heshin must have been referring to the beginning of a trend that, in the 1950s, the poet Abraham Shlonsky termed "Canaanism."

In sum, Poʻaley Tsiyyon recognized the historical necessity of cooperation between Eretz Israel and the Diaspora, including the forces at work there, as a great and indispensable reserve for the building of Eretz Israel.

By so doing, however, Poʻaley Tsiyyon did not equate the two temporarily or, a fortiori, in the future. After all, Eretz Israel was to be the venue of the Jewish ingathering. The party did not ignore the quantitative strength of Diaspora Jewry and the vital forces embodied in the very existence of Jewish nationhood there, but argued that the fledgling Yishuv surpassed the Diaspora in quality, since great changes in the Jewish character, the harbingers of revolution for the Jewish masses, were already evident there.[31] At the Poʻaley Tsiyyon convention in 1913, several party members criticized the newspaper *HaʼAhdut* for focusing mainly on the trifling if not meaningless problems of Palestine and disregarding main events in the Diaspora. Advocates of the newspaper's policy replied that the paper was foremost an organ of the workers of Palestine and added that the importance of Eretz Israel is chiefly qualitative, not quantitative, that is, not only for its future as the venue of the Jewish ingathering, but also, and mainly, for the *original* creative work that is beginning to take place there. That year, one could already speak about originality in organizing self-defense—Ha-shomer—and in cooperative labor rural settlement, as in Deganya.

Even during the doldrums of the Second Aliya, when it was clear that the struggle for Jewish labor was not succeeding and that large-scale private or public Jewish capital was not flowing to Palestine, Yitzhak Ben-Zvi believed that in Eretz Israel, as opposed to the Diaspora, the foundations for a normal Jewish society had been laid—a society that, like other nations' societies, controlled its national economy and was capable of political autonomy. By expressing these matters in a public forum,[32] Ben-Zvi showed that he really did believe them, even though reality did not reinforce his convictions.

Nevertheless, even though he defended Zhitlovsky against his attackers, Heshin felt it his duty to speak out against Zhitlovsky's "galutic" ideology with all possible vehemence. In a debate that they conducted on the pages of *HaʼAhdut* in 1914, Zhitlovsky set forth several basic assumptions that were widely accepted in the Diaspora at that time and that represented an original synthesis of his own, so to speak, between the "labor in the present" of Hibbat Tsiyyon and its historical rival, the Bund. This led Zhitlovsky to a sort of

national Dubnowism of a Socialist complexion, which views the Jewish
national entity in Palestine (the Yishuv) as an inseparable part of Klal Yisrael,
in accordance with the following premises:

1. The Diaspora has a national future. It is not dying but rather living and functioning. Therefore, the concept of "renaissance"
   should not be attributed solely to Palestine.
2. For this reason, the Yishuv is not meant to replace life in Diaspora but rather to augment this life and complement the national
   renaissance process that the Diaspora is currently experiencing.
3. The doubt hovering over the political existence of the Yishuv is
   more severe and tangible than that threatening the Diaspora.
4. It is the small Yishuv, not the large Diaspora, that needs the
   Yishuv–Diaspora relationship. This is because Palestine will
   never be able to take in the entire Jewish people; only a minority of Jews will be able to settle there. Therefore, a "return to
   Zion" is out of the question. The quantitative and, perforce, the
   qualitative weight (according to the rules of historical materialism) will always belong to the Diaspora side.
5. In view of all the foregoing, there is no point in developing a Hebrew culture because such a culture will never become a mass
   culture in the Diaspora and is liable to drive a wedge between the
   small Yishuv and the Jewish people in exile.
6. The Hebrew language is the romantic vision of a handful of
   individualists.

The article concludes with an emotional appeal: "A great disaster will
befall our people if they dig a chasm between the Diaspora and Eretz Israel,
if they rend the nation into Jewish and Hebrew tribes. We must unite as one
people with one language. In all matters that separate us, let us direct our
hearts toward one culture."[33]

The response to these remarks, which must have reverberated
strongly among party members in Palestine, was presented by Heshin in his
article, "Heavenly Renaissance, Earthly Renaissance."[34] At the outset, he
accuses Zhitlovsky of an overly rational view and of disregarding historical and psychological factors. Farther on, he rejects Zhitlovsky's thesis
about the obvious progression of development toward a national renaissance in the Diaspora. However, since he is also unwilling to embrace the
widely held view that the Diaspora is dying out, he proposes a balanced assessment of the situation: "Galut is a chronic illness of sorts that does not
entomb its victims but embitters their lives [. . .]. It is a never-ending game

between the force that extinguishes and the force that sustains, with neither able to vanquish the other. It is a global and interminable drama."

The life-sapping power of galut, the exilic mind-set, reveals itself in the destruction of the original folk-cultural strengths of the Jewish people and in Jews' absorption of foreign culture.

> Therefore, the earthly center for which we hope is not only an "added increment to galut" or an "elevation" of galut life, as Dr. Zhitlovsky would have it, but the essence of national life, an essence that will return life to its natural state and restore its inner freedom. There, in the Hebrew national center, our folk strata will unite and form an indivisible national bloc that will allow no foreign force to invade its recesses, and our lives will find their national uniqueness and manifest themselves freely.[34]

By implication, one may also conceive of a stance that emphasizes the quality of Eretz Israel and its supreme importance for the Jewish people in categorical affirmation of the Hebrew reality-in-formation, destined to come into being in Palestine, and not in categorical negation of the reality of the Jewish Diaspora. Ben-Gurion took a similar position on the Eretz Israel–Diaspora relationship in 1917. In his remarks on the prospects of mass aliya in the aftermath of the Balfour Declaration, he said:

> Our old knapsack will also be measured by means of a new ruler. We will pack everything that is large and important enough for the path we are taking; we will cast aside everything that is small, rotten, and galutic, so that it will disappear together with the bad heritage of the dead past. Thus [the latter] will not cast its shadow over our new souls and will not desecrate the redemption.[35]

The ambivalence of Po'aley Tsiyyon-Palestine toward the Diaspora, which oscillated between repudiation and acknowledgment of the vital relationship with the latter, affected relations between it and sister parties in various countries that belonged to the World Union of Po'aley Tsiyyon. The problem was especially severe in the case of the parent party, Po'aley Tsiyyon-Russia, headed by Borochov.

From its earliest years, Po'aley Tsiyyon-Palestine had been trying to carve itself a special niche in the World Union. Its aim was based on its pioneering nature, that is, its being the practical fulfillment of the Po'aley Tsiyyon ideology in Eretz Israel. In the pursuit of this aspiration, the party in

Palestine did not demand extra entitlements for itself but called on members in the Diaspora to follow in its footsteps and asked affiliated parties to provide it with organized assistance—all of which, without waiving its autonomy and decision-making prerogatives, in accordance with needs in Eretz Israel and the interests of Po'aley Tsiyyon particularly and the workers of Palestine generally.

To reinforce this stance, it was necessary to draw a clear boundary between the party in Palestine and the parties abroad. Ben-Zvi sums up the differences between them in his article, "Unzer arbayt in Eretz Yisroel."[36] Po'aley Tsiyyon-Palestine is unique, he said, in that it is fulfilling the principle of territorial ingathering in Eretz Israel in practice; the other parties embrace this principle in theory only. The party in Palestine is affected directly by realities in Palestine directly; the parties in Diaspora are affected only indirectly.

Thus, what Po'aley Tsiyyon in Palestine demanded of the Union is that it focus all efforts on assisting it, that is, to fulfill the theory by means of financial aid, *shipments of arms,* and encouragement of aliya.[37]

The dividing line did not create a dichotomy of fulfillers and helpers, of the vanguard and the rear. Instead, and also, it created a dichotomy of those who have a flexible ideology that changes in accordance with the reality in Palestine and those who adhere to ideological principles set forth in the Diaspora. Ben-Gurion stressed this difference in a debate at the sixth party convention (1910).[38]

In his opinion, those who lacked the wisdom or the will to come to grips with the ideological changes that had occurred in the worldview of the party in Palestine had left both the party and the country. By implication, the shift from the accepted Diaspora views to the new views that had formed in Palestine was so extreme as to have forced many to abandon the party, if not the country. The ideological buffer had taken shape not only due to conscious thought but also due to the special emotional attitude of Palestine Po'aley Tsiyyon toward Eretz Israel and its upbuilding, a passion that the members abroad did not share. Rahel Yanna'it expressed this in her remarks about the tasks that the third world convention of Po'aley Tsiyyon would have to tackle. She came to the gloomy conclusion that

> After listening and pondering—[I believe] a dense fog will again spread between us and our comrades on the outside; and everything that we've created, with its ups and downs, its ebbs and flows, will not be close to their hearts. The full reality and development of Eretz Israel will be as vague and, perhaps, as incomprehensible to them as it had been before. To recognize life, to

take action in regard to life, and to be powered by life—you cannot do these from afar. . . . From afar one cannot take creative action at one's own initiative; one can only help and support others in what they're doing.[39]

Such a state of mind among members of party in Palestine also led to an overt collision between them and the World Union administration abroad. In 1911, Ben-Gurion published an open letter to the Union,[40] severely criticizing it for having decided to send an emissary (Leon Hasanovich) to Argentina to examine the attitude of the JCA (the Jewish Colonization Association) toward the Jewish settlers there. Hasn't the World Union got any goals but this one? Ben-Gurion asked. If it does, would it perhaps give some indication of its actions in other fields? After showing that the Union had done nothing in Eretz Israel, he presented it with two goals: socionational labor in the Diaspora and the same in Eretz Israel. However, as stated, nothing was being done in the field. If so, why is the fate of the Jews in Argentina more important to the World Union than that of the workers in Palestine? Of course, the provocations of the JCA (Jewish Colonization Association) officials in Argentina should be resisted, but why should they be considered more dangerous to the socialist workers than the provocations of the Alliance Israelite Universelle emissaries in Palestine? Thus, the demand of Po'aley Tsiyyon-Palestine for assistance and support from the World Union, a demand that was not fully requited, caused some friction between the entities. The emissary to Argentina, Leon Hasanovich,[41] provided an indirect response to this demand by stating that "our party is not only for labor in Palestine." He also complained, in contrast to Ben-Gurion, that the Union was not doing enough to organize workers in the Diaspora.

The issue led to a clash between the Palestine delegates and the Diaspora delegates to the third Po'aley Tsiyyon World Union convention. The dispute began when one of the Palestine delegates stated vehemently that the only true Zionist labor was that in Palestine. This precipitated a tumultuous response by most of the Diaspora delegates, who attempted to prove that socialist Zionist labor could take place in the Diaspora as well.

Concurrent with (although not in contrast to) the vanguard activist stance of the Palestine delegates, the Diaspora delegates set forth a program of Zionist Socialist labor in the Diaspora. The main planks of the program were the following: (a) strengthening the class and national organization of the Jewish worker; (b) instilling Zionist awareness among Jewish proletarians; and (c) amassing resources for the building of Eretz Israel, and so forth. All of these actions, in their opinion, stemmed from one basic premise: that the future of all Jewish workers was associated with Eretz Israel.

Although the conference resolutions stated that the Union would encourage "needed and appropriate" workers to settle in Palestine, the editorial board of *Ha'Ahdut* summed up the debate and the resolutions in the following way:

> The main thing elucidated in these debates is the social difference that exists in the attitude toward Zionism and Eretz Israel labor between *those in Eretz Israel* and *those in the Diaspora.* Here, Zionism is not only yearnings and hope for the future but also labor in the present and a matter of life; there, in the Diaspora, all surrounding life is totally divorced from that future ideal, and the living, active connection that affects at every moment and *provides a ceaseless impetus to labor* is absent. [emphasis mine][42]

This seems to be the best explanation for the development that occurred in the party's attitude toward its siblings in the Diaspora and its rivals in Palestine. As the members increasingly pulled away, ideologically and psychologically, from the sharing of an ideology with the Diaspora, their distance from their ideological rivals in Palestine, their de facto partners in the effort being made there, steadily diminished.

This brings us to the stance of Po'aley Tsiyyon and Ha-po'el ha-Tsa'ir on two issues: the Hebrew language and the problem of the Yemenite Jewish workers in the moshavot (the farming settlements). The former began with controversy and continued with consent; the latter began with consent and continued with disillusionment and schism.

THE LANGUAGE ISSUE

Although the national language question was a focal point in the credic outlooks of both historical rivals, the Bund and the Zionist Labor Movement, there was a fundamental difference between the parties not only as to which of the two languages was the national one, but also in regard to the role of each. From the standpoint of the Bund, Yiddish and its culture were not only valuable in themselves, but also offered the only barrier against Jews' tendencies to assimilate into modern society. In Palestine, in contrast, Hebrew and its culture, apart from being manifestations of the nation's origins and roots, were meant to reshape the nation. Thus, the two—the preservative cultural revolutionism of the Bund versus the revolutionary cultural conservatism of the Labor Movement—squared off against each other. The former defended the Yiddish language and sheltered it from the social revolution; the latter wished to transform Hebrew into a primary medium in the fulfillment of the national revolution. This explains the vast difference between the movements in their attitude toward Klal Yisrael from this standpoint. In the Bund doctrine, only the Yiddish-speaking segment of World Jewry belonged to the Jewish people, whereas the Zionist Labor Movement wished to integrate, by means of Hebrew, Jews who spoke various languages into the new Hebrew-Jewish nation. Thus, the Bund made the objective cultural reality into a principled approach in its national outlook, whereas the Labor Movement defined the construction of the new culture as a way to establish a different national society. This aspiration created a clashing dialectic tension in Po'aley Tsiyyon circles and a clashing polar tension in Ha-po'el ha-Tsa'ir.

Yosef Aharonowitz, editor of the journal *Ha-po'el ha-Tsa'ir,* viewed the Hebrew-language issue in terms of absolute principle. He did not consider Hebrew important as a useful way to unify the members of different Jewish ethnicities and cultures who were gathering in Eretz Israel, although he did not disregard this utility. From his standpoint, what counted was the "factual side," as he expressed it: "The Hebrew language is our historical language, and only by its means can we cleanse ourselves of the imprint of Gypsyism, and only with it can we extend the historical thread that links all generations and invest our lives with the coloration of a cultured people, a living and spiritually self-sustaining people."[43] His party rendered this outlook into a "sanctified principle," so to speak.

Unlike Ha-po'el ha-Tsa'ir, which considered Hebrew a central ideological tenet from the outset, Po'aley Tsiyyon was quite undecided about the choice between Hebrew and Yiddish. Its indecision stemmed not from belittling the value of Hebrew in the national revival process but the opposite: the members of this party, aware of the national importance of both languages, became confused to the need to choose between them.

In his memoirs,[44] Yizhak Ben-Zvi attempted to explain this confusion among members of his party by tracing it to the cultural reality of multiple languages and ways of life that typified the early twentieth-century Yishuv. It seems, however, that the vacillations of Po'aley Tsiyyon originated mainly in this party's inner worldview and not from the cultural realities in Palestine. At the very outset of the history of Po'aley Tsiyyon in Eretz Israel, even before its constituent groups coalesced at the Ramle convention in 1906, three linguistic tendencies—Yiddishist, Russian, and Hebrew— fought for primacy in party circles.[45] These trends were articulated by groups of members from different parts of Russia, but there was also an ideological basis. For example, a Po'aley Tsiyyon group from Crimea, positioned on the party's left flank, opposed a synthesis between the national and the class interest that members of the other groups supported, and it advocated the use of the Russian language. After this group left Palestine, this attitude toward the language issue vanished as well. However, the pro-Yiddish and pro-Hebrew forces continued to fight. After Ben-Zvi settled in Palestine in 1907, Poʻaley Tsiyyon began to publish a Yiddish-language newspaper called *Der Anfang*. Although the paper was not long-lived—it came out in only two editions—its swift demise did not end the language dispute within the party. The debate continued throughout the Second Aliya era until Poʻaley Tsiyyon ceased to exist as an independent party upon the formation of Ahdut ha-ʻAvoda in 1919. However, as we will see below, the issue remained controversial in that setting, too.

The internal disputation in Poʻaley Tsiyyon was echoed at the party's conventions. At the third convention (1908), Ben-Zvi and Ben-Gurion represented different leanings.[46] Ben-Zvi favored the publication of the party newspaper in Yiddish for an ideological reason (to maintain Diaspora-Yishuv relations) and for a practical reason (so that a majority of workers would be able to read it). Ben-Gurion, in contrast, considered the necessity for a party organ in Hebrew a corollary of the party's wish to organize the workers of the Old Yishuv first of all and the expectation of large-scale immigration from Africa and Asia, where Yiddish was a foreign language. The irony was that Ben-Gurion, the fanatic warrior for Hebrew, was forced at this convention to expound on the merits of Hebrew in Yiddish! In his opinion, the language question was different in Eretz Israel than anywhere else. Even at that early juncture, he predicted a leading role for the Jews of the East in aliya. Therefore, in his opinion, the determining question from the standpoint of the Yishuv and of Klal Yisrael was, "Will the Jews speak different languages or one language?"[47] If an example of a principled national outlook contrasting that of the Bund were needed, these remarks capture it.

Both disputants' positions were characterized by an ideological and practical approach to the problem. For Ben-Zvi, the focal point of the unity question was in eastern Europe, whence aliya would emanate; for Ben-Gurion, the focal point was Palestine and aliya would originate in the eastern countries. Thus, the Palestinocentrism that typified Ben-Gurion's worldview and his many years of political activity already found expression in this very early period of his public endeavors.

The debate at the convention ended with a compromise between the two outlooks, albeit with an explicit and clear tendency toward Ben-Gurion's stance. A majority of 11 to 5 resolved that the party organ would be published in Hebrew. To compensate the pro-Yiddish delegates, a 13 to 2 majority resolved to publish the Poʻaley Tsiyyon information pamphlets in both languages.[48] However, the debut of the Hebrew-language journal—

Ha'Ahdut—was delayed for another two years or so. The difficulties that brought about this postponement were not only technical and budgetary but also internal and ideological.

In 1910, at the sixth party convention, the opponents of Hebrew repeated with greater vehemence their objection to the publication of the newspaper in Hebrew. Their obstinacy was based on both principled and practical rationales. First, they did not recognize Hebrew as the one and only national language of the Jewish people. Second, they expressed concern that the use of Hebrew in Palestine, while Yiddish remained dominant in the Diaspora, would drive a wedge between the segments of Jewry in the two locations. Third, believing that even in Palestine a majority of prospective readers of the paper were Yiddish speakers, they expressed doubt about whether a Hebrew-language paper would have any influence over this part of the Yishuv.[49]

Ben-Gurion responded to these charges at length—this time in Hebrew—several months later. "They said much about the *Ha-'Ahdut* newspaper and the Ha'Ahdut publishing house but forgot about national unity and workers' unity. Our people is torn and fragmented. The jumble of languages is keeping the Hebrew workers apart. Should we widen the gap by using several languages, or should we lower the barriers and heal the rifts by [using] our one national language?" In daily life and for speaking and propaganda purposes, Ben-Gurion was willing for lack of choice to acquiesce in the use of different languages. However, in the fields of culture and written communication, he considered it an unpardonable sin to succumb to temporary practical needs, "because this is a cardinal question that goes to the root of our national existence and our future as a healthy and unified people in its country."[50] Thus, paradoxically, Ben-Gurion, like his Bundist rivals, considered language the factor that would shape the new nationhood. He would have Hebrew replace Yiddish, of course, but this would occur in the national territory.

Alexander Heshin developed this trend of thought further in his debate with Dr. Chaim Zhitlovsky in 1913. Zhitlovsky, visiting Palestine that year, expressed orally and in writing the idea of making Yiddish the daily vernacular there. He based his view on the strength and efflorescence of Yiddish culture among the millions of Jews who dwelled in the Diaspora and the menace of national schism that the use of two languages might cause. Heshin countered by claiming that Zhitlovsky overestimated the strength of Yiddish culture in the Diaspora. In Heshin's opinion, Jewish intellectuals evinced a steadily rising tendency to assimilate because they were attracted to the surrounding culture and regarded Yiddish culture with contempt and emotional rejection. These intellectuals were in a vise—they rejected the national culture in its Yiddishist mantle and were rejected by Gentile culture and society.

The Hebrew culture and language were their one remaining hope because, although culturally assimilated, they felt themselves to be part of the nation in the national-history sense. They could express this connection only in Hebrew, "because only in Hebrew can one feel the historical links that bind us into one golden chain and [one] living and special national acceptance."[51] Thus, Heshin invested the Hebrew language with a unifying significance that transcended current realities. For him, like his political rival Yosef Aharonowitz of Ha-po'el ha-Tsa'ir, it was Hebrew that connected and unified the nation's past, present, and historical future.

Apart from the historical national significance that Po'aley Tsiyyon attributed to the Hebrew language as a catalyst of national unity on an old-new cultural basis, this party considered it an instrument for the reinforcement of Jewish national autonomy in Palestine. Perforce, Po'aley Tsiyyon demanded the creation of an autonomous Hebrew education system and categorically rejected the school systems affiliated with the Jewish benevolent societies Alliance Israelite Universelle and the Esra society. In their opinion, the existence of these institutions in the Yishuv was evidence of the Yishuv's national immaturity, for they served the political and cultural interests of their home countries.

In the heat of the debates concerning the language of instruction at the Hebrew Technion in Haifa, Ben-Zvi suggested to the directors and supporters of Esra that they learn a lesson in national renaissance from their neighbors. "The Arabs, who have awakened in a national renaissance, have not been seeking the patronage of any foreign government." As the Arabs maintain their national integrity and vehemently demand their national rights in Palestine, "whom should we approach to assert our rights, and on what basis? On the basis of a high school under French authority? [He was referring to the intention of the Herzliya Gymnasium to seek French patronage]—or on the basis of a *technikum* under German authority? Aren't we destroying our whole future by this foreign politics?"[52]

The Po'aley Tsiyyon people were also concerned that a Technion that taught in German and not in Hebrew might be more useful to the Germans' imperial interests than to the Jews. After all, a German-language technical school would also train young Arabs, and the result would be that "they, not we, will receive those posts in Eretz Israel that the Technion will prepare them for, because they are stronger than we are."[53]

In contrast to these dangers, they stressed the supreme and primary importance of the Hebrew language as a political and cultural instrument for the attainment of Turkish recognition of the Jews' national rights in Palestine. A circular disseminated by the party's central committee explained this in so many words:

. . . Insofar as we are unified by our language and insofar as our language becomes a cultural and economic factor, so will its influence in the country grow and so will its rights and, perforce, ours too, be recognized as a special people and not as a collection of diverse religious communities, as has been the case thus far. We have been aiming for this from the day the national idea began to pound in our hearts, and we mustn't give it up under any circumstances.[54]

Notwithstanding the principled and practical rationales that the majority in Poʻaley Tsiyyon expressed in favor of Hebrew, after the pro-Hebrew decision was adopted in principle in 1908 and in practice in 1910 with the debut of its Hebrew-language journal *Ha'Ahdut,* and despite the party's extreme stance on the question of the language of instruction at the Technion in 1913, the intraparty debate was not yet over.

The language polemics resumed at the last Poʻaley Tsiyyon convention, held in 1919.[55] The fires were rekindled by party members who had reached Palestine with Jewish Legions from the United States and Great Britain. Here an additional issue found its way into the language debate: the political unity of the Palestine labor movement. Those who sought an official status for Yiddish in Palestine, although not equal to that of Hebrew, objected to union with Ha-poʻel ha-Tsaʻir for an additional reason: the latter's uncompromising zealotry in the matter of Hebrew. As for the issue itself, the pro-Yiddish camp argued that pro-Hebrew fanaticism and opposition to Yiddish might dissuade thousands of Jews from settling in Palestine.[56]

Countering them, Ben-Zvi—while admitting that Yiddish had once served as a barrier against assimilation in the Diaspora and acknowledging the need to assist recently landed comrades in this respect as well as in others—ruled out any official or semiofficial status for Yiddish in Palestine. The debaters also reexamined the question of national unity. Ben-Zvi warned his colleagues that opposition to the primacy of Hebrew in Palestine might only "sow disunity among the brethren."[57] Ben-Gurion, staunch in his Palestinocentric and rather elitist outlook, proclaimed, "Anyone who wants to live in Palestine should know that he is not going to the people but, on the contrary—the people will go to him."[58]

At the end of the debates, the convention adopted a compromise motion on the language issue that, practically speaking, reaffirmed the party's stance since 1908. To wit, it resolved to sustain the long-existing party resolution "to disseminate party information in additional languages, as required."[59]

The Yiddishists, whose proposal virtually to equalize the status of Yiddish with that of Hebrew did not even come up for a vote, demonstratively walked out of the convention. Thus, the schism in Po'aley Tsiyyon on the eve of the formation of Ahdut ha'Avoda became a fact. It is no small paradox that one of the causes of the schism, and the measure that symbolized it, was the unity dispute with its Bundist cultural aspect.

THE YEMENITE-JEWISH WORKER

Another arena of struggle for Jewish national unity generally, and that of the Yishuv particularly, was the encounter between Jewish workers of European and Yemenite origin. The cultural and psychological disharmony, not to mention the tension, that came to light in this encounter attested to the existence of an ethnic problem within the small and select labor collectivity.

Until Yemenite Jewish workers began to appear in the moshavot, social contact between the Ashkenazi workers there and the "Old Yishuv" generally, and its non-Ashkenazi segment in particular, had been scanty. Therefore, despite appreciable differences in the two societies' life realities and mind-sets, the paucity of relations averted direct confrontation. This changed when Yemenite Jews made their appearance in the moshavot. Ostensibly, the concepts and actions of the *olim* from Yemen were not far removed from those of the young immigrants from eastern Europe. Both came to Palestine in the Second Aliya. By turning to farm labor in the moshavot, many of the Yemenite Jewish immigrants theoretically came into proximity with Ashkenazi workers and had identical interests and goals that focused on the cause and the struggles of the Second Aliya—the "conquest of Hebrew labor."

Furthermore, the Zionist Labor Movement had been looking forward to the aliya of "Oriental" Jews. As I showed above, in the Hebrew language debate the hope was expressed that mass aliya from the eastern countries, as heralded by the immigrants from Yemen, was one of the principled and practical rationales in favor of Hebrew. Many Labor Movement members pinned hopes on the Yemenite-Jewish workers as the "redeemers of Hebrew labor" in the moshavot, believing that these Jews, accustomed the climate of Palestine and willing to live frugally, would find the adjustment to farm labor in the moshavot easier. Thus, it was not by chance that Shemuel Yavne'eli, who went to Yemen to stir up aliya passions, targeted the Jewish working class that he found there. History, however, is often replete with tragic paradoxes. The very people who had been looking forward to aliya from Yemen, those who had fulfilled the ideal of Hebrew labor, soon began to disapprove of the phenomenon and the tendency to consider Yemenite-

Jewish workers surrogates for Ashkenazi ones. Their resistance was by no means the only manifestation of their theoretical and practical attitude toward the Yemenite-Jewish workers, but it was a second and additional facet of a social reality that was rife with contrasts and contradictions, of a groping and errant community struggling doggedly and indefatigably for the attainment of its national goals, notwithstanding its many failures and few successes. Thus, the attitude of the Ashkenazi workers and their leaders toward the Yemenite-Jewish workers was an inseparable part of this web of uncertainties. The daily contact between the two groups of workers accented the differences between them: between a Western culture and way of life and an Eastern tradition, between a nonreligious collectivity and a staunchly pious one, between a group of young people infused with revolutionary social consciousness and another that entertained a conservative worldview. It was difficult to instigate a dialogue between them. Not only did they fail to find a common language but some of the Ashkenazi workers soon realized that these "redeemers of Hebrew labor," the Yemenite Jews, were actually obstacles to the fulfillment of this ideal, as if there were not enough obstacles to begin with. After all, the struggle for Hebrew labor had dual significance: national and social. From the national standpoint, it meant using Hebrew labor to acquire a national status. From the social standpoint, its goal was to bring wages and working conditions up to a level at which Jewish workers from Europe could get by, since otherwise there was no chance of forming a Jewish labor collectivity or class in agriculture. With cheap Arab labor available, the contradiction between these desiderata became evident. The Yemenite-Jewish worker, frugal, quiet, patient, and acquiescent in low wages to support his family, embodied this tragic contradiction by his very presence in the moshavot. He seemed to constitute living proof, Jewish proof and not Arab, that there was no room for the Ashkenazi worker in these localities.

This caused disgruntlement among Ashkenazi workers, who accused "the Yemenites," as they called these Jews, of lowering the wages of Jewish workers in the moshavot and crowding out the Ashkenazim. The public debate that began to take shape in 1910 gives evidence of the severity that the labor parties and their trade unions attributed to this question. Amidst all this, a clear contrasting tendency developed in the Labor Movement to view the Yemenite-Jewish workers as alternatives to Ashkenazim in the struggle to establish the primacy of Hebrew labor—a tendency of which Yavne'eli's mission in 1911 was a practical manifestation.[60]

The first person to decry the tendency to seek alternatives to Ashkenazi workers was Yosef Aharonowitz, who did so on both moral and national grounds. From the moral standpoint, he condemned the instrumental attitude that was being taken toward the Yemenite Jews as human beings, with the intent to transform them, due to their nonresistance to social expectations, into a tool for the "conquest of Hebrew labor." From the latter standpoint, he considered this tendency even riskier than the menace of Arab labor:

> . . . We are creating for ourselves *a rival more dangerous than the previous one:* against the previous rival, we fought by means of the devotion of the Hebrew worker, the quality of his work, his utility to the moshava in the present, and the power of the national idea in the future. However, we neither may nor can fight the [new] rival because he has the advantages we listed above, and he is making the existence of young people who come from the outside altogether impossible. [italics mine]

After expressing this grave evaluation, which can be explained only in view of the constant dread that beset the Second Aliya people, Aharonowitz added,

> Those who advocate replacing the Ashkenazi laborers with Yemenites may be right from the logical standpoint, but this substitution, even if we favored it in all its aspects, is impracticable because the few remaining young people who are attracted to Eretz Israel do not, for the most part, find any source of sustenance other than work in the moshava, and if this labor becomes impossible for them, not only will we have to close the gates in the newcomers' faces but we will also have to deport the old-timers, since it will not be possible to reduce the wages that they have already earned by their immense toil.[61]

Two members of Ha-po'el ha-Tsa'ir, Eliezer Yaffe and Yosef Bussel, debated this question about two years later at an assembly of Galilee workers. Yaffe seconded Aharonowitz's attitude; Bussel opposed it. "If the Sephardim work in the moshavot," Yaffe ventured, "what will we have gained? In what respect do they have an advantage over the Arabs from our standpoint? Their Jewish names? Generally speaking, too, when we come forth to 'conquer life,' we cannot choose the good jobs, [keep them] for ourselves, and leave the inferior jobs to the 'easterners.'"[62]

Bussel, a leading personality in the Deganya collective, opposed this view on decidedly practical grounds. In his opinion, Ashkenazi workers could not dominate labor in the moshavot because they aspired to be free and did not wish to be enslaved; under the conditions in the moshavot, only workers from the eastern countries could establish the dominance of Hebrew labor. He countered Yaffe's accusation—that, practically speaking, he intended to discriminate between Ashkenazi and non-Ashkenazi workers by proposing to leave the difficult and "inferior" jobs to the latter—by asserting: "We don't want to absolve ourselves of the hard jobs and hand them over to the Easterners. We want to create a Jewish Yishuv and not the most wretched working class in the world."[63] Bussel's reply did not resolve the moral dilemma. If he wished to prevent the formation of a wretched class of farm workers by means of labor settlement—this is what Bussel intended, after all—why did he leave the function of the moshava farm worker in the hands of Jews from Yemen and other countries in the East?!

The members of Po'aley Tsiyyon, too, were not of one mind on this issue. Rahel Yannait articulated the outlook of those who largely agreed with Aharonowitz. Countering party members who hoped to establish the dominion of Hebrew labor by means of the Yemenite-Jewish worker, she argued that "The main thing is not only to dislodge the Arabs and replace them with Jews but to reinforce the Jewish agrarian working class and enable it to exist and develop. The Yemenite does not raise the worker's status; he lowers it."[64] The way to change things, in her opinion, was to secure the standing of the Ashkenazi worker, not the Yemenite, in the moshavot.

Ya'akov Zerubavel expressed a totally different view. His remarks, which reflect the state of emotion and mind of both sides in the debate, deserve to be quoted at length. Zerubavel complained bitterly that those who several years earlier had looked forward to the arrival of Jewish workers from Yemen as aids in achieving the primacy of Hebrew labor in the moshavot had now changed their minds and opposed their advent in the settlements.

> The source of the error is that they actually want to solve the problem of the Jewish worker in Russia or somewhere else. And since that element cannot penetrate the agrarian system for the time being, they consider the penetration of other Jews valueless. However, *according to our worldview, the main thing is to solve the Jewish national question at large,* and in this respect *there is no difference between the Ashkenazi element and the Sephardi one; what counts is to create a self-sustaining Jewish society here, and if the Yemenites can make it happen—all the better.* [emphasis mine][65]

Ben-Gurion seconded Zerubavel's opinion. To strengthen his comrade's national outlook with its inclusive unity perspective, Ben-Gurion presented the practical rationales. Here, as in the Hebrew-language debate,
Ben-Gurion stressed the aspect of practical utility in the problem of principle. The root of the crisis in Hebrew labor in the moshavot, he said, is not
the paucity of jobs but the Ashkenazi worker's failure to adjust to farm
labor. This explains the tendencies of Ashkenazi workers to leave moshavot
and to migrate from one moshava to another. This, he believed, makes the
attempt of Yemenite workers with families to hold jobs in the moshavot "a
phenomenon of supreme importance in Yishuv life, for here is the key to
a radical solution of the Hebrew labor question."[66]

This important phenomenon was gauged not only in "conquest of
labor" terms but also at the political level. In Ben-Gurion's estimation,
"The entry of the Yemenite workers also strengthens our political stance;
by their means we enrich ourselves by boosting the number of Ottoman
subjects in our settlements."[67]

Thus, the Yemenite Jews' political function was to bolster the electoral strength of the Yishuv, in which a majority of inhabitants held Ottoman citizenship. Later on, Ben-Gurion launched an anguished and
furious attack on the manifestations of national disunity and individual
estrangement that accompanied the Yemenite workers as they took on jobs
in the moshavot. "[Their entry] is leading to one of the most painful
wounds in the body of our people: shattering of limbs, disintegration, and
separation into Ashkenazim, Sephardim, [and] Yemenites." There was
nothing novel about these phenomena, Ben-Gurion admitted. Ashkenazim, too, experienced estranged treatment in the moshavot due to class
contrasts. However, the Yemenites' situation was different.

> The Yemenites' foreignness is of a different kind. Here, apart from
> the class difference, there is a "national" difference. This foreign-
> ness is not only *de jure* but also—and mainly—a state of mind.
> What we have here is two levels of Jews: the first level—just plain
> Jews, without a modifier, and the second level, "Yemenite Jews."
> Although we know that the process of uniting the exiles and tribes
> is neither short nor easy, this knowledge does not absolve the
> worker of responsibility for these adverse phenomena; the worker
> must be not only the builder of the Yishuv but also its teacher, in
> the broadest and deepest sense of the word.[68]

For this reason, when the Yemenites were wronged in the apportionment of plots in Moshav Ganei Yehuda (a workers' cooperative farming set-

tlement near Rishon Lezion), Ben-Gurion did not flinch from addressing himself overtly to those responsible for this embarrassing act and to those who had acquiesced in it.

The terms of apportionment were as follows: (1) every member would receive seven dunams (one dunam = 1/10 hectare); (2) all members of the moshava of Ganei Yehuda would receive equal plots; and (3) fifty to sixty dunams of the 350 dunams allocated for the moshav were set aside for a moshav (workers' cooperative) of Yemenites, in which twenty settlers would receive land. Pondering this information, Ben-Gurion asked sarcastically,

> Will the members of the committee that was elected to pre-pare a plan for the workers' moshav please advise us about the following three things: (1) what does the word "member" mean? Is this esteemed title reserved only for those privileged to hold Russian passports, or can any worker put on that crown? (2) Why should a special pale of settlement be set aside for peo-ple from Yemen? (3) Why does a "member" need seven dunams if a "Yemenite" can make do with three?[69]

Worse still was the affair surrounding the settlement of Yemenite Jews near Qevutsat Kinneret in the Galilee. Due to cultural differences, ideological misunderstandings, and clashing interests between the personal wishes of the Yemenites and the collective will of the members of the Kinneret collective, the Yemenites were forced after nearly twenty years of struggle (1912–1932) to renounce their wish to settle next door to Qevutsat Kinneret.[70]

That very year, *Ha'Ahdut* published a letter from a worker in Petah Tiqva who described the situation of Yemenite workers in that locality. The Yemenite workers, the author explained with emphasis, received lower wages than Ashkenazi workers for the same labor. At the end, the author quoted a Yemenite worker as saying caustically, "There, in our country, we were in physical exile, and here, in Eretz Israel, we're in physical *and* spiritual exile."[71]

The publication of such remarks in an official organ of Po'aley Tsiyyon-Palestine indicates that the party leadership was increasingly sensi-tive to the discrimination that Yemenite workers faced in the moshavot. However, the party had not yet decided how to evaluate the Yemenite work-ers' contribution to the "conquest of labor" and ruled, notwithstanding the discrimination, that "The Yemenites' cultural level threatens to some extent to dislodge Hebrew labor from the high status it occupies wherever it has created a niche for itself."[72]

The ninth convention of Po'aley Tsiyyon (1913) adopted a resolution that struck a compromise between the two attitudes toward the Yemenite workers problem: "Immigration from Yemen is not a solution to the problem of farm workers, but it is a positive phenomenon as a solution to the problem of labor for the Yemenites themselves and an important [development] for the Yishuv in Palestine."[73] The resolution then urged the Ashkenazi workers to oppose the discrimination being practiced against their Yemenite comrades and to strive to integrate the Yemenites into labor organizations, farms, and collectives. However, the ideological and ethical dilemma that the organized labor movement encountered due to its theoretical and practical attitude toward the Yemenite workers in the moshavot also led to attempts to sweep the matter under the rug. At the Po'aley Yehuda convention in 1913, the issue was left off the agenda and came up for debate only after a group of delegates applied pressure. This convention adopted a resolution similar to that taken by Po'aley Tsiyyon at its ninth convention, held the same year.[74]

Po'aley Tsiyyon did not content itself with its resolution; it also came out with a passionate article decrying the attitude toward the Yemenites, especially on the part of the workers at large:

> We can only be ashamed and bury our faces in the ground in view of this disavowal of the ideal of national and proletarian solidarity. . . . If dozens of the hundreds of Yemenites who have come here choose to return to exile in Yemen and go back to living in slavery, disgrace, abuse, and contempt at the hands of their Gentile tormentors, so as not to suffer from strife at the hands of their brethren in Eretz Israel or from unemployment, the guilty parties are not only our farmers who regard the Yemenites as slaves but also the Ashkenazi workers who stand aside and take no interest in their fate, their situation, and their living conditions, and neither reach out to them nor do anything to ease their spiritual and material plight. It is a saddening mistake for which no self-justification or apology exists.[75]

The language debate and the attitude toward Yemenite-Jewish workers in the moshavot were paradoxical and painful reflections of the attempt of the Zionist Labor Movement to overcome the diversity, the contradictions, and the cultural and social contrasts of the realities in Second Aliya Palestine. The paradox that typified these debates originates in an internal contradiction that resided in the very aim to achieve unity.

The language controversy among members of Po'aley Tsiyyon led to such discord among the disputants as to be one of the causes of the 1919 rift.

The pro–Hebrew zealotry of the majority of members severely impeded the reception of immigrants in the party and was occasionally a factor in their re-emigration. What is more, in the mid–1920s the Palestinocentric stance of Po'aley Tsiyyon, pronouncedly reflected in the language debate, drove the World Union of Po'aley Tsiyyon to the brink of schism, as I show below.

It was the yearning for and expectation of the immigration of Jews from the east, coupled with the hope that the immigrants would abet the struggle for the primacy of Hebrew labor in the moshavot, that led to the great disillusionment with this population group when it stepped into the field of labor in the moshavot. The situation put the Ashkenazi workers, collectively, to a test that they did not fully pass and left them with a guilt complex that they could not shake off.

These phenomena, however, should be judged against the historical reality and the workers' final goals within it. The purpose of struggling for Hebrew against Yiddish as part of the Palestinocentric outlook was not to split the Jewish people but to achieve a new unity among members of a nation that spoke many languages. Were Yiddish to be legitimized, so might other languages that the immigrants spoke.

Here it is proper to emphasize that the Bund, as a party of the grass roots, was on firm logical ground in criticizing the goal of reviving Hebrew at the time. However, the party misread the purpose of the resurrection of Hebrew, which, as stated, was not disunity but its diametrical opposite, unity.

The same may be said about the Yemenite workers issue. Acquiescence in the poor wage terms meant abandoning labor in the moshavot to Arab and Yemenite-Jewish workers, that is, renouncing the goal of establishing a class or a public of Jewish farm workers of European origin. Since the foreseen mass immigration was expected to originate in eastern Europe, this would deal a blow to the prospects of such immigration and the immigrants' productivization.

Thus far we have described two paradoxes in the Second Aliya's aspiration to national unity. However, there was a third paradox: the attitude toward the Zionist Organization (ZO). From their inception, both parties (Po'aley Tsiyyon-Palestine and Po'aley Tsiyyon-Russia) criticized the ZO severely for doing little to promote the settlement enterprise in Palestine. The leading critic was Po'aley Tsiyyon-Palestine. Although this party opposed the resolution adopted by Po'aley Tsiyyon-Russia in 1909 to secede from the ZO, its disappointment and frustration led Ben-Gurion to consider establishing an alternative to the ZO. Back in 1907, he stated in a letter to a friend that "Zionism ceases to exist wherever it is fulfilled."[76] This statement implies an instrumental attitude toward Zionism that Ben-Gurion held throughout the Second Aliya period and afterwards as well. Thus, in 1910, after the Young Turks rebellion led to changes in the Ottoman Empire, he proposed the establishment in Eretz Israel of a pan-Jewish political organization that would represent the Yishuv's interests vis-à-vis the authorities. His proposal spoke of depriving the ZO of its political functions in Eretz Israel and handing them to the new political organization, which would belong jointly to the Jews of the New and Old Yishuvs. The reasoning, he explained, is that "What Zionists abroad think isn't so weighty; what we see here in Eretz Israel counts for more."[77] The point of his adage was not to trivialize the Zionist Organization's activities in Palestine but merely to limit them to economic and cultural affairs. In the political field, in which the ostensible democratic reform had created an opening for political action on a territorial basis, the role of the ZO was over.[78]

Another reason for Ben-Gurion's outlook on the establishment of an alternative political organization to the Zionist Organization in Palestine was the severe criticism that Po'aley Tsiyyon-Palestine had leveled against this organization's modus operandi. The debate about the party's status in the ZO was the direct outcome of the resolution of the sister party in Russia, headed by Borochov, to secede from the ZO. Three approaches were visible in these debates. One demanded secession from the ZO for the reasons that Borochov had cited, foremost disillusionment about the possibility of cooperation among clashing classes within one organization. Those of the second persuasion, including Ben-Gurion, proposed the formation of two organizations, one of *fulfillment Zionists,* those who did the practical work in Palestine, and another of *donor Zionists,* which would provide the fulfillment Zionists with financial aid and political support. The third view, held by the majority, advocated remaining in the ZO and expressed hope that the political balance of forces within the ZO would change so that the fulfillment-Zionist working class would attain a position of influence.[79]

As I show below, these ideas lived on in the Zionist Labor Movement of the 1920s.

To bring this chapter and the era to a close, we may say that the ab initio views of the Bund and the Zionist Labor Movement entangled both movements in a thicket of contrasts and contradictions. The Bund adhered to the concept of Jewish nationhood but found its basis difficult to define; it introduced the idea of national cultural autonomy but refrained from defining its complexion—class or pan-national—explicitly. In the Labor Movement, negation of the Diaspora, despite its extremism, did not advocate the disengagement from the Diaspora that Po'aley Tsiyyon expressed. However, the "mobilization" of Yemenite Jewish workers for the "conquest" of Hebrew labor, as a part of the total national effort, created a deep cultural and social abyss that separated workers of the two ethnicities. The Bundists did not have to deal with this contradiction, since they distinguished among types of Jews from the very beginning.

However, due to their ab initio position, both movements were susceptible to tensions. Were it not for this position, the nationally centrifugal trends—the absolute class view in the Bund, and the radical "Canaanite" leanings, which found various forms of expression as early as the Second Aliya, in the Labor Movement—would surely have become dominant in each of them.

Nevertheless, the proportional difference between the Bund's disunifying eastern European national outlook and the unifying—Klal Yisrael—national outlook of the Labor Movement, notwithstanding all its difficulties and contradictions, deserves reemphasis.

The political litmus test of these differences and contradictions would be administered in the next period, the interwar era, when both movements operated in democratic systems that were open to all sorts of possibilities of action within the framework of Klal Yisrael.

CHAPTER 3

FROM CLASS TO PEOPLEHOOD
The Polish Bund, 1917–1932

"Wipe out Zionism" [Likvidirn dem tsiyoynizm].

—A Bund slogan in 1929

The Polish Bund was born in a new political reality but carried the genes of the Russian Bund's "old ideology." The democratic Polish republic was a far cry from autocratic Czarist Russia. It carried the tidings of democratic governance, equal civil rights for all, and cultural self-determination for its national minorities. The last-mentioned hope, however, soon gave way to severe disillusionment. The Polish national majority, roughly two-thirds of the population, rejected the principle of a multinational Poland and, therefore, denied the minorities the status of collective national equality while extending formal civil rights to non-Poles as individuals. The minorities in Poland—Ukrainians, Germans, and Jews—were trapped by this political contradiction between democracy in theory and a repression by the national majority in practice. The trap was different and more powerful for the Jews than for the others, because the Jewish minority, unlike the Ukrainian and the German, was dispersed across the entire country. This placed the Jews in a state of unmitigated friction with the majority population in all parts of the country, as the historical religious tension between Poles and Jews, along with traditional modern anti-Semitism, was augmented by political and national confrontation.

This clash in interwar Poland, between theoretical civil democracy in theory and practical nationalist autocracy, was especially difficult for the Bund. Unlike and in contrast to other political parties, the Bund considered the Jews not only equally empowered citizens of the Polish state, but also an inseparable part of the multinational Polish nation. Thus, whereas a large absolute majority of Jews in Poland perceived the country as a place of residence, Bundists viewed it as a homeland. The disillusionment that set in among Bundists before the Polish Republic was more than a few years old stemmed not only from the Polish national majority, but also from the Polish Socialist Party (the PPS), which also repudiated the multinational principle and spurned the Bund's offer to establish, on this basis, a federative general socialist party.

In addition to these factors was the thorough rupture between the Bund and the Third International (the Comintern), that is, the Bolshevik Communist Party in the Soviet Union, in 1920–1921. The reason for this, of course, was the Bund's rejection of the famous twenty-one terms for enlistment in the Comintern. Had the Bund accepted these terms, it would have been liquidated as an independent party and taken over by the Communists, as indeed happened in the Soviet Union. In this state of ideological and political disengagement from international Communism, which did not acknowledge any form of Jewish nationhood, political logic favored the formation of pan-Jewish national front—a political Klal Yisrael—through which the Jewish parties would maximize their strength in struggle for Jews' civil and national rights. The Bund, however, refused from the outset to join such a front. From this standpoint, it replanted its erstwhile political attitudes, dating from the 1905 revolution in Russia, in the new political soil.

The Bund's rejectionism gathered strength and ferocity after the war due to the Balfour Declaration, the Jews' greatest international and national political achievement since their dispersion. This achievement, as even the Bund leaders admitted, catapulted the Zionist movement to a vastly higher status in the Jewish street. Thus, Zionism, which had stimulated the coalescence of the Russian Bund's national outlook, became a political menace to the Polish Bund. After all, Zionism, more than any other Jewish political party or movement, represented the Klal Yisrael outlook in its broadest national sense. Cooperation with Zionism, however limited, was tantamount to recognition of Zionism as a leading force in Jewish affairs. The Bund could not acquiesce in this. Furthermore, Zionism continued to gather momentum in the Jewish street until the Fourth Aliya crisis of 1926–1929 applied the brakes. This crisis strengthened the Bund's confidence in itself as an alternative Jewish political force. This self-confidence climbed steadily as Jews who had settled in Palestine flowed back to Poland and peaked in the aftermath of the 1929 Arab violence in Palestine. For the Bund, then, Zionism was the hostile antithesis, the "opposing other," by means of which it resisted the Klal Yisrael outlook both in the heyday of Zionism and when that movement had to retreat in view of its failures.

The Bund's struggle against Klal Yisrael politics intensified in the early 1920s for another reason: the internal controversy in the party concerning the terms of enlistment in the Third International under the leadership of the Russian Communist Party and, at the end of that decade, the question of joining the Second Social Democratic International.[1] Did the victory of the moderate central leadership in both of these struggles, which divided the party into two camps of almost equal strength, also have an effect on Klal Yisrael politics?

Just as dramatic political changes prompted no substantial change in the national outlook of the Polish Bund, so did the passing of generations in the party's leadership (see below) engender no changes in its policy. The leadership of the Polish Bund—the topic of concern in this study, along with that leadership's worldview—was composed of two groups. The first group was comprised of Henryk Erlich, the authoritarian leader; his unofficial deputy, the practical-minded Wiktor Alter; Emanuel Nowogrodzki, the organizer; and others. Among the second group were veterans of the "Vilna dynasty"—Arkady Kremer, Vladimir Kossovski (Nahum Mendel Levinson), Benish Mikhalevich, Yekutiel Portnoy (Noah), and younger members who did not belong to that circle, such as Jacob Pat, Y. Y. Trunk, and Leivik Hades, to name only a few.[2]

Political authority in the party was wielded by the first-mentioned group; comradely honor belonged to the veterans. Apart from frustrations and personal disappointments, which the members of the "Vilna dynasty" in the Polish Bund also shared, there was no perceptible intergenerational tension within the party leadership. One possible reason for this was that the veterans, whose political culture had formed under underground conditions in Czarist Russia, were unaccustomed and even unsuited to overt political action in a climate of relative public democracy. At the ideological level, too, which was so important to the Bund, the Russian veterans and the Polish arrivistes did not adopt perceptibly different approaches. The internecine fault lines ran not between the groups but within each— in particular with regard to the Klal Yisrael issue.

Since the Polish Bund was a centralized political party, run by a authoritarian central committee (the Z.K.), its two leading figures—the party chairman, Henryk Erlich, and his deputy, Wiktor Alter—deserve attention. They came from families that belonged to the Jewish hasidic bourgeoisie but both men had extensive general schooling, were well versed in Polish literature, and loved music. Alter was also schooled in the natural sciences. Erlich was ten years older than Alter; active in the Russian Bund before and during World War I, he had been the youngest member of the party's central committee before the war began. Alter rose to prominence in the Polish Bund only. Erlich was the fiery political leader and ideological prophet of the Bund; Alter was the high priest of applied ideology. He was so aristocratic and loyal as to sacrifice himself willingly for his elder comrade. Both had the gift of public and personal courage, and both set examples for their colleagues, who showered them with affection and admiration. They divided the party's main spheres of activity between themselves: Erlich wielded political authority as the party chairman and as the editor of main Bund organ, the *Folks Tsaytung,* whereas Alter focused on praxis and social thought. Alter's main concern was the image of the future Socialist society as a democratic egalitarian organism; in this regard he displayed pronounced Utopian tendencies, which we assess below.

The Polish Bund took its first political stance on the national issue—a theoretical stance only, of course—at its first convention, held in December 1917. The convention resolutions, pursuant to the resolutions of the Russian Bund convention (which were published in the same pamphlet)[3] stated that only cultural autonomy could guarantee the national minorities' collective rights, insofar as a capitalist society could guarantee them at all. Therefore, the Jewish working class, along with the other Jewish classes, demands national-cultural autonomy on behalf of the Jewish people as a national minority (*far das yudishe folk in Poyln, als a natsionale minderheit in land*).[4] Ostensibly, then, the Bund's political interests intersected with those of the other Jewish classes, creating a Klal Yisrael of sorts, albeit limited in terms of territory and time. This, however, was not so. The fourth paragraph of the platform, devoted to the Bund's attitude toward the other Jewish parties—the Volkists, the Dubnowists, the Zionists, the religious parties, and, in particular, the Bund's rival for the affections of the working class, Poʻaley Tsiyyon—explicitly ruled out cooperation with these parties in view of the Bund's uncompromising struggle against them. In contrast, the platform stressed that for the sake of the future Socialist regime the Bund must aspire, and make every effort, to achieve unity between itself and the Polish working class in order to create a joint Polish Socialist Party of class complexion.

This picture definitely contained an internal contradiction that reflected the traditional internal debate about national autonomy that had characterized the Bund since it was first discussed at the Fourth Convention in 1901. This is because the debate sent two mutually exclusive messages: talk of autonomy for Polish Jewry and exclusion of the Bund's ideological adversaries, who accounted for a large majority of Jews, from the political collectivity, the *klal*, of the Jewish people. In the past, the autonomy issue was purely academic; now, however, the new reality seemed to have made it practical. Accordingly, Klal Yisrael and autonomy issues that could once have been obfuscated no longer lent themselves to such treatment. Therefore, the convention adopted a resolution that meant, practically speaking, a retreat of the Bund from the Dubnow-style national autonomy idea as phrased, with his consent, at the All-Russia convention in 1917.

As noted in the previous chapter, the debate between Vladimir Medem and the majority in his party reflected this intra-party controversy, the results of which were typical of the internal political tradition of the Bund—a contradiction that stymied movement toward a political solution.

The Bund's resolution at its convention in Poland, with its two clashing planks, attests to the internecine academic and political debate in 1917–1922 not only about joining the Third International, but also in regard to how the party should affiliate with the Jewish people. A public debate between Wiktor Alter and Vladimir Medem in 1919 on the pages of the party journal *Lebens Fragn* was typical of the ideological ambivalence and political confusion that beset the party.[5] Young Alter, who had not been tested in the crucible of the Russian Bund's debates on the national autonomy issue, expressed a bivalent outlook, ideological and political, in which the two values were mutually exclusive. In the first outlook, Alter recognized the existence of the Jewish nation—eastern European, of course—and in the second he ruled out struggle for national autonomy at that time—a period that he regarded as a transitional era between capitalist and Socialist rule. He stated explicitly that "national autonomy" is only one possible way of assuring the Jews' national existence and presumed that in the future, under a different form of governance, conditions enabling the Jews to express their nationhood differently would mature. Admittedly, aiming to "seized the rod at both ends," he stressed that that if it were a matter of bourgeois society, he would favor national autonomy. Under the current revolutionary transition conditions, however, the party should stop using national autonomy as its battle cry.

Vladimir Medem, the veteran leader whose back carried the scars of the Russian Bund's debates on this question, countered Alter's arguments aggressively. He mentioned the dangers that the Jewish people faced during this period of transition. He noted trends of disintegration and fragmentation that the Jewish public was evincing. Most of the Polish proletariat, he said, was inimical to the goals of the Bund. The poison of national hatred flowed freely in the veins of the Polish people. It would take generations to treat the illness of national hate. It was the Bund's duty to speed the process of recovery from opposition to cooperation. To accomplish this, the party should be strong so that it might take up a central and leading position in shaping the Jewish national framework under the new political conditions. By implication, the party should struggle for the adoption of the national program, that is, cultural autonomy for the Jewish people. In Medem's opinion, this is the right time to fulfill the ideas on this topic that the Bund had taken up twenty years earlier.

Medem undoubtedly came out clearly in this dispute in favor of a Klal
Yisrael organization, whereas Alter opposed it. As the 1920s advanced, as I
show later in this chapter, Alter also changed his views somewhat and moved
toward what I call the "proletariat Klal," but not necessarily in the staunchly
Marxist-Bundist sense. On the basis of these doctrinary premises—which the
Polish Bund never repudiated at the theoretical level—the party adopted a
limited political flexibility that typified its modus operandi throughout the interwar period. In 1918, the Bund boycotted the kehilla (Jewish community
administration) election campaign; five years later, in 1923, it changed its
mind after a strident internal debate. In its aforementioned 1918 platform, the
Bund ruled out all cooperation with other Jewish national parties; three years
later, in 1921, it established CYSHO—the Central Organization of Jewish
Schools—in conjunction with other progressive but non-Marxist Socialist
parties: Left Po'aley Tsiyyon, the Volkists, and Yiddishist circles. Notably, although the Bund was the largest faction in CYSHO, and even though one of
its senior leaders always headed it, it never attained a majority there.

The change in views was definitely related to the end of the internecine struggle between the Left and the center in regard to joining the
Third International. Erlich, leader of the center, which disapproved of the
ultimative terms of the Soviet Communist Party that controlled the International, emerged victorious in the intra-party tussle. This achievement enabled him to adopt a more practical approach toward the kehilla elections.
However, he did not conceal the political goal that inspired his decision.
Candidly he stated that the Bund would deign to participate in the elections
only to dislodge the reactionary and nationalist regime of the clericalists
and the Zionists in the kehillot. Since Erlich considered this regime worse
than Polish nationalism, he thought any political opportunity to replace it
should be exploited.[6] In other words, dialectically, in accordance with Erlich's concepts, the Bund would participate in a shared national setting in
order to infringe upon the bourgeois image of Klal Yisrael principle, which,
in part, the kehilla represented.

For Erlich, the struggle against Klal Yisrael had ostensibly contrasting
aspects. Even as he persuaded his party to take part in the kehilla elections,
he furiously opposed a proposal by the Zionist leader in Poland, Itzhak Gruenbaum, to seek state funding for the teaching of both languages, Yiddish
and Hebrew, in the Jewish education system. Erlich, categorically ruling out
any agreement between the Bund and the Zionists, accused Gruenbaum of
Machiavellian chicanery. After all, Erlich asserted, Gruenbaum "knows we
will never compromise on the language issue. No force in the world will
ever require us to share the front with Gruenbaum on this question." Erlich
was especially wrathful because Gruenbaum, leader of the Kolo (the Jew-

ish political bloc in the Polish Sejm), had persuaded the leaders of the bloc to support his bilingualism proposal to the exclusion of any other alternative. In Erlich's opinion, Gruenbaum's motion was meant to help the government to withhold funding from Yiddish-language schools. Therefore, he declared an uncompromising war against the "Polish and Jewish anti-Semites" (the Zionists and Agudath Israel), who were attempting to deprive Jewish citizens of the only instrument with which they could maintain their cultural autonomy—the school system that would conduct most studies in their national language, Yiddish.[7]

Behind this unequivocal rejection—"no force will ever . . ."—stood a worldview. Two years earlier, shortly after CYSHO was founded, Erlich published an article in the organization's monthly journal entitled "The Struggle for the School," in which he demanded Polish budget funding for Jewish schools. In this article, he developed his anti-Klal Yisrael theory. According to Erlich's outlook, the Jewish proletariat and liberal bourgeois circles had cooperated sporadically to develop Jewish culture, but only until World War I. The postwar era, after all, was typified by social polarization that was exacerbating the class struggle in all social domains, including culture. This, in Erlich's opinion, led to a fundamental difference between the bourgeoisie and the proletariat in regard to this question. For the bourgeoisie, the national school is one way of controlling the masses. For the proletariat, in contrast, it is a matter of life or death. Hence, only the proletariat has a genuine interest in the struggle for national culture. Furthermore, Erlich continued, there is a substantive difference between the cultural autonomy that the bourgeoisie advocates and that for which the proletariat struggles. The bourgeoisie wishes to drive a wedge between the Jewish people and its surroundings, insofar as this is possible. Therefore, it struggles to create an inclusive, multipurpose autonomous organism of which education is only a part, and a system of national schools that depends on it.

Erlich decried this functional "Klal Yisraelism." In his opinion, the proletariat categorically opposes an all-out separation of Jews from their surroundings, except, of course, the degree of separation needed to maintain the national culture. National culture is maintained mainly by promoting the Yiddish language, which in Erlich's opinion, is the only substance of national autonomy according to the Bund outlook. In all other matters, the Jewish proletariat should cooperate with the general Polish Socialist labor movement.

Erlich, the dogmatic rationalist whose optimism verged on Utopianism, asserted that the struggle for the national culture is an interest of the entire working class in Poland and a pillar in the edifice of Poland's multinational Social Democratic Party.[8] Erlich wrote in this vein even though he admitted that some of the Polish Socialist movement, which he termed "anti-Semitic,"[9] together with the nationalists and the Zionists, opposed state assistance for Jewish schools that taught in Yiddish. His article was so extreme that the editorial board believed it necessary to remark that some of its contents represented the author's views only. However, the board was composed of representatives of the "partial Klal Yisrael" in CYSHO,[10] whereas Erlich headed a political party.

Nevertheless, both decisions—to participate in the kehilla elections and to establish CYSHO, the Yiddish-language school system, in conjunction with other parties that were not overtly proletarian and Marxist—reflected a balanced practical political calculus of sorts. Although this calculus was limited—the extremist ideology remained dominant in the Bund—it created a fissure in the wall of isolation ("separatism") as Erlich termed it—that the Bund had built around itself.

A REEXAMINATION OF A PARTY'S OUTLOOK

The climate of political compromise, on the one hand, and the sharpening of antinationalist class ideology, on the other hand, forced the Bund intelligentsia to reexamine the party's national outlook in view of changes of time and place. The opportunity to perform this inquiry was provided, symbolically, by events surrounding the thirtieth anniversary of the Bund in 1927 and, especially, the Fourth Aliya crisis, which, as noted above, strengthened the Bund's hopes and ideological self-confidence.

The debate was opened by the essayist Benish Mikhalevich, a member of the "Vilna dynasty" group in the Polish Bund leadership. Mikhalevich was a person who linked the two eras in the history of the development of the Bund's national thought; he was also Vladimir Medem's successor in the continuity and contents of this thought. Accordingly, to monitor the change of views that occurred in segments of the Bund after Medem, it may be instructive to trace the development of Mikhalevich's national thinking. Back in 1910, according to C. S. Kazdan,[11] a dispute erupted between Mikhalevich and A. Litwak concerning national "neutralism," that is, whether or not to accept the historical perspective of nationhood that either continues to develop or vanishes. Litwak, a member of the "Vilna dynasty," was the troubadour of natural Jewish peoplehood. The Jews' Yiddish culture, he said, requires neither proof nor intellectual justification. Accordingly, not only did he reject the "neutralism" formula categorically, arguing that it had made no inroads among the Jewish masses, but he also found a material contradiction in the doctrine that nourished it, the Bund's national outlook. In Litwak's opinion, the contradiction is rooted in the contrast between the theoretical premise of neutralism and the Bund's practical, political, and cultural activity among the Jewish working masses. This activity, he continued, is sharpening the masses' national consciousness and shaping their social awareness. Thus, the Bund, although ostensibly "neutralistic," is teaching the Jewish working class to take the national fate of the Jewish people into its own hands. In response, Mikhalevich swiftly defined these remarks "revisionist." In a polemic article against Litwak, published in 1910 in the American journal *Di Tsukunft* under the title, "Neutralism or Nationhood,"[12] Mikhalevich searched for a way to resolve the contradiction that his comrade, Litwak, had noted. At the level of principle, Mikhalevich covered no ground that Vladimir Medem had not covered five years earlier. His only addition, but an important one, was an attempt to tackle the alleged contradiction that Litwak had pointed out. Mikhalevich argued that "neutralism" means, on the one hand, negating the idealistic spiritual concept of national eternity, and, on the other hand, favoring the folk-level cultural national reality that the masses exude naturally and profoundly. This reality need not be "saved"; one must merely assure its unimpeded development. This is accomplished by social democracy, which lays the national problem atop a solid foundation of authentic peoplehood. In other words, Litwak accepted Jewish nationhood as an existing principle whereas Mikhalevich acquiesced in it after the fact.

Less than ten years later, after the February 1917 revolution and the Bund convention in Russia—where the demand for national-cultural autonomy was again expressed—Mikhalevich took up the national question again. Now, however, in view of the Bund's consent to the establishment of a pan-Jewish national organization in democratic Russia, his discussion focused on the Klal Yisrael principle. In this matter, Mikhalevich quickly erected a barrier against the "danger" that the Russian regional political formula of Klal Yisrael might be construed as a national pattern for world Jewry. To accomplish this, he reiterated the postulate that his predecessor, Vladimir Medem, had broached in 1911: that national unity must rest on a shared sociocultural basis. In view of the large cultural differences among Jews in different countries, especially western Europe vis-à-vis eastern Europe, they have no national common denominator save religious faith, which the Bund rejects categorically. If this is the case, then "The question of 'Am 'Olam [the eternal people] should be dislodged from its place of honor."[13] To reinforce his sociocultural argument, Mikhalevich based himself on the Jewish historical experience, which attests to a lack of solidarity among the segments of the Jewish people, such as Sephardi versus Ashkenazi communities and western European versus eastern European communities. Even the Zionists, with their Klal Yisrael ideology, could not deny the existence of this disunity, a structural element in the Jewish experience. World War I and its political results, foremost the establishment of the nation-states, had accelerated the centrifuge that was pulling Jewry apart. Thus, it is both illogical and hopeless to call, as did the champions of Klal Yisrael politics, for an elected assembly of all European Jews. Mikhalevich proposed an alternative: under the new postwar conditions, an attempt to apply Medem's idea concerning a world organization of Yiddish speakers, for the purpose of fostering Yiddish and Yiddish culture, might succeed and should be made.

This idea, another outgrowth of Medem's thinking, makes one wonder about those Bundists of the Marxist-materialist persuasion who were attempting to base Jewish nationhood on Jewish culture—a line that was so conspicuous in Mikhalevich's argument. Even if one concedes that language is a shaping factor in social reality, one must continue to doubt whether a culture, even in its broadest sense, without additional framework factors such as territory and an economy, can sustain a people undivided amidst a historical process of constant change. Even if one might accept these premises, more or less, with regard to the large collective of Jews in eastern and Central Europe—which had a pronounced national-cultural complexion—it is difficult to accept them in respect to the Yiddish-speaking Jewish communities in the rest of the Diaspora. Not only did historical development in the Jews' immigration countries thoroughly disprove Mikhalevich's argument, but even his own remarks contain a contradiction between his belief in the existence of a "Yiddishist" world Jewry and his analysis of the formation of nation-states, a global political development. Even Mikhalevich would admit that the creation of additional nation-states was intensifying the fragmentation of the Jewish people, and the only unifying factor that Jewry retained was the religious faith to which many Jews subscribed. Even that, however, was fated to slacken and eventually to vanish in the course of historical development.

By acknowledging the unifying national role of the Jewish religion in the past and even in the present, Mikhalevich, consciously or not, verged on the historical outlook of Simon Dubnow—a logical thing to do, considering that in 1917 there was also a political rapprochement between "Bundism" and "Dubnowism," as a national and political historical point of view, in the matter of establishing an autonomous and democratic national setting for all Russian Jews. However, it would be a mistake to think that this slight and incomplete move toward Dubnow, viewed in the historical and political context of the issues, affected Mikhalevich's outlook significantly. Mikhalevich remained a zealous fighter against assimilation in its Bolshevik-Communist version, on the one hand, and against Zionism, on the other. He likened the latter to the clericalism of Agudath Israel because it, too, "bound itself" to the Holy Land. Mikhalevich continued to resist Dubnow's conviction that the Jewish national interest always takes precedence over the class interest. In his opinion, since class always precedes peoplehood (*folk*), a national whole (*klal*) cannot exist as long as a class society exists.[14] Therefore, he also dismissed Itzhak Gruenbaum's Zionist initiative to establish the Minorities Bloc in the Polish parliament, in the belief that such an organization would be national in character.

This political stance led him to the sweeping conclusion—which much of the Polish Bund leadership, including Erlich, adopted—that instead of one Jewish people there are in fact two nations. This view was expressed on the occasion of festivities surrounding the opening of the Hebrew University of Jerusalem in 1925. The two nations, in Mikhalevich's opinion, were the Jewish bourgeoisie, champion of the elitist Hebrew culture, and the Jewish proletariat, bearer of the folk Yiddish culture. The two are locked in uncompromising class and cultural struggle.[15]

Notably, Mikhalevich wrote this in 1925, a peak year in Jewish immigration to Palestine (35,000). For this reason, and with the United States imposing severe limitations on immigration to its shores, an illusion formed that large-scale mass Jewish immigration to Palestine might offer Polish Jewry a meaningful solution for its hardships. In Palestine itself, the Yishuv made practical and theoretical progress toward national autonomy. Some voices in Zionist labor circles demanded territorial autonomy for the Yishuv in areas that had a Jewish majority. These developments, and the hopes that accompanied them, paradoxically served the interests of the Bund. After all, the Bund accepted the verdict of objective historical development, which was fragmenting the Jews into culturally differentiated groups. Thus, Jews of Hebrew culture could co-exist with Jews whose predominant culture was German, French, or Anglo-Saxon. They would join the minority of persons of Jewish origin who were no longer numbered among the Jewish people, that is, the large and decisive majority whose language and culture were Yiddish. No sincere neutralist could deny that the process of Jewish emigration from eastern Europe to the West was prompting segments of the Jewish people to disengage from the whole. Thus, the entire problem was not the emigrants' Zionism but that of those who remained, the Bund's political rivals for the leadership of Polish Jewry.

As stated, the Fourth Aliya crisis erupted about two years later and, from the Bund's perspective, demonstrated the nullity of the Zionist illusion as a solution for the Jewish masses, on the one hand, and the correctness of the Bund's approach, on the other. Therefore, the re-exploration of the Bund's national views on Polish peoplehood and Polish statehood ceased to be an ideological issue only. It now included political inquiry as well, in a series of fields: autonomy, religion, and trade unionism, or what this study calls the "proletarian Klal Yisrael."

Mikhalevich began this investigation with a two-part article entitled, "Our National Program in View of Praxis."[16] Most of the article presented a historical survey of the development and consolidation of the Bund's national outlook and its "mythological" stopovers, from L. Martov's speech to the fourth convention, the tussle at the London convention, the 1905 revolution, and so on, up to the time of writing.

The members of the "Vilna dynasty" welcomed this sort of historical narrative and ideological analysis; they cited it in their memoirs as a crucial factor in their personal political experience. This reflected the understandable personal narcissism of people who had held their ground against everyone around them and maintained a fighting political movement. It also reflected, consciously or not, the Marxist "historicist" outlook, according to which history, in its materialist senses, has present-day meaning as a factor that affects the analysis. After he rejected the mechanistic Marxist outlook and its reverse, the spiritual and idealistic attitude of his opponents, the Zionists and the Dubnowists, Mikhalevich set forth the Bund method. Thus, the main contribution, if not the innovation, of this article is its coherent and lucid definition of nationality according to the Bund outlook—primary a historical definition that regards nations as collective entities formed by shared historical conditions of fate and culture.[17] If so, the Jews are a people like any other. (*Yidn zenen a natsie tsugleykh mit andere natsies.*)

Paradoxically, this comprehensive sociohistorical approach was not vastly dissimilar from the Zionist historical outlook. Like the Zionist view, it linked the fate of the nation to its historical fate, both as the way the nation was shaped the past and as a process that would affect its future. This explains Ahad Ha'am's concern about the centrifugal process among Jewish centers—a concern that, as we recall, the Bund leaders also noted. To brake the process, Ahad Ha'am wished to establish the Jews' sociospiritual center in Palestine. It explains Herzl's dread of the anti-Semitic menace; to deflect it, he aspired to establish a Jewish state. It explains Borochov's view that, in consideration of global socioeconomic trends that were crowding out Jews from labor markets, only a national territorial base would solve the problem that beset both warring classes of the Jewish people. Thus, the Zionists, the Dubnowians, and the Bundists had both a common theory and common methodological way of thinking about the shaping of the Jewish nation in the historical and social process. The difference was that Dubnow considered Jewish existence a national anomaly whereas the Zionists and the Bundists, who regarded Jewish nationhood as a normal historical phenomenon, realized that for Jewry to exist it needed normal conditions that were subject to historical processes. The Zionists regarded the risk of Jewish assimilation as an inherent ingredient of historical and social development; the Bund, in contrast, presumed the possibility of a future situation in which all national collectives would vanish. Neither the Zionists nor the Bund viewed the future with equanimity and helplessness; instead, each chose to confront it in its political, social, and cultural activity, but in opposite ways.

The purpose of presenting matters this way is to underscore the paradoxical similarity between these two mutually opposed movements, even though Mikhalevich's article did not feud with Zionism, which, at the time, as stated above (during the Fourth Aliya crisis), had ceased to be a dangerous adversary in the eyes of Bund leaders. The rival from their standpoint was the Yevsektsia (the Jewish affairs department of the Soviet Communist Party) in Soviet Russia, which purported to offer an alternative Jewish national model to that of the Bund. Mikhalevich decried what he called the pragmatic or practical approach of the Yevsektsia, which affirmed the existence of a Yiddishist Jewish culture but acquiesced in non-recognition of the Jews as a nationality in the Soviet Union. In the USSR, the fate of the Jewish national culture belonged to a party bureaucracy instead of the democratic representatives of the Jewish people. Therefore, too, the Jews were not represented in the congress of Soviet nationalities, and the entire future of Jewish cultural self-determination was shrouded in doubt because it was not based on the people's democratic will. Thus, for the Bund, the Yevsektsia's "class" approach was as illegitimate as the Zionists' postwar national aspirations to establish national autonomy with broad political powers—a modern version of the Synod of the Four Lands—in the short-lived independent Ukrainian state. The Zionists' approach had failed in the past and that of the Yevsektsia was fated to fail in the future. By so expressing himself, Mikhalevich predicted the future of Jewish culture in the Soviet Union.

In that case, the practical answer to the Jewish national question, in view of reality, is of course national-cultural autonomy. At the level of principle, Mikhalevich had not changed his mind at all. The change was reflected in his practical political approach. Considering the Zionists' previous efforts to take control of Jewish autonomy in the Ukraine, and considering the present reality of nationalist and clericalist political dominance in the Jewish communities of Poland, Mikhalevich opposed fellow Bundists who continued to depict autonomy as an interest of the Jewish working class. Thus, he proposed, on the basis of political experience (*derfarung*), to desist from the struggle for autonomy under nationalist slogans coined by the other parties in the Jewish street—versions that had nothing in common with the Bund's cultural autonomy idea. Instead, he proposed focusing on several main issues in the kehillot (Jewish community administrations), such as the status of religion and the Yiddish versus Hebrew controversy. He also urged the party to take the struggle over these matters into a broader arena than the Jewish street, that is, to transform them into questions of concern to the Polish working class at large. After all, the separation of religion from the social and political organism—the kehilla in the Jewish case—and the choice of a national language of instruction in schools were general issues that transcended the purely Jewish interest. In practical terms, the proposal did not aim to ease the internecine Jewish tension by transferring the causes of the tension from the Jewish street to the general public domain. Its intent was quite the opposite: to recruit an external force that would intervene in both areas of intra-Jewish controversy—the status of religion and the national language—and settle them on the basis of universal criteria or principles. After all, Mikhalevich had no doubt that the Bund's outlook was closer to that of the Polish Socialist labor movement than to that of the Zionists or of the religious circles.[18]

Thus, Mikhalevich drew a clear dividing line between "political autonomy," to which the Zionists and their fellow-travelers aspired, and the Bund's idea of "cultural autonomy." The latter idea marked a retreat from the basic premise in this regard—expressed in the platform that the Bund enunciated in 1917, upon the establishment of independent Poland—which advocated Jewish national autonomy and contained a genuine reflection of the Klal Yisrael idea, albeit faint and limited to a specific political sphere. Now that the Zionists were on the decline, as stated, Mikhalevich reversed even this small degree of Klal Yisrael-ism and exchanged the limited national connection for an alliance along social-class lines, that is, with the Polish proletariat. Mikhalevich was not the sole proprietor of these ideas; soon other Bund personalities would seek to take the party out of the kehilla.[19] By then, however, Mikhalevich would no longer be alive.

Mikhalevich also wished to invest the Bund notion of national-cultural autonomy with universal meaning—pursuant to the Austrians Otto Bauer and Karl Renner but surpassing them. In his opinion, this is the political actualization of the supreme proletarian ideal (*der hekhster proletarisher ideal in der politisher farvaltung*)—an ideal no less important than socialist organization of economic life. Furthermore, he regarded cultural autonomy as a fundamental of a free multinational Socialist society (*grindzayl fun der sotsialistisher gezelshaft*).[20] By arguing this way, he ranged farther than his teachers, Bauer and Renner, who had been among the founders of the Austrian Marxist national school of thought. They invested a real situation, in which territorial peoples exist, with a Socialist theoretical basis; he elevated multinationalism, in all its complexions and types, to an ideal of Utopian significance. The studies that Mikhalevich collected in this book include a brief article about Utopian Socialism,[21] in which, following Karl Johann

Kautsky, he defined Utopian Socialism as a preparatory phase of sorts for scientific Socialism. In a paradoxical paraphrase of this view, one may say that scientific materialistic Socialism, for Mikhalevich, was the basis for the realization of Utopian Socialism in its egalitarian, multicultural social and national sense.

Mikhalevich's articles constitute a theoretical summation of the Bund's approach to the national question in the interwar period. This summation, it seems, was amenable to the entire Bund, that is, its two wings—the Left, which ogled the Third International, and the Right, which wished to join the Second International, as indeed happened in 1930. One gets the impression that Mikhalevich's summation did reflect a Bundist consensus, since the movement press, which thrived on disputation and polemics in its revolutionary culture and reality, did not respond to it polemically.

Moreover, two years earlier, Vladimir Kossovski, a pioneer articulator of the national outlook of the Bund, published an article in *Di Tsukunft* that expressed the party's attitude toward the national autonomy idea clearly and explicitly. Kossovski decried party colleagues who, in view of the reactionary clericalist-Zionist control of the kehillot, thought it best to limit their demands to proletarian cultural autonomy only. Kossovski considered this politically unrealistic. First, the concept of "working class" was not sufficiently defined in its sociological and economic senses. Second, the autonomous mechanism would not have resources for special needs, beyond its state funding, unless the bourgeoisie came aboard. Third, non-Jews perceived the Jews at large as a minority endowed with national characteristics. This led him to an unequivocal conclusion: "If the slogan of 'cultural autonomy for the working masses' is offered, it means, practically speaking, the forfeit of all general autonomy."[22] In other words, national-cultural autonomy, by being national, is a Klal Yisrael form of cultural organization. Thus, for the class-oriented Bund, national-cultural autonomy became national trap of sorts—a trap from which no class or political consideration could release it as long as it upheld the principle of national-cultural self-determination.

Thus, Kossovski and Mikhalevich agreed that national autonomy in a capitalist society is not only impossible but also undesirable due to the bourgeois nature of such a society, which the social reality renders unavoidable. As an alternative, they proposed the development and encouragement of the Yiddish language in the ways and with the methods that the Bund was invoking in Poland. Notably, however, both intellectuals inadvertently expressed a prophecy that would have a paradoxical outcome. Both Mikhalevich, in a "Utopian spirit," and Kossovski, in his materialistic analysis, believed that a European state structured in the form of a federation of nations would eventually come into being. Kossovski even gave it an up-to-date name, "the

United States of Europe." However, they hinged this development on the triumph of Socialist governance, whereas today this vision is gradually becoming a reality on the combined basis of a capitalist market economy and
social-democratic social governance.

Generally speaking, the writings of Kossovski and Mikhalevich reflected the Bund's tendency to "realistic Utopianism" on the national issue
as well, that is, a tendency to define itself as the standard bearer, in the
world Socialist movement, of the exalted ideal of cultural autonomy as an
inseparable part of, if not a basis for, the future Socialist society. Mikhalevich, like most of the Bund leadership, was a Utopian. He viewed Utopian
Socialism favorably[23] as a phase that would prepare the Marxist theory for
society and its trends of development. Marxism, in turn—as his writings
imply—should lay the social foundations for a Utopian, variegated egalitarian social edifice composed of national-cultural autonomies.

The dividing line between the Zionists' political-autonomy idea and the
cultural-autonomy concept of the Bund, as drawn by Mikhalevich, is indicative of the historical fate of the two movements. Both failed to attain any
degree of autonomy in the interwar period, and both failed to attain equality
in civil rights—in the political domain in Poland and in the national domain
in Soviet Russia. However, the Bund continued to cling to its Utopian dreams
even as reality dashed them with rising intensity, whereas the Zionists, especially those in the labor movement, created in Palestine the autonomy that
they had not managed to attain in the Ukraine and Poland.

Notably, the "Bundist autonomy" idea clashed with the Klal Yisrael
concept, which was manifested in the aspiration to "Zionist autonomy." The
Bundist vision was foremost a *class* concept; that of the Zionists was *national*. Bundist autonomy was rooted in the Yiddishist cultural reality of the
Jewish masses in the here and now; Zionist autonomy rested on the multilingual Jewish reality in the Diaspora and the Hebrew reality in Palestine.
Consequently, the Bund's fanatic Yiddishism created theoretical and practical partitions among the various segments of the Jewish people, whereas
the Hebrew culture, although no less fanatic, aimed to attract and unite
them. This also explains Zionists and Bundists fought each other so fero-
ciously over the language of instruction in Jewish schools—Yiddish only
versus Yiddish and Hebrew.

Notwithstanding the intellectual tenor of the Klal Yisrael debate,
which began with Vladimir Medem before World War I and lasted up to
Mikhalevich in the late 1920s, there was no visible contradiction between the debate and the overt politics of the Bund in interwar Poland.
This does not imply, however, that the Bund was susceptible to unmitigated dogmatic rigidity on this issue, as on others. Changing realities

definitely nudged the Bund toward greater flexibility on several issues, even though the decisions in those matters were accompanied by vacillation and intense internal disputes. Such issues included participation in the kehilla elections, joining the Second International, and the successful attempt to establish a general federation of Jewish trade unions that, although under Bund management, was not part of the Bund's organizational infrastructure. Inherent in this initiative, led by Wiktor Alter, the second-ranking leader of the Polish Bund, was the principle of the Jewish proletarian Klal as an alternative to the traditional Klal Yisrael in its ideological and political senses.

In 1927, an article by Alter touched off a polemic debate in the Bund ranks. Its bland title, "Remarks on Bundist Issues," concealed the explosives that the author had planted in its contents.[24] Alter's programmatic article was built of three segments: (1) a principled stance on Socialist Party ideology in view of changing times; (2) proof of the first premise—that the ideology should respond to changing times—analyzing developments in the Bund's outlook during its thirty-year history; and (3) articulation of a practical approach toward the construction of a joint political edifice of workers of different if not clashing worldviews in the Bund party leadership.

Alter began his article by distinguishing between two types of Bundists. One comprises those who believe they have discovered the absolute, immutable Socialist truth that was set forth in the past. Alter likened them to religious fanatics who believe the laws of the Torah were given at Mount Sinai and transmitted en bloc from generation to generation. The second type of Bundist, on whose behalf he argues, regards a political party not as a fossil but as a living, growing, and developing organism that regularly adapts to changing historical circumstances. In Alter's opinion, the Bund, like other Socialist parties, underwent important ideological changes in its thirty-year history. At first, it assumed that it represented working-class interests only and set forth to defend them. Today, in contrast, the Bund, like other social democratic parties, "has moved far away from these primitive assumptions" (*dozike primitive bagrifn*). By explaining matters this way, Alter inadvertently justified Simon Dubnow's indictment of the Bund, in his famous 1906 article, for its refusal to join the pan-Jewish organization in defense of Jewish rights at a time of national emergency.

The social democratic socialist setting that Alter wanted his party to join—the Second International—had long since abandoned the "political illusion" attitude toward the working class. Instead, it aimed and strove to broaden the social and political basis of the working class, an aspiration flowing from the awareness that capitalist society had tumbled into a severe crisis that undermined the status of the petty bourgeoisie, which had wanted to form an alliance with the working class. The working class also knew that in the absence of such an alliance, its political likelihood of rising to power in a democratic society was small.

Alter related similarly to the Bund's attitude toward the impoverished and numerically diminished Jewish masses in Poland: the party, he said, must present itself as their ally. The current state of affairs offers the possibility of fulfilling the dialectic rule in which, under certain circumstances, quantity becomes quality (*Di kvantitet zal aribergeyn in kvalitet*). Thus, by forging an alliance with the impoverished petty bourgeoisie, the Bund would improve its chances of gaining political influence in the Jewish street and in Poland. This possibility frightened its rivals.

From the organizational standpoint, Alter continued, the Bund should earn the sympathies of the distressed Jewish masses and begin to shape its future image. Although he did not explain what he thought that image should be, Alter hinted that the Bund, unlike the Communist Party, is essentially a democratic entity. As such, it has experienced ideological and structural changes over the years, due to the influence of social forces that had joined it. In Alter's opinion, it is this proletarian democratic nature that gave the Bund its strength and guided it through the harsh ordeals that it had experienced in its thirty-year history. Therefore, "In the future, on the basis of the democratic partisan experience, every Jewish worker who carries the revolutionary passion and is willing to assume the obligation that flows from his being a party member should be given the right and the possibility of shaping together with others the fate of his class by means of his party."[25]

These remarks do not elucidate the organizational structure that Alter had in mind. Perhaps, on the basis of his analysis of the Bund's internal ideological changes as it shifted from the national outlook and "neutralism" toward nationalism to a positivist attitude toward Jewish nationhood—one may infer that he would allow different ideological currents within the party to engage in unrestricted struggle. It is more likely, however, that Alter wished to establish a united labor organization patterned after the CYSHO school system, which, although ideologically pluralistic and multipartisan, was controlled by the Bund (even though the Bund lacked a majority in its governing institutions) and administered by people who, alongside reform-minded Yiddishists, sought the revival and efflorescence of Yiddish culture with revolution zeal.

This led Alter to an original and surprising stance, relative to the rest of his party, toward religious workers. He assumed that the impoverished masses to which the Bund would beckon were nearly all religious, and that in this arena the Bund might find itself in direct confrontation with Agudath Israel for their souls. Thus, Alter proposed that the party distinguish between the political clericalism of Agudath Israel, which it should resist unflinchingly, and religion as the individual's own business (*a prayvater inyan fun yedn yokhid*), as Western social democratic parties normally considered it. To preempt the shock that this might inflict on his comrades, Alter emphasized swiftly that recognition of the individual's right to religious faith did not signify, in any sense, a retreat from the Bund's belief in an open secular society. His intention was to separate religion from politics; only thus would religion become the individual's personal affair. His prescription would also further the struggle for the open secular society, one of the fundamentals of which was religious tolerance.[26]

Even if these remarks reflected a rather strong "divide and rule" intention vis-à-vis Agudath Israel—apart from their vision of the future proletarian society—they were very significant in regard to the "proletarian Klal Yisrael" outlook.

Alter expressed a similar approach toward the Bund's second ideological rival, the Zionist-leaning workers. In regard to them, however, he took a different point of departure. Alter viewed the clericalism of Agudath Israel as a dangerous rival that should be fought uncompromisingly, whereas he judged Zionism to be a total failure. His conviction in this matter gathered strength after he visited Palestine in 1924 and published a series of articles that are discussed below. Zionism failed, in Alter's opinion, because Palestine could not offer the eastern European Jewish masses a response to their economic and political distress. Even under optimal conditions—mammoth financial investments and six-digit annual immigration—the desired national solution for the Jewish people would not be attained. This is because natural increase in Poland would almost offset Jewish emigration from Poland to Palestine, however large in scale—especially at the time of the Fourth Aliya crisis in 1926–1929, when more Jews left Palestine than immigrated to it. Therefore, the question is not whether a solution exists elsewhere; instead, a solution should be sought in Poland. On this basis, the Bund should co-opt the Zionist minority in the Polish Jewish working class. This thinking followed the Bund's glittering victory over Zionism—the Zionism that, in his opinion, had once purported to embrace (*arumtsunemen*) and represent Klal Yisrael, and now had become a fringe movement among the Jewish bourgeoisie. Zionism's downfall, he wrote, revealed not only the ideological untruth but also the political futility of the Zionist Klal Yisrael view. For this reason, even though not all workers accept the Bund worldview, the Bund, as a party struggling for the liberation of all oppressed people, must reach out to the impoverished Jewish masses, be their worldview as it may. Therefore, the slogan should be: "If you agree with our demands and are willing to participate in our struggle, then come with us, even if you believe in the Torah and even if you favor Eretz Yisrael [*Palestine*]!"[27]

Alter placed an exclamation point after the proper noun "Palestine" to emphasize the innovative audacity of his remarks. However, he linked the practical explanation to Socialist logic. Had a general Socialist Party come into being in Poland, he wrote, it would have to include not only the Bund but also workers of Zionist persuasion, albeit without accepting the Palestine solution. Furthermore, "the idea of the working-class unity is a consequence of the Bund's comprehensive worldview. It should be central in [the Bund's] attitude toward other labor parties and in the consciousness of every Jewish worker and laborer."[28] Alter did not entertain the delusion that the small labor parties would vanish in the near future and merge into the large party, the Bund. He only hoped, he said, to instill in all of them the consciousness and sense of practical responsibility (*praktisher farantvortlekhkayt*) that anyone who fragments the labor movement must assume. If that happens, it will be an important step in the right direction of unifying the labor movement on a democratic basis. As an outgrowth of this feeling, he hoped, it would be increasingly realized that the safest way to achieve de facto unity is to strengthen the Bund. For the Bund, the unity issue is not merely a Jewish problem but a general one. Since it operates within a Jewish framework—for the time being—the Bund concentrates on the Jewish working class. However, had unity in the Polish street come about, the Jewish street would never have taken up the issue. Importantly, these rules, Alter writes, also apply to the Jewish Communists if they would accept the democratic principles on which the comprehensive proletarian organization should be based.

In a nutshell, Alter's article proposes the establishment of a ideologically diverse organization of Jewish workers—religious, Zionist, and Communist. This organization would be led by the Bund, both as the largest Jewish labor party and as a ideological framework based on principles such as tolerance of different and clashing views, internal political democracy, struggle to improve the living conditions of Jewish workers and masses, and recognition of the Poland as the homeland, in theory and in practice, of the Jewish masses that dwell there.

Alter did not propose a future reorganization of the Bund party. He definitely wished to maintain the party structure while tailoring its worldview to changing realities. As an interim phase, and to build mutual trust, he settled for the establishment of a Jewish labor congress that the Bund would convene in 1923. Six hundred delegates from ninety-one towns, including 434 delegates affiliated with the Bund, would attend. Thus, the strength of the Bund would be much greater in this organization than in CYSHO—70 percent as against 40 percent.

Alter's article was accompanied by a remark from the editors: the author, they said, had touched upon a series of important problems in his typical unorthodox (*apikores*) way and responded to them on his own counsel. These views, in the editors' opinion, deserved further discussion and investigation in any case. However, Alter's article did not instigate a far-reaching debate in the party ranks, possibly because the Bund was preoccupied at that time with a much more crucial and immediate question from its standpoint—whether or not to join the Second International. The debate over this issue—which lasted for more than two years, was divided almost equally between proponents and opponents, and was eventually resolved by a very small majority—displaced all other concerns in the center of political life. Furthermore, the party central committee, chaired by Alter's senior comrade Henryk Erlich, who subscribed to the Bund's ideological spirit and political path more zealously than Alter, may have removed the matter from the agenda. Evidence of this is that Erlich himself did not take a public stand on the issue.

Only historical figures from the glorious Bundist past in Vilna and philosophically inclined intellectuals took part in the public debate. Erlich, who also edited of the Bund's daily newspaper, the *Folks Tsaytung,* evidently decided not to disseminate his comrade's heretical views widely. Therefore the debate over the article unfolded in the movement's intellectual monthly journal, *Unzer Tsayt.*

The most acrid response came from Noah (Yekutiel Portnoy), who, as a nearly legendary figure from the underground days in Russia, commanded a status of honor and admiration in the party at the time of the debate. Noah rejected Alter's basic "Dubnowian" claim that the Bund intended to defend the labor class only. In his opinion, even if this accusation was basically true, the Bund, like every other Socialist Party, targeted a much broader population than the narrow proletarian base from which it had grown and on which it rested. However, the adoption of this broadbased goal, which always referred to the impoverished Jewish masses, did not mean that the party should transform itself into an ideologically pluralistic entity that would, for example, reconcile itself with religious faith. Since the Bund had declared war on the power-hungry political clericalism that had grown in the soil of religious faith, clericalism and faith were inseparable, even if Alter believed to the contrary. Zionism should be treated the same way. Although Zionism had stumbled, it had not yet collapsed; therefore, the Zionists' nationalist worldview is inseparable from their conviction that Palestine is the center of the present and, especially, the future Jewish national reality. Hence, the whole idea, in Noah's opinion, is merely an exercise in intellectual hairsplitting.[29] E. Moss, one of the party intellectuals, also categorically dismissed Alter's premise that religion is the individual's personal affair. He believed in an all-out struggle against religion and urged the party not to limit itself to the political dimension of the matter, that is, the aspiration to achieve a separation of religion and state. From this standpoint, the conflict between Bund-style revolutionary socialism and religion was one of substance.[30] The literary critic David Einhorn also dismissed Alter's approach, not only due to Bundist political or ideological rationales but also because, in his opinion, Socialism—because of its Utopian complexion—is itself religious and therefore offers an alternative to any historical religion.[31]

B. Mikhalevich, a member of the "Vilna dynasty" and a contemporary of Noah (Portnoy), whose serpentine confrontation with the national issue was discussed above, came to Alter's defense. He accused Moss of taking a obsolete scholastic-maskilic attitude toward religion. Regarding the religious emotion as a favorable phenomenon in itself, he also construed Socialism as a form of religion-of-the-future or part of the Utopia that the historical process would bring about. In his opinion, the working class, which expresses the solidarity of humankind at large, is religious, and more so, today's proletariat, with its worldview and spirit, already carries the future religion. The proletariat, Mikhalevich said, "is building today the temple of the socialist religion" (*der templ fun der sotsialistisher religie*).[32]

Alter's "heretical" and provocative idea was consumed in the flames of passion that flared in the internecine struggle over whether to join the Second International—the Erlich-Alter leadership was barely able to push that decision through—and in the orgy of anti-Zionist criticism that followed the 1929 Arab violence in Palestine. The Bund's political response to the bloodshed in Palestine verged on ideological pathology. The party called a mass rally under the slogan, "Liquidate Zionism" (*Likvidirn dem tsiyonizm!*).[33] Newspaper articles after the rally gloated over the plight that had befallen Zionism, which had previously stumbled over the Fourth Aliya crisis and had now prompted the enraged Arab masses to rise up in resistance against the "Zionist invasion" of their country.

Alter and Erlich had only one remark to offer about the "pogrom" against the Jews of Hebron: the bloodshed in Palestine might lubricate the wheels of Zionism instead of proving its failure, on the one hand, and it showed that the Bund was right, on the other.[34] This reaction attests that despite their thundering declarations of victory over Zionism, the Bund leadership was not sure that Zionism had indeed been liquidated.[35] Therefore, following the rule of capitalizing on a political advantage, the Bundists stepped up their attacks on Zionism with the intention of dealing its ideas a *coup de grâce*.

The party leader, Erlich, led the onslaught personally. He defined the call of the Palestine labor movement for the formation of a joint front against anti-Semitism as the hypocrisy of a "fatty Klal Yisrael" (*das gedikhte sotsialistish Klal Yisroeldike shmalts*).[36] He accused the Rothschild family, the allies of Zionism, of having been in contact with Hitler, leader of the Nazi Party, even before his accession to power, in order to destroy the German labor movement.[37] Instead of forming a "false" alliance with the Jewish bourgeoisie and the Zionists, Erlich called for the convening of a labor congress in Europe for the purpose of organizing resistance to fascism and anti-Semitism.[38]

As the Bund categorically ruled out the political Klal Yisrael, its public expressions of total allegiance to Poland as the homeland of the Jews who dwelled there—and not a place of exile that must be tolerated—gathered strength. It was the Bund's historical role, according to Alter, to reinforce this sense of homeland among Polish Jews, despite the difficulties and hostility amidst which they lived, by striving relentlessly and in various ways to topple the walls of the Jewish ghetto.[39]

Less than two years later, Erlich reinforced Alter's remarks with the imprimatur of leadership. Erlich launched into an effort to explain the ostensible contradiction between the Bund as a separatist Jewish party and its Socialist worldview, which fully intended, among other things, to breach the ghetto walls that isolated the Jews from the surrounding society. He explained the fact of the Bund's separatism by arguing that it was not an ideal in itself; it reflected neither an adherence to the erstwhile Bundist organizational tradition, nor an abandonment of the traditional goal of joining a general social democratic party as an autonomous player. The Bund maintained its separate existence, according to Erlich, because "conditions in Poland have not yet matured for the establishment of one united party, since the Socialist Party of the socialist proletariat has not yet decided to transcend its national framework to become a countrywide party and evolve from a Polish Socialist Party into a Socialist Party of Poland" (*tsu vern fun a poylisher sotsialistisher partey a sotsialistishe partey fun Poyln*).[40]

The unmistakable inference in this assertion is that the Bund, unlike the PPS, continued to adhere to the traditional national outlook that it had proclaimed since it had been founded, an outlook that demanded, at varying degrees of intensity, the right to maintain cultural-national autonomy within a broad social-democratic setting.

By the time these remarks found their way to print, Hitler had acceded to power in Germany. They attest not to the blindness of the Bund leadership—since no one at that time predicted World War II and its horrific results—but rather to their tragic intrinsic paradox, not only in regard to Germany but also, and especially, with regard to the Poles. Furthermore, not paradoxically but in full cognizance, the Bund leadership opposed the

Klal Yisrael notion ideologically and politically and favored a "Klal Poland"—if one can use such a metaphor to define the concept.

CRITICISM OF THE BUND'S NATIONAL OUTLOOK

What did the Bund's sympathizers, of all people—those whose outlooks approximated the Bund's for years and who had helped the party considerably in its public activity—think about the party's anti-Zionist fulmination and its dismissive attitude toward any attempt to create a common Jewish front? The term "sympathizers" refers mainly to the Yiddishist intellectuals in Warsaw and New York, authors such as Shalom Asch and Melech Ravitz, trade-union leaders, heads of the Arbeter Ring in the United States, and so forth. The two most conspicuous public figures among them were the poet and essayist Abraham Liessin (1872–1938), the well-known editor of the Yiddishist monthly journal *Di Tsukunft*, and Abraham Cahan (1860–1951), the charismatic editor of the large American Yiddish daily newspaper, *Forverts*. Both men were of the social democratic persuasion. Liessin, a contemporary of the founders of the Bund, had belonged to the party since early adulthood. Before World War I, he had been for some time a member of the Bund's "Committee Abroad," based in Switzerland. Cahan, although not a card-carrying party member, did much to help the Bund raise funds in the United States. One may say that Liessin and Cahan reflected the two facets of the Bund, the national and the cultural—Liessin as a grassroots natural Yiddishist and Cahan as a political intellectual who preached for Jewish cultural integration in the United States.

Liessin's public dissociation from the Bund's anti-Klal Yisrael ideology and the perceptible schism between Cahan and the leadership both took place in the mid–1920s. Our use of two separate terms, disassociation and schism, reflects two different types of public reverberations. Paradoxically, Liessin's criticism of Bund doctrine was ideologically much more significant than Cahan's, which was mainly political. Liessin's critique was positive and indirect; Cahan's was negative and direct. This may explain why the Bund treated Liessin, whom it respected, forgivingly, whereas Henryk Erlich, the Bund leader, who had few equals as a political polemicist, doused Cahan with boatloads of condescending contempt.

The indirect and direct dispute between these two men and the Bund is somewhat reminiscent of the war of words between Simon Dubnow and the Bund twenty years earlier. Then, too, the debate focused on the Klal Yisrael issue and Zionism. There was a difference between the discussants: Dubnow and the Bund, although somewhat similar in their national outlooks, were ideological and political rivals, whereas Liessin and Cahan were ideological partners and political allies of the Bund. This is why their views matter—not only due to their standing in Jewish public circles, but also because of their ability, instead of offering an alternative to the Bund's ideological outlook and political path, to point to slight but meaningful changes that could be made in them.

Liessin published two articles, which, although more than a year apart, form one essay centering on the Klal Yisrael issue. Their very titles bespeak this focus: "Palestine and Diaspora" (1926), and "Remarks upon the Thirtieth Anniversary of Zionism and the Bund" (1927).[41]

Pursuant to Herzl, Ahad Ha'am, and his own comrades in the historical leadership of the Bund, Liessin traced the importance of Zionism to three factors. Following Herzl, he considered Zionism a national movement that created a barrier against assimilation. He even repeated, almost verbatim, one of the main ideas in Herzl's keynote address at the first Zionist Congress—an idea that did not attract as much public attention as the "Jewish state" concept—that Zionism is meant to return assimilated Jews to the Jewish people before it returns the Jewish people to its country. Under the influence of Ahad Ha'am, he wrote (in an almost literal paraphrase of the famous sentence), "I do not believe that Zionism will offer a significant solution to the problem of the Jews [di frage fun idn] but I do believe it can solve significantly the problem of Jewishness [di frage fun idishkeit]." Like his contemporary Bundist comrades, Liessin, with his balanced outlook, believed that Zionism had furthered the coalescence of the Bund's national outlook for the very reason of the party's opposition to it and struggle with it for political leadership in the Jewish street. In the same context, Liessin claimed that it was actually the Bund that prodded Zionism into political action and struggle for the national rights of Russian Jewry. He offered as an example the well-known Helsingfors program, which called for the establishment of Jewish national autonomy—largely pursuant to a similar demand that the Bund had raised five years earlier.

On the basis of these premises, Liessin praised the establishment of the Jewish national center in Palestine, which he termed "a lovely and wonderful experiment" (a shaynem un vunderlikhn experiment). In his opinion, the Jewish labor movement, which was also national in consciousness, should not oppose it since it also transmitted the socialist message in its most exalted Utopian sense. This made Liessin into a "Socialist Ahad Ha'am" of sorts. He followed Ahad Ha'am's lead not only in regard to the national center in Palestine, but also—and mainly, in reference to the Klal Yisrael principle—concerning the Palestine-Diaspora relationship. Liessin advocated a national synthesis of the two collectives. After all, without the vitality of the Diaspora, the center in Palestine would not have come into being and could not exist as a center without continual Diaspora support,

whereas the Diaspora could exist in the national sense without the lumi-
nance emanating from the center in Palestine. Without Palestine, "we would
be no more than Gypsies, with neither a past nor a future" (*nit mehr vi
tsigeyner—ahn a nekhten ahn a morgn*). This led him to a conclusion that
was totally contrary to the outlook of his Bundist comrades: only a synthesis of the great Diaspora and tiny Palestine makes the Jews a wondrous and
original phenomenon among the nations, since the Jews had managed to
merge, internally, their historical Hebrew culture and their constantly
renewing Diaspora culture.

After legitimizing Zionism in the eyes of his Bundist comrades,
Liessin set forth in his second article to place the Klal Yisrael outlook on a
solid ideological footing. He judged the Bund and Zionism to be the two
most important movements in the past century of Jewish history, since each
movement, in its own way, significantly impeded the assimilationist flow
among Jewish youth. In this sense, each movement played a separate national role: Zionism affected the intelligentsia in the main, whereas the
Bund had attained an important position of influence among the Jewish
masses. Thus, "Zionism gave the people an intelligentsia while the Bund
gave the intelligentsia a people" (*Be'et der tsiyoynizm hot gegebn dem folk
a inteligents, hot shoyn der Bundism oykh gegebn der inteligents a folk*).
The Bund revealed the Jewish masses to the intelligentsia, and this discov-
ery gave the intelligentsia a sense of national and social mission that was
manifested in struggle for Jewish rights in the Diaspora and the establishment of the national and social center in Palestine. Thus, according to
Liessin, the Zionist intelligentsia was a Jewish Narodnya Volya of sorts that
turned to the Jewish masses in order to consolidate their national image.
The Bund, in turn, represented the masses, without which the intelligentsia
could not play this historical role. Therefore, Liessin remained at heart a romantic and Utopian Bundist whose national consciousness—acute, popular, and intellectual—prompted him to seek a synthesis of these two
worldviews as a path to Jewish national continuity.

Liessin's viewpoint not only contradicted the Bund's outlook on the
national issue at large but also clashed at specific points with impressions
that Wiktor Alter had gained during his visit to Palestine in 1924. A year before Liessin's first article was published, Alter documented those impressions in a collection of articles.[42] In one of them, he defined the cooperative
enterprise of the Zionist labor movement as a "dual utopia" (*di topelte
utopia*) composed of the Socialist enterprise of the "labor society" generally and collective settlements specifically. In this respect, Liessin's two articles were an indirect response of sorts to Alter's book and a topical
critique of the comments on the Yishuv that appeared in it.

Liessin's articles were followed by a series of articles that Abraham Cahan published in his newspaper after his own fact-finding trip to Palestine in 1925. In these writings, Cahan praised the constructive Socialist enterprise of the labor movement and, in particular, the Histadrut (the General Federation of Jewish Labor in Palestine), although he accompanied these remarks with pointed criticism and doubt about the future of this project in its present form. Cahan's writings sparked a lively debate between opponents and proponents of his view in the pages of *Forverts*.[43] Erlich, writing in the Bund newspaper in Poland, responded to this series of articles with characteristic furious derision. He defined Cahan's remarks as a pro-Zionist posture that corresponded well with their author's assimilationist worldview.[44] Seven years later, the two conducted a public debate in the American and Polish Jewish press—an exchange that was subsequently published in a separate pamphlet.[45]

The Cahan–Bund debate related only indirectly to the Klal Yisrael issue. The debate had been touched off by caustic remarks by Cahan against the Bund due to leftist positions, very close to those of the Communists, that Bund leaders had taken at the Second International in their criticism of the German Social Democratic Party's "rightist" and conciliatory policies concerning cooperation with the Communists as a counterweight to the rising strength of the National Socialist Fascists.

Cahan, holding the Bund to a general reckoning, argued that the political line it had adopted and the education it gave its youth were increasingly blurring the difference between it and the Bolshevik Communist Party in the USSR. From there he segued, almost inevitably, into severe criticism of the Bund's attitude toward the Jewish people at large. This reflected Cahan's equation of Communist leftism with anti-Semitism. The root of this evil, Cahan alleged, was the Bund's Bolshevik and antinational fanaticism. By expressing himself this way, he paraphrased Simon Dubnow's famous remarks more than a generation earlier. The Bund, Cahan charged, does not have a view of the entire Jewish people; from its standpoint, there is no such thing. Its sole concern is for the "revolutionary" Jewish working class; the rest of the Jews "can go hang themselves and drown" (*Di iberige idn megen zikh hengen un trinken*).[46] Cahan cited the Bund's elitist class outlook, which represents only a miniscule portion of the Jewish people but purports to speak for the impoverished Jewish masses. Condescendingly it wishes to lead these masses by adopting the hypocritical formula of proletarian democracy, which is nothing but a fig leaf for a Bolshevik-style dictatorship.

Cahan's critique, unlike Liessin's, did not address itself to the Bund's attitude towards Zionism and the settlement enterprise in Palestine. Cahan placed special emphasis on the Bund's ideology and its antireligious, and perforce antipopular, mind-set. This argumentation led him to conclude that, "The Polish Bund could have played a very important role in the lives of Polish Jews had it only been able to free itself of its fanaticism. It must take a broad look at all of society and focus on the tragedy of Polish Jewry from a broad point of view, with greater warmth, and with abundant tolerance. That is how Socialists—not Communists, but Socialists"[47]—behave in all countries, Cahan concluded.

Erlich's response was no less pungent than Cahan's criticism. It spoke in great detail about the Bund's political stance as a general labor movement but very sparingly about the Bund and the Jewish people at large. Erlich contemptuously rejected Cahan's charge that the Bund was oblivious to the fate of the Jewish masses in Poland. He traced the source of these groundless accusations against the Bund, and against him personally, to Cahan's being an "principled assimilationist" (*a printsipieler asimilator*) from the national standpoint. In accordance with this general worldview, Erlich alleged, Cahan was easy prey to the Zionists' "Klal-Yisraelish and even Jewish-clerical phraseology" (*klal yisroel-dige un afilu idishlakh-klerikale frazeologie*).[48]

Parenthetically, it is worth noting that the ultraorthodox and the Bund leveled the same charges against Zionism. Both blamed it on assimilation, although for different reasons. Neither should the shared origin of this claim—extreme and uncompromising fanaticism—be overlooked.

As for the matter at hand, Cahan undoubtedly exaggerated in his generalized accusations against the Bund. After all, the Bund's attitude toward Jewish religious culture did not resemble its attitude toward Jewish poverty. Never in its history had the Bund delegitimized the Jewish masses because of their religiosity; instead, it aspired to change their ways of life and transform them "from a people to a class." Therefore, Erlich was correct in vehemently denying Cahan's claim that the impoverished Jewish masses were not of interest to the party; after all, it was the Bund that had created the mythical ethos of Jewish poverty (*das idishe aremkeit*). However, the labels that Erlich attached to Cahan—"Zionism and clericalism"—indicate that his "accusations" against him contained much truth, since the Jewish masses were in fact largely poor but also largely religious and, to a very significant degree, pro-Zionist. These two categories were excluded from the Jewish Klal that the Bund, under Erlich's leadership, regarded itself as representing.

This, however, does not mean that the Bund was monolithic in its attitude toward Jewish tradition and the Jewish masses' emotional connection with Palestine. As stated above, Alter did not rule out an alliance with religious or pro-Zionist workers at the trade-union level. Furthermore, one of the most prominent intellectuals in the party, Dr. Liebmann Hersch, who had studied statistics at the University of Geneva, expressed an original view in this matter. In 1927, in response to Liessin's articles, he published a series of articles in Liessin's newspaper under the headline, "From Statistics to Politics, to the Debate over Zionism."[49] In these articles, he attempted to prove the absurdity of the Bund's view of Zionism as a Jewish migration movement and its intrinsic riskiness as a political movement that diverts the Jewish masses from their true mission, as the Bund saw it. As he wound up his remarks, however, he concluded that there is room for an association of "lovers of Palestine" (*liebhaber fun Eretz Yisroel*) that would express the profound connection that the Jewish masses felt for the Jewish historical homeland. By so expounding, Liebmann Hersch wished to separate totally the existing grassroots Zionism from Zionist Organization politics. Although he personally doubted that this was at all possible, the very articulation of such a view, which did not delegitimize Liessin's approach outright, shows that the Bundists, and especially the party's intelligentsia, did not have a monolithic attitude toward the national complexion of Zionism, especially when even the political and intellectual leader of the Bund, Wiktor Alter, did not categorically delegitimize Zionism as a grassroots idea.

In sum, on the eve of Hitler's accession to power in Germany, Bundists felt that their party was about to vault to leadership in the Jewish street. They felt this way mainly due to the difficulties that had overtaken the Zionist movement and the worsening economic and civil situation of Polish Jewry in view of the ascendancy of the anti-Semitic movement, which had led to an escalation of anti-Jewish economic discrimination. In the Bund's typically paradoxical manner, the party was not inspired by the undermining of the Jews' status in Poland to rapproach with the rest of Polish Jewry to create a common front in defense of national interests. In fact, it did the opposite, retreating into separatism and dissociating itself from the interests of Klal Yisrael in favor of the class interest.

In retrospect, the tragic paradox is inescapable: the worse the international situation of European Jewry due to the rise of Nazi Fascism, and that of Polish Jewry due to the escalation of anti-Semitism in that country, the more vehemently and acridly did the Bund oppose Klal Yisrael politics. To buttress its opposition, the Bund argued that there is not one Jewish nation but two—a dwindling bourgeoisie and a growing proletariat—and that neither national compromise nor even temporary political cooperation between them is conceivable. The only hope for the hard-pressed, persecuted Jewish masses, the Bund claimed, is the struggle of the proletariat at large, of which the Jewish working class is an inseparable part, against European reactionism. Therefore, the idea of a united Jewish national front for struggle against anti-Semitism is not only illegitimate from the class ideology standpoint, but also useless from the practical political perspective. The two leaders of the party, Erlich and Alter, and the veteran ideologue, pundit, and member of the "Vilna dynasty," V. Kossovski, stated this explicitly.[50]

This approach was logical in Poland during the tenure of Marshal Pilsudski, in which anti-Semitism was restrained, and in Europe preceding the Nazi accession in Germany. The logic stemmed not only from the Bund's worldview, but also from its structural Utopian optimism. Thus, the Bund leaders straddled the border between grassroots and intellectual anti-Semitism in Poland and Nazi rule in Germany, cooperating with others in protesting the ascendancy of fascism but not included among those who feared for the fate of their own people.

CHAPTER 4

BETWEEN THE "ZIONIST KLAL" AND THE "HALUTSIC KLAL"
The Zionist Labor Movement in the 1920s

Only there, in Prague, did we realize that there is an abyss between those of us who came from the Diaspora and those from Palestine. Even if the abyss does not create a separation—it differentiates and defines.

—Simon Rawidowicz, at the First World Convention
of Ha-po'el ha-Tsa'ir, Prague, 1920

World War I originated in conspiracies among unwise rulers and convergences of powerful imperial interests, and it culminated in messianic expectations borne on the wings of revolutions of February and October 1917 in Russia; the vision of eternal global peace under the League of Nations; and the resolution of the national minorities problem on the basis of President Wilson's Utopian ideas. These hopes had a significant effect, to put it mildly, on the civil status of Jews in eastern and Central Europe. A particularistic Jewish political achievement augmented these universal phenomena. The Balfour Declaration and the League of Nations' award of a mandate for Palestine to Britain denoted international recognition of the Jewish people as a member of the global community of nations and entitled the Jews to build their national home in their historical homeland. Practically speaking, these events endowed the concept of Klal Yisrael with international recognition.

The Balfour Declaration ostensibly gave the Zionist Labor Movement the dramatic development it needed to blaze its trail to new and broad national horizons in the political and social construction of the Jewish national entity in Eretz Israel. After the initial euphoria ended, the Declaration sent two ripples of tension through the movement. The first ripple ran between the movement and the Jewish masses, whose spontaneous passion did not metamorphose into systematic and broad support for the settlement enterprise in Palestine. Against the backdrop of declining resources, the traditional tension born in the Second Aliya gathered strength—tension between the Palestinocentric "halutsic klal," which insisted that the Zionist effort be concentrated on Palestine, and the "Zionist klal," which espoused a "labor of the present" (*Gegenwartsarbeit*) that aimed to strike a balance between the construction of the national home in Eretz Israel and concern for the political and cultural aspects of Jewish existence in diaspora. This struggle lasted until the late 1920s and ended in compromise.

Three political entities that belonged to the halutsic klal took part in this struggle: the Ahdut ha-ʿAvoda party, established in 1919 in a merger between Poʿaley Tsiyyon in Palestine and the nonpartisans; the veteran Ha-poʿel ha-Tsaʿir Party; and the nonpartisan He-haluts youth movement, established in 1917, which conducted most of its activity in the1920s in Poland. These entities were differentiated in their public complexion. Ahdut ha-ʿAvoda and Ha-poʿel ha-Tsaʿir were Yishuv labor parties, whereas He-haluts was an organization of young people who prepared to "make aliya," that is, to move to Palestine for good; it had no political intentions and lacked a consistent ideological doctrine. At its outset, it was made up of Socialist groups and movements that were close to Ahdut ha-ʿAvoda and non-Socialist but purely nationalist groups that identified with Ha-poʿel ha-Tsaʿir. In all, one may describe He-haluts as ideologically pluralistic and monistic in terms of the mission it undertook. Theoretically and practically, He-haluts was a confederation of youth movements and of individuals who joined its training collectives independently. From the political standpoint, it was organizationally independent of the country-level Zionist organizations, especially the Zionist Organization in Poland, and it answered to the call of the World Zionist Organization. Accordingly, the three entities were institutionally linked by the General Federation of Jewish Labor in Palestine (the Histadrut), which members of He-haluts joined after they reached that country. Their strength in the Zionist Movement during that decade derived not from their political power but from the pioneering ethos that they expressed and fulfilled. Even though the Zionist Movement never totally identified with the radical vanguard spirit of this ethos, it could never ignore it.

The halutsic klal's dispute with the Zionist klal carried an internal contradiction that contemporaries of the Utopian mind-set seem to have overlooked. On the one hand, the pioneers demanded a totally Palestinocentric policy, that is, a focusing of the entire national effort on the He-haluts groups that engaged in "fulfillment." On the other hand, they affirmed the democratic political nature of the Zionist Organization, without giving thought to the clash between the radical avant-garde attitude of the pioneering ranks and the political compromise without which democratic rule cannot occur. They learned to make peace with compromise by the end of the decade, but it was a dynamic, not a static, compromise—a "creeping" compromise, so to speak, in which they gradually moved part of the way toward their goals. However, as stated, the political starting line in the early 1920s was a radical one that tended toward the alternative of creating a pan-Jewish national entity that would replace the Zionist Organization.

As explained in chapter 2, in the early days of the Second Aliya, Ben-Gurion defined his principled attitude toward Zionism by stating that wherever it was fulfilled it ceased to exist. To use contemporary terminology, this was an early "post-Zionist" turn of phrase. Additionally, as noted above, Ben-Gurion distinguished between Zionists who personally fulfilled Zionism and those who enriched it with material donations. Paradoxically, then, those who fulfilled Zionism theoretically stopped being Zionists. This led Ben-Gurion to the idea that two Zionist organizations should be set up, one of donors and one of doers, with the former nothing but an instrument that would funnel resources to the latter.

After the Balfour Declaration, this alternative was replaced with another. The "Zionist fervor" of the Jewish masses gave birth to the idea of establishing a world Jewish congress *"in lieu of the Zionist Congress"*— as expressed in an editorial in the Ahdut ha-ʿAvoda journal, *Kuntres,* in 1919, on the occasion of the calling of a national assembly of Jews in Palestine.[1] A year later, Yizhak Ben-Zvi refined the idea and set it on the tripod of world Jewry, the Zionist Movement, and—in the future—"the world Zionist organization of the Jewish worker, which will come into being for the labor of building our country." A special place in this structure was reserved for the organized Yishuv, of course. It is also noteworthy that the Zionist activist Ben-Zvi regarded "the people that resides *in this country, in all of its segments, religions, and classes,"* as a partner in this organization, which would devote itself to the building of Eretz Israel.[2] Notwithstanding these remarks, one doubts that the leaders of Ahdut ha-ʿAvoda were absolutely committed, even at the intellectual level, to the idea of the Jewish Congress as an alternative to the Zionist Organization. As political realists, they realized from the outset that they lacked the power to change objective reality. Even in their alternativist reflections, they did not intend to dismantle the Zionist Organization but only to make it part of an expanded national framework.

Nevertheless, Ben-Gurion, the progenitor of the alternativist outlook, did not let the idea rest. In the midst of the economic and social crisis at the end of the Third Aliya, he repeated his proposal from the Second Aliya era, now a decade old, to establish a separate entity alongside the Zionist Organization that would enlist organizations and individuals that sustained the building of Jewish Palestine. Henceforth, in his view, the important national political duties would belong to the Zionist Organization. However, the ZO would have to relinquish responsibility for the building of the country because "it has shown itself to be utterly inept in this domain and is but . . . an unnecessary and disruptive buffer between the people and the fulfillers of Zionism." The correct alternative player in this capacity is the Labor Movement, whose historical role it is "to be not only the doer but also the doing." Therefore, Ben-Gurion insisted, as he had demanded four years earlier, in his speech at the last convention of Po'aley Tsiyyon in Palestine in 1919, that "national resources should move directly from the people to the builders of the country with no intermediaries, and the builders should answer to the people directly from their labor with no need for proxies."[3]

Ben-Gurion based his idea on a revolutionary Utopian plan that was also of his parentage: transformation of the Histadrut (the General Federation of Labor) into an egalitarian, disciplined, and centralized "confraternity of labor," in which every member would be subordinate to the collective. The goal in this regard was to make legions of volunteers available to the national society for its constructive enterprises, just as the Palmach—*pelugot mahats* or elite combat units—were established as in the 1940s to furnish this society with military defense. Therefore, in Ben-Gurion's opinion, the weakness of the Zionist Movement was sufficient reason to establish a confraternity of labor. "Thus far," he explained, "most of us thought that the Zionist Organization is the conduit through which Zionism would be fulfilled, and we planned our steps accordingly. This idea has proved false. From my standpoint, it's absolutely clear: *we must find a different instrument* [emphasis mine]. The instrument that can do this is the Federation of Labor in Palestine."[4]

The idea was to circumvent the Zionist Organization by establishing a halutsic fulfillment organization that would turn directly to the Jewish people. The organization envisaged, the confraternity of labor, would supplant the Zionist Organization and the nonexistent world Jewish Congress in matters related to the building of Jewish Palestine. Thus, the unorganized Jewish people, the segment of the nation that was not subject to institutional discipline, was asked voluntarily to support an avant-garde that would engage in Zionist fulfillment, something like an order that answered to no institutional democratic authority save its own organization—the confraternity of labor.

To understand better the Palestinocentric "alternativist spasm" that gripped Ben-Gurion during those years, one should also note his attitude toward the various currents in the international labor movement in 1919–1920. He believed it vastly important to enlist Po'aley Tsiyyon in the Second International as a Palestine party and not as a representative of a world organization of Jewish workers, as the heads of the World Union of Po'aley Tsiyyon demanded. In a letter to Shlomo Kaplansky, he explained that these terms of admission might be faulty in other times "but are altogether praiseworthy now, because the immediate need is to underscore *the Palestine element of our national independence*. There is no lovelier historical symbol than having the representatives of Hebrew Socialism in Eretz Israel appear as *the first national emissaries of the Jewish proletariat*."[5] This was a diametrically anti-Bundist way of expressing the issue. The Bund came to the International as the representative of a territorial Jewish party, whereas Po'aley Tsiyyon purported to represent the Jewish national proletariat vis-à-vis the world on the territorial basis of Palestine.

During those years, the newly established Ahdut ha-'Avoda was also gripped with hopes of the impending revolution. In 1920, it assisted in the establishment of the Vienna International, an amalgam of parties that wished to unite the entire international labor movement. In discussions among members of the Po'aley Tsiyyon-Palestine delegation, Ben-Gurion and Yizhak Tabenkin expressed an ideological and psychological affinity for Bolshevism and some delegates did not categorically reject the idea of joining the Third International, provided that the latter recognize the Jewish national and Socialist enterprise in Palestine and change its authoritarian and undemocratic methods of governance.[6] From this standpoint, Ahdut ha-'Avoda and the Bund held similar positions on both principles, democracy and national recognition.

Obviously, Ahdut ha-'Avoda not only failed to take even the first step toward the fulfillment of these matters but also dismissed them categorically. In keeping with the practice in this party, Ben-Gurion, the supreme leader of the Labor Movement, had a penchant for extreme Utopian plans whereas Berl Katznelson, the indefatigable keeper of the party's moral and spiritual flame, remained staunchly practical. Therefore, Katznelson expressed a view opposite to that of Ben-Gurion. In his cautious estimation, "today, with all its flaws, the Zionist Congress is *the only supreme Jewish institution* that nurtures and, in small measure, creates grassroots instruments for the purchase [of land], settlement of the country, building, and immigration."[7]

Just then, at the XIII Zionist Congress (August 1923), the critical if not alternativist outlook of Ahdut ha-'Avoda was put to a rather difficult test of principle against the leadership of the Zionist Organization. It happened when the president of the Congress, Chaim Weizmann, took up a plan to expand the "Jewish agency" by co-opting famous Jews who were not necessarily Zionists, and not on the basis of democratic elections, in order to place their influence and wealth at the service of the enterprise in Palestine. His proposal met with stiff opposition from various circles and personalities in the Zionist

Organization. The leading opponents were the Polish Zionist leader Itzhak Gruenbaum; Nahum Goldmann, a leader of the liberal group at the Congress; and Ze'ev Jabotinsky, who would soon resign from the Zionist Executive and establish the Revisionist Party as an opposition to Weizmann's policy. Ahdut ha-'Avoda, as part of the World Union of Po'aley Tsiyyon (Right), also sided with the opponents.[8]

The opponents, including the Po'aley Tsiyyon delegates, considered the plan a political menace and a threat to the foundations of the Zionist Movement. From the political standpoint, they feared that since most candidates for admission to the expanded "agency" held British citizenship, they might prefer British over Zionist interests at a time of crisis. Katznelson warned the supporters of Weizmann's motion that they would "deprive Zionism of its only weapon—its being a political movement that answers only to itself." Katznelson also expressed concern about an ulterior intention in the motion to create a bourgeois alternative to the grassroots, democratic Zionist Movement as the builder of the Yishuv and the Jewish society in Palestine, "by means of and in accordance with the working class, because the country has no other builder."[9]

Thus, Ahdut ha-'Avoda, which had espoused the idea of a "halutsic alternative" within or even without the Zionist Organization, was clearly upset about the possibility of an undemocratic and non-Zionist alternative—a takeover of the Zionist Organization by the wealthy. However, since Ahdut ha-'Avoda belonged to the Zionist klal as a matter of principle and had no framework in which to operate save the Zionist Organization, and since the financial resources of the Labor Movement, albeit meager, came solely from the Zionist Organization, the party had no choice but to compromise with political reality, that is, to abstain in the voting on Weizmann's motion. Young Moshe Shertok aptly explained his party's vacillations: "The urge to take this step"—to vote no-confidence in the leadership—"was powerful. However, *the sense of responsibility, anxiety* for the fate of our rickety structure in Palestine, which any gentle push could topple, overcame the wish to vent the accumulated wrath against Weizmann for several years."[10]

Thus, the halutsic klal was a trap of sorts for Ahdut ha-'Avoda within the Zionist klal. At that time, if resources for the Palestine enterprise had been available elsewhere and had those resources been turned over to the Labor Movement, as Ben-Gurion had demanded, the movement would surely have fulfilled its alternativist penchants. However, this did not occur because the entire constructivist enterprise of the Labor Movement, which was also its political base, depended on the Zionist Organization generally and on Chaim Weizmann particularly. The leader of Ahdut ha-'Avoda had been aware of this since the beginning of the party's contacts with Weizmann immediately after the war.[11] This relationship was especially important in the 1920s, when the Labor Movement needed Weizmann to consolidate its position as a leading force in the Zionist Movement. The paradox was that the greater the national and social pretensions of the halutsic klal became, so did the dependence of this klal on the Zionist klal.

Ben-Gurion, unlike Katznelson and Shertok, had not yet internalized—at least outwardly—the notion of an oppositionist mode that does not rupture the democratic institutional framework. About a year after his debate with Katznelson, his Utopian leanings drove him to flights of political fancy. At the party Council in 1924, Ben-Gurion "took the bull by the horns"—he actually used this expression—and unveiled for his comrades a world-spanning alternative political vision. Instead of membership in the Zionist Organization, which he believed to be crumbling, he envisaged an alliance with the British Labour Party, which would climb to power in Great Britain, and even revealed a change in the political line of the Soviet government. He hoped to obtain economic aid from the former and the opening of gates for large-scale halutsic aliya from the latter. In his customary way, Ben-Gurion always carried his Utopian vision to a practical political or social conclusion. To prepare the Labor Movement for these political possibilities, in his opinion, it was necessary to weld the movement into one large and strong political party.[12]

In this round of the debate, Ben-Gurion's rival was the journalist and intellectual Moshe Beilinson, who had foreseen the outcome of Ahdut ha-'Avoda's serpentine development in the Zionist Organization, as he had in other matters on which the party was undecided.[13] Beilinson sought to persuade his comrades to withdraw their opposition to Weizmann's plans to expand the Jewish Agency. He, too, "took the bull by the horns," but not from the point of view of his leader, Ben-Gurion. "If we really wish to fulfill our enterprise," Beilinson wrote, "we must liberate ourselves of several slogans that, let us admit, are suitable for Europe but have become barren utterances for us." The reason, he said, is that "we have a permanent and unique goal, building the country." Since the goal sanctifies many of the means, it should be attained "*in all ways*. . . . Only from this point of view should we discuss expanding the Jewish Agency, and for this principle all other principles should be set aside."[14] Beilinson was referring to those who, citing democratic principles, objected to the admission of unelected people to the leadership of the Zionist enterprise on the basis of their fame or wealth. In his opinion, the preservation of "the purity of democratic principles" would eviscerate the movement's constructivist power.

Pursuant to his opposition to basing the national politics of Ahdut ha-'Avoda on rigid democratic "principles," Beilinson also came out against the "principle" of class struggle and urged the movement to demonstrate explicitly that its methods and tactics were decided "not by the interests of the class struggle but by the interests of building the country." Class struggle as a way to protect the interests of the workers should, in his opinion, be replaced by a national policy of distributing the effort and the personal sacrifice among all classes. This policy, he believed, would entitle the Labor Movement to be "the legitimate successor to Congress Zionism as the leadership of the Jewish freedom movement and . . . the living core of the Jewish revolution." Only in this manner, he asserted, could "a true Jewish Labor Movement be established and organic socialism be fulfilled."[15]

"Organic Socialism" was a concept that Beilinson had coined as a contrast to class socialism. In terms of Socialist concepts, the line between Ahdut ha-ʿAvoda and the Bund undoubtedly ran here, even though both entities defined themselves as social democratic parties and belonged to the Second International. It is also this distinction that defined the Labor Movement as an organic part of Klal Yisrael. The movement became such, as I show below, without foregoing the class definition in the political and cultural sense—a definition that became important precisely at the time that the accepted "class struggle" formula was steadily being abandoned in theory and in practice.

Beilinson's remarks presaged two social and political developments that persuaded Ahdut ha-ʿAvoda to abandon its alternativist schemes and begin to move toward full integration into the Zionist Organization leadership, with the intent to attain full primacy in the ZO at some future time. The first development was the ascendancy of the Jewish bourgeoisie in the Yishuv due to the Fourth Aliya, which seemed to offer an alternative way to build the national society. The second was the establishment of the Revisionist Party under Ze'ev Jabotinsky in 1925—a party that purported to offer an alternative to Chaim Weizmann's leadership. Both developments endangered the status of the Labor Movement in the Zionist Movement and the Yishuv. Amidst its ideological distress and political concerns, on the one hand, and in its aspiration to attain a leading status in Zionism, on the other hand, the Ahdut ha-ʿAvoda ideologues were increasingly willing to admit that the party needed an ally in the Zionist Movement and that this ally was Chaim Weizmann. Indeed, for all practical purposes Ahdut ha-ʿAvoda lifted its objection to the idea of expanding the Jewish Agency, and Weizmann invested his full stature and presidential power in the defense of the Labor Movement when rightist circles assailed the movement and savagely accused it of wasting national funds on social experiments that were doomed to fail from the outset.

About two years later, the bourgeois alternative withered as the Fourth Aliya tumbled into severe economic crisis. This reinflated the Labor

Movement's self-confidence as the locomotive of the Zionist building enterprise. Consequently, the process of merger between Ahdut ha-ʿAvoda and Ha-poʿel ha-Tsaʿir, which concluded with the formation of the Palestine Labor Party (Mapai) in 1930, accelerated. So did the movement's political rapprochement with Chaim Weizmann, which became an official alliance that endured until the XXII Zionist Congress in 1946, after World War II and the Holocaust.

In sum, there were three main approaches toward the Zionist klal in Ahdut ha-ʿAvoda's political exertions. Katznelson favored cooperation with the Zionist bourgeoisie as a national and Socialist necessity, even though the Labor Movement would have to make painful concessions on its account. The determining principle, in his view, was the comprehensive nature of the Labor Movement's national responsibility. Beilinson, as stated, considered this cooperation a manifestation of the rooted "organic socialism" of the Palestine Labor Movement. The third approach was that of Ben-Gurion and Tabenkin, for whom the supreme and determining test for the Zionist Organization was the constructivist act. In 1927, Weizmann seemed to be leaning toward accepting the report of the "committee of experts" that had drawn critical negative conclusions about the economic condition of the cooperative settlement venture, citing mismanagement of the cooperative aspect of the enterprise. In view of this menace, Tabenkin, according to E. Golomb, proposed a direct appeal to the Jewish masses in cooperation against Weizmann with the leader of the Zionist opposition, Ze'ev Jabotinsky.[16]

Ben-Gurion's response was more complex than his predecessor's and, therefore, more adaptable to the political situation. During the "committee of experts" crisis, Ben-Gurion proposed to resign from the Zionist Executive. In response to critics who feared that this would cause the Zionist klal to disintegrate, he exclaimed, *"I'm not afraid of disintegration*, I am not deterred by an ultimatum, I am fighting for the Zionist Organization to do its duty"[17] due to his conviction that the Organization had the strength to do it. Therefore, he proclaimed that he would demand uncompromising struggle against the Zionist Organization by the workers at large unless the ZO changed its policy. The secession of the Histadrut from the Zionist Movement gave Ben-Gurion a way to beat a tactical retreat from the threats of resignation and disintegration. Indeed, about a year later, at the 1928 session of the Ahdut ha-ʿAvoda Council, as the unity talks between his party and Ha-poʿel ha-Tsaʿir were well along, Ben-Gurion stated that despite the harsh criticism that his comrades had leveled against the Zionist Organization, "Come what may—they won't drive us out of the Zionist Organization."[18] On the eve of the founding ceremony of the expanded Jewish Agency, he defined the expanded Jewish Agency as "a vital necessity for us and the only basis for our development." He made this assertion with typical unassailable vehemence that treated everything he had said in the past with utter disregard. Then he admonished the critics of this political decision: "We have a principle that is greater than the democratic *example*. It is the building of Eretz Israel by *the Jewish people*."[19]

The roots of the political decision in which Ahdut ha-ʿAvoda moved away from setting up a halutsic klal as an alternative to the Zionist klal and shifted to an oppositionist status in the Zionist Organization and, eventually, to integration in the Zionist leadership were planted in the awareness, born in the Second Aliya period, of the role of the working class in the national building enterprise. The problem that Ahdut ha-ʿAvoda inherited from the Second Aliya was how to integrate the interests of the working class, as Poʿaley Tsiyyon termed it, or the working public, to use the Ha-poʿel ha-Tsaʿir term, with the national interest without allowing the Zionist Movement to transform the workers into tools and have them sacrifice themselves on the altar of this enterprise.

The solution, which aspired to reconcile the two not totally identical interests, was found in a cooperative Socialist program that aimed to build an egalitarian national society in Palestine by means of national wealth. According to the outlook behind the plan, the class struggle should be prosecuted in the form of a rivalry between the capitalist method and the Socialist method in building the national economy and society.

The capitalist wealth versus Socialist wealth approach reflected a compromise of sorts. The previous approach, expressed by the Poʿaley Tsiyyon delegation in 1920, envisioned the construction of a fully cooperative society with a population of one million Jews in Palestine in the coming ten years.[20] The "class struggle in Zionism" phrasing, adopted at the Party convention in 1923, reflected the spirit of compromise between the cooperative Utopianism of Poʿaley Tsiyyon and the realistic Utopian constructivism of Ahdut ha-ʿAvoda. It was a comprehensive wording that saw class struggle in all aspects of working-class realities in Palestine: the workers' standing in trade-union struggles, the Zionist Organization, municipal government, and building the cooperative society in urban and rural areas. In other words, as the resolution stated: "In all manifestations of struggle and creative endeavor that aim to impose labor in all aspects of popular, national, and economic life"—Ahdut ha-ʿAvoda saw "the Hebrew worker's path toward the creation of the Socialist Hebrew community in Eretz Israel" in all of them.[21]

Since the resolution mingled the ideological and the political motives of Ahdut ha-ʿAvoda inseparably, it is immaterial from the historical perspective to ask which motive preceded which and which is cause and which is effect. What is more, the contemporaries of those involved did not differentiate between the two at all. From their standpoint, and from that of their Bundist rivals, ideology always had political significance and politics always had an ideological motive; otherwise, neither would have meaning in reality. There is no doubt, however, that politics was the pragmatic fundamental in the politics-ideology nexus; it was politics that forced ideology to adjust to the changing reality. Indeed, this is what happened in Ahdut ha-ʿAvoda in view of the dual crisis that overtook it during the Fourth Aliya. The crisis originated in the concern that a bourgeois alternative to the Labor Movement as the locomotive of the national society-building endeavor was taking shape in Palestine. It continued with the economic emergency that rocked the Yishuv and inflicted a painful blow on the Labor Movement. However, it was precisely due to this crisis Ahdut ha-ʿAvoda came to the third stop on its path to labor leadership of the enterprise as part of the Zionist Klal.

According to the new formula, the collapse of the bourgeois alternative left only one surviving agent that could carry out the national mission: the workers. For this reason, the very definition of the workers as a class in the organizational, ideological, and social senses aggrandized their power in their struggle for national hegemony. However, this definition, according to Berl Katznelson, was not directed toward the conduct of a "class struggle" in the literal sense; instead, it pertained to the creative force of the class. Therefore, "In the generation of fulfillment, in regard to the problems that socialism faces, a basic distinction should be drawn between socialism of *producers* and socialism of *consumers*—between a socialism that considers the front of *national product* its point of departure and a socialism that considers the front of *distributing and delivering [national] product* its point of departure."[22] It is this that distinguishes the constructivist halutsic Socialism in Palestine, and even the Bolshevik form of Socialism in the Soviet Union, both of which endeavor to build a new society, from Western social-democratic Socialism. Of interest here is the likening of Bolshevism to the halutsic movement as parties that undertook to build new societies on behalf of their respective nations. This explains why the class definition of the Zionist Labor Movement was so important to Berl Katznelson. In discussions with Ha-Poʿel ha-Tsaʿir members before the merger into one party, Katznelson repeatedly stressed the importance of assuring the class nature as well as the Zionist nature of the united party. In other words, the emphasis should now shift from routine class struggle in the political and economic domains to "the class nature of the united party."[23] Moreover, if the party is to assume a national role of the highest order, then the class spirit and mentality, in the organizational, economic, and cultural senses, becomes a national instrument of the highest order. Thus, despite

numerous differences in substance and praxis, the Bolshevik Party and the
Zionist Labor Movement positioned themselves at the forefront of social and
national revolutions.

Here we find a noteworthy distinction between the Bund and Ahdut ha-
ʿAvoda in regard to the Socialism-nationalism nexus. In both parties, the national outlook had an important influence on class politics and vice versa, but
in different ways. For Bundists, the national outlook was one of the factors in
the party's opposition to joining the Russian or Polish social-democratic
party, and the class outlook of the Bund categorically ruled out cooperation
with Klal Yisrael on a national basis. For Ahdut ha-ʿAvoda, in contrast, the national condition of the Jewish people made the working class a leading force
due to the party's Socialist perspective. Thus, the national historical imperative made the Socialism-nationalism nexus an "organic" one, as Moshe
Beilinson put it; that is, it contained no contradiction in terms of the consciousness of that generation and it both could and should reflect the entire
reality of society. For the Bund, in contrast, the "organic" relationship between class Socialism and grassroots nationalism was partial only and confined mainly to the cultural domain. Thus, the contradictions and contrasts
that the intersection of socialism and nationalism created for the Bund were
less severe than for Ahdut ha-ʿAvoda. The paradox is that the limited national
contrast kept the Bund from joining a general Socialist Party, whereas the
profound social clash between Socialists and the bourgeoisie in the Zionist
Organization prompt the former to insinuate themselves into such a party.

Thus, the ideological process that set out to explicate and justify integration of the class into the Zionist klal, a process that began during the
Second Aliya, culminated with the formation of Mapai in 1930. Its first
phase was the constructivist Socialist outlook that took shape at the end
of the Second Aliya and the early 1920s, by force of which the Histadrut
was established as a multidisciplinary workers' organization that by complexion and purpose was ideologically related to and financially dependent
on the Zionist Organization. In the second phase, under Beilinson's inspi-
ration and by means of Katznelson's phrasings, the constructivist halutsic
working class was tasked with the political function of leading Zionism to
its national destiny by means of the united party, Mapai. However, as suggested above, the aspiration of Ahdut ha-ʿAvoda to leadership of voluntary
political entities such as the Zionist Organization and the Histadrut subjected it to a stress test between the anvil of democratic political culture,
based on compromise, and the hammer of the avant garde's radical spirit.

In the Histadrut, Ahdut ha-ʿAvoda espoused the avant-garde ideal of
abolishing political parties and establishing a "workers' community," to use
Katznelson's expression, but failed to bring this about. In the Zionist Orga-

nization, the party hoisted the banner of regimented halutsic activism and came away with partial success, but only because this spirit was congruent with Chaim Weizmann's Zionist outlook. Beyond political intentions and stratagems, however, Ahdut ha-ʿAvoda's membership in the family of democratic, pluralistic organizations forced it to deal with the principled question of the essence of correct democracy. This had a considerable effect on the party's sense of belonging to the Zionist klal. The concept of "correct democracy" was not an intrinsic matter that pertained to the proper and desired contents of a democratic regime; instead, it related to an extrinsic task: attaining the national goal. Thus, the assessment of democracy was a function of its performance and contribution to the attainment of external goals. For this reason, the national goal became a criterion for the evaluation of both Socialism and democracy. Therefore, the combination of constructivist Socialism and regimented democracy became the two-pillared infrastructure of the Ahdut ha-ʿAvoda worldview. From this standpoint, the party's encounter with the Zionist parliamentary democracy that followed World War I and the Balfour Declaration, amidst a political climate that carried messianic tidings, led to disillusionment.

Katznelson articulated this collective mood in his party in notes that he took at the first conference of the Zionist Movement after the war, held in London in 1920. He wrote with bitter derision about the time wasted on nitpicking points of protocol, the acridity invested in the debates, the parliamentary formal procedure, and the participants' failure to get around to any part of "the main work itself." In his perturbation, he called the phenomenon "this disease that eats away at our gatherings, our meetings, everything we set out to do. How wretched our public activity is; it adheres firmly *to all the dregs of external parliamentarianism,* demanding enormous prattle and finding no direct, energetic, and focused path toward useful action but rather a path of talk, talk, and talk." Pursuant to his "naughty" reflections, as he sarcastically called them, he asked a question that is so typical of radical groups: "So what is this whole democracy thing, with all its rules and regulations, its drums and bells, all this plenitude that weighs on us, *if we can't enhance the public's ability to act?*"[24]

When one ponders these statements and other remarks by Katznelson's comrades at that time, one must of course distinguish between the attitude toward democracy as a form of governance, which was favorable if not crucial from their standpoint, and the acidic criticism of institutional parliamentarianism as an entity that animates action in society. Ahdut ha-ʿAvoda experienced this tension between ideological principle and daily social and political action in the Histadrut. In both institutions, Ahdut ha-ʿAvoda attempted to bridge the gap between principle and praxis by mobilizing regiment-type elites for the specific goal of building the new society: the "army of labor" in the Histadrut, as Ben-Gurion proposed, and the halutsic organizations in the Zionist Movement.

Moshe Beilinson set out to tackle this question—the tension between the pioneering avant garde and the democratic movement—at its intellectual level.[25] As his point of departure he stressed the importance of the revolutionary avant-garde, which was related to the people and expressed its will, unlike an entity that treats the people with condescension and disregard. This positive avant-garde, he said, thereby expresses and fulfills the democratic will of the people even if it does so without the people's formal consent. Beilinson then shifted from the general to the specific matter of concern to him, the Zionist Movement. The movement, in his opinion, is democratic neither because a majority of Jews support it, nor because it follows democratic procedure but because its idea and the people's will are one and the same. Alternatively, as some Zionists argued, the Zionist idea "corresponds to the needs of the Jewish people, and therefore we consider the Zionist Movement a truly democratic movement irrespective of whether a majority of Jews embrace the Zionist idea or not."

Consciously or not, this was undoubtedly a "Zionist variation" on Jean Jacques Rousseau's concept of the "general will," in which the nation needs to be educated until it gets to the root of an idea and understands it, and only then will be free. It was in accordance with this principle, in Beilinson's opinion, that Herzl and Weizmann had led the Zionist Movement on behalf of the Jewish people. Thus, the movement became the Jewish avant-garde. Beilinson, a forceful and consistent opponent of all manifestations of dictatorship, especially the Leninist Bolshevik version of his time, was aware of the intrinsic danger of the formula. To avoid it, he elevated the halutsic movement to the status of an avant-garde within an avant-garde, so to speak—the avant-garde of the Zionist Movement—that educates by means of personal fulfillment. The result, he said, is a synthesis of sorts between the pioneering and the grassroots ethoses, which are interdependent due to the limits of their strength. The outcome of the synthesis will be "neither pioneerism alone nor a mass movement alone, but a pioneerism that achieves its takeover in a process that inflicts pain on the masses . . . and surmounts the indifference of the people."[26]

Beilinson's principled rejection of democratic formalism was more sweeping than Katznelson's emotional rejection. Beilinson, motivated by "the Zionist general will," dismissed the clash between the Zionist klal and the halutsic klal in the Zionist Organization by terming both the carriers of the avant-garde idea, the antithesis of formal democracy. The two were differentiated only by the will and the preparedness to undertake personal fulfillment in the here and now, as the halutsic movement demanded of its members. Katznelson translated Beilinson's formula into political principle in his justification of Ahdut ha-ʿAvoda's support of the Jewish Agency expansion plan. Katznelson did not deny that the composition of the new institution, which would include nonelected representatives, was flawed in formal democratic terms. However, he said, "The main thing for us is aliya and rural settlement—*under any conditions, and not pure democracy without them.*"[27]

Thus, in accordance with the ideological principle of the Zionist "general will"; the political interest of the Labor Movement, which had no organizational alternative; and the social constructivist will; Ahdut ha-ʿAvoda found a way to acquiesce in the Jewish Agency idea and opened the door to leadership of the Zionist Movement.

The halutsic klal and Zionist klal dichotomy was not the only bone of contention in Ahdut ha-ʿAvoda during those years. Concurrently, the party waged a struggle within the World Union of Poʿaley Tsiyyon over the Hebrew and Palestinocentric nature of this union.

In July–August 1920, the World Union of Poʿaley Tsiyyon convened in Vienna and split into two—Right and Left. The main and immediate issue in dispute was Poʿaley Tsiyyon's participation in the Zionist Organization and the acceptance of Ahdut ha-ʿAvoda as a member of the Union. The left flank demanded, in the form of an ultimatum, that the Union secede from the Zionist Congress; the right wing of the party and the Ahdut ha-ʿAvoda leadership ruled this out totally, believing it better to split the Union than to resign from the Zionist Organization. Katznelson's explanation of his party's stance planted the seeds of a dispute that would erupt in Poʿaley Tsiyyon Right: "The main issue is not the Congress but the entire active program of building a socialist Palestine in our spirit."[28]

The dispute that evolved from then on originated in the expression, if not the concept, of "in our spirit." This is also what distinguished between the tension in the Zionist Organization and the discord in the World Union. The first time it came up, "in our spirit" was merely a state of mind due to lack of power. The second time, it concerned the politics of the power that the Yishuv did possess.

The policy of the Ahdut ha-ʿAvoda leaders was to expand the dimensions of the halutsic klal by establishing the Histadrut in 1920, to strive to effect a merger among the labor parties (which did take place about ten years later), and to attempt first to merge the two Diaspora unions with which it was associated—Poʿaley Tsiyyon and the ZS (the Zionist Socialists). Their efforts in this vein lasted for about three years (1923–1925), amidst tripartite disputation among Ahdut ha-ʿAvoda, Poʿaley Tsiyyon, and the ZS over three issues—the extent of autonomy that Ahdut ha-ʿAvoda had carved out for itself in the World Union, the nature of constructivist Social-ism, and the status of Yiddish and Hebrew in the Diaspora. In regard to all three issues, the Ahdut ha-ʿAvoda leaders drew a boundary between them-selves and their partners in dispute. They portrayed themselves as people who gave labor in Palestine precedence over everything and accused their opponents of considering political-organization interest supreme. What is more, they included both rival camps in the Diaspora—Poʿaley Tsiyyon and ZS—among the latter. By so doing, they created a Socialist-Zionist version, so to speak, of the struggle between "labor of the present" and building the national Yishuv in Palestine.

It is mainly the third dispute—the "language dispute" between Yid-dish and Hebrew—that concerns us here. This dispute, which threatened to split the camp, had historical roots in the contretemps surrounding the lan-guage of instruction (Hebrew or German) at the Technion in Haifa in 1913, compounded by a contemporary motive: the struggle with the Bund in Poland for leadership of the Jewish working class, whose language was Yiddish. Nor should one ignore the Bundist syndrome in this debate among Zionist Socialists in reference to the national importance of the Yiddish language. However, the material difference between the two ap-proaches—one that rejected Klal Yisrael and one that made every effort to sustain it—is manifested in the outcome of the dispute.

The two protagonists in the language quarrel were Poʿaley Tsiyyon and ZS. ZS was the more extreme in its demands, insisting on principled recognition of Hebrew as the only national language of every future au-tonomous Jewish organization in the Diaspora and on freedom of instruc-tion in both languages in Jewish community school systems. Poʿaley Tsiyyon, in turn, demanded recognition of reality: Yiddish as the national language of the Jewish masses in the Diaspora and teaching of Hebrew in schools that would, of course, use Yiddish as their language of instruction. In the Poʿaley Tsiyyon view, the "Hebraist" principle reflected an elitist ap-proach that would be off-putting to the Jewish masses. This had an anti-Socialist significance because it would lead to an alliance with the Jewish bourgeoisie. As a compromise, Poʿaley Tsiyyon proposed a diglossic ap-proach: recognition of Hebrew as the national language of the Yishuv and of Yiddish as the national language of Diaspora Jewry.

The Ahdut ha-ʿAvoda representatives, wishing to preserve the in-tegrity of the halutsic klal, accepted neither of these radical outlooks. In-stead, they bruited what I call a "progressive compromise": the World Union of Poʿaley Tsiyyon would recognize the exclusivity of the Hebrew culture in the Yishuv and, in regard to the Diaspora, would leave it as "an open question for each country to decide."[29]

The compromise motion was not adopted at once, due to the dispute as such and due to its underlying factors. The leaders of Poʿaley Tsiyyon in the Diaspora were unwilling to accept the Ahdut ha-ʿAvoda demand for a preferred status of "moral hegemony by virtue of the enterprise and the location," as Katznelson phrased it. In Katznelson's opinion, which he did not conceal, the Labor Movement in Palestine and the Poʿaley Tsiyyon Party in the Diaspora were *very far apart.*" Therefore, he demanded that his comrades in the World Union "keep up with us,"[30] that is, accept the Ahdut ha-ʿAvoda prescription. This would have the effect of transferring the center of gravity in Union activities to Palestine, especially in regard to the encouragement of aliya among members. At the time, most ʿolim (Jews who "made aliya") were members of halutsic youth movements that had nothing to do with Poʿaley Tsiyyon.

In politics, of course, to "keep up" usually means to compromise. This is exactly what happened. To avert a schism in the World Union after Ahdut ha-ʿAvoda's threat to secede, the two sides concluded an agreement in 1925 that rested on three principles: (1) each party in the Union, and not only Ahdut ha-ʿAvoda, would be allowed to maintain its own policies in regard to culture and language of instruction; (2) the Yiddish language and the struggle of the Jewish proletariat are culturally, if not organically, related. As for the ZS Party, the candidate for admission to the Union, it was agreed that (3) if the party agreed to teach Yiddish in its schools, especially in Lithuania (where the language of instruction was Hebrew), the opposition to its admission for the purpose of creating one world union would be lifted. A short time later, in a dramatic act of conciliation, the two unions merged to form the World Union of Poʿaley Tsiyyon-ZS.

The stance of the Poʿaley Tsiyyon leaders was affected by three factors: their own natural cultural affinity for the Yiddish language, their ideological awareness that Yiddish really was the language of the simple Jews whom they wished to represent, and political competition among erstwhile comrades and current rivals for the sympathies of these Jewish masses. One of these rivalries, with Poʿaley Tsiyyon Left, the Bund's ally in organizing the CYSHO Yiddishist schools, concerned this very point. Here, however, the material difference between Poʿaley Tsiyyon Left and its former comrades, not to mention the Bund leadership, became apparent. Where the Bund and Poʿaley Tsiyyon Left rejected all compromise in the matter of national status for both languages, Yiddish and Hebrew, Poʿaley Tsiyyon Right accepted it. The reason: they were an inseparable part of the three spheres of the national klal—the Jewish (Klal Yisrael), the Zionist, and the halutsic. These, of course, were the three pillars on which Ahdut ha-ʿAvoda rested and without which it could not exist.

Therefore, all the alternativist ideas that were widely held by party members during this decade were trends of thought and desiderata and not political programs.

Ahdut ha-ʿAvoda was the pillar of the halutsic klal. It was flanked on one side by the politically moderate Ha-poʿel ha-Tsaʿir Party and on the other by the He-haluts movement, the radical advocate of Zionist fulfillment. Thus, the dualistic trait of Ahdut ha-ʿAvoda—ideological radicalism coupled with political pragmatism—was divided, as it were, between the two, with He-haluts exhibiting the former and Ha-poʿel ha-Tsaʿir the latter. Contrarily expressed, Ahdut ha-ʿAvoda absorbed the traits of both parties on its flanks. However, He-haluts was unique vis-à-vis the two parties. It was not a political party that felt itself responsible for the building enterprise of the Labor Movement; therefore, it absolved itself of the need to make the constant compromise between principle and reality that is unavoidable when a movement decides to enter politics as a path of return to history, as had happened to the Zionist Movement and its constituent labor parties. However, the two parties were radical in different ways. Ahdut ha-ʿAvoda may be defined as pragmatic-radical and Ha-poʿel ha-Tsaʿir as radical-pragmatic. The difference in emphasis also points to the difference in the parties' political behavior in the Zionist Organization.

OTHER HALUTSIC VIEWS

The Ha-poʿel ha-Tsaʿir approach was severely radical in its attitude toward Palestinocentric Zionism and pragmatic in its political view. Members of this party regarded themselves as unconditional participants in the Zionist Organization. Unlike the leaders of Ahdut ha-ʿAvoda, they did not entertain alternative political fantasies as Ben-Gurion did and did not feel estranged from the Organization as did Berl Katznelson. In both the conscious and the personal senses, they were "in." Weizmann took a liking to Yosef Sprinzak, the veteran leader of the party; the two were very, very close. Weizmann and Chaim Arlosoroff, the young star in the Zionist policy firmament, had a father-son relationship. Furthermore, Weizmann had much in common with the practical-minded Eliezer Kaplan. Such relations with leaders of Ahdut ha-ʿAvoda did not exist at the time, although Ha-poʿel ha-Tsaʿir remained ultraradical in respect to the Zionist priority of action in Palestine.

The Palestinocentric spirit was predominant at the first world convention of Ha-poʿel ha-Tsaʿir and Tseʿirey Tsiyyon, held in Prague in March 1920. Its most extreme exponents were A. D. Gordon and Eliezer Yaffe; the latter was the most extreme delegate from Palestine in terms of negation of the Diaspora. These delegates, of all people, were given affectionate and appreciative treatment by intellectuals of Western cultural background, such as Martin Buber and Felix Weltsch, as the author Ya'akov Rabinowitz reported. According to Rabinowitz, the "Western" Zionists and the people of Palestine, especially members of the Bar Kokhba circle in Prague, shared the awareness that "If no moral innovation takes place, then the whole cause of Palestine isn't worth it." One intellectual, the young philosopher Simon Rawidowicz (our last chapter discusses his worldview after Israel was established) summarized his notes from the conference in a different vein: "Only there, in Prague, did we realize that there is an abyss between those of us who came from the Diaspora and those from Palestine. Even if the abyss does not create a separation—it differentiates and defines." He also noted the contrast between the Jewish intellectuals and creative artists, who were mired in a state of "exhaustion and a sense of dead-end," and those from Palestine, "whose souls are folded into that little corner of the beloved, terrible homeland." The entire reduction process, he said, is meant to whet the conquering will: "Only from a point of concentration can a human being conquer and envelop anything that exists in reality."[31]

The dispute over the expansion of the Jewish Agency and the crisis following the report of the committee of experts put the attitude of Ha-po'el ha-Tsa'ir toward the Zionist Organization to a severe test for two contrasting reasons: the relationship with and admiration of Chaim Weizmann, coupled with acknowledgment of dependency on him; and trepidation about allowing "foreigners" to join the leadership of the Zionist enterprise—a concern that the conclusions of the committee of experts had confirmed and reinforced. Indeed, important personalities in the party, such as Yosef Aharonowitz and Eliezer Yaffe, vehemently opposed the idea. Yaffe even turned in his party card to protest the party's assent to Weizmann's scheme. From the very beginning of the dispute, however, the majority resolved not to sever relations with the Zionist Organization leadership, a conclusion that the Ahdut ha-'Avoda leadership did not reach until the end of the Jewish Agency debate. From the political standpoint, at the XIV Zionist Congress (1925), the Hit'ahdut (unity) faction (Ha-po'el ha-Tsa'ir) tipped the scales between the proponents and opponents of the idea. Thus, for lack of choice, the opponents of the Jewish Agency plan accepted the terms that Ha-po'el ha-Tsa'ir proposed. The terms rested on four policy principles: (*a*) unrestricted aliya, (*b*) expansion of agricultural settlement, (*c*) defense of Hebrew labor, and (*d*) encouragement of Hebrew language and education. It is these conditions, which ultimately became a political achievement for Ha-po'el ha-Tsa'ir, that bound the party to the Zionist Organization ab initio. After all, within no framework other than the ZO could the conditions come to pass. Therefore, this was a struggle for the building of a society on the basis of purely political conditions. Basically, Ahdut ha-ʿAvoda was in the same situation, but due its political spirit and the Utopian propensities of several of its leaders, the points agreed upon by Ha-poʿel ha-Tsaʿir at the beginning of the dispute, albeit after severe vacillations, were accepted by Ahdut ha-ʿAvoda at its end. The outcome of the Jewish Agency debate, as stated, was the creation of a conduit that would lead the Labor Movement to primacy in the Zionist Movement on the basis of the united party, Mapai, and the political and ideological alliance with Chaim Weizmann. In other words, the attainment of the goal—hegemony in the Zionist Movement—was sketched out by Ahdut ha-ʿAvoda but the path to it was paved by Ha-poʿel ha-Tsaʿir. From then on, the halutsic klal became an "organic" part, to use Beilinson's term, of the Zionist klal and, by its mediation, of Klal Yisrael as well.

This development was most evident in the changes that occurred in the ultra-halutsic Zionist attitude of the He-haluts movement toward the Zionist Organization, as portrayed in Yisrael Oppenheim's comprehensive and painstaking study of He-haluts in interwar Poland.[32] The conclusion drawn in the first part of the study, which discusses the 1920s, is that He-haluts, including most of its constituent youth movements, was the most consistent and extreme negator of exile in the Zionist Movement. Oppenheim attributes this mentality to the influence of the authors M. I. Berdiczewski and, particularly, Y. H. Brenner and A. D. Gordon. It seems to me that one may expand the circle of influence and also attribute the mentality to the youthful *esprit* of the Second Aliya, with its extreme moral negation of the Diaspora, as shown in chapter 2 of this study. By the 1920s, however, the Second Aliya people had aged and matured. This effect, combined with their parties' political interests, weaned them of the "youthful" style that is typical of radical movements at their outset. In He-haluts, for opposite reasons, this mentality was dominant. In other words, paradoxically, Brenner and Gordon came back into style in Poland of the 1920s, at least in this respect, and exerted greater influence than they had wielded over participants in the Second Aliya.

Thus, a negation-of-the-Diaspora style that even the Second Aliya had not invoked was rampant in the press of the halutsic movements. Diaspora Jews were described as slaves who "creep along the ground like worms in the dust" or "cringe under the heavy yoke of the do's and don't's that our forebears bequeathed to us." The religious strictures have extinguished the "holy flame that had kindled in the Hebrew heart; the light of life and the joie de vivre have gone out." In other words, the Jews' national characteristics have been ruined and distorted only by the hardships of their external political and social environment but also, in part, by the Jewish religion that shapes their internal lives. To counter the historical and cultural religious tradition of submission to the dominant Gentile and suppression of the national spirit of innovation and rebirth, a different historical tradition should be posited. This alternative tradition regards halutsism as an extension of the other fabric of Jewish history, "woven of leading fighters in the conquest and defense of Eretz Yisrael—all those who rebelled against the foreign occupiers [of our land] and the exilic fate of our people. These are the Judges, those who returned to Zion from Babylon, those who went to the pyre in the Inquisition in Christian Spain, the victims of the Chmielnicki violence, the masses who followed the lead of Shabbetai Zevi, and also the Jewish masses who adhered to the religious code until [the advent] of pioneering Zionism, which has inherited the intransigent heroic spirit of those who sustain the national life and renaissance."[33]

These remarks, written in 1925 by a leading young personality in the Ha-shomer ha-Tsa'ir movement, Mordechai Orenstein (Oren), mark both a continuation and a change relative to the historical outlook of the Second Aliya. The Second Aliya people, especially the romanticists in Po'aley Tsiyyon, regarded themselves as a renaissance of the fighting spirit of their rebellious forebears.[34] They also drew a dividing line, as Ben-Gurion did, between the "Jewish histories" in exile and the resurgent national history in Eretz Israel. However, the youthful Oren viewed the issue differently. From his standpoint, the line of continuity of national intransigence and rebellion against the surroundings extended from Palestine to the Diaspora and back. None of this diminishes the extreme nature of the historical view and the attitude toward the current Jewish reality, which has a uniqueness of its own. In this view, the rebellion against exile is borne not on values external to it but rather, and also, on values that have been intrinsic to it throughout Jewish history. Hence, extreme negation of Diaspora does not fracture Klal Yisrael but actually reinforces it by revealing national traits that had been marginalized by what the He-haluts minions considered the degenerative exilic religious tradition and socioeconomic reality.

The question is whether He-haluts, as a movement that avoided the political-party orbit, remained free of the pragmatic political considerations that concerned the Palestine labor parties with which most of its members identified. As Oppenheim remarks, "The fundamentally negative assessment of the status of the Diaspora and the prospects of sound national existence there did not change later on either, as stated." It actually became more acrid in the second half of the 1920s. However, as the public standing of He-haluts gained strength in the Polish towns and cities that Jews inhabited, so did the organization's practical interest in developments in daily Jewish life there, even as it continued to reject that life in radical terms.

The same may be said about the Zionist Movement. In the first half of the 1920s, He-haluts seceded from the Zionist Organization in Poland after a series of clashes with the Zionist leadership about the "labor of the present" policy, which He-haluts opposed with condescending contempt. Concurrently, relations between He-haluts and the Histadrut in Palestine gathered strength, thus aggravating the tension between He-haluts and the Zionist Organization in Poland, because this augmented the tension concerning national action with the ideology of class contrast. This convergence of He-haluts and the Labor Movement in Palestine, however, also strengthened relations between He-haluts and the World Zionist Organization, under whose umbrella it continued to shelter itself without forgoing its principled disagreements with the WZO in respect to the appropriate practical meaning of Zionist ideology: the radical meaning, which positions Palestine at the forefront, or the moderate one, that of "work of the present," which seeks a political equilibrium between Palestine and the Diaspora.

It is worth mentioning here that He-haluts's place within the halutsic klal was even more problematic than its place in the Zionist klal. In the World Zionist Organization, He-haluts was the rebellious member of the family. In the Histadrut, too, some members of He-haluts persistently adhered to their rebellious radical line. The Yosef Trumpeldor Labor Brigade, established by members of He-haluts to transform the Labor Movement in Palestine into a countrywide commune, entered into a confrontation with the Histadrut leadership. This radicalism eventually led to the dismantling of the Brigade for two reasons: internal clashes within the Brigade and political struggles between its leaders and the heads of the Histadrut.

Consequently, an important contingent of members of the Brigade, foremost their leader, M. Elkind, returned from Palestine to Soviet Russia. This action of collective "dissent" left a deep scar in the collective consciousness of the Labor Movement in Palestine, but not because of the very fact of their leaving the country. Re-emigration had been a typical occurrence in the young pioneers' society since the Second Aliya days, but then the emigrants were individuals who fled the battlefield of fulfillment surreptitiously, quietly, and without caustic remarks. The case of the emigrant group from the He-haluts Labor Brigade was different. These pioneers left Palestine in a collective demonstrative act against the Jewish Socialist national enterprise. It was a ceremonial collective public conversion, so to speak, from the "religion" of Socialist Zionism to the "religion" of Bolshevik Communism. Furthermore, as out-converts tend to do, they escalated their rejection of Zionism by also abandoning, practically speaking, Jewish nationality. In this respect, they went even farther than Zionism's historical rival, the Polish Bund.

The secession from Zionism of the Utopian leftists of the Brigade is the exception that proves the halutsic Zionist rule. The "halutsic Zionists" waged their struggle from within and never quit, even when beset by severe heretical reflections. This was so not only because of their Zionist convictions, which did not always pass the test of "heresy" and ideological exclusivity, as in the case of the Labor Brigade, but also because Halutsic Zionism did not succumb to the political urge to shatter the organizational framework of the Zionist klal, as the Revisionists did in the mid–1930s when they established a parallel national structure—the New Zionist Organization, the National Federation of Labor, and the National Military Organization. Furthermore, as we have seen, Zionist convictions did not prevent several leaders of Ahdut ha-ʿAvoda from reflecting aloud about the formation of an alternative setting to the Zionist Organization, without resigning from the Zionist Movement.

Thus, there was something in addition to conviction that kept the Labor Movement, with its three segments—the youth movements, which were under the He-haluts umbrella; the political parties; and the Histadrut—in the Zionist Movement from start to finish. The extra "something" was constructivism, which, as a worldview and a way of life, made the Labor Movement totally dependent on the Zionist Organization and its leader, Chaim Weizmann, for the financial means to assure the existence and advancement of the new society that the movement was building in Palestine. Thus, paradoxically, the very factor that bound the Labor Movement to the Zionist Organization gave the movement a tendency toward fierce criticism of the ZO without the will, the interest, and the ability to secede from it.

The strengthening of this "organic" relationship—again, to use Beilinson's expression—with the Zionist Movement in the 1920s meant a strengthening of the hegemony of the halutsic culture within it, even before the Labor Movement rose within it to a state of political dominance. This came about due to two different phenomena, as noted above: continuance of the halutsic enterprise despite the hardships and the numerical growth of the youth movements, especially in Poland. This stood in marked contrast to the painful crisis of the "bourgeois" Fourth Aliya in the second half of the 1920s, which gave Zionism a scare and abetted a spirit of alternativism that sought a substitute for the Labor Movement in building the Jewish society in Palestine.

The gradual but steady tightening of halutsic hegemony in the Zionist Movement also led to changes in the movement's attitude toward the Diaspora. Although "negation of the Diaspora," with its basic principles and its economic, social, political, cultural, and ethical manifestations, did not vanish, it lost its hard edge. This was due to an increase in the political power of

the Labor Movement in the Diaspora countries, which led to a rapprochement between the movement and Diaspora Jewish life, and to the movement's need to obtain political backing from the Diaspora. Thus, the
Diaspora increasingly became a participant in the establishmentarian Zionist political outlook of "labor of the present"—the outlook that tried to strike
a balance between the building of Palestine and education and reinforcement
of the Diaspora; between the Zionist-fulfillment elites and the masses that
supported them, between the new Hebrew culture and the existing Yiddish
one, between Utopia and reality; and, generally speaking, between the Zionist klal and the Jewish klal, that is, Klal Yisrael.

      This state of affairs, of course, resulted in a clash between the sense
of moral hegemony in Zionism, to use Berl Katznelson's phrase, and recognition of the lack of political power to lead it. This situation seemingly
changed in the early 1930s, when the Labor Movement ascended to political leadership of the Zionist Organization.

      To sum up this decade from the standpoint of the Bund and the Zionist Labor Movement, one must answer the question that was posed at the
beginning of this section of the study: In what respect were the two entities
differentiated in their political methods vis-à-vis Klal Yisrael? The question
is pertinent because the movements' political situations were not totally different. In their respective situations, one of the players, the Labor Movement, integrated totally and easily into the Zionist klal establishment
whereas the other, the Bund, totally disassociated itself from the Jewish klal.
In both cases, this is not exactly what happened. The Bund belonged to the
Conference of Jewish Communities and spearheaded the conference of Jewish trade unions, not all of which belonged to the Bund, whereas the Labor
Movement, was mired in perpetual disputation in the Zionist Organization
from the beginning of the decade to its end. Both movements were riven by
internal discord on the issue of joining a broad-based national organization
and entertained thoughts about seceding from such an organization due to
disillusionment with the movement's paucity of influence over it. This reflects both movements' Utopian intentions of directing the respective organizations in view of their anticlericalist or halutsic-constructivist proletarian
worldviews. The interesting thing is that neither seceded—for national political reasons—and in the coming decade, under different conditions and for
different reasons, each rose to political importance if not hegemony: the
Bund in the Jewish communities of large Polish cities and the Labor Movement in the Zionist Organization. This similarity, however, is external only.
There was a great difference in the essence of the two radical movements' affiliation with their respective pan-Jewish national political settings. The
Bund joined the Conference of Jewish Communities for declaredly political

reasons; its sole intent was to struggle against the forces of Zionist nationalism and religious reaction—that is, Agudath Israel—from within. Its purpose was not to strengthen the Jewish klal but the opposite, to fragment it even more severely. For this reason above all, and not only due to its class ideology, it attracted the opposition of most segments of Jewry. Therefore, even at the pinnacle of its strength, it remained a minority within its people. In contrast, the Labor Movement in the Zionist Organization, due to its pioneering constructivism, was recognized as a force that acted on behalf of the entire Jewish people, even when its vision was not acceptable to a majority in the Zionist Movement and was continually and severely criticized by circles on the movement's Right flank. Therefore, the Labor Movement was always perceived as an inseparable part of the Zionist Movement and attracted the sympathies of various circles and personalities within it, including the patronage of the president of the movement, Chaim Weizmann—a matter of crucial importance from its standpoint. What is more, its pioneering enterprise was appreciated and supported by non-Zionist Jewish circles as well.

Furthermore, the Labor Movement, like the Bund, had a sense of "family" that ruled out secession from or rupture in the Histadrut and the Zionist Organization. The Second Aliya members who led the movement could not imagine themselves outside this partnership, even though relations with them were tense, as were relations among the Bund leaders themselves. In the Zionist Organization, too, relations between the president, Chaim Weizmann, and the Labor Movement had a strong element of emotion and intimacy. Therefore, from their standpoint, the world outside these settings was a sociopolitical "desert."

This is not to say that the Labor Movement acted without political calculus. Indeed, it never concealed its intention to lead the Zionist Movement. However, in contrast to the Bund, due to its Zionist ideological principles, the Labor Movement never excluded portions of the Zionist Movement as possible partners in the national struggle. The Bund, when it joined the Conference of Communities, ruled out ab initio the majority of potential partners in community leadership—Agudath Israel and the Zionists—due to its Marxist class worldview. The reason for this was rooted in a crucial difference between the two movements' "centrism" ideologies. The Palestinocentrism of the Labor Movement was meant to serve Klal Yisrael, whereas the Poland-centrism of the Bund, which concerned itself mainly with Polish Jewry, aimed to overturn the ideology and politics of Klal Yisrael.

CHAPTER 5

THE TRAGIC ILLUSION

In our life and death, we feel ourselves bound to our homeland, Poland.
—Wiktor Alter, August 1939

In the period between Hitler's accession to power in Germany and the eruption of the Warsaw ghetto uprising, the policy of the Bund on the Klal Yisrael question came to its heroic and tragic end. This denouement found symbolic expression in late 1942 when the Bund joined the Jewish Fighting Organization, which was headed by the halutsic youth movements, and in May 1943, when the party's representative in London, Szmuel (Arthur) Zygielboim committed suicide in active identification with his comrades who had perished in the Warsaw ghetto uprising and the millions of Jews who had been cremated and murdered in the extermination camps. Zygielboim's action was also a cry of protest to the enlightened world and the Polish government-in-exile, which had abandoned the Jews to their fate. Thus, those who had disapproved of Klal Yisrael during their lives marched with Klal Yisrael to their death. However, the Bund's attitude toward Klal Yisrael at the end of *this* period gives no evidence of its attitude at the beginning of that time. The opposite is the case. This is not to say that the Bundists were oblivious to the looming disaster that the leaders of other Jewish parties sensed or predicted. Such a degree of grim foresight lay outside the limits of anyone's imagination. All of them, however, definitely understood that the political standing of the Jewish people had changed. For the first time in the history of the peoples, a state that pronounced world Jewry to be its national enemy had come into being. The novel situation forced segments of Jewry to enter into a "solidarity by negation," one that stemmed from external pressures and not necessarily from internal consciousness. Did this form of national solidarity include the Bund, whose leaders were not blind to the "Fascist menace"? The discussion in this chapter will revolve around this question.

141

From the time of the Nazi accession in Germany, the Bundist press consistently and vehemently warned about the Fascist menace that loomed over all of Europe. It did so more for ideological reasons than as the product of political analysis. Thus, the Bund loudly implored the European labor movement to mobilize for struggle against Fascist rule everywhere and spoke out with special vehemence against the specter of a Fascist takeover in Poland, with all the implications this would have for the Jewish population of that country. The leaders of the Bund were among the first to grasp the belligerent intentions of Polish anti-Semitism in the first half of the 1930s, which viewed the Jews as a menace to the Polish nation. However, the Bund construed this anti-Semitism not as a particularistic objection to Jews but as one of many aspects of global Fascism. Therefore, because it treated the war on Fascism mainly as a general problem, the Bund did not change its views about organizing Klal Yisrael on a political basis to defend European Jewry against the rising tide of anti-Semitism. This aggravated the party's internal contradiction between ideological theory, which numbered the Jews among the victims of the expected menace of Fascist rule, and political action, in which no change whatsoever took place. In terms of the ranking of issues that concerned the Bund on the basis of their importance, it was business as usual. On the spectrum of lightweight to heavyweight issues, the following appeared: in 1934–1935: a public debate took place on the question of the Jewish settlement project in Birobidjan. Several participants in the debate saw in this enterprise an intention to establish a culturally autonomous territory as a way of solving the Jewish question under Communist rule. These theorists ruled out the Birobidjan program for two reasons: its goal of artificially separating Jews from society at large and its paradoxical resemblance, in their opinion, to the Zionist Ahad Ha'am's doctrine of the spiritual national center. The other participants were willing to acquiesce in the Birobidjan venture provided that its intentions did not transcend a partial solution to the problem of employing Jewish workers.[1] Although the debate between these approaches was politically barren, it articulated an important and very meaningful principle in the Bund's worldview: staunch ideological objection to a linkage between the Jewish national and cultural autonomy question and any piece of territory. Emigration of Jews to Birobidjan or to some other territory for reasons of economic hardship was another matter.[2] Thus, the Bund created the focal point of another conflict with the Communist regime, even if that regime seemed inclined to meet the Bund's demands in respect to cultural and national autonomy. This opposition, of course, was backed by the Bund's suspicion and distrust of the Soviet Communist tyranny. The Bund's general criticism of the Soviet dictatorship did not put an end to the disputation between its left and right wings, even though the party had already joined the Second International. The main spokesman of the left flank was the veteran Vladimir Kossovski, one of the last stalwarts of the "Vilna Dynasty", whereas the spokesman of the right flank was a member of the young generation, Wiktor Alter. The dispute between the two, which we take up below, concerned how far a social-democratic party should go in its efforts to form a political alliance with the progressive petit bourgeoisie. Kossovski ruled out such an alliance, believing that the petit bourgeoisie had Fascist leanings, whereas Alter affirmed it. The debate between the two, although intellectual in nature, acquired political significance later on, when the Bund under the leadership of Erlich and Alter appealed to the impoverished Jewish masses, as we will see below.

The Bundists conducted significant political debates about whether or not to collaborate with other forces to establish a joint front against the Fascist menace and the anti-Semitic threat. These points tested the Bund's "separatist" policy in principle and in practice. Paradoxically in reference to the political situation but logically in terms of the Bund's doctrinary worldview, the worse things became the stronger the party's separatist political leanings were. This was reflected in the party's opposition to the anti-Fascist Popular Front, both in western European countries and in Poland. The reason for this opposition was the Bund's concern about a Communist takeover of this organization and its aversion to political alliances with the liberal bourgeoisie. Instead, the Bund fervently supported the idea of establishing a "pure" proletarian front for the anti-Fascist struggle. It was even willing to co-opt the Communists into such an organization, provided that they accept the principles of "proletarian democracy"—a concept with which the leaders of the moderate wing in the Bund amused themselves and that is discussed at greater length below.[3]

The intrinsic paradox in the separatist approach was even more blatant in the context of Jewish nationhood. The Bund leadership defined the World Jewish Congress, which had been established to combat the anti-Semitic tide, as a political organization of the Klal Yisrael "bluff."[4] The reference, of course, was to the founding statement of the Congress in August 1936 in Switzerland, which defined the goals of the new entity as "assuring the existence of the Jewish people and promoting its unity." The Bund could not acquiesce in a Zionistic statement such as this, with its emphasis on Jewish unity. Worse still, the Congress was headed by three individuals who were identified with Zionism: Stephen Wise (head of the Congress), Nahum Goldmann (chairman of the Executive Board), and Louis Lipsky (Chairman of the Governing Council). However, even were the Congress not redolent of Zionism, the Bund, true to its worldview, could not join it.

After all, the leaders and founders of the Congress considered the Jewish problem an international one. The Bund, in contrast, perceived it in purely local terms (*doyikayt*), that is, it regarded Jews as equally empowered citizens of their countries of residence and stipulated that they should struggle against their assailants there. This stance, of course, was contrary to the politics of Klal Yisrael.

Thus, the Bund steadily stepped up its attacks against the driving force in Klal Yisrael politics, Zionism. The Bund's anti-Zionist propaganda found a sharp-edged sword in the form of the "Ha'avara" (Transfer) Agreement between the Jewish Agency and the Nazi regime, under which the property of German Jews who emigrated to Palestine was transferred to Palestine in the coin of German industrial goods. The Bund was not only the critic of this agreement; most non-Zionist Jewish organizations objected to it, because they had proclaimed a boycott of German goods. However, the Bund's criticism of Zionism was unique in its ferocity. The party leader, Henryk Erlich, termed the Zionists "Hitler's agents in the free world." The Bund also identified Zionism with Ze'ev Jabotinsky's Revisionist movement and considered it, as such, a collaborator with the anti-Semitic government of Poland. Things went so far that Erlich termed Zionism and anti-Semitism "Siamese twins" (*siamer tsviling brider*)[5] and accused Zionism of being willing to sacrifice the Jews of central and eastern Europe on the altar of its Palestinocentric ideology and politics.

It is noteworthy, however, that when the "Arab uprising" erupted in Palestine in April 1936, the Bund responded in a different rhetorical tenor than it had adopted in 1929, evidently because its leadership was aware of the role of Fascist agents in inciting the uprising. Thus, unlike their behavior in 1929, they refrained from attacking Zionism as the main cause of the violence, and the killings, and murders that it occasioned. Reportage about the events in Palestine in the Bund press was largely topical if not critical of the intentions and complexion of the Arab national movement.[6] Even Shlomo Ben-Yosef, who was hanged in Palestine, was treated understandingly due to his idealistic motives, although disapproval of the Revisionists' attempt to make him into a national hero was expressed.[7] What is more, the Arab terrorism was condemned.[8] Although the party indeed adopted a more balanced approach toward the doings in Palestine, this attests in no way to a change in its attitude toward the Zionist enterprise there. Paradoxically, here, too, the Bundists found evidence of similarity between the Fascists' incitement to violence and the Zionists' wish to establish a Jewish national home in Palestine.[9] This negation of the Zionist enterprise, just as Fascism was gaining strength and the situation of European Jewry was becoming increasingly precarious, originated not only in the Bund's ideology but also in the "Utopian optimism" that had typified the movement throughout its history. Accordingly, the louder the voices of opposition to the advance of German Fascism became, the more vigorously the Bund leaders strove to disseminate optimistic political and social assessments about the imminent inevitable demise of Fascist and Nazi rule.

The Bund's demonstrative optimism had several facets. In international affairs, its leaders attempted to convince the party members that economic development and social processes in the Fascist-controlled countries would bring these regimes to their knees. Thus, less than four months before World War II began, Wiktor Alter published an article titled "Marx Avenges Hitler."[10] Several days before the German forces invaded Poland, Erlich expressed his confidence that Germany could be defeated in a military offensive by France and England from the west and by Poland from the east.[11] Alter was even more optimistic. In his dialectic view, the aftermath of the ascent of Fascism and the social processes and cultural developments would themselves lead to the disappearance of the Old World phenomenon known as nationalism. Accordingly, the triumph of reason over nature (*der zig iber di natur*) would occur in the progressive Socialist society that would soon take shape.[12] By April 1939, Alter saw indications of a Fascist-Hitlerist Waterloo and Erlich discovered that the Fascist regimes were losing supporters despite their political achievements.

The Bund's optimism, of course, spilled from the international arena onto the local stage, that is, Poland. Here the movement had solid proof. The party's grand achievements in municipal elections in the large cities, foremost Warsaw and Lodz—where it had earned a majority of the Jewish votes—infused its traditional political optimism with fighting spirit. Therefore, when its leaders received proposals for the establishment of a united Jewish front for war on anti-Semitism in Poland, it rejected them vehemently and with more than a touch of derision and condescension. Instead, they proposed the formation of a joint proletarian front for the same purpose.[13] The Bund's argument was that it and the political Zionist Jewish bourgeoisie differed at the level of principle not only in their class affiliation, but also in substance, in their assessment of the political future of Polish Jewry. Both sides regarded large-scale emigration from Poland and emigration to Palestine as a partial solution to the problem, but only the Bund, in accordance with its worldview, believed that the political struggle should be fought to victory in the Jews' places of residence. In the opinion of Erlich and Alter, the municipal election results proved that not only the Jewish proletariat was close to the Bund, but also the Jewish masses favored this approach.[14] Therefore, the Bund came out fervently against the climate of despair that the Zionists, they alleged, were inculcating among Polish

Jews. V. Kossovski termed the XXI Zionist Congress, held on the eve of the war, a conference of despair. Indeed, the delegates parted in a melancholy frame of mind, especially when they took leave from those who were returning to Poland. Kossovski reserved special contempt and mockery for Po'aley Tsiyyon Left, which had resolved to return to the Zionist Organization.[15] To countervail this "Zionist despair," as the Bund spokesman attempted to portray it, the party offered "Bund optimism." Thus, Shlomo Mendelsohn expressed vehement opposition to an attempt by the leaders of the World Jewish Congress to internationalize the issue of discrimination against Jews in central and eastern Europe. This, he said, would abandon Polish Jewry to a state of political passivity and force them to place their trust in international institutions. To change the situation, he prescribed struggle to replace the nationalist regimes in these countries with social-democratic rule.[16]

The Bund derived its optimism not only from political analysis of possible ways to solve the question of Polish Jewry that had considerable logic at the time, but also from unconditional patriotic loyalty to Poland. A month before World War II began, Alter, in response to an article by Moshe Sneh, asserted that while Zionists were conditionally loyal citizens of Poland, the Bund had such a string civic sentiment that "in our life and death, we feel ourselves bound to our homeland, Poland" (*Mir filn zikh oyf lebn un toyt farbundn mit unzer land, mit Poyln*).[17]

The tragic paradox that pervaded these matters would not become clear until after the Holocaust, by which time Alter was no longer among the living. However, Alter's pathetic and poetic elocution—borrowed from the great Polish poet, Adam Mickewicz, in his poem, "Lithuania, You Are My Homeland"—contains a terrifying symbolism in the phrase "in our life and death." In fact, systematic readers of the Bund press cannot rid themselves of the imagery of the *Titanic:* the sinking ship, limited possibilities of rescue, and the band continuing to play flagrantly surreal "ideological waltzes." By and large, the Polish people did not want Jews in its midst. Those averse to the Jews included some of the Socialist democrats with whom the Bund wished to confederate.[18] One cannot say that the Bund leadership was stricken blind, since it spearheaded the struggle against anti-Semitism and clashed for decades with the Polish Socialist Party (PPS) over the Bund's right to its own national autonomy within the general framework. The leadership knew that the Bund was being spurned but never ceased to strive and offer its outstretched hand in cooperation. Since Poland was both the existing and the desired "homeland," the Bund chose a posture of separatism and isolationism vis-à-vis Klal Yisrael. Its separatism was more severe and consistent within the Jewish constellation than in the general Socialist domain. In the general orbit, the party belonged to the Second International, albeit as part of the oppositionist left wing, and was willing under certain conditions to collaborate with its sworn enemy, the Communist Party. What is more, even though it rejected the principled demands of the PPS, the Bund thirsted to collaborate with that party on any occasion. In contrast, it summarily and vehemently rejected all offers that it received to join any pan-Jewish national setting.

What, then, was the underlying reason for the Bund's partial or total separatism, especially in a period of emergency and impending war, to which—as stated—its leaders were not blind? What is the difference between the courage to remain separate and fight for one's principles, a commendable thing, and the Bund leaders' blind zealotry, which they maintained even on the brink of perdition in the Warsaw ghetto? The answers, of course, are rooted in the politics of the Bund as a party that steadily amassed power in the Jewish street in the second half of the 1930s until its leaders became convinced that their movement represented the political will of the Jewish masses. This notion was buttressed by the party's traditional class-national worldview, which utterly rejected the Klal Yisrael outlook. For these reasons, the Bund always preferred a class alliance to partnership with the Jewish people at large. This outlook was accompanied by practical political considerations, such as cooperation with the PPS in municipal elections and relations with the left-wing Polish resistance during the Nazi occupation. These explanations, however, do not plumb the psychological and ideological roots of Wiktor Alter's statement: "Poland is our homeland in our life and death." His utterance reflects the consciousness and the conviction, preceding any practical political calculus, that Poland would eventually cease to be a foreign country for Jews and become a benevolent homeland. This belief, invested with idealistic motives and explicit Utopian fundamentals, dictated the Bund's policies and decisions in the cultural, social, and political domains.

Three personalities represented the three aspects of the Bundist "public thinking": Y. Y. Trunk, Wiktor Alter (the party's second-ranking leader), and Henryk Erlich, the leader of the movement and the senior personality in the Bund parties worldwide. None of the three came from the impoverished Jewish world for which the Bund fought. Their families belonged to the Polish middle and upper bourgeoisie. Trunk, in fact, was the offspring of an affluent family. All three were broadly educated and loved Polish and German literature and music. The three of them encircled the Bund in a rampart of isolation and separatism that created a triple barrier between the party and the Jewish people at large. Trunk burnished the rules of cultural difference, Alter fortified the social separatism, and Erlich raised the political hurdle. Among the three, only Trunk of all people, the product of an affluent upbringing, was immersed in the grassroots Jewish cultural reality. At least two of the three—Trunk and Alter—were "tainted" with pronouncedly romantic and Utopian leanings. The thinking of each personality had a particular point of specificity: the nexus of ideology and culture for Trunk, the issue of society and politics for Alter, and the relationship of ideology and policy for Erlich. Trunk was neither a political leader nor a distinguished example of an "inside intellectual" as I define this term, a personality who has his/her own unique manner of expression. Instead, he was a loyal party member who marched to the beat of the party's central committee. He considered Erlich the supreme party authority, whose word was law. Presumably, then, everything that he published and said in respect to the Bund's worldview had the endorsement of the party leadership. Trunk's two collections of articles, published in the second half of the 1930s, constitute the most systematic and probing discussion of the socialism-and-nationalism question from the perspective of the Bund since Vladimir Medem's famous essay, "Social Democracy and the National Question," in 1906 and his articles in 1911.[19]

Y. Y. TRUNK—THE "INSIDE INTELLECTUAL"

The difference between Medem's approach and Trunk's, apart from the distance in time that separated them, is rooted in their respective points of departure. For Medem, separate Jewish nationhood is mainly part of the east European reality, and this remains the case even where similar Jewish realities exist, for example, in the United States and in Argentina. The future of these similar realities is not assured; social and cultural logic indicates that they, too, will eventually vanish, as happened in western Europe. For Trunk, in contrast, Jewish nationhood is predicated on the very fact of Jewish dispersion and is based not on a specific territory but on its language and culture. The difference between the two approaches was mainly intellectual, not practical. After all, both thinkers advocated "labor of the present" in the field of Yiddish culture. From the intellectual standpoint, however, they were differentiated by their assessments of future developments. The difference, it seems to me, was as follows: Medem remained a "prognostic neutralist" while Trunk was a "principled nationalist," for whom Jewish nationhood is a principle not conditioned on any future historical process. In terms of cultural endeavor in the here and now, there was no difference between them.

In the field of national outlook, Trunk added a dimension to the edifice that his intellectual precursors in the Russian Bund had erected in their debate with their teachers and rivals in the Russian and European Socialist movement. The general attitude of Socialism toward the national question seems to have changed in several phases. Lenin and Plekhanov, following

Marx, took a pragmatic political approach to the national movement. Those who served the cause of the revolution, especially among large peoples such as the Poles, were privileged with recognition and support. Small peoples' revolutionaries, in contrast, were denied recognition. Karl Kautsky softened this attitude and regarded the nation as a corollary of protracted economic relations within the confines of a given territory and an entity with a language of its own. Karl Renner took this notion a step farther, stating that a nation need not be linked to a territory and is mainly a social and spiritual partnership. Otto Bauer took another step toward the intellectual definition, arguing that nations are collectives that were created by a partnership in historical fate. The Bundists, foremost Medem, rested Jewish nationhood on the foundations of regional Jewish culture in eastern Europe. Trunk, in contrast, following Kautsky and Bauer, based nationhood on the language and its culture against the background of historical development. By so doing, he circumvented all the theories of his teachers, the thinkers of social democracy. Whereas they considered language and its culture one of several significant shaping factors of national consciousness, Trunk defined language as the predominant factor in the coalescence of any nation, not only the Jews. By so postulating, he also outpaced all of his Bund predecessors and comrades who debated the national question.

To reinforce his argument, Trunk cited the multinational Swiss example, which proves that shared territory and a unified state do not create a single nation. In contrast, the German-speaking citizens of Germany, Austria, and most provinces of Switzerland do, in his opinion, constitute one nation, albeit a nation divided among three sovereign states. The same, he suggested, applies to the Greek Diaspora in ancient times, which sustained its Greek national identity even when disengaged from its historical territory.

Trunk also used the example of the German nation, fragmented among three sovereign states, to challenge his predecessors' firm conviction that it is an uninterrupted shared history that gives a nation its contours. By so arguing, of course, Trunk meant to refute the views of thinkers and historians, especially Heinrich Graetz and Simon Dubnow, who predicate the unity and continuity of Jewish history on an intellectual, religious, national, or messianic shared destiny (*a gemaynsomer shikzal*). In his contrasting opinion, Jewish history is but a loose collection of diverse histories (*a loyze zamlung fun farshidene geshikhtes*). In his opinion, only a history that reveals, as it progresses, intellectual forces that create a shared culture is a shared history. A history that does not create a shared culture, such as that of the Jews, even if endowed with some common elements, is very hard to define as a national history. Therefore, the only setting in which the intellectual national partnership takes form is the *national language*. The language is a product of the

collective effort, an expression of the "collective psyche" and not the "individual psyche," as Trunk put it; it is this that gives society its solidity and
shapes its overall intellectual image (*formet psikhish ire velt-farshtelung*). If
this is so, according to Trunk, then every multilingual state such as Switzerland or Belgium is made up of different nations.[20]

Just the same, Trunk seems not to have acquiesced totally in this likening of the Jewish nation to the German one, or of either nation to the Flem-
ish and the Walloons in Belgium. After all, these two non-Jewish nations
constituted a majority in their places of residence in the binational or multinational states. In this sense, the Jews cannot establish a national canton
even in areas where they are populous. For this reason, perhaps, Trunk took
up the old debate, more than a generation previous, about whether the Jews
are a nation or a race. As we saw in chapter 1, representatives of the Bund
and heads of the Russian Social Democratic Party had debated this issue at
the famous conference in London in 1903.

Trunk's recourse to the race-and-nation distinction in the second half
of the 1930s, by which time Nazi racism had overtaken Germany in full
fury, is puzzling, because he does not dismiss the racial definition categorically. In his opinion, race is an abstract historical factor (*raseh iz an ab-
strakter koyakh, vos historish ekzistirt er zikher*). He meant to say that the
trait of "race" is found in the concept of the historical myth of Jewish existence. Thus, he accepted part of Nietzsche's definition of the Jews as a race
and as more than a nation. A nation, unlike a race, is an outgrowth of reality and nationhood denotes a historical and biological perception (*Natsie iz
a geshikhtlekh biologisher bagrif*). Again one wonders why Trunk was not
deterred by the problematic nexus of nationhood and biology. Evidently
blinded by his Bundist optimism, Trunk failed to see the dangerous significance of this nexus and, therefore, did not hesitate to use terms of race or
biological nationality that, he said, both philosemites such as Nietzsche and
anti-Semites such as the Nazis used. None of it mattered to him because at
least ten million Jews around the world had a meaningful national image:
the Yiddish language, the only evidence of the sense of general partnership
that controlled the Jewish "togetherness" (*Dos iz der ayntsiker baviz fun
dem gemaynzamen konstruktivn velt-gefil vus dominirt als natsionaler element in der daziker yudisher gemaynzamkayt*).[21] Although language is ar-
guably the basis of any nation's national partnership, the Jews are different
from other peoples because they have already lost about one-third of their
numbers, the fraction that no longer speaks Yiddish and does not live within
the Yiddish culture. What remains, therefore, are those eight or ten million
Jews who live with their national language. No other people has such a rate
of linguistic national assimilation, despite the great migration from Europe

to new continents. Thus, Trunk, like Medem, drew the contours of the Jewish people to include Yiddish-speakers only. However, unlike Medem, Trunk did not link the Jewish national future with the historical process, irrespective of its results. From his standpoint, Jewish nationhood is a timeless principle and phenomenon that needs no justification.

The linguistic circumscription of the Jews' national basis steered Trunk into an uncompromising head-on clash with Zionism. The issue at stake, after all, was neither the likelihood of building a national home in Palestine nor the dispute about which of the two languages—Yiddish and Hebrew—is the Jewish national tongue, but the very definition of the Jews as an 'am 'olam, a world people. Is the Jewish cultural basis narrow from the outset and will it steadily contract as the years pass and the times change, or is it wide and diverse in all respects—social, political, and cultural? Under these terms of debate, the a priori pluralism of Zionism collided frontally with the class and cultural Yiddishist monism of the Bund. However, Trunk, as a dialectic polemicist, attempted to turn the tables and depict Zionism, of all things, as a movement that undermines the basis on which Klal Yisrael exists. To prove it, he cited the goal in the Zionist cultural policy of establishing the dominion of Hebrew in Palestine, and were that not enough, the Zionists also chose to use the Sephardi pronunciation of Hebrew and not the Ashkenazi one! Trunk regarded this as clear evidence of a deliberate intention on the part of Zionism to distance itself, if not to divorce itself, from the Jewish people—precisely when the Jews' national existence was in jeopardy, especially in the Zionists' own eyes. In this respect, assimilated Jews and Zionists should be judged identically: both are attempting to escape from the Jewish people and the fate that, according to their worldview, awaits it. However, the assimilated run away from Jewry as individuals whereas the Zionists wish to tear a chunk from the Jewish body, territorialize it, change its image, and mold "human dust" into a normal nation (*fun der tseshtoybter "yidisher" stadie makhn a yidishe natsie*).[22] Thus, the Zionist worldview embodies the greatest of paradoxes: "to flee from the Jews together with the Jews," that is, "to tear a piece from the Jews' hide out of love for the Jews."[23]

Trunk's critique of Zionism also gives rise to a fascinating paradox. His remarks make him sound more faithful to the Klal Yisrael principle than the Zionists. That, however, depends on the cultural definition of Klal Yisrael. Trunk defined Klal Yisrael as Yiddish-speaking Ashkenazi Jewry alone. For him, the Sephardi segment of the Jewish people no longer lay within the contours of the Jewish klal. This was the opposite of what the Zionists meant and did. Trunk knew what the Zionists had in mind by instituting the Hebrew language in Palestine. He even accepted this logic of this action, which he considered an erroneous one, since it flowed from the wish to unite the Jews and weld them into a single nation. But if the goal was to integrate the Sephardim into Ashkenazi society, why, he asked in amazement, was the Sephardi pronunciation of Hebrew introduced instead of the Ashkenazi? Trunk regarded this act as proof of the Zionists' intent to abandon the Jewish people. After all, the Sephardim have no common spiritual and psychological ground with the overwhelming majority of Ashkenazi Jews and are an insignificant minority among the offspring of the historical Jewish people—a minority that does not participate in the comprehensive, universal Jewish reality. It is a nationally impotent (*natsional-impotent*) minority, a "withered branch" (*trukener boym*) that no longer draws sustenance from the vibrant roots of Jewish life.

Deep down, Trunk believed, the Zionists knew this truth. However, they were suspending themselves on that withered Sephardi branch because their entire ambition was to uproot the living tree of the Diaspora Yiddish culture, which is essentially the reflection of the rooted reality of a people. Thus, in Trunk's opinion, the Zionists were attempting to dissociate themselves not only from exile, but also from the Jewish masses, due to the elitist condescension that typified their worldview and conduct. Evidence of this, he believed, was their introduction of the Sephardi pronunciation of the Hebrew language instead of the Ashkenazi pronunciation, which the Jewish masses accepted for use in prayer. All of which, of course, for the cause of a Jewish unity that would be attained by abandoning the majority of the Jewish people.[24]

This, Trunk opined, is the result of the Zionists' misunderstanding and misinterpretation of Jewish history. Following Simon Dubnow, Trunk argued that the Jews are essentially an extraterritorial people. Even when Jewry dwelled in its historical homeland, Eretz Yisrael, most Jews lived elsewhere most of the time. The inevitable conclusion, then, is that the national essence of the Jewish people is one of world history (*velt geshikhte*) and this, indeed, is the Jews' national territory.[25] Here, in the vastnesses of a world history that transcends territory, Jewish history took place in the past and takes place in the future, whether the Jews wish it or not.

These remarks, published in 1939, shortly before the war, give further evidence of the tragic innocence that typified the leaders of the Bund in their assessments of historical developments and the international situation. This innocence originated in the indefatigable Utopianism and, consequently, the chronic optimism of the Bund leadership.

From Trunk's perspective, the global essence of the Jewish people was always inseparably related to the Jews' universal mission. It is true that Trunk, the Marxist, carefully refrained from interpreting the concept of "mission" in theological terms. Specifically, he seems to have meant it to denote the "Jewish destiny" doctrine of the Reform Movement. Accordingly, he defined the Jews' secular "mission" as a "line of life" (*lebens linie*). This interpretation led him to the Utopian idealistic conclusion that neither individual and collective life can exist without a clear mission (*bashaynferlekher*) and that the absence of a mission is tantamount to the absence of character (*misielazikayt iz dos eygene dos karakterlazikayt*).[26] A life without a mission is historically meaningless, especially in respect to the Jewish nation, a "world people." It is this historical state of affairs, in his opinion, that gives rise to the historical identity between the Jewish mission and the Socialist ideology. Consequently, even though Trunk refrained from identifying the Jewish national mission with the Jewish theological mission, these were actually two variations on one theme. The Reform Movement spoke of a Jewish religious mission; the Bund championed a Jewish Socialist mission. For both movements, the "deity"—history—had done the Jews a kindness by dispersing them among the nations.[27]

Thus, in sum, Trunk fashioned a realistic Bundist Utopia made up of three tiers: an upper tier of the universal social democracy, a middle tier of Socialist nationhood, and a lower tier of Yiddish culture. The common denominator is what I call "realistic Utopianism," that is, premises that were not unhinged from reality. However, since the emphasis in these premises was on the Utopian aspect and not on the realistic one, the premises proved to be tragically erroneous. Indeed, one could believe logically that the Jews' hope under the political circumstances of Europe in the 1930s, and in the sense of the future world, lay with democratic Socialism. Nor would it be totally incorrect to think that the solution to the problem of the national minorities in Europe, in the progressive and egalitarian society that would come into being there, lay in the granting of cultural autonomy to all nationalities that did not constitute a majority in any political territory, as the Bund asserted. Furthermore, it was realistic to believe that, in a Jewish society millions strong, Yiddish culture could blossom as an expression of the Jewish national traits and style.

Although the Polish majority in the interwar period did not accept the Bund's multicultural autonomism outlook, one might presume that in the future, after the triumph of Socialism in Europe, Yiddish culture could be recognized as a Jewish national culture of equal value to the cultures of all peoples. On this point, it is worth noting that when Trunk spoke of those ten million Jews living amidst Yiddish culture, he did not draw class distinctions among them as his party customarily did at the time it was founded and in the 1920s. No longer was it a matter of two nations but of one people. The change evidently had to do with the ascent of anti-Semitism and the Bund's positioning of itself at the front rank of the defenders of Polish Jews of all strata and creeds.

However, the reconciliation of Trunk's beliefs and reality poses intellectual and the logical difficulties that cannot be ignored. Indeed, no social democratic thinker, even Otto Bauer, the mentor on the national question, recognized the Jews as a nation entitled to cultural-national autonomy. Even when Social Democrats bruited the idea of personal autonomy, they connected it with the existence of territorial autonomy in a region of a multinational state. In contrast, the Bund, and Trunk in particular, detached Jewish personal autonomy from any realistic national foundation—historical, economic, and, particularly, territorial. All that remained of "real reality" were the interrelated elements of language and culture—language as an expression of the culture, which, according to Trunk, is the totality of the people's ways of life, and language, which invests the cultural ways with style and form. Even if we accept Trunk's basic view of language as one of the components of real life, like territory, economy, and history, it is hard to see how a nation can be sustained in history solely on the basis of the language and its culture. Furthermore, Jewish society in eastern European evinced not one Yiddish culture but at least three: the Orthodox, the Yiddishist-modern, and the Zionist-national. Only 40 percent of Jewish children attended the Jewish school systems of Agudath Israel (Orthodox), Tarbut (Hebrew-Zionist), and CYSHO (Yiddishist).[28] In the second half of the 1930, 60 percent of Jewish children attended public schools. Even had the Polish government accepted the Jewish national demand to finance the Jewish organizations' schools, one strongly doubts that a majority of Jewish children would have been enrolled in them. The Bund and its partners attempted to implant the Jewish secular culture, in its Socialist version, especially among members of the public that had progressive leanings.

In this context, it is worth noting remarks in the Warsaw ghetto diary of the historian Emanuel Ringelblum, who as a member of Po'aley Tsiyyon Left and an activist in the CYSHO system was nearly as passionate about Yiddish culture as Trunk. Thus, commenting about the choice of the Polish language in the debut performance of a play in the Warsaw ghetto theater, Ringelblum explained that "There is no good theater in Yiddish. Second—it points to the severe and conspicuous assimilation in the ghetto. The public loves to speak Polish; in the street one hears very little Yiddish." As he explains it, members of the educated class in the ghetto conducted many debates about the matter. Some attempted to explain this in psychological terms, as the Jews' contrarian way of showing the Germans that the ghetto walls cannot separate the Jewish reality from Polish culture. However, Ringelblum added, "I think it is proof of a great linguistic assimilation *that had already been evident before the war* [emphasis mine] and has become more conspicuous in the Polish-speaking street. It did not draw attention as long as the streets were mixed, but today, with the streets Jewish, we see how great the decline is." Here Ringelblum made an inference, as did, partly, the surviving Bundists—including Trunk—only one generation after the Holocaust: "In the absence of territorial concentration, we are doomed to total assimilation."[29] Importantly, "linguistic assimilation" is not a new and modern phenomenon in Jewish history. At various times the Jews have used languages other than their national one in daily life. However, in cultural domains where language was not the Jews' national indicator, they maintained a distinct religion, the organizational institutions of that religion, and a spiritual and psychological relationship with Eretz Yisrael. In contrast, the Bund, unlike Zionism, attempted to build a new Jewish nationhood that was totally detached from these Jewish historical fundamentals.

Paradoxically, Trunk's attempt to base a comprehensive Jewish nationhood on Yiddish culture and Socialist consciousness undermined its own foundations. After all, world Jewry was neither culturally Yiddish nor politically Socialist. Thus, the Bund's universal multicultural ideology was unwilling to acquiesce in multiculturalism in Jewish society, even in the period of transition between capitalism and Socialism.

Of course, Trunk's national and Socialist idealism was not typical of the Bund as a party that, by nature, invested much in political disputation and very little in conceptual explorations of principle. It was, however, an inseparable part of the cultural and psychological reality of the party's educated elite and political leadership. Therefore, many leading Bundists regarded Trunk's "idealistic" views as supplements of sorts in the party's "psyche"—a "psyche" that does not reveal itself in daily political activity but is indispensable for the part of Bund life that concerns futuristic ideas.

Trunk was not the only person in the Bund and its intellectual periphery who viewed the Jews as a world people. The history teachers in the CYSHO system, which the Bund headed but did not control, wrestled with this question at the levels of curricular contents and methodology. Specifically, they debated the proper way to teach history at the various levels of the CYSHO schools. Two topics that relate directly to our study were articulated in these discussions: the global nature of Jewish history in the dimensions of time and space and the relationship between national history and general history. The Klal Yisrael question lurked in the background of both. The CYSHO history teachers took up these two problems at their first conference, held in Vilna in 1925.[30] However, the most important debate in terms of its scope and timing took place at the national conference of CYSHO teachers in Vilna on January 7–8, 1939.[31] Several dozen history teachers from all schools of the system in Poland participated in the gathering. The conference was opened by C. S. Kazden, director of the system, and by S. Mendelsohn, who delivered the keynote address, "Trends and Tasks in Teaching History in the Jewish General School (CYSHO)." Mendelsohn, a CYSHO associate and one of the leading intellectuals in the Bund, spoke in favor of history as a main subject in the schools. He stressed the need to find the correct blend of Jewish and world history generally and Polish history particularly. In so doing, he acknowledged the vast quantity of historical material and questions of ideas and values that accompany the study of various historical eras. Therefore, he proposed that the focus be placed on eras that gave rise to great and revolutionary ideas of progress.

Three motions for debate were tabled. One of them (proposed by N. Fludermacher) was of a national complexion; it proposed in a Dubnowian vein to focus on Jewish history as the creator of its own national culture and stated explicitly that no matter how important general history might be, Jewish national history was more important. The second motion (by M. Teichman), who in the spirit of the Bund's two-track national thinking proposed to focus exclusively on teaching the Jewish history of Polish Jewry and the role of Polish Jewry in its millennium in that country. The third approach (that of N. Miner) favored a balanced integration of general and Jewish history.

After a lengthy debate, the compromise motion won a decisive majority of forty-eight votes, the national motion received six, and the countering motion three.

The overall curriculum that the conference put together in the spirit of the majority resolution included Jewish history from the Patriarchs to the present, along with general history. Thus, from the historical perspective as expressed in the curriculum, the distant past and the very near present were linked by one unbroken national thread. This comprehensive view of the Jewish people in terms of time, geography, and culture was definitely influenced by Dubnow's national historiographical outlook. It is true that, in regard to the present, the curriculum overlooked both the Zionist enterprise in Palestine and the Zionist Movement, apart from mention of the Po'aley Tsiyyon party alongside the Bund. In all, however, it was a curriculum for the teaching of the history of Klal Yisrael.[32]

The political identity of the authors of the curriculum is hard to determine. The historians Raphael Mahler and E. Ringelblum, members of Po'aley Tsiyyon Left, were members of the committees that debated the curriculum. The decisive matter in terms of trend of thought and purpose, however, was the final curriculum, which, as stated, was pan-Jewish. This trend of thought shows that the educators—the history teachers, in this case—were closer in spirit to Y. Y. Trunk than to the leader of the Bund, H. Erlich, in regard to the Klal Yisrael question.

WIKTOR ALTER—A PRACTICAL POLITICAL LEADER

Wiktor Alter was not an author and essayist like Y. Y. Trunk; he was a practical political leader. Nevertheless, he, too, gave evidence of Utopian tendencies. For Trunk, these tendencies largely determined his belief in the existence of Jewish nationhood; in Alter's case, they affected his social worldview. Thus, from this standpoint and others, the difference between the two was in the point of departure. Trunk was a Socialist Jew and Alter a Jewish Socialist.

In early 1932, Alter published two articles that described the phases of transition from Socialist governance to Socialist society. The first stage after the assumption of rule, he says, would be a transitional period from capitalism to Socialism. The primary goal during this time would be to improve the masses' standard of living by increasing production. Production would be increased by nationalization of the main means of production, an appropriate government budget, comprehensive long-term economic planning, and progressive taxation. As a Social Democrat, Alter did not prescribe an all-out Soviet model of nationalization. In fact, he warned against the formation of a state-capitalist regime of Communist complexion and urged caution against overconcentration of economic power in bureaucratic hands. Accordingly, he envisaged a dual economy, part nationalized and part private. Banking, basic industries, and natural resources would be state-owned; trade, crafts, and services would be private. The state would supervise the private economy by controlling credit and applying a monetary policy that would abolish the gold standard.

The purpose of state planning, according to Alter, would be to keep the levels of production and consumption in alignment. Unemployment would be eradicated by putting all productive forces to work and creating jobs that would not be dependent solely on profit. Correct planning, Alter hoped, would make it possible to effect the correct allocation of resources between investments and consumption and, thereby, raise the masses' standard of living.[33]

To this point, Alter's ideas did not deviate from routine Social Democratic thinking in interwar western Europe. However, when it came time to describe the future Socialist regime he penetrated the realm of Utopia, with its idealistic yearnings and material contradictions. The supreme goal of the Socialist regime, in his opinion, is freedom, meaning the right to individual and collective self-determination (*zelbstbashtimung*). The entire Socialist movement that comes to power in a given state must subscribe to this principle inclusively and comprehensively, since freedom is both the basis of sound public life and a condition for changes in the direction of a progressive society.

Accordingly, from the political standpoint, the Socialist movement should reject Communist governance out of hand due to the party dictatorship that it practices. The appropriate goal of tomorrow's Socialist regime is to exchange the concept of "dictatorship of the proletariat" for "democracy of the proletariat" and to assure this by enacting a suitable constitution. This document, in turn, should ensure a proletarian majority in all elected institutions of state; supervision of the elected entities of the regime; and separation of the executive and the legislative branches. Alter considered the "parliamentary democracy" method an alternative to a liberal capitalist regime in which the moneyed elites exert control. In his Socialist Utopia, the people would rule the roost by means of the continual hegemony of the working class.[34]

This is definitely a subdued and idealistic phrasing of the "people's democracy" formula, which was riddled with internal contradictions precisely because its intentions were good. After all, according to social common sense, even irrespective of historical examples, individual and collective freedom could hardly be assured by allowing one portion of the public to rule in perpetuity. One might think that way, of course, but only on the basis of the Utopian premise that all people will eventually be equal and form one class. Alter's thinking stations him between Bolshevik totalitarianism and a traditional Social Democratic outlook that sanctifies liberal parliamentary democracy. The radical Social Democratic idealism that led him to compose basic guidelines concerning the "democracy of the proletariat" also influenced his assumptions about the status of the Jews.

The main questions Alter faced were: will the Jewish question (*di yidn frage*) be solved under the future Socialist regime in Poland, and will the Jews' national struggle end with the eradication of all current forms of discrimination against Jews in the future regime? Alter attempted to employ a full measure of caution in answering these questions, emphasizing that he spoke on his own counsel, since the party had not yet subjected the matter to systematic debate and due to his unwillingness, evidently prompted by reluctance to be called Utopian, to engage in prophecy. All he meant, he explained, was to point to social and cultural trends that were taking place in the Jewish public scene. He wished to evaluate these trends under the assumption—an unchallengeable assumption according to his worldview—that anti-Semitism would be gradually eradicated under the future Socialist regime and Polish Jewry would then arrive at a crossroads: assimilation into the new society or national self-determination within it.

The first path led to self-obliteration, as was occurring in Soviet Russia by means of use of the Russian language, acquisition of modern schooling, integration into new occupations, and intermarriage. This trend, which, in his opinion, the Jewish national bourgeoisies and especially the Zionists deemed so illegitimate as to be a national disaster, was acceptable to him as a favorable objective phenomenon. Just as forced assimilation should be opposed on behalf of the human right to freedom, so should resistance to volitional assimilation be considered unjust and artificial (*umborekhtikt un falsh*).[35] Therefore, one should neither support nor resist assimilation; if this is the individual's free will, why not allow him to invoke it? This, of course, is an extreme and idealistic individualist approach of the sort that Alter was unwilling to allow others in respect to the type of regime that they wished to have in the future Socialist society. On that topic, his mind was already made up. The reason is clear: he took a favorable view toward assimilation in the sense of the integration of nations that would occur in the future society. Thus, for Alter, in contrast to the Zionist outlook, nationhood in itself is not an absolute principle and the individual should not be sacrificed on the altar of "Jewishness." In his opinion, such a phrasing is a vacuous and unethical nationalist slogan, a translation of the Hitlerist "babbling" about the purity of the German race (*Hitlerisher plapleray vegn der 'rayner daytsher raseh'*).[36] As such, it is contrary to the positive and objective historical process of national integration within a Socialist society. It is very hard to explain Alter's frighteningly harsh manner of expression toward Zionism— even in its own time, shortly before the war—as a slip of the tongue in the heat of debate. These remarks were written in reasoned consciousness as part of the anti-Zionist polemic, as we have seen above.

The second path, which Alter also accepted even though it clashed in principle with the first path, was nationhood. Like the assimilation trend, it originated in the living and effervescent reality of the Jewish grassroots in Poland. Thus, both paths derived their justification from reality: assimilation from the dynamic reality in the Soviet Union and nationhood from the effective reality in Poland. Both roads, according to Alter, originate in the Jews' right to individual and collective self-determination as a national minority in the Socialist Poland of the future (*zelbstbashtimungs-rekht fun der yidisher natsionaler minderhayt*). Accordingly, he proposed a rational Utopian and tolerant relationship between them. Alter was consistent in his free Socialist way of thinking. Therefore, in contrast to the views of several of his party comrades, he argued that freedom of choice in national self-determination also legitimizes the attempt to establish Jewish autonomy in Birobidjan—provided that this be prompted by individuals' free choice. What is more, Alter recognized the Jews' right to aspire to a state of their own. However, theoretical rights may become political reality only under special conditions. Accordingly, Zionism, in its attempt to transform the Jews' "abstract 'right'" (*abstrakte 'rekht'*) to statehood into a political instrument, is inflicting inestimable damage on the Jewish masses. This imaginary right, he warned will be exploited in the existing capitalist and nationalist society to deprive the Jewish masses of their right to struggle for civil equality and nondiscrimination in access to the labor market. Thus, Zionism is a menace because it creates the illusion of a solution for the Jewish masses outside their current places of residence, in the hope that the regime change will coincide with a ground-up improvement in their situation. Therefore, the territorial national alternative to Zionism is the idea of Jewish autonomy in Birobidjan, because instead of purporting to solve the Jewish question it offers Soviet Jews who so desire the possibility of establishing a limited territorial national environment for themselves. Thus, according to Alter, an opponent of the Soviet Communist regime, it was actually in the USSR that two ideal solutions for the Jews—assimilation and downscaled nationhood—would come to pass, provided that they not be implemented forcibly. Could both be actualized in a future Socialist Poland as well? Alter, the realist, answered in the negative. He assumed that the positive process of assimilation would gather speed under the new regime, but conditions for the establishment of Jewish territorial autonomy did not and would not exist in Poland. However, precisely due to the imbalance between the reality of assimilation and the reality of territorial autonomy, Alter believed that in Socialist Poland a solution would also be found for that segment of the Jewish people that would wish to maintain its culture and nationhood (*natsional zayn*), and that this solution would reflect a true relationship of Socialist fraternity (*oysdruk fun emesdiker briderlechkayt*).[37]

Thus, Alter became the successor to the "neutralist" concept that Vladimir Medem broached thirty years earlier. However, whereas Medem had treated it chiefly as a theoretical issue, the Soviet example made it a practical problem for Alter. Consequently, Medem's Utopian and futuristic neutralism became Utopian and realistic in Alter's hands. In other words, something that Medem considered a long-term historical possibility had begun to come to pass in the USSR as Alter looked on. This made Alter Medem's successor not only in awareness but also in knowledge. From this standpoint, however, the views of Trunk and Alter collided frontally. Jewish nationhood was a principle for Trunk and only a possibility for Alter. In this sense, Alter became the great challenger of the Klal Yisrael concept as a fundamental of the Jewish national consciousness.

This approach, well tailored to Alter's outlook as a practical politician, was manifested in his plan to organize the Jewish workers in a joint union—led by the Bund, of course—and thereby to establish a Jewish "proletarian klal" of sorts. The Bund's victories in the kehilla (community-administration) elections in the large cities encouraged Alter to persevere.

However, he knew that the path to the goal was long and difficult due to the unorganized petit bourgeoisie nature of Jewish society, a society of individualistic "human dust" (*der tseshtoybter kleinbirgerlakher individualizm*) in the accepted Socialist jargon. Of course, beyond the intent to organize the Jewish "human dust" into a fighting proletariat, Alter and his comrades wished to offer an ideological, political, and organizational alternative to the Zionist outlook of Klal Yisrael.

Alter aimed barbs of derisive criticism at advocates of the establishment of a joint Jewish national front for war on anti-Semitism and the discriminatory policies of the Polish government. Alter called this idea, which Moshe Kleinbaum (Sneh) had fathered, an "old refrain" that was as contrived in the present (*azoy falsh haynt vy nekhtn*) as it had been in the past. Genuine national unity of the Jewish "masses" could be a positive thing provided that it have clear and agreed-upon goals, that is, national and social liberation of the Jewish masses and a strong and inseparable partnership with the Polish masses in struggle for the establishment of a Socialist society. For this reason, all Jewish organizations and parties of capitalist, clerical, and nationalist complexion must be excluded from the fighting social organization that the Bund wished to form.[38] Consequently, the Bund, as noted above, ruled out all collaboration with the bourgeoisie. The exclusion was not limited to the Jewish bourgeoisie; the Bund refused to join the anti-Fascist Popular Front in Poland and, of course, staunchly opposed Moshe Kleinboim's (Sneh) idea of establishing a "Jewish front" for war on anti-Semitism.

However, Alter did wish to spearhead an action of significance that would transcend the organization of Bund-led Jewish trade unions. Therefore, he proposed an initiative for the establishment of a "Histadrut," a general federation of labor, of Jewish workers in Poland that would include dirt laborers and intellectuals, subcontractors who themselves were workers (*kalopnikes*), petty artisans who sold merchandise directly to consumers, unorganized unskilled workers, and the jobless. This idea, reminiscent of one of the principles on which the General Federation of Jewish Labor in Palestine had come into being, had been brought up by Alter in the 1920s, as we recall. The party had rejected it back then. Now, however, several years later, in view of the objective need to establish a Jewish national and Socialist organization on a broader basis, Alter approached his party with a track record of success. The success in question took place at the Bund-sponsored Congress of Jewish Trade Unions in 1936. The congress had been attended by representatives of trade unions from forty towns, who represented some seventy thousand organized workers, some of whom neither belonged to the Bund nor identified totally with its worldview. The credic basis of the Congress, according to Alter, was freedom of thought and unity of action (*frayhayt fun gedank—distsiplin un tot*).[39] In fact, what he envisaged was a Bund-headed grassroots proletarian federation that would have three components—trade unions, the school system (CYSHO), and the people's movement—as a political organization that would offer an alternative to the traditional Jewish establishment and the modern Jewish organizations, and from which the new Jewish society, Socialist, democratic, and of high cultural character, would grow. The Jewish masses' cultural level was as important to Alter as it was to every Utopian thinker who had preceded him. In this respect, too, he followed the lead of his mentor, V. Medem. Therefore, he inveighed against what he considered the cultural vacuum in the Jewish environment (*der kulturlazikayt in unzer yidishe sviveh*). His criticism, he explained, was meant not to prettify the Jews in Gentile eyes but to elevate them in the cultural sense. As an example, he cited the raucous behavior of Jewish audiences at the theater. What he had in mind was the need for a cultural grassroots revolution, a cultural renaissance (*kultur renesans*) that would take place only as a result of a supreme effort to overcome the Jews' internal weakness and backwardness (*goyver zayn di aygene shvakhkayt un aygene opgeshtanenkayt*)—all of which as an obvious precondition for the creation of the "new man," who would be different, better, and more beautiful (*mir viln zayn andersh, mir viln zayn beser, mir viln zayn shener*). The Utopian alternative lay not only in the formation of a grassroots "proletarian klal" in lieu of Klal Yisrael, but also in the creation of a new Yiddish Jew in lieu of the new Hebrew Jew whom the Zionists wished to create.[40]

Thus, Alter's thinking moved in three Utopian concentric circles. The outermost circle, the Socialist one, focused on the principle of individual and collective freedom. The second circle, inside the first, was the Jewish one; in its midst was the issue of improving the status and the cultural level of the poor Jewish masses. In the middle of the third circle, the Bundist revolutionary one, stood the revolutionaries, the new people of the new Jewish era that would dawn.

HENRYK ERLICH—A PARTY LEADER THROUGH AND THROUGH

Unlike his two comrades, Henryk Erlich, the party leader, was free of overt Utopian leanings. Unlike Trunk, he was loathe to toy with reflections about Jewish nationhood, and unlike Alter he did not concern himself with how the Jewish people would exist in the future Socialist society. He was a party leader through and through, a prodigious and sharp-tongued political publicist. As an exceptionally zealous defender of the absolute truth of the Bund, it was he who strengthened and fueled the party's isolationist trends.

He played this role in the early 1920s, during the debate about the terms for joining the Comintern; in the uncompromising war on behalf of Yiddish and against Hebrew in Jewish schools; in regard to the moderate Socialist parties in the Second International and the Polish Socialist Party—the PPS—of which Erlich demanded, as a condition for the Bund's joining it, that it redefine itself as a Socialist Party of Poland (*a sotsialistishe partey fun Poyln*—SSP) instead of a Polish Socialist Party; in his insistence on the political principle of "hereness" (*doyikayt*), that is, of Jews' affiliation with their countries of residence, which precluded the possibility of establishing an international organization of Bund parties and left behind a political archipelago of "Bund islands," of which the large Polish one is the most important but not the decisive one;[41] and, of course, in his uncompromising and furious opposition to the Klal Yisrael idea, which found dramatic expression in a public exchange of letters with his father-in-law, the historian Simon Dubnow.

In 1937, ahead of the Bund's fortieth anniversary festivities, Erlich wrote to Dubnow and asked him to give the party his public congratulations. The very fact that Erlich would contact Dubnow, the anti-Socialist national intellectual and an opponent of the Bund for thirty years, is puzzling. It may have been prompted by Erlich's awareness that at that time, with Jews being persecuted in many countries such as Germany and Romania, and being attacked in Palestine (*Palestina*),[42] a "Klal Yisrael of national distress" was taking shape. Under such circumstances, it would be proper to ally with a famous relative whom the Jews accept, whose non-Zionist national outlook was known universally, and with whose books the CYSHO schools taught Jewish history. Here, however, Erlich was in for an earth-shaking surprise. The Jewish state of emergency in the late 1930s had made Dubnow a strong supporter of Zionism. What is more, he expressed this view publicly in a personal letter of response to his son-in-law.[43]

The very title of the article reflects two different approaches on Dubnow's part. One was his unchanging and ultracritical attitude toward the Bund's national "isolation" policy, against which he had inveighed years earlier, after the 1905 revolution in Russia. The other was his change of heart about Zionism, which he now defined as a people's movement (*folks bavegung*). The letter itself was terse, sharply worded, and vehement in its stance, which, as stated, had not changed in thirty years. In Dubnow's opinion, the traditional anti-Klal Yisrael separatism of the Bund was exceptional in comparison with any social democratic party in Europe. The chief concerns of such parties in Britain, France, and Germany, for example, were the overall national interest. For the Bund, the main thing was a national separatism that took no account of changing times and the Jews' steadily rising distress.

Dubnow dismissed Erlich's remarks about the Bund being representative of the will of the Jewish majority after its electoral successes in 1936–1938. These victories, said Erlich, had made the party the leader of the Jewish majority, and only with the Zionist nationalists and the clerical Orthodox would it be unwilling to cooperate in any way and form. Insofar as the Bund's attitude toward Agudath Israel was concerned, Dubnow agreed with Erlich. Agudath Israel, in Dubnow's opinion, had displayed fanatic opposition to all pan-Jewish political cooperation from the time it was founded, in what Dubnow defined as "sectarian Orthodoxy" (*trenungs ortodoksie*). Embedded in this concurrence of views, however, was a barbed arrow that Dubnow launched at the Bund. The Bund's attitude toward Klal Yisrael, he claimed, was similar to that of Agudath Israel. Just as the former feared religious nonconformity and free and progressive thinking, so did the Bund dread progressive national outlooks, including those of Jewish Socialist movements. This gave rise to a bizarre and unholy alliance between the clericalist Agudath Israel and the Marxist Bund, both of which refused to take part in two initiatives that sought to wage a collaborative war on anti-Semitism: a joint congress of Polish Jews and the World Jewish Congress.

Thus far, as stated, Dubnow had not broken new ground relative to the anti-Bund arguments that he had expressed thirty years earlier. Then, however, came the surprising novelty. Dubnow, who had disapproved of Zionism for most of his life, not regarding it as a comprehensive solution to the problems of Jewish peoplehood—he felt the same way about the spiritual-center prescription of his friend and rival, Ahad Ha'am—now admitted that Zionism was right. The reason, he said, was that Zionism had become the broadest grassroots manifestation of the aspirations of the Jewish masses, including both sworn Zionists and fellow-travelers. Dubnow confidently asserted that all democratic and national forces in the Jewish public domain, apart from assimilated groups, considered the rebirth of the national center in Palestine the greatest marvel in Jewish history (*der grestn vonder fun der idisher geshikhte*). Admittedly, Dubnow remained a vehement opponent of the negation-of-the-Diaspora doctrine and the Zionists' spirit of "chosenness," but he could not understand, let alone accept, the unwillingness of a Jewish Socialist Party to cooperate with a grassroots Jewish movement—Zionism—that had earned the esteem and political support of most social-democratic parties in western Europe. Only the Bund was unwilling to share a table even with Socialist Zionists who were actualizing their Socialist ideals in Palestine. Dubnow himself, although a non-Zionist, who consistently resisted the negative traits of the Zionist Movement, could not grasp how it was possible to oppose Zionism on behalf of the Jewish masses while these masses would only be too pleased to have an opportunity to reestablish their lives in the Jewish colonies and towns of Palestine.

The matter, Dubnow continued, was rooted in the organic flaw (*der organisher feler*) of the Polish Bund, which considers itself the representative of part of the Jewish people, the Jewish proletariat, instead of an inseparable part of Jewry at large. Hence, his characterization of its worldview as "sectarian Socialism" (*trenungs ortodoksie*), in an analogy to "sectarian Socialism" (*trenungs sotsializm*).

Importantly, these remarks give no evidence that Dubnow had fundamentally changed his historical worldview and his assessment of Zionism. Dubnow regarded Zionism as an especially important historical phenomenon in its "Ahad Ha'amic" cultural sense, but he opposed political Zionism, believing that it failed to offer a realistic answer to the existential problem of the Jewish people. There is no doubt that, in view of the new situation, he deemed the Zionist solution to be more significant than any other possible response. However, he never abandoned his belief in the idea of a Jewish national autonomy that would shape form mainly in eastern Europe. Shortly before the war began, he repeated this idea in a conversation with a journalist.[44]

Erlich's reply, published about three months later, was seven times as long as Dubnow's letter.[45] Although written with due deference to Dubnow, it treated the aged historian, who was distant from and therefore unfamiliar with day-to-day politics, with more than a bit of disdain. Erlich expressed critical amazement that this historian, a stickler for meticulous accuracy in historical research, was sloppy in dealing with the sources that determined the Bund's outlook. Then Erlich launched a sweeping, angry, bold, and politically uninhibited attack against the Zionist Movement. This indicates how offended Erlich was by Dubnow's "Zionist" stance and how important he considered Zionism as the main rival of the Bund. For this reason, the article was also published in installments in the party newspaper, *Naye Folks Tsaytung*.

One may discern two sections in Erlich's letter: ideological clarification of the Bund's attitude toward the Klal Yisrael concept and the political attack on Zionism. First, Erlich set out to refute Dubnow's claim that the Bund had never considered itself an organic part of the Jewish people. Erlich considered this a falsehood that had been concocted by the Bund's opponents and that had clung to the party from the time it was founded. The truth, he said, is the opposite: the Bund has always belonged to the Jewish people, that is, to its grassroots segment, the Jewish majority. This shows that the Bund has always aspired not only to represent the Jewish proletariat, but also to be the standard-bearer of the Jewish masses in their struggle for social and political liberation.

Erlich's definition of the Jewish people as a social-class klal, as opposed to a historical and national klal, led him to the crux of his dispute with Dubnow. Erlich sought to distinguish between the goal of unifying the klal of Jewish progressive forces and the concept of Klal Yisrael, which Dubnow stressed in his letter.

In Erlich's view, there was an ab initio ideological differentiation among the various segments of Jewry, whereas according to Dubnow's approach, these contrasts are inconsequential in comparison with the national necessity of membership in Klal Yisrael. Erlich was pleased with Dubnow's exclusion of Agudath Israel, the isolationist Orthodox movement, from the progressive partnership. However, he suspected that Dubnow would welcome Agudath Israel willingly and happily if it agreed to join the klal that he proposed. Erlich was unquestionably right about that, since Dubnow's point of departure was Jewish nationhood as an all-embracing and diverse phenomenon. For Erlich, in contrast, it was the Jewish working class and the impoverished folk strata, which he distinguished a priori from the rest of the Jewish people, even though he considered the Bund, particularly at the time of the exchange of letters, an inseparable part of the Jewish people.

Erlich's principled arguments about the Bund's attitude toward Klal Yisrael served as a preface of sorts to his answer to Dubnow's main question: why was the Bund so categorically unwilling to collaborate with the Zionists at this time of historical emergency?

Notably, notwithstanding his claim that the Bund represented the Jewish majority, Erlich admitted that the Fascist ascent to power in Germany and the tide of anti-Semitism in other countries, much of the Jewish people had lost its faith in *galut* (exile—the term that Dubnow used). Accordingly, the leaders of the Bund knew that the political support they received from the large Jewish electorates in the cities of Poland was ephemeral and nebulous. Erlich blamed Zionism for this due to its twenty years of political activity since the Balfour Declaration and saw no reason whatsoever to change the party's negative attitude toward it even though the historical situation had changed. Furthermore, the correctness of the Bund's criticism of Zionism was becoming increasingly clear as time passed. Thus, in Erlich's opinion, it had been shown that the settlement enterprise in Palestine was a valueless and very expensive venture that provided a "solution in miniature" to the basic problems of the Jewish people. This was so even if it offered a chance to establish Jewish statehood in a small part of Palestine. Such an entity would be a dwarfish parody of a state, in which the implacable opposition of the Arab and Muslim world to a Jewish state in that region would imperil life at all times. In the best case, then, the most Zionism could achieve is the creation of a new Jewish tribe, a small, Hebrew-speaking tribe that lives in Eretz Israel. To attain this achievement, which is devoid of historical and existential meaning for the Jews, Zionism consciously impairs the very existence of Diaspora Jewry in two senses: by seeking out self-serving cooperation with anti-Semites, the blood-enemies (*unzer dam-soyne*) of the Jewish people, and by opposing all political action meant to improve the Jews' situation in the various countries of Europe. Therefore, he repeated the equation—off-putting even in his time—of Zionism to a Siamese twin of anti-Semitism (*a siamer bruder fun anti-Semitizm*). Then, rising to the occasion, Erlich accused Zionism of willingness to sacrifice the fate of millions of Diaspora Jews on the altar of its Palestinocentric interests insofar as these interests clashed with those of Diaspora Jewry. The Bund, in contrast, as Polish Jewry's largest political party, came to the Jews' defense against the anti-Semitic attacks. Thus, his remarks led to a paradoxical conclusion. Zionism, which preaches the ideological and political principle of Klal Yisrael, actually eschews this principle by abandoning the Jewish masses to the anti-Semites, whereas the Bund, which rules out the Klal Yisrael outlook in principle, actually defends all Jews against anti-Semitism, irrespective of class and creed.

Although Erlich's remarks break little fresh ground, they deserve our attention at the ideological and political levels in terms of their factual truth and historical significance.

Erlich was imprecise, to put it mildly, when he countered Dubnow by asserting that the Bund had always considered itself an inseparable part of the Jewish people. The editors of *Di Tsukunft* commented about this in a footnote at the end of the article. The previous chapters in this study, especially chapter 1 (which discusses the Russian Bund), paint a different picture—one of struggle between two equally powerful groups: "nationalists," who considered themselves an integral part of the Jewish people, and "internationalists," who regarded themselves primarily as an integral part of the international working class.

In the political domain, in his frothing critique of the Zionist Movement and its attitude toward the Jewish people, Erlich cannot be faulted for what he, like his rivals, the Zionist leaders, did not and could not foretell. In 1938 and afterwards, the plight of the Jews was known but their physical extermination unforeseen. Therefore, our criticism of Erlich's views should relate solely to matters in which he had knowledge.

Erlich correctly believed that a solution for the Jewish masses would not be found in Palestine, let alone in a rump Jewish state that would be established in only part of that country. Therefore, the Diaspora and its millions of Jews would continue to exist and their welfare would entail struggle. He also knew, however, that no Zionist leader in his time, from

Weizmann to Gruenbaum, from Ben-Gurion to Jabotinsky, believed in the possibility of the quantitative eradication of the Diaspora. Indeed, Jabotinsky's evacuation plan and Gruenbaum and Sneh's emigration plan spoke of the departure of about a million Jews from Poland over a ten-year period. The Zionists and the Bund leaders also agreed that natural increase would replace much of the depletion occasioned by the feasible extent of annual immigration. Erlich also knew about the Zionists' efforts to establish a joint front to defend Jews from anti-Semitic attacks and the hostile policies of the government that did not prevent such assaults. After all, the Bund had rejected all the Zionists' offers to collaborate with them. Furthermore, both Erlich and the Zionists knew that there was no international solution to the Jewish problem. At the International Refugee Conference at Evian (July 1938), no realistic international program to address the question of Jewish refugees, foremost from Germany, had been bruited. In contrast to this futile endeavor, the Bund and the Zionists had two principled conceptions that, while totally different from each other, shared the quality of skepticism about the viability of international solutions. The Bund argued that the Jews' problem should and could be solved in their places of residence; the Zionists argued that the problem of the Jewish refugees—at that time, this referred to several hundred thousand German Jews—should and could be solved largely in Palestine. None of them, as stated, imagined the emigration of millions of Jews from Europe to any destination, let alone Palestine. Therefore, Erlich's allegation that the Zionists were sacrificing the fate of Diaspora Jewry on the altar of Palestine can only be termed a deliberate political smear. The libel was reinforced by Erlich's ideological interpretation of the negotiations that Zionist leaders were conducting with the government of Poland to ease the Polish Jews' plight by resettling some of them in Palestine. Erlich, as stated, considered these contacts the reflection of an ideological kinship between Zionism and anti-Semitism, that is, the "Siamese twin" nexus. Notably, a year before the Dubnow–Erlich dispute, Abraham Liessin, congratulating the Bund on its fortieth anniversary, indirectly asked the Zionists and the Bund to pool their forces. Both movements, in his opinion, were acting on behalf of Jewish nationhood— Zionism for its minority in Palestine and the Bund for the majority in the Diaspora. The article was published shortly before Liessin's death and became his national-ideology will, so to speak.[46]

The historical significance of Erlich's anti-Zionist polemic should also be understood within the limitations of the time and the place. At the time, all the Zionists wanted and considered possible was to obtain a Jewish state, albeit a small one. Such a state would offer an answer to the distress of the small number of Jews who would settle there. It would also provide a solution for the Jewish people at large, since the establishment of a nation-state would normalize the Jews' status in the global community of nations. The Bund, true to its worldview, totally rejected both: an exit route for some Jews and a nation-state solution to the problem of the Jews as a world people. The way to normalize the Jewish condition, in Bundist thinking, was to integrate the Jews politically and socially into the societies where they lived. Here lies the root of the unbridgeable dispute that history decided so tragically. Symbolically, the tragedy for the Bund became evident in full fury in the Warsaw ghetto and in London in 1942–1943, a time of supreme danger for Klal Yisrael. In both locations, the Warsaw ghetto and London, at that fateful hour for the existence of the Jewish people, the traditional Bundist tension between the dogmatic, all-inclusive separatist ideology and the occasionally pragmatic political approach toward special issues was unmasked. In the Warsaw ghetto, the Bund leadership spent some ten months, between early 1942 and October of that year, discussing whether to join the Jewish Fighting Organization that had been established by the Zionist youth movements and parties. The final decision in favor of joining was made mainly due to pressure from leaders of the Bund youth movement, Tsukunft, who overcame the opposing separatist stance of the older leadership.[47] In London, in contrast, Shmuel (Arthur) Zygielboim, the Bund's representative to the Polish government-in-exile, consistently refused to collaborate with Jewish political entities that contacted him several times in this matter.[48]

Both approaches, the political rejectionism in Warsaw and the ideological rejectionism in London, belonged to the Polish Bund tradition. In Warsaw, a debate went on among those who, for pronouncedly ideological reasons, considered cooperation with the Polish Socialist Party preferable and also ideologically and practically necessary. Bund members in the ghettos of Vilna and Bialystok, in contrast, were unable to stay aloof in the midst of a joint effort to salvage the dignity of the Jewish people—a cause of supreme importance and value to the youth of both camps. In London, Shmuel Zygielboim persistently adhered to his separatist stance in fealty to the Bund's core ideology. This ideology drew sustenance during those wretched years from the assumption that it would be the Bund that would represent the majority of Polish Jews at the end of World War II. This was the conventional wisdom among surviving members of the Polish Bund leadership who had managed to escape from Poland and find shelter in the United States. In New York, too, Bund leaders refused to cooperate with Zionist and religious organizations in representing the cause of Polish Jewry vis-à-vis the Polish government's representative in the United States. Leivik Hades, a member of the Bund central committee and a journalist of the highest stature, explained this political stance in the dialectic terms that were typical of the Bundist ideological tradition. In his opinion, precisely at that time of emergency, as the hardships of the Jewish masses mounted, the foundations on which the Bund ideology stood were expanding and gathering strength (*Di bazeh far der bundisher ideologie hot zikh gvaltik vitgebraytert*). He based this view on the dialectical premise: the greater the distress of the Jewish masses, the more clearly they would see that only the Bund's solution to this problem—the triumph of world Socialism—is correct.[49]

A year earlier, a member of the Bund organization in New York, Emanuel Nowogrodzki, had affixed himself to the Utopian vision of the Polish Bund. He publicly expressed his belief that the Bundist solution for the Jewish masses in Poland was still realistic and not mystical, as his opponents claimed. The political and social trend toward progress, equality, and Socialism, which had begun with the French Revolution, was still valid and was borne on the shoulders of that very action—the proletariat. In lieu of the traditional Jewish messiah, a new messiah-in-the-flesh was arising. As Nowogrodzki expressed it, the Bund also believed in the internal power of the Jewish masses and proved this during its years of existence as a Jewish Socialist Party. Therefore, the conclusion is not to run away from the Diaspora home, as Utopian Zionism proposes, but to transform the Diaspora into a home by joining the international proletariat in its struggle.[50]

Notably, some of the Bund's opponents also believed in the continued existence of a Jewish collectivity in postwar Poland. That very year, in a letter to Nahum Goldmann, Moshe Kleinbaum (Sneh) stated that it would be necessary at the end of war to fight for European Jews' civil status and their unrestricted right to live "full Jewish cultural lives" in their countries of residence. Two years later, the press of the Po'aley Tsiyyon Left party in the ghetto stated that a large proportion of Polish Jews might look forward to a future in their country.[51] However, they were differentiated from the leaders of the Bund by the Utopian belief of the latter in the Jews' organic integration into the Polish people. As stated, for the Bundists the future Socialist Poland was a homeland; for the Zionists it was a state of exile.

After Zygielboim's suicide, the Bund leadership in New York posted a new delegate to London: the intellectual of the group, a member of the young generation, Dr. Emanuel Szerer. At the beginning of his political activities, Szerer, too, sought to integrate into the institutions of the Polish political leadership in London. However, after most of his attempts failed, he softened his separatist stance and was even willing to collaborate with the General Zionist leader, Itzhak Schwarzbard, in efforts to provide war refugees with relief.[52]

Does the Bund's oscillation during the war between ideological dogmatism and political pragmatism, manifested particularly in its decisions in the Warsaw ghetto and other ghettos, indicate that, under those circumstances, it drew a line between politics and ideology? The turnaround in the Bund's stance in the Warsaw ghetto in regard to the ZOB was not an aberration in the political history of this movement. In the early 1920s, for practical political considerations that clashed with the separatism principle, the Bund leadership, after a harsh internal debate, decided to take part in elections for the community administrations. In the early 1930s, it opposed the demand of the radicals, headed by the well-known Shmuel Zygielboim, to secede from the association of community administrations because the clericalists and the Zionists controlled the association at the de facto level. The establishment of the Congress of Trade Unions on a non-Bund basis also attests to political pragmatism. These political actions, like the Bund's stationing itself at the forefront of the opponents of the anti-Semitic tide in Poland, fissured the party's rampart of Utopian isolationism but did not undermine the foundations of that rampart, as this chapter has shown. However, the demonstrative and tragic suicide of Shmuel Zygielboim on behalf of his beleaguered people, and the desperate heroism of the Bund fighters together with members of the Zionist youth movements in their last battle for national and personal dignity, were symbolic acts in which the ideological and political taboo against cooperation with the Zionists was broken and the Bund cried out on behalf of Klal Yisrael. Both symbolic actions—of those who fell alone in battle and of the one whose suicide remained a mute outcry—attest to the strength of Jewish national solidarity.

CONCLUSION

This episode of the Bund's "reporting to the front" in defense of Klal Yisrael at times of distress and disaster concludes with the tragedy that befell its two revered leaders, Henryk Erlich and Wiktor Alter, who perished in Soviet prisons in late 1942. Their march to death in the Soviet gulag went via Klal Yisrael. Both men escaped to Soviet-controlled eastern Poland after Warsaw fell to the Germans. They were immediately arrested by the secret police and charged with anti-Soviet activity, collaboration with bourgeois organizations, and criticism of the Ribbentrop-Molotov pact. Both were sentenced to death in the summer of 1941, but in September 1941, shortly after the Nazi invasion of the USSR, they were released and taken to Moscow. Their release came at the initiative of Laurenty Pavlovich Beria, head of the security services. His intention was to establish an international Jewish anti-Fascist committee that would help the militarily beleaguered Soviet Union to marshal political and military support in Britain and the United States with the aid of Jewish public opinion. This, in my opinion, proves that the myth of the *Protocols of the Learned Elders of Zion* was still considered somewhat valid. Now, however, the Jews were deemed to be a benign element in terms of Soviet interests. According to Beria's proposal, Erlich would chair the committee, Alter would serve as his secretary, and the famous Soviet Jewish actor, Solomon Mikhoels, would be deputy chairman and representative of Soviet Jewry on behalf of the Supreme Soviet.

Beria asked Erlich and Alter to prepare a memorandum for Stalin about the essence and function of the committee. The two Bundists complied and the document was sent to its addressee in October 1941. Two months later, both men were rearrested and placed in prison, where they died—Erlich by suicide in May 1942 and Alter by execution nine months later, in February 1943. The reasons for the change in attitude toward them are not totally clear; the explanations that exist are based on conjectures that fall outside the purview of this discussion.[53]

For our purposes, the main item of pertinence is the memorandum to Stalin, which expresses consciously and, perhaps, unconsciously the principles of Klal Yisrael as they apply at a time of emergency and existential national peril. The memorandum spoke of the Jewish masses and their fate under the Nazi yoke, a fate closely and inseparably related to the freedom of other national groups that share the same state. Thus, the document refers to *the Jewish people*, and not only the Jewish proletariat, as a people equal in status to other peoples. However, the memorandum also stresses that the Jewish masses are living under an especially harsh regime of Nazi repression, one that in its acts of brutality and humiliation surpasses the treatment meted out to the other occupied peoples. Therefore, Erlich and Alter wrote, the Jewish masses in the occupied countries should struggle for their national and social liberation in concert with the other peoples.

The role of the Committee, according to the memorandum, would be to encourage "the totality of Jewish society" in all countries, in all possible ways and with all possible means, to combat Nazism by raising aid for the Jewish masses in the occupied countries and for Jewish refugees in the free countries, foremost the Soviet Union. To accomplish this, the Committee would organize the refugees in the USSR and serve as a liaison between them and their brethren in the countries at war with Germany. It would also conduct political propaganda in the United States and Britain, by means of Jewish organizations, to raise aid for the Soviet Union in the form of military equipment and food.

The stunning thing in the memorandum is its recourse to the "Zionist" idea, born in World War I, of organizing "Jewish battalions" within the British army. The idea resurfaced in World War II with the establishment of the Jewish fighting brigades in Palestine. Now Erlich and Alter brought up the idea of establishing a Jewish army unit in the United States and other countries that would be annexed to the Red Army. They proposed to promote the idea by launching a public propaganda campaign in the United States—all of which in addition to a Jewish national fundraising campaign for the Jewish refugees who had fled to the Soviet Union.[54]

Obviously, one cannot accuse these men of imitating the Zionists. Their model for emulation, without a doubt, was the Polish national leader Josef Pilsudski, who in World War I established a Polish legion in Austria that had fought valiantly against the forces of Czarist Russia. Just the same, the main point is the very idea of establishing a Jewish national unit under the Red Army umbrella. This idea was not radically dissimilar from the propaganda that Revisionist groups in the United States disseminated about a year later in favor of the establishment of a Jewish quasi-army of volunteers for war against Nazi Germany.

Thus, the "cat" of the Bund emerged from the "bag" of the Jewish distress. Erlich and Alter's memorandum was in fact one of the supreme expressions of concern for Klal Yisrael. Admittedly, the document did not yet denote a conscious return to Klal Yisrael; only decades later, after the Holocaust, did Klal Yisrael become a matter of principled consciousness and political resolution in Bundist thinking. Even so, however, it pointed to the Klal Yisrael national complexion of the Bund, as manifested in actions that quite often clashed with the party's declared ideology.

CHAPTER 6

BETWEEN PIONEERHOOD AND PEOPLEHOOD
The Zionist Labor Movement, 1930–1947

We want aliyah so that the 'olim will save the country.
—David Ben-Gurion, 1933

We've got to realize that today's Diaspora is tomorrow's Eretz Israel.
—Berl Katznelson, 1934

In the early 1930s, the Labor Movement acquired a new status in the Zionist Organization. The movement that had once commanded a "moral hegemony" in Zionism, as Berl Katznelson put it, became its executive political organ, thereby fulfilling David Ben-Gurion's ambition. The change was occasioned by an internal Labor Movement initiative and developments within the Zionist Organization. In 1930, the Palestine Workers' Party (Mapai) was established in a merger between Ahdut ha-ʿAvoda and Ha-poʿel ha-Tsaʿir. The merger handed Mapai a decisive majority in the Histadrut and, thereby, made it a leading political force in the Yishuv. In 1931, Chaim Weizmann resigned the presidency of the Zionist Organization due to criticism of his policy of appeasement toward Britain. Concurrently, the Revisionist Zionist Party, an opposition to Weizmann and the Labor Movement, seceded from the Zionist Organization in a process that began in 1931 and ended in 1935. These two developments—the resignation of the authoritative leader and the departure of the spirited opposition to his policies—created a political void of sorts in the Zionist Organization leadership. The Labor Movement filled this void by dint of its power, which would henceforth be based on more than 40 percent of delegates to Zionist Congresses from then until the establishment of the State of Israel. Thus, the movement completed its takeover of the "Zionist klal." Its campaign of conquest had begun during the Second Aliya with an effort to "conquer Hebrew labor" that, although unsuccessful, brought it to the consciousness of

Zionists at large. The campaign had continued with the onset of a successful attempt to "conquer the land" by laying the foundations of cooperative
rural settlement, the progenitor of the pioneering Zionist ethos. From that
point the movement climbed to centrality in Yishuv society by founding the
Histadrut, the General Federation of Jewish Labor in Palestine, in 1920, and
by conquering the pioneering youth movements for the construction of the
new society in Eretz Yisrael. The process was culminated by the "political
conquest" of the Zionist Organization, against the background of the Fourth
Aliya crisis, which dashed the hopes of Zionist-bourgeois groups of taking
over the leadership of the Yishuv and the Zionist Organization. Each phase
in this campaign of conquest had its own ethos: the demonstrative self-sacrifice of the Second Aliya immigrants, the pioneering passion of the Third
Aliya, and the personal and collective mobilization, especially in the cooperative settlements, during the national emergencies of the mid–1930s Arab
uprising and World War II. Notably, the conquest would not have been possible had the Labor Movement not earned appreciation, esteem, and reward
for its service on behalf of the Zionist enterprise, that is, its role as the
spearhead of action in rural settlement and defense. Consequently, the constructivist enterprise and the political status in the Zionist Organization
became increasingly interdependent.

The question at the forefront of this chapter is this: after it acquired
political hegemony in the Zionist klal, did the Labor Movement also develop a consciousness of national responsibility vis-à-vis Klal Yisrael?
And if it did, was this a generally accepted stance or was there a difference in attitude between members of the elitist pioneering movements
and the pragmatic political leadership?

Importantly, these questions were not central in the Labor Movement's daily affairs, since even at that time of massing clouds of emergency
in the Jewish firmament, the Yishuv continued to pursue its political and
social routine, devoting most of its attention to the continual quest for financial resources to sustain the labor economy; the war on unemployment;
efforts to induce a stronger flow of pioneering immigration; political sparring with the Revisionists over the division of labor and the right to strike;
and additional mundane matters. Furthermore, the Labor Movement leadership was in the throes of a diminution of Zionist thinking that, more than
it attested to a narrowing of intellectual horizons or even to psychological
imperviousness, reflected the power of concentration with which the Jews
were being given relative latitude to act on behalf of their national cause.

Nevertheless, it is appropriate to ask whether the leadership really
regarded its "mundane" political actions—debates about the makeup of the
Zionist Organization coalition, apportioning of immigration visas by this or

that key, arrangements with the Revisionist Movement to govern labor relations in Palestine and subordinate them to the discipline of the majority in the Zionist Organization—as the be-all and end-all? Or did the leaders have a vision that transcended such matters? Did they have a historical consciousness that advised them that the Zionist Movement and the Jewish people were approaching a crossroads that could be sensed even though it had not yet come into sight? Or did ideological continuity and constructivist "narrowing of horizons" in their devotion to the labor enterprise thwart a more comprehensive view of matters against the background of the changing times?

The first answers to these questions were proffered by David Ben-Gurion and Yosef Sprinzak in their keynote speeches at the Mapai founding convention in January 1930.

Ben-Gurion's speech was an impassioned and thrilling rhetorical combination of old ideas that had accompanied the Labor Movement since its inception in the Second Aliya and new intentions that might come to pass in the future. Describing the essence of the Zionist Labor Movement, he extolled the movement by coronating it with "messianic" utterances that he had been coining over the past generation. He spoke about "Hebrew redemption," "Zionist fulfillment," "historical mission," "sanctity of the homeland," and "the Zionist will." With his customary disregard of the audience that had been hearing these remarks for years—since the Second Aliya, in fact—he reemphasized the national mission of the working class, which "is wholly pledged to identification with the Zionist enterprise" and has no interest other than this identity, singly or collectively. After all, "its personal interests [and] its class interests are indistinguishable from the Zionist interests in this country."

As stated, there was nothing novel about these remarks, but under the new historical circumstances—the shock following the Arab violence in 1929; the Shaw Commission and its dire conclusions, the policies of the British Labour government; and the weakening of Chaim Weizmann's grip on the Zionist Organization—they sounded like a call for a sweeping takeover of the Zionist Movement leadership by the united Labor Movement. To be sure, Ben-Gurion could not have predicted Weizmann's resignation about a year later, at the XVII Zionist Congress, and the Labor Movement's ascent to a position in the coalition leadership of the Zionist Organization. However, no leader matched his sense of historical timing, and evidently his remarks were again influenced by it now. Therefore, he stated with emphasis, and not for the first time, that the working class was unique in that its national mission took precedence over its class consciousness. Although the two were not mutually exclusive, the working class knows its historical mission: "to cease to be a class, to cease to be a part" and, thereby, "to become an entire nation." Here, then, he expressed the formula, which he had articulated a year earlier in different terms, of moving "from a working class to a working people."[1] Thus, he not only resolved the seeming contradiction between the national destiny and the social vision of the working class, but also proved the working class' responsibility for the interests of the national klal. The Bund, in his opinion, lacks such an awareness because it is an anomalous proletarian phenomenon—an "appendage of another people's labor movement." Unlike the Bund, the Zionist Labor Movement in Palestine had assumed the function of "building a country, establishing sovereignty, and bringing a people over here." What is more, it had a chance of accomplishing its mission, as the only national Jewish labor movement that is "a Labor Movement with territorial prospects, with sovereign prospects, with great responsibility at the level of peoplehood." This unity, according to Ben-Gurion, can exist only by virtue of "absolute faith" in "one path" and "only one idea" upon which such unity may be built. As far as he was concerned, this idea could be expressed in various ways. Aware of the historical sensitivity of his partners in Ha-po'el ha-Tsa'ir to the concept of Socialism, he argued that one could either define it as Socialist Zionism or forgo the Socialism. What counted was the national and cooperative nature of the action taken.

Ben-Gurion's willingness to waive the concept of Socialism lest it drive a wedge between the new partners—Ha-po'el ha-Tsa'ir and Ahdut ha-'Avoda—came at a price. He demanded that his comrades, especially those in Ha-po'el ha-Tsa'ir, stop distinguishing between the Labor Movement in Palestine and its counterpart in the Diaspora. His ostensible purpose was to tone down the radical negation-of-the-Diaspora ideology that was typical of Ha-po'el ha-Tsa'ir and, especially, of the Ha-po'el ha-Tsa'ir of the past. In fact, however, Ben-Gurion was looking ahead to the day when Eretz Israel and the Diaspora would be united. Therefore, turning to the extreme negators of Diaspora, he argued that "It is a not a drawback for an idea to have been imported from the Diaspora. The Zionist idea itself was imported from the Diaspora. And at day's end, the Diaspora is *our main source of nourishment, [the source] on which we depend, and in which all our trust and future lie—the Jewish people.*"[2] By expressing himself this way, he indicated that important segments of the Labor Movement still leaned toward dissociation from Diaspora Jewry. These were unquestionably some of Ben-Gurion's strongest remarks about the Klal Yisrael idea. He rested the idea on a three-way unity: political, which had come to pass in Palestine with the establishment of Mapai; historical, as revealed in the national mission of the working class, which had now been vested with the political mechanism, the united party, to carry out its task; and the national—which creates an inseparable bond between the new Jewish Palestine and the old Diaspora. Two years later, Ben-Gurion would give this ideological view a far-reaching national-political interpretation.

Yosef Sprinzak's keynote speech, in keeping with the nature of the person and his party, lacked these messianic pulsations. However, it did contain some very vehement statements about the Diaspora. They originated in Sprinzak's pioneering-elitist ideological and political worldview. Thus inspired, Sprinzak told his audience about a conversation he had held with a group of emissaries who were about to visit the pioneering youth movements in Poland. His remarks, if lifted out of their historical and cultural context, might sound like the articulation of a "tyrannical" Palestinocentric ethic. ". . . In your work in 1930," Sprinzak told the emissaries, "you must begin preparing the reserve for 1935. *Take the boy* [the expression may be a reference to the removal of the biblical Benjamin from Jacob's home by his brothers] *kidnap him from his parents' home so that we may build the national home.*" He referred not only to the preparation of young people for aliya, but also to greater intensity in Hebrew education. Sprinzak, the pragmatic politician, did not intend merely to remove the "boy" from exile; he also sought to wrest control of the Diaspora street from the ascendant Bund. He made particular note of the need to persuade the Jewish masses of the correctness of the "expanded Jewish Agency" idea, which aimed to give the entire Jewish people "a stake in building the house of Israel."[3] By so speaking, he seemingly denied any contradiction between Diaspora-negating pioneering elitism and an appeal to Diaspora Jewry at large—Klal Yisrael—to take part in the national effort. By implication, Ben-Gurion and Sprinzak borrowed a little from each other, but each expressed the idea differently and envisaged a different pace of implementation. Indeed, Ben-Gurion's progression "from class to people" and from the "halutsic klal" to the petit bourgeois "Klal Yisrael" was rapid; it would take place over less than three years, from 1932 to 1935. This turnabout was related to the change in Ben-Gurion's own political status in 1933, when he resigned as Secretary of the Histadrut to chair the Zionist Executive. Importantly, however, it was not functionalist in its essence, since it predated his appointment as Chairman of the Zionist Executive. As stated, it began with the formation of Mapai and solidified at the Mapai Council meeting at Kefar Yehezkel in 1932.

In his lecture at the Kefar Yehezkel gathering, Ben-Gurion established a historical and moral tautology between the Socialist Zionist outlook and the Klal Yisrael idea. He did this by way of negation, arguing that the Yishuv urban class "is progressively destroying Klal Yisrael in this country, because this Klal Yisrael is unsuited to the class cravings of this gang, and there's no guarantee that the Jewish bourgeoisie won't betray the Hebrew language as well."[4] In remarks he made in a far-ranging article more than twenty pages long, Ben-Gurion softened these expressions but broadened their meaning. The origin of the Klal Yisrael idea, he said, is not in the working class: "General Zionism had *one precious asset* that it did not acquire from the working class, and in which [the General Zionists] took pride: the 'Klal Yisrael idea.' Now, who is more anxious than a bourgeois Zionist about *'national unity' and the integrity of the national organism?*" The question was not meant to be sarcastic, since Ben-Gurion admitted that some workers in the Diaspora related suspiciously to this concept and to all its political and material meanings. His allusion to the Bund was clear and explicit, even though he also aimed his remarks at Po'aley Tsiyyon Left. The worker in Palestine, in contrast to members of both parties, assumed explicit responsibility for the fate of Klal Yisrael.[5]

Nevertheless, even though the Labor Movement in Palestine outperformed all other class groups in demonstrating allegiance to the Klal Yisrael idea and resolve in its struggle to unify it, the Zionist bourgeoisie in the Yishuv decided that "Klal Yisrael, from which the worker has not been expelled or, at least, within which he has not suffered a diminishing of rights—has one fate only, destruction, because this Klal Yisrael is not suited to the brutes' cravings for class rule."[6] At the time, these remarks referred not only to the bourgeois General Zionists in Palestine but to world Zionism at large.

The crisis that befell the Zionist Movement, Ben-Gurion explained, originated in the fact that "General Zionism," which accounted for most bulk of the Zionist Movement to that time, "*is steadily voiding itself of national contents and is becoming a Zionism of class interests*" [italics in the original]. Thus, not only is it attempting to shove the Zionist working class out from under the Klal Yisrael umbrella, but it itself has ceased to be Zionist in its conduct. Consequently, "*This class Zionism begins by shirking responsibility and concern for any Zionist enterprise in which it has no self-interest and ends by repudiating, overtly assaulting, and undermining basic and main Zionist values wherever they values clash with the class interests of the 'Zionist' bourgeoisie*" [italics in the original].[7] Ben-Gurion's hyperbole about "repudiation" and "assaulting" was meant, of course, to cause General Zionism to shoot itself in the foot with the weapon that it had aimed at the "class" Labor Movement, as the General Zionists termed it. Thus, Ben-Gurion stationed the "old" Labor Movement, rooted in the Second Aliya, against the "new" General Zionism. He admitted that both sides had class interests but stated that they should be tested in reference to the overall national interest. From this standpoint, "the worker's class interest and the general national interest are one and the same."[8] Of course, he judged the interests of the Zionist bourgeoisie to be the exact opposite. Thus, Ben-Gurion was influenced by Marxian doctrine but not in the sense that Marx had intended. Just as Marx distinguished the working class from all other classes in that it does not control its own property and, accordingly, has no interest in protecting it, so did Ben-Gurion differentiate between the working class and the other Zionist classes in its constructive pioneering function, which derives its nourishment from national property.

Ben-Gurion's remarks at this occasion caused no commotion in the central committee. Most of the discussants, who in large part came from the cooperative rural settlement sector, expressed shared concerns: ineptitude in the party's performance, the weakness of the Histadrut in protecting the Jewish worker, disappointment in the Zionist Organization for failing to promote the settlement enterprise adequately, and so forth. Even Yitzhak Tabenkin, the champion of pioneerism, did not challenge Ben-Gurion's class-transcending premises, possibly because he was impressed above all by Ben-Gurion's sweeping attack on the Zionist bourgeoisie and his proclamation of the imminent replacement of the Zionist Organization leadership along class lines. Some, in contrast to Tabenkin, took reasoned exception to the general criticism of the Zionist bourgeoisie and also pointed to the Labor Movement's weakness in the Jewish street. This led them to believe that the Movement had no chance of replacing the decaying Zionist Organization leadership and prompted them to resurrect the 1920s alternativist idea of establishing a broad grassroots organization that would replace the Zionist Organization.[9]

The disapproval of the party "pragmatists" of Ben-Gurion's passionate remarks about the destiny of the Labor Movement and his sweeping criticism of the Zionist bourgeoisie did not deter him from discussing in greater depth the dynamic essence of his outlook, which signaled a transition "from class to people." However, most of Ben-Gurion's theoretical reflections were aimed at the practical domain of his public life. In this case, his political intuition evidently told him that large grassroots and bourgeois circles in the Zionist Organization might construe the slogan in a manner dangerous to the Labor Movement, that is, as an attempt to engineer a Socialist takeover of the "Zionist klal." Therefore, in his next speech, at the party convention in late 1932, he hurriedly explained what he had in mind. First, he drew a distinction between the subjective Zionist worldview—religious, bourgeois, or Socialist—and the objective needs of Zionist fulfillment. Thus, in his opinion, even were the Labor Movement not Socialist, its Zionist actions in rural settlement and pioneering should be exactly as though it were. This did not imply, he said, that "Socialism and Zionism are fully, totally, and intrinsically

identical." On the contrary, he quickly stressed. "If we take Zionism and
Socialism as theoretical concepts, then they are totally different in both their
theoretical contents and their human carriers." Zionism as a national movement aims to create a normal Jewish society in Eretz Israel; Socialism as a
social movement aspires to transform society at large. "The two concepts are
not mutually exclusive," he added, "but neither ideologically or topically do
they overlap." Sociologically, too, they are different movements: Zionism is
a grassroots multiclass national movement; Socialism is a single-class movement that transcends nationality. Thus, he concluded emphatically, "Our
equating of Zionism with Socialism is not informed by an objective intrinsic
identity of Zionism and Socialism that ostensibly exists independently of
ourselves, in the abstract. There is no such identity. Instead, it flows from an
identity of the carriers of Zionism."[10] Thus, the identity originates not in the
objective nature of the class but in the subjective choice of individuals and
groups. This choice, he was firmly convinced, required the Zionist Labor
Movement to breach the limits of the objective class definitions. Otherwise,
"The Labor Movement will not carry out its mission faithfully and com-
pletely unless it learns how to become a people's movement." Thus far, Ben-
Gurion explained, the Labor Movement and Klal Yisrael were separated by
a dual barrier: "One barrier that we erected and another barrier that others
erected." The former barrier was based on the youthful rebellion of the pioneers who had settled in Palestine. By totally negating exile (*galut*) in their
actions and lifestyle, they distanced themselves from the Jewish masses,
which have remained in the Diaspora. Consequently, "Many are blinded to
the true value of the Labor enterprise, *the class structure oveshadowed the
national contents of our movement and its formation.*" The "others" who
erected the second barrier were the opponents of the Labor Movement,
whom Ben-Gurion termed "the false prophets of barren rhetorical Zionism."[11] As a result, the active and leading entity in the Labor Movement, "the
pioneering movement, has withdrawn too severely into its corner and its private niche." Therefore, despite its thousands of members, it is too weak to
influence the actions of the Zionist Movement.

Thus, Ben-Gurion considered both definitions of the Labor Movement in Palestine—an objective social entity of class nature and a subjective Zionist pioneering choice—inimical to the Klal Yisrael idea.
Therefore, he demanded that the movement open its ranks to the Jewish
masses without Socialist-class or pioneering-ideology conditions. After
all, he reasoned, any Jew who settles in Eretz Israel as a worker objectively
fulfills the aspirations of the Zionist Labor Movement without diminishing
the guiding potency of the movement's pioneering and Socialist ideals. In
a small way, Ben-Gurion's statements mirrored the Bund's basic argument

against the very possibility of a synthesis of Socialism and nationalism. At the most, the Bund maintained, the two could coexist under certain social conditions, with Socialism in the lead, of course. For Ben-Gurion, in contrast, it was Zionist nationalism that commanded primacy.

In sum, Ben-Gurion's two lectures may be termed—in a paraphrase of Berl Katznelson's well known headline at the end of World War I— "Heading for the Next Days"[12]—"heading for the existing Klal Yisrael."

This time, Ben-Gurion's cumulative remarks touched off a dispute among the party delegates, in which the two traditional outlooks in the Labor Movement—that of "from people to class" and that of "from class to people"—that I pointed to in the introduction to this study, found expression.

Most advocates of the "from people to class" approach were members of the kibbutz movement, along with a few old-timers from the Second Aliya. They warned Ben-Gurion about the danger of blurring the clarity and singularity of the pioneering Labor Movement by reaching out to the Jewish petit bourgeoisie, which, in terms of its occupational and psychological profile, could not possibly identify with Labor Movement values, let alone to integrate into the new society in Palestine. Some also saw in the idea of a transition from class to people a Communist pattern of action (reminiscent of the Soviets' New Economic Policy in the 1920s) if not a Fascist political predisposition. There were also practical rationales, some arguing that the Labor Movement is by essence unfit to take political action at the present time, since its entire intellectual and practical world is future-oriented in all respects. Furthermore, the petit bourgeoisie, by its nature, cannot walk with the Labor Movement down the same path. Additionally, some voices, while not ruling out Ben-Gurion's initiative to form a political alliance with the Zionist petit bourgeoisie, affirmed the historical relationship between Zionism and progressive social forces at large, foremost Socialism. Furthermore, the nexus of Zionism and Socialism had rescued many young Jews from the tentacles of Communism.[13]

The two veteran leaders, Yosef Sprinzak and Berl Katznelson, took the middle ground, urging an appeal to the grassroots coupled with painstaking preservation of the singularity of the Labor Movement. Sprinzak urged the party to make a political effort to capture the Jewish street from the Bund *and* from bourgeois Zionism by involving itself politically in community life and striving to improve the living conditions of the impoverished Jewish masses, displaying initiative and "offensiveness" in all fields of Jewish life. However, this progression "from class to people" had only one intent: negation-of-the-Diaspora amidst an attempt to transform the petit bourgeoisie people into a pioneering working class following the outlook of the historical Ha-poʿel ha-Tsaʿir. Therefore, Sprinzak stressed:

We want a party that *will know how to negate, repudiate, and
deny the public reality that is rampant in the Diaspora today*. We
want the contours form of the Party's systems to contrast with
every manner of social relations that has taken shape in Diaspora
life, [a party] that in its actions will present a total contrast to the
belligerence and rowdiness that are commonplace today in Jewish affairs abroad. We want a party whose members will know
how to uphold its moral and social imperatives and that, in its
own behavior [and] cultural activity, will know how to elevate
the personal and collective Jewish culture in the Diaspora.[14]

These cultural and value yearnings were not strikingly different, at
their Utopian cultural level, from those expressed by the Bund leaders
V. Medem and W. Alter. However, as stated, the debate was mainly of political nature and intent. Here it is worth elucidating the differences between
Sprinzak's views and Ben-Gurion's. Sprinzak wished to reinvigorate the halutsic elite so that it could lead the Jewish masses but seriously doubted that
the party, Mapai, had the strength to lead the Zionist Organization. Ben-
Gurion held the opposite view. He believed that this was a politically op-
portune moment to climb to the leadership, and he was right. Thus, in terms
of Klal Yisrael politics, Sprinzak remained in the clouds of the halutsic
ethos whereas Ben-Gurion was willing to come to Earth in order to take the
helm of the Zionist leadership.

Following the accepted practice at Mapai conferences, Berl Katznelson summed up the debate. He agreed with Ben-Gurion about the political
goals that Mapai should adopt but took exception to their ideological basis
and, especially, to their "Bundist" tenor in regard to the nonidentity of Zionism as a national idea and Socialism as a social worldview. Katznelson did
attempt to explain Ben-Gurion's surprising remarks by arguing that he must
have had practical reasons for making them, that is, to facilitate cooperation
with non-Socialists. However, since his intention might be construed as the
need to forsake Socialism, Katznelson proclaimed emphatically that "I don't
accept that outlook." One could be a non-Socialist Zionist or a non-Zionist
Socialist, he explained, as long as one acted in a reality that included points
of intersection between these divergent outlooks. "But we are speaking
about Zionism and Socialism as we [would speak of] ideas, perceptions. And
no worldview can be built on the basis of two ideals when it is acknowledged
that the ideals are different and do not intersect." Therefore, "anyone who
wishes to treat Zionism and Socialism as two different ideas will do both a
disservice." This is because "Then Socialism will be trade unionism, an aspiration to improve the working man's conditions, an utterly primitive out-

look that lacks every human ideal, that in no way aspires to social, national justice, women's liberation, and so forth." This being the case, "Any advocacy of national political sovereignty that does not recognize the equality of every individual in his nation reduces the national idea to a sham." The Zionist Labor Movement is unique in world Socialism—in its Democratic-Socialist and, especially, its Communist segments—because "Only we have seen the synthesis." Admittedly, he quickly added, "we also formed alliances with other Zionists, but *complete Zionism* is ours and any other form is a contradiction." Thus, "We have no practical or educational need to relinquish *this precious property of ours.*" Consequently, "We will not be able to establish a comprehensive national outlook as class contrasts and class power disappear. But the wish to transform the class into a force also requires [us] to be cautious about the falsifications of Orthodoxy and the truculence of the pious, which also clash with the class outlook."[15] For Socialism, after all, class is a means and not an end. Socialism abhors the idealization of class. The Jewish labor movement, that is, the Bund, in his opinion, has made class ideology an instrument for the factionalization of the Jews and has made the petit bourgeois Jew into the antithesis of Socialism. "Let us then free ourselves of these falsehoods." The party should "defend the limits" and should be aware that "Not always can one defend a class by calling it one."

In bringing this charge against the Bund, Katznelson was right and wrong. Bund leaders in the 1920s had in fact spoken about "two [Jewish] peoples," the proletarian and the bourgeois. The proof was the debate between Wiktor Alter and his comrades, in the late 1920s, about the need to find paths to dialogue and cooperation with the impoverished Jewish petit bourgeoisie. Alter, as stated (in chapter 3), stayed within the class framework whereas Ben-Gurion reached out to the people at large. Both, however, were inclined to breach the narrow class setting—the proletariat one, as in the Bund's thinking, and the halutsic one, as with the Labor Movement. Therefore, as anti-Semitism and Fascism mounted in and after the mid-1930s, the Bund positioned itself at the forefront of the defense of the Jewish masses.

From Katznelson's standpoint, a decisive role in the fulfillment of the national enterprise had been reserved for the collectivity of class-conscious workers since the Second Aliya. Thus, it was the unique sense of "together" that would abet the cohesion of the Jewish national society, and not the other way around. In this sense, in his opinion, it was necessary and important to distinguish between the socionational situation in the Diaspora and that in Palestine. In reference to the Diaspora, the "class phraseology" of the Bund should not be accepted, since the Jews' social condition there was abnormal, unlike that of the peoples among which the Jews dwelled. However, when one compares the Diaspora with Palestine, one finds a paradox: the normal class distribution that does not exist in the Diaspora has already taken shape in Palestine. However, neither the working class nor the Labor Movement erects a barrier between itself and people; the opposite is the case. The integration of Socialism and nationalism lowers the barriers that separate them. Katznelson did admit that the two entities, the class and the people, had not interrelated smoothly in the past. This, he explained, was because the Zionist Labor Movement had inherited a "maskilic" tradition—a tradition of condescension that originated in the Jewish Enlightenment—and "did not have a people's outlook on class." As proof, Katznelson noted the movement's aloofness and estrangement from the "eastern Jews." He considered this dissociation not only a national disgrace but a blemish in the sense of class as well, because "The entire halutsic enterprise is worth doing only insofar it does not confine itself to the circle of He-haluts." After all, "It is our consciousness that *we are acting on behalf of the entire Jewish people,* but in fact we were less cognizant than anyone else of the simple path *to the ordinary Jew,* the candidate for our movement, who is ours in a deeper sense than the formal mission of the Histadrut." This is because "Socialism demands that we give him an opportunity to change his life. Failing this, it has no right to posture as Socialism. Such a movement is aristocratic, proletarian in terms of ideals but devoid of grassroots roots in essence."[16] Therefore, the Labor Movement should seek paths to people's hearts. Instead, the movement sends its message mainly to very young people, in utter disregard of people who are still young and have "beards and sidelocks," as he put it. To reinforce his arguments, Katznelson concluded emphatically, "In no other labor movement in the world do you find such conduct."

Notably, for Katznelson, the Labor Movement's zealous pursuit of the "Zionist klal" stemmed from its loyalty to Klal Yisrael and not the other way around. "We realized [from the outset]," Katznelson asserted, "that the Zionist enterprise *is not one in which one part of the nation would participate and another part would have no foothold whatsoever.*"[17] Only due to "the vulgarization of the class ideology," in which even large portions of the Labor Movement in Palestine were complicit, "have we gone so far as to neglect this truth." Katznelson was referring both to the attitudes traditionally held in the Second Aliya period and the 1920s and also to Yosef Sprinzak's remarks. In contrast and in full accord with Ben-Gurion's political goals, he stressed that a Labor Movement that aspires to the Zionist leadership ought to make strenuous efforts to mobilize the Jewish masses for the Zionist enterprise. This, in Katznelson's opinion, is *a bitter and tragic necessity,* since "It is not a question of a mere coalition, the sort of thing that everyone does; it goes much farther than that" because of the disparity between the magnitude of the national mission and the paucity of political strength to lead the nation toward its fulfillment. To Katznelson's mind, the way to resolve the existential national contradiction that the Labor Movement faced is not by political action but by applying education—among the young above all but for the masses as well.

Thus, the debate among Mapai stalwarts in 1932 revealed three attitudes toward Klal Yisrael. The first was held by members of the cooperative settlement movement, which followed the elitist pioneering tradition of personal Socialist Zionist fulfillment. This outlook, by necessity and conscious choice, drew a line between the Jewish masses and the select groups that were acting to build the future. The second approach, that of Berl Katznelson, was an ideational and political synthesis. Katznelson explained the integration of Zionism and Socialism as a necessity for the fulfillment of national goals, and to apply it at the political level pioneering working class would have to reach out to the masses—to act not only *for them* but also *with them*. In this matter, relating to the pioneering movement's crucial role in mobilizing the Jewish people for Zionism, Sprinzak and Katznelson were in full agreement except with regard to the Zionism–Socialism synthesis.

The third position, Ben-Gurion's, may be defined as a practical existential one. Ben-Gurion noted the material distinction between Zionism as a national idea and Socialism as a social aspiration but insisted that a combination of both doctrines be fulfilled in the act of building the Jewish national society. Accordingly, in the existential sense, Ben-Gurion viewed his goal of building a political coalition in the Zionist Organization on behalf of national endeavor, under the leadership of Mapai or of the Labor Movement, as both Zionist *and* Socialist for the individual and for the many individuals who would play an active role in building the society in Palestine.

The difference between the isolationist approach of the rural settlement leaders and Katznelson's and Sprinzak's integrative approach was one of politics and psychology, not of essence. Both sustained an organic integration of Zionism and Socialism. The first-mentioned, however, demanded dissociation from the people for the sake of this integration; the latter expressed the need to reach out to the people. In contrast, Katznelson's approach was differentiated from Ben-Gurion's at the level of substance. After all, only a minority of Jews and Zionists were Socialists, and the separation of Socialism from nationalism generally, and in the Zionist formula particularly, meant the marginalization of Zionist thinking and action. This would soon become implicit in Ben-Gurion's "Zionist-etatist" doctrine as Chairman of the Zionist Executive and it recurred years later, after the State of Israel was formed, in the "Israel-etatist" outlook that Ben-Gurion championed as Prime Minister in the Government of Israel. Admittedly, there is no doubt

that for Ben-Gurion, with Katznelson's support, and for everyone who followed in their footsteps, the imposition of Labor Movement hegemony on
the Zionist movement was the goal. In practice, however, the accelerated
movement toward the "Zionist klal" gradually led him to a schism within the
"halutsic klal."

The debate over the "from class to people" question, which was mostly
theoretical in 1932, became political in 1933–1935 in two urgent contexts:
how to apportion immigration visas to Palestine after the Nazi accession
to power in Germany stimulated European Jews' interest in emigrating, and
the Ben-Gurion–Jabotinsky accord, concluded in London in 1934. At issue in
the first context was how to divide up the quota of immigration visas that the
Mandatory Government had allocated to the Jewish Agency. Until then, the
party key that was accepted among the members of the Zionist Organization
political coalition had always given "halutsic" aliya (pioneering immigration)
the highest priority. In view of the upturn in for visa applications, however, the
Zionist Executive came under public pressure to reserve some of the quota for
prospective immigrants of the middle class who, although not defined as
"pioneers," undertook to become rural settlers. When the Mapai Council debated this issue in January 1933, the two traditional attitudes, "from people to
class" and "from class to people," collided.[18]

The former approach was articulated by the senior personality in Ha-
po'el ha-Tsa'ir, Yosef Aharonowitz, and the latter was represented by David
Ben-Gurion. Aharonowitz expressed his views in extreme terms: Eretz Israel, he stated, is meant not for the Jewish masses but only for the select
portion of Jewry, the one capable of shouldering the burden of building the
new society. In a critique of Ben-Gurion's approach, he argued that Ben-
Gurion's inclination to reserve a larger quota of immigration visas for the
bourgeoisie was devoid of practical value; "In Zionist terms, he added, "it
would be a sin." After all, if the bourgeoisie were expected to become rural
settlers, then every piece of land placed in these private hands at the expense of cooperative settlement would no longer serve the national interest.

As for the moral question that preoccupied Ben-Gurion—"Is our conscience clean, are we not doing others an injustice?"—Aharonowitz retorted
flatly, "We're not doing an injustice; we're doing the opposite: we are defending Zionism. The injustice is being done by others who wish to turn matters
upside-down."[19] In his opinion, the bourgeoisie should be encouraged to invest
in Eretz Israel but not to settle there because it is unfit to build a country. Its arrival would impair the building enterprise and the immigrants themselves
would not stay for long, as had happened during the Fourth Aliya crisis.

David Ben-Gurion, in contrast, took an "etatist" Zionist-klal stance even
though he had not yet become Chairman of the Zionist Executive

(a promotion that would occur in August 1933 at the XVIII Zionist Congress). In his opinion, the upsurge in aliya applications left no choice but to reserve some visas for petit bourgeoisie circles, since "It is impossible to be in a situation for several years where Eretz Israel is a place of refuge but we take the stance—which is also of no utility to us—that 'certificates' [immigration visas] are for a certain kind [of Jew] only." He then asked the kibbutz representatives how one could imagine that immigrants might follow only one path, that leading to the kibbutz, since some would opt for a different one.

To reinforce his position, Ben-Gurion invoked a principled argument and an original historical assessment. In principle, he stressed, the Labor Movement had always accepted the notion that, rather than aliya being meant to save 'olim (Jewish immigrants), "We want aliya so that the 'olim will save the country."[20] By saying this, Ben-Gurion revealed a fundamental Zionist truth and set a political rule that would be manifested twenty years later, when Israel experienced mass immigration. Practically speaking, however, in all waves of immigration, the immigrants were rarely appreciated as saviors of the country. Even Ben-Gurion himself did not wage an all-out struggle—as he made sure to do in other fields—to invest this unifying ethos, the very core of the Zionist Klal Yisrael idea, with greater substance in daily national life.

Yosef Sprinzak occupied the middle ground. He admitted that psychologically he identified with his colleagues who criticized Ben-Gurion's plan. For reasons of political common sense, however, he advised against turning the issue into a problem of principle. Zionists at large, he explained, might construe such a move as evidence that the Labor Movement was concerned only for itself in apportioning "certificates" and had thereby abandoned the severely distressed petit bourgeois Jewish masses. Therefore, he proposed a compromise approach that would create a way to increase middle-class aliya without forsaking the interests of the pioneering movement so that the latter could maintain its status as an elite of "doers." For example, he opposed a motion by his colleague Eliezer Kaplan to allow working members of the petit bourgeois to join He-haluts on an individual basis. "If we expand He-haluts so that it admits ordinary [Jews]," Sprinzak warned, "*it will not be halutsic.*" By the same token, if the Labor Movement continues to toe the rigid halutsic line, then "The people will hate us even though we will be building its future."[21] Unbeknownst to him, he was foretelling the outcome of relations between the kibbutzim and the mass immigration of the 1950s. In both periods, the 1930s and the 1950s, the pioneering settlement movement and the masses of immigrants were culturally estranged. In the years at issue in this discussion, however, they were buffered by an ideological outlook that no longer existed twenty years hence.

In November 1933, pursuant to this debate, Berl Katznelson spoke at a labor meeting in Tel Aviv about his impressions of a visit to central and eastern Europe.[22] Emotionally he recounted evaluations of the state of Diaspora Jewry that had been expressed in a debate at the Mapai Council. He described the plight of Jewish refugees from Germany, who were being packed into cramped, dark rooms and made to queue for bowls of soup; he spoke about the economic distress of the Jewish masses in Poland, the decline in national culture, thuggish aggression in the Jewish street, the shallow nature of the critical debate in that country, and the inability of Western Jewish organizations to help Jewish refugees who wished to emigrate from their countries of residence. This led Katznelson to "a few conclusions about what we might do and what roles we might play in the Diaspora." In view of the situation, these remarks were seemingly meant as a backdrop for a transition from a "from people to class" attitude to one of "from class to people." Katznelson admitted that his movement had once had a dialectical attitude toward the Diaspora that was manifested in the awareness and belief that deliverance for the Diaspora would be achieved by dissociation from the Diaspora in favor of building Palestine. It was this viewpoint that had furnished the Labor Movement with moral justification for meeting its needs at the Diaspora's expense, especially when the needs included young people who would be torn from their parents and induced to abandon their communities. Now, Katznelson said, the situation had changed. The Yishuv had amassed material and human wealth, whereas the Diaspora was steadily losing ground and finding the basis of its existence increasingly unstable. Therefore, the Yishuv should offer it a brotherly helping hand. This, however, would not only benefit the Diaspora but also "*secure ourselves*" [italics in the original], since "we've got to realize that today's Diaspora is tomorrow's Eretz Israel." Therefore, "Those whom we discuss today dismissively and contemptuously will constitute Eretz Israel tomorrow. They will provide the forces for the building [enterprise]." The conclusion was Palestinocentric, of course: "In concern for what will be in this country tomorrow, we ought to turn around and extend a hand to the Diaspora." However, Katznelson's Palestinocentrism was "balanced," so to speak. It no longer aimed to exploit the Diaspora but proposed to assist it by offering it the only service it could render, acceptance as an equal partner in building the Jewish future in Palestine. The aliya Katznelson sought was not an influx of pioneers who would join the new labor society but rather working people from the withered, persecuted Jewish middle class, which, as Katznelson described it, paraphrasing the biblical account, "did not know Joseph." This, in his opinion, was the challenge that the Labor Movement would have to meet at the present time. Katznelson's attempt to bind Eretz Yisrael and the Diaspora in psychological unity as a precondition for practical unity led him, in a natural and obvious progression, to young people. In a lecture that year at a meeting of council of the Ha-no'ar ha-'Oved youth movement, he described the economic hardships and cultural decline of Diaspora Jewry, especially in Poland, in even bolder terms.[23]

In his remarks to the young people, as in his lecture to the audience of workers, Katznelson expressed his greatest concern about "psychological relations between young people here and there. . . . Young people in Palestine," he admitted, "do not feel that they are the youth of the nation, do not feel connected with the Jewish masses, and even when they acknowledge their connections with the Yishuv they do not consider themselves part of the Jewish people at large." Thus, it had been since the Second Aliya period. Palestine-born members of the *moshavot* (noncooperative "colonies") had also felt this way when A. D. Gordon proposed that they establish a joint organization. Nothing whatsoever had changed since then: "The young Jews who climb down from the benches of the high schools and go abroad to study are a long way from understanding Jewish life there; the baggage they prepare for their departure is skimpy." This has to do with the fact that "Many young people in Palestine have scanty and weak Jewish roots that are implanted neither in the pioneering enterprise nor in the Jewish people. Therefore, many dangers lurk for them." Consequently, not only for the young people but generally speaking, "The satiated, self-satisfied Yishuv, resting on its placid laurels, is turning the Zionist idea of 'negation-of-the-Diaspora' as a way of life into estrangement from Jewish life and Jewish distress." By implication, "negation-of-the-Diaspora" means the opposite of dissociation from the Diaspora. It denotes full partnership with the Diaspora by study of the past and creation of a psychological bond in the present. The current situation is quite the opposite: study of contemporary Jewish life is avoided, "as if we are nothing but members of an aristocratic people in the past and a sovereign people in the future—and [as if] there is no Jewish people at the present time, with its agonies and sufferings and effervescence and needs. We ought to educate youth to be not only citizens of their country, but also of their people."[24] By expressing himself this way, the radical Zionist, Berl Katznelson, of all people, accepted the Bund's criticism of Zionism. By building the Yishuv in Palestine, Katznelson admitted, Zionism was disengaging from Diaspora Jewry. However, there was a fundamental difference between them: what the Bund considered a deliberate policy, driven by Zionist ideology, Katznelson viewed as a natural cultural phenomenon that is essentially anti-Zionist and, therefore, contrary to the Klal Yisrael perspective as well. Accordingly, they reached different conclusions. The Bund, practically speaking, wrote off the Yishuv as a negligible and unimportant part of the Jewish people. By so believing, it became as much a "negator of the Yishuv" as some segments of Zionism were "negators-of-the Diaspora."

To Katznelson's mind, in contrast, exile (*galut*) was an inseparable part of the Jewish resurrection. That very year, the Labor newspaper *Davar* ran an article by Katznelson under the headline, "Destruction and Uprooting." In the article, Katznelson expressed pained protest about a decision by the leadership of one of the youth movements to require members to attend summer camp on the Ninth of Av—"the very night when the Jewish people laments its destruction, enslavement, and the bitterness of its exile."[25] Even when this is done without prior intent, the very unawareness of the act is the most troubling thing of all. After all, "What is the value and the product of a liberation movement that lacks *rootedness* and indulges in *forgetfulness,* [a movement that] instead of developing and deepening its members' sense and knowledge of [their] origins, blurs [their] memory of whence they came and cuts the fibers along which the movement feeds its marrow?"[26] Remembrance of the destruction of the Temple, and the preservation of this remembrance throughout those generations of exile, constitute the origins of the "renaissance movement" and "the strength of the vital, coherent symbol that produces fruit in a people's history." Thus, remembrance of the destruction, the sense of exile, and the ardor to create a renaissance are one and the same, not only as a heritage, but also as a spiritual and cultural reality that must exist today and in advance to tomorrow.

Many responded to Katznelson's remarks and most of them were critical. The critics dealt mainly with the negative attitude of the Orthodox toward the national renaissance endeavor and everything it embodied. Katznelson responded to them in an article titled "Everlasting Origins."[27] Here, countering the critics, he argued emphatically that the worldview and cultural reality of the Labor Movement shared some of the religious tradition of Klal Yisrael, since "The nation's memory knew in very simple ways *to inspire every Jewish soul around the globe at one heavy moment."* Therefore, mourning for the destroyed Temple on the Ninth of Av is an unsurpassable way to express the connection between the Jewish renaissance movement in Palestine and the worsening situation in the Diaspora countries after the upturn in anti-Semitism and, in particular, the Nazi accession in Germany. Accordingly, those in Palestine should not assert that they have been redeemed "until our exile ends."[28] By implication, the basic concepts of Klal Yisrael speak not of partial redemption of the Jewish people but only of total redemption. This explains the importance, in Katznelson's eyes, of transmitting this heritage from his generation to the young people who had been born and were being raised in Palestine. They must be taught that had this historical heritage not been maintained, albeit in religious form, the Zionist Movement would not have fathered the likes of Hayyim Nahman Bialik, Yosef Hayim Brenner, and Aharon David Gordon, who in their yearnings to return to Eretz Yisrael embodied the continuation of Yehuda Halevy's poetry.

Katznelson's remarks were not devoid of political calculus; they were meant to encourage cooperation between the Labor Movement and the two Religious Zionist factions—the Mizrachi movement and the Ha-poʻel ha-Mizrachi organization—that participated in the Zionist Organization and the Histadrut. Katznelson, like Wiktor Alter, considered religious faith the individual's own business and ruled out religious coercion as a spiritual and political phenomenon. However, the reasoning of Klal Yisrael politics prompted Katznelson, unlike Alter, to take large steps for the cause of collaboration with the religious workers who belonged to the Histadrut. When members of Kiryat Hayim opposed the construction of a synagogue that very year, he told them, "If you ask me what I want, a Socialist health service without Ha-poʻel ha-Mizrachi, with a non-kosher kitchen, or a kosher kitchen with Ha-poʻel ha-Mizrachi, I would choose the partnership with Ha-poʻel ha-Mizrachi. Socialism has to balance its profits against its losses."[29] Indeed, from the national standpoint, this balance sheet was much more meaningful, if not fateful, for the Labor Movement than for the Bund.

A year after the debate over the aliya policy, Mapai tumbled into a pregnant political controversy over the Ben-Gurion–Jabotinsky accord, signed in London in 1934. The purpose of this agreement was to regularize relations between the Zionist Organization and the Revisionist Movement in two respects: the status of the Revisionist Party in the Zionist Organization and relations between the Histadrut and the Revisionist Party in Palestine in regard to labor relations and, particularly, the right to strike. The accord was comprised of two parts: a political agreement signed by Ben-Gurion on behalf of the Zionist Executive and a "labor agreement" that was presented to Mapai for discussion and, after a passionate debate, was handed over to a plebiscite of Histadrut members—which defeated it by a narrow majority.[30]

The first agreement, pertaining to the Zionist Movement, directly addressed the question of the existence of a Zionist klal but was not debated by the Labor Movement. Instead, the movement, especially in its Mapai faction, heatedly discussed the possibility of an agreement on labor relations with the Revisionist Party, which was very widely viewed as a Fascist movement. However, the Klal Yisrael question came up in full fury in the course of this tumultuous debate.

Yitzhak Tabenkin, champion of the halutsic-class ethos, explicitly labeled the Revisionists as Fascists. The Bundists also drew this analogy, but of course they overstated the case and extended it to Zionism at large. For Tabenkin, a loyalist of the dialectic way of thinking, the working class' right to strike was an absolute entitlement that no player or agreement should restrain. It is this right that lends the class the historical strength that carries "the ideal to its people and to all peoples," he said.[31] The Bund would surely have accepted this phrasing had it been stated in a non-Zionist context. As for Zionism's goal of building a new society, a goal of Utopian or ideal complexion, Ben-Gurion also would have agreed with it but would have rejected its methods of struggle for reasons of political interests.

From Ben-Gurion's standpoint, it was the political change in the standing of the Labor Movement in the Zionist Organization—from a minority to the political mainstream—that entailed a change in the movement's perception of the Zionist klal. "For all these years," he explained, "we have imposed our Zionist doctrine by means of others. Now there are no others. Now we must go the rest of the way by ourselves."[32] This is a necessity from the standpoint of Zionist-klal politics, "not because our strength in the Zionist administration is about to decline in the Executive; it is about to increase—there is no doubt whatsoever that this matter is conditioned on the logic of Zionism in [the process of] its fulfillment. We must be adamant about this."[33] Thus, the "halutsic-klal" has become the political leader of the Zionist klal. This development, in Ben-Gurion's opinion, means a transition from a class that has a halutsic interest, which is also partly a Zionist interest, to a class that represents the Zionist interest at large. Thus, just as Ben-Gurion had repudiated the Zionism-as-Socialism equation three years earlier, he now expressed doubt about the absolute identity of the interests of the working class and those of Zionism. They overlapped only partly, he said. "The sum of the interests of all Palestine workers does not fit into the historical interests of Zionism and is not identical. . . . Our mission is on behalf of Zionist history."[34] Notably, Ben-Gurion did not intend to identify with all parties and movements in the Zionist Movement. He and his comrades agreed that this was not the case. Instead, he put forward a far-reaching and novel claim of principle: the ideal of the Labor Movement and the historical mission of Zionism are not exactly one and the same. A generation later, this line of argumentation led him out of the Zionist Organization. Therefore, he asked his colleagues to admit only that the social processes that were prompting masses of Jews to move to Palestine and transforming petit bourgeois Jews into workers and farmers there fulfilled the Zionist vision even if these Jews were not motivated by materialistic ideology or a Socialist Utopian vision. Later he repeated this claim, too, in reference to the immigration of Jews from Islamic countries. In the 1930s, it reflected the early coalescence of Ben-Gurion's *mamlakhtiyut* (etatism) outlook, in which policymaking tilts in the direction of the Jewish klal "insofar as the interests are Zionist interests, even if they are not Labor interests." To fulfill and manage these diverse interests, political enforcement power was needed. The Zionist Organization had no such power at the state level because it did not represent a state. "A state fights against anti-statist phenomena by statist means. We are not a state and we do not have the tools of a state. We are a 'quasi-state' and we have quasi-state needs. Let us not forget the great difference between a state and a 'quasi-state.' There is an enormous difference."[35]

Katznelson, unlike Ben-Gurion, pinned no hopes on the political agreement with the Revisionists in the Zionist Organization. In his view, the Revisionist Party was intrinsically incapable of accepting the yoke of "Zionist-klal" discipline. However, he did favor the "labor agreement" because it created a class-based avenue of dialogue between workers on job. He regarded this chance as a great achievement for the unity of the "Zionist-klal." After all, "In terms of political Zionism, I consider it [a way to] remove innumerable obstacles in our political war against the Revi-sionists."[36] Thus, more than Katznelson valued the agreement in itself, he regarded it as a weapon in the struggle against the Revisionists—a weapon that might prevent fissure in the Zionist Organization.

Therefore, Katznelson took heated exception to Tabenkin's approach because he considered it a manifestation of separatism from the opposite direction, the dogmatic Left. He rejected the sanctification of the unlim-ited right to strike and asked his comrade pointedly, "Is that why you're a man of 'Ein Harod?"[33] Zionist passion aside, Katznelson made an ideo-logical and political argument: not every national authority in labor rela-tions is Fascist. Such authorities exist even in countries that have deep-seated democratic traditions, such as Britain. Ultimately, Katznelson ruled, "Our supreme national authority *is* 'Ein Harod! The national author-ity built 'Ein Harod. 'Ein Harod was built neither by the class struggle in its conventional European form nor by the works of private capital."[38]

Katznelson was aware of the paradox of 'Ein Harod as a symbol and an expression of national authority. 'Ein Harod represented the crux of the Labor Movement's strength as a servile elite, a strength that originated mainly in its separatism vis-à-vis Klal Yisrael. Katznelson appreciated the strength of this halutsic Zionist separatism and acknowledged its erstwhile contribution. However, he expressed concern that the separatist strength, which had once been constructive, might now become a destructive factor in view of the changes in the state of Diaspora Jewry. Therefore, "It is time to dispose of the 'I am, and there is none but me' [Zeph. 2:15] way of thinking, the notion of

'I'm the nation and everyone else is the enemy.' One cannot apply governing power that way, let alone attain it. In some matters, you have to listen to the soul of the people."[39]

The direct and indirect political and ideological debates over the Klal Yisrael question came to an end with the polemics surrounding the "London agreements."

These debates had greater practical political significance than their predecessors in the 1920s, because the Labor Movement had in the meantime risen to political leadership in the Zionist klal. For this reason, just as Chaim Weizmann fought to expand the Jewish Agency on behalf of a Zionist interest that was identical with the interest of Klal Yisrael, so did Ben-Gurion now prod his movement to begin a "from class to people" progression that denoted, above all, national responsibility. Here we should again note the principal difference between the Bund and the Labor Movement. In the 1930s, as we have seen, the Bund expanded its sphere of national responsibility to include groups outside the working class, that is, the impoverished Jewish masses, and defense of the Jews against anti-Semitic attacks at large. However, the Bund never moved beyond eastern Europe Jewry, whereas the Labor Movement, by extending its dominion to the Zionist klal, eventually expanded its auspices to the global "Jewish klal," Klal Yisrael, as well.

A short time later, historical events, political developments, and global crisis forced Klal Yisrael to abandon all ideological debate in order to fight for its existence. In view of the Arab uprising in 1936–1939; the Palestine partition plan that followed the recommendations of the Peel Commission; the 1939 White Paper, which aimed to revoke the Balfour Declaration; the beginning of World War II; the efforts to establish a Jewish army; awareness of the Holocaust; and preparations for political struggle toward the establishment of a Jewish state, the Klal Yisrael question ceased to be the topic of ideological political debate; instead, it became an existential problem.

The decade between 1936 and the end of World War II (1945) may be divided into two periods in terms of Klal Yisrael. The first period is 1936–1939, when the Palestine question became increasingly central on the Jewish agenda due to the Arab uprising, the national debate over the establishment of a Jewish state, and the Jewish refugee problem, which defied comprehensive solution. During the second period, starting with the beginning of the war, Klal Yisrael became a problem of both the Zionist klal and the Jewish klal—initially in the quest for ways to rescue Jews and later, at the end of the war, in the struggle to resettle the Holocaust survivors in Palestine.

The debate and controversy over the partitioning of Palestine affected the Klal Yisrael issue in several ways. First, the issue was evident in the role that anti-Zionist and non-Zionist players, such as the rabbis of Agudath Israel, the leaders of the American Jewish Committee, and the heads of the Bund played in it. Their involvement in the matter alongside the parties in the Zionist Movement transformed the Jewish state question into a Klal Yisrael problem. Second, the Zionist leadership under Weizmann and Ben-Gurion became convinced that the Mandate regime could not answer the Jews' distress and that, therefore, a small state in the Mandate area, which would provide a partial solution to this distress, was preferable to a Mandate that would prevent it.[40]

Precisely here, however, the paradox that public leaders regularly face stands out. It was Berl Katznelson, who understood the distress of the eastern European Diaspora better than any other leader, who opposed partition. Others, such as his comrade Ben-Gurion, believed that in the absence of Jewish statehood, under the existing political circumstances, Zionism would find itself helpless to build the national society and to rescue those who needed it. This is exactly what happened. When the war broke out, the Zionist Movement and the Jewish people at large, lacking a sovereign state that could be a crucial ally for the anti-Nazi forces, tumbled into a state of helplessness in all matters pertaining to the rescue of Jews.

In recent years, a series of important studies has been written about the actions of the Zionist Organization and, especially, its Executive in Palestine, which was headed by the Labor Movement. The titles of these works—"Leadership in a Trap," "Mute," "Awareness and Helplessness," "Arrow in the Mist"—attest to the movement's plight.[41] Indeed, at first, until 1942, the mist enveloped all leaders in *ignorance* of the extent and essence of the disaster of European Jewry. Afterwards, when *awareness* of the magnitude of the Holocaust, they were helpless in finding a way to effect rescue amidst the international political, military, intelligence, and material realities.

The impermeable blanket of mist drove a wedge of sorts between the leadership, headed by Ben-Gurion, which indefatigably and surreptitiously tried to poke holes in it despite its scanty political strength and limited financial resources, and the Yishuv society, the Zionist Organization, and the Labor Movement, the last-mentioned of which carried on as if nothing had changed. The movement's business as usual behavior may be judged in two ways: to its discredit, as a reflection of disregard of the situation, or understandingly, as a focusing of thought and effort on the one field in which it could apply the Jewish will and power on behalf of the national cause. In this sense, the ability to deal with the normal amidst the abnormal, consciously or not, generated a great deal of collective strength that, under the given situation, dictated the order of feasible national priorities. Therefore, the members of the Mapai Central Committee busied themselves with mundane issues: internal party affairs, Histadrut elections, relations with the Mandatory government, the struggle between Weizmann and Ben-Gurion, the Biltmore program, and so forth. The party forums did not subject the ongoing murder of Klal Yisrael to direct debate; even indirectly the matter came up only a few times. The Jewish Agency Executive, headed by Ben-Gurion, treated the topic differently, repeatedly debating it in all of its tragic significance and in two contexts—rescue possibilities and the preference of some candidates for rescue over others. The latter issue came up in view of the possibility that the "rescuers" would have to distinguish among non-Zionist or even anti-Zionist Jews and loyal Zionists, especially members of pioneering youth movements. Ben-Gurion equivocated on this tragic question. Once he spoke about rescuing *every* Jew whose life was in danger; on another occasion he stated vehemently that "For the future of this country, young people and children are more important"—more important not only than non-Zionists but even than Labor Movement veterans.[42]

In fact, however, the tragic choice did not exist. In the few rescue opportunities that presented themselves, the Zionist Movement organs did not differentiate among candidates. In its essence and in historical terms, however, the debate is reminiscent of the choice made by R. Yohanan Ben-Zakkai, who set out from besieged Jerusalem, with the permission of the Roman emperor, to save Yavne and its sages. From the standpoint of Ben-Gurion and his Labor Movement colleagues, the Yishuv was no less important for the Jewish nation—Klal Yisrael—than Yavne and its sages were, in the view of R. Yohanan, for the Jewish religion and faith. Both were convinced that the nation's survival depended on a handful of individuals— sages or pioneers.

Nevertheless, the Diaspora was an inseparable part of the Zionist worldview of the leaders of Mapai, Ben-Gurion, Tabenkin, and Katznelson— as Jewish masses who would settle in Palestine after the war, as warriors for Jewish dignity in the ghetto uprising, or as a national culture from which no divorce should be contemplated. The Fifth Mapai Convention, held in October 1942, only a few weeks before explicit reports about the systematic annihilation of European Jewry arrived, devoted itself totally to internal dissension that would eventually cause the party to split. Ben-Gurion, however, used the occasion to deliver a lecture about the state of the nation. In the spirit of his interpretation of the Biltmore resolutions, he looked forward to the "transfer" of millions of Jews to Palestine after the war, assuming that they could not rebuild their lives in their countries of residence, especially Poland.

As he articulated his vision of mass aliya, which surpassed even Herzl's imagination in its magnitude, he revealed something, as if en passant, that evidently troubled him greatly and attested to the "separatist" trends of thought that members of the pioneering elites entertained.

> There are ideologues among us who say that Zionist ideology says nothing about Jewish refugees. [That] Zionism was not created for refugees. [That] Zionism is the product of our tradition and our love of [our] country, the product of our consciousness and our will to establish complete lives and live in towns and villages, [attend] our university, speak Hebrew, develop our industry, and so on. But this Zionist ideology has nothing to do with refugees. We would be Zionists even if the Jews were not in trouble. Zionism does not depend on Jewish troubles.[43]

Then Ben-Gurion countered the allegation of those unidentified ideologues:

> I do not know if Zionism needs the Jewish troubles or not and I do not know what Zionist ideology is. [This is not the time to probe] the metaphysical essence of Zionist ideology. What has ideology-shmideology got to do with us? *There's a Jewish people that's being wiped out.* There will be millions of Jews whom, if Hitler doesn't annihilate them, will we be able to rescue and bring here and bestow on them that same life, that *human Jewish face,* and this deep involvement, this sense of homeland, and this sense of independence—like ours—or not?[44]

Notwithstanding his vision of mass aliya, Ben-Gurion remained a realist. Convinced that he knew his fellow Jews, he was sure that not all would wish to resettle in Palestine. He reasoned that if the United States opened its gates to immigration after the war, "[most of the] Jewish masses might flow to America and only a minority will come here." However, he stated with a firmness that proved accurate after the war, "I tell you that America will not open its gates. The American Jews are afraid of such a thing." The United States would be willing to help solve the refugee problem in other countries. However, the prewar international experience proved that the Jews' problem could be solved only in Palestine, and this should be stated in full awareness.

> There has never been so tragic a question (a tragic question is one that pertains to the lives and expectations of millions of people) . . . for the Jewish people than the present one: does this

address exist or does it not? [I do not ask this in view of] Zionist
ideology. Zionist ideology did not teach me what can be done in
Palestine. No ideology could have taught it to me. I learned it in
this country. Apart from Zionist ideology, there's a country here
named Eretz Yisrael.[45]

Ben-Gurion's impassioned, enthusiastic remarks allude to a contrast
between Zionist ideology and the existential Zionist experience in Palestine. This was probably no slip of the tongue. After all, acknowledgment of
the occasional contradiction between ideology and reality had been part of
Ben-Gurion's baggage since the Second Aliya, by which time he had already determined that reality would dictate the nature of Socialism in Palestine. Therefore, he was able to replace his "from people to class" outlook,
which assigned the pioneering Labor Movement a starring role in the fulfillment of Zionism—as he had argued during the Second Aliya and in the
1920s—with a "from class to people" approach in the 1930s and a vision of
mass "transfer" of Jewish refugees after the war. Thus, one may understand
how, when Ben-Gurion visited Germany after the war, he regarded the
Holocaust survivors, too, as a collective that had no choice, even if it
wanted one, and as leverage for the building of Palestine alongside the
other sources of leverage, the pioneers and the grassroots, that were already
at work in the country.

Thus, at the convention where he doomed Mapai to political schism,
Ben-Gurion conducted himself with a sense of national disaster, even
though he did not know its magnitude. Furthermore, as was his wont at
fateful times, he entertained Utopian hopes instead of allowing himself to
drown in despair. Thus, his feverish imagination envisaged the hundreds of
thousands, if not millions, of Jews who would come to Palestine in the aftermath of the disaster. He even saw the possibility of building enormous
ships that would deliver them to the country's shores.[46]

Several months later, after the Warsaw ghetto uprising, Yitzhak
Tabenkin spoke about the pioneering elite's responsibility to the Jewish people, most of which had already been annihilated in Europe. During those
terrible days, as the sounds of the ghetto rebels' gunfire fell silent, he considered it important to stress the importance of upholding Jewish dignity.
However, he added emphatically, the pioneer who fights for his people's dignity should not be liberated from the Jewish historical heritage and should
retain the memory of the Jewish life that has been destroyed. Thus, he asked:

May we turn aside and liberate ourselves from the dominion of
this memory, from the imperative of this death? The millions of

Jews are gone; we have no others to replace them. We lack three or four million Jews not only as millions of individual people but also as millions who had lived together and were a *center* . . . The 'mother-Diaspora,' the mother of Judaism, our own mother, your mother. We are the descendants of those Diaspora Jews. They preserved that fraternity, that profound altruism, that Jewish history, and they carried the sense of [Jewish] *unity*.[47]

The supreme expression of this Jewish unity is the upholding of Jewish dignity. The partners in this [endeavor] are, on the one hand, the Zionists, from Ahad Haʿam and Bialik and from the Kishinev pogrom up to the pioneering movements and, on the other hand, the Bundists, since "that party took up the cause of Jewish independence, demanding the Jewish right to self-organization, the Jewish right to fight, from the stand against the anti-Semitic Czarist regime in Russia to the Warsaw ghetto uprising." Therefore, this tradition connects "*in proud steadfastness* . . . from Hirsh Lekert to Zygielboim to Toussia and Sagan in one line, one education."[48] Thus, the Bundists (Zygielboim), the stalwarts of the halutsic movement (Toussia), and members of Poʿaley Tsiyyon (Sagan) are all part of the fighting Jewish klal.

Whereas Tabenkin placed fighters at the forefront of the unifying and cohesive reality of Klal Yisrael, Katznelson placed there "the oneness of the Jewish fate, the intergenerational partnership." As early as 1940, he told his colleagues, "We should relive the Crusader era, the Inquisition era, and the Chmielnicki era not only as days of violence but also as days of *heroism*. We should open the 'book of tears' and similar [books] to ourselves, our youth group leaders, and our schoolchildren."[49]

Four years later, shortly before his death, Katznelson gave a lecture to the Mapai "Young Guard"[50] in which he spoke in anguish about the uncoupling of Yishuv youth from the cultural heritage of the Diaspora. He also presented evidence of indifference among young Jews in Palestine about the very fate of Diaspora Jews. The Bundists' claim that Zionism was engineering a divorce between the Jewish klal and segments of the nation might come true, he warned bitterly. Then he asked, "Whom do we regard as the carriers of Zionist fulfillment? Theoretically, we say, it's the Jewish people. But are we living in such a way that the concept of *Jewish people* is real for us or not?" [italics in the original].[51] Katznelson expressed the gist of his concern in the confused idea, which beset him constantly at the time, that the Bundist prediction—that the Zionist and Hebrew Yishuv in Palestine would deliberately divorce itself from the Jewish masses in the Diaspora—would indeed come to pass. Then, within a few generations, "The Hebrew child in the Yishuv, deep inside, will not feel that he is part of the Jewish people, even if he has some idea about Jewish independence or Jewish Socialism. And if large-scale aliya transpires, we may become not a small tribe but a large tribe, but a *different* tribe" [italics in the original].[52]

The intriguing thing here is that the name of the movement's stubborn and uncompromising historical rival, the Bund, came up at this fateful hour in Jewish history. It surfaced not only due the fear that its anti-Zionist predications would come to pass but also because, throughout its history, its members had defended the national cause heroically. The leaders of the Bund did not reciprocate Katznelson's high-mindedness. However, the difference between the movements in their interrelations stemmed essentially from different perceptions of Klal Yisrael. In the teachings of the Labor Movement, the Bund belonged to Klal Yisrael despite its refusal to take part in it. The Bund did not share this feeling toward the Labor Movement. We find the most pronounced manifestation of the Labor Movement's attitude in remarks by Katznelson in 1944, shortly before his death, at a seminar of the Socialist Youth, an organization of young members of Mapai.[53] His messages to these young people had threefold symbolic significance. First, since they were articulated very shortly before Katznelson's death, they may be regarded as his ideological and intellectual historical testament to the successor generation. Second, his remarks were informed by explicit knowledge of the annihilation of European Jewry and the world whence the pioneering Labor Movement had emerged. Third, other currents of Jewish Socialism, foremost the Bund, to which Katznelson devoted much space in his descriptive sociocultural writings and ideological analyses, had been devastated as well.

Katznelson drew up a historical reckoning with the Bund, in which he stressed the ambivalence with which much of his movement had treated the rival movement. On the one hand, he continued the historical debate with the Bund that his movement had conducted from its first day. The main target of his polemic was the Bund's national separatism. Katznelson, like Dubnow in his time, censured the Bund for shirking "overarching national" responsibility so egregiously as to refuse to cooperate with Zionist groups in Jewish self-defense during the violence of 1905. From that point of departure, he proceeded directly to the Bund leadership in New York in the 1940s, which, in the very midst of the national devastation in Europe, continued to struggle furiously against Zionism and, in particular, against the Biltmore plan. He expressed rhetorical bewilderment about how "Jews, the few war refugees who had reached America from Poland, believe it their duty there to serve as agents of the Jewish workers in Poland, who may be dead by now, in thwarting the building of Palestine" because the Bund still considered itself an inseparable part of Poland even though Polish Jewry had been annihilated.[54] If the sin of national disunity were not enough, Katznelson also accused the Bund of inadvertently abandoning the Jewish masses to their tragic fate. He claimed that the Bund, from the time it was formed to the beginning of the war, had opposed not only aliya but also emigration in general and emigration to the United States in particular, which "might have saved another million Jews." Even that did not perturb the Bund's conscience; "instead of searching its historical soul, to this day it rests on the laurels of its hoary notions."[55] The reason, he continued, was the ideological and psychological tradition of the Bund, in which the theory of class struggle "required it to be *'broigez'* [embroiled in quarrel] *with Klal Yisrael, to stand apart from Klal Yisrael.*" Therefore, it had never developed "the willingness *to influence Klal Yisrael.*"[56]

Apart from the matter of emigration, these comments added nothing new to the traditional national polemic against the Bund. However, Katznelson concurrently delivered another historical assessment that, while hardly augmenting our understanding of this movement, attested to his own outlook on Klal Yisrael. Katznelson regarded most public endeavors of the Bund and its members as nationally important even if the Bund did not mean them to be so. In regard to Hirsh Lekert, the "Trumpeldor of the Bund," as I have termed him, he admitted, "He meant not to avenge the dignity of his people" but to defend the dignity of the proletariat. Just the same, "Even Lekert's revenge was invested with national importance, although he did not have this in mind: the very fact that a Jewish worker takes up the cudgels of war and forfeits his life for it."[57] Thus, the Bund, which objected to terrorist actions, transformed its sacrifice into a national ethos. Forty years later, Katznelson continued, it was Shmuel Zygielboim, who considered himself foremost a Socialist and a Jewish citizen of Poland, who "in his act of suicide showed himself to be a symbol of Jewish suffering, the most spirited manifestation of Jewish anguish, which no Zionist expressed in that situation as he did." By behaving as he did, Zygielboim proved to be not a narrow-minded member of a political party or a class but a *"national hero."*[58]

Underlying these personal acts of heroism and self-sacrifice was the revolutionary culture that the Bund had managed to implant in parts of eastern European Jewish society. As Katznelson put it, the Bund had demonstrated its merit not only by defending the Jewish worker against the oppression and exploitation of the Jewish bourgeoisie, but also by rebelling, "in a very great human effort," against the "intellectual dilution" that had overtaken the impoverished masses in the Jewish street. "It is the Bund that introduced the Jewish workers to the concepts of Socialism, struggle against exploitation, the will of the worker to acquire schooling, to learn, to develop."[59] As such, Katznelson admitted, "The Bund had tremendous influence on Zionist youth." For this reason, "[We had such] respect for its organizational strength, its control of the masses, that we negated ourselves somewhat. We respected [the Bund] because it engaged in *action* [italics in the original] at a time when Zionist youth had not yet done so."[60] Furthermore, at a time when Zionist youth still groped for the correct path with uncertain and false steps, the Bund's actions abounded with optimism about the possibility of solving the Jewish problem in the Diaspora countries.

Katznelson's remarks marked the continuation of a Zionist Labor Movement tradition of sorts that Ber Borochov had fathered forty years earlier. In 1906, after the revolution in Russia failed and the entire labor movement in Russia was at a nadir, Borochov cited the Bund in very favorably terms for the way it had coped with the crisis. "At that time," he said, "it revealed itself as *the only group* that did not lose touch with the living, with the working masses." As the other parties crumbled and the intelligentsia retreated from the public arena to its personal affairs, the Bund "continues to serve as the organic avant-garde of the movement, firmly implanted in the proletariat, its very flesh." Borochov, who termed himself a "principled opponent" of the Bund and considered the Bund's attitude toward the Jewish question fallacious and its politics harmful, nevertheless spoke out in appreciation of its activities. "As we acquaint ourselves with the Bund, we acquaint ourselves with the Jewish labor movement."[61] Even if Borochov wrote these lines in view of his disillusionment with the Zionist Organization, which prompted Po'aley Tsiyyon in Russia to secede from it in 1909, and even if he said it only as part of his vain attempt to forge a proletarian alliance with the Bund, his appreciation of this party at a time when the Labor Movement was "puny" was undoubtedly sincere.

All in all, Katznelson considered the Bund an unexceptional phenomenon in the exilic period of Jewish history. The Bund is powered, he said, by "the recondite force that acts in Jewish history, the force that seeks to sustain the Diaspora and fears the Zionist dream."[62] The Bund's outlook and feeling, he continued, are shared by liberals who believe in the naturalization of the Jews in their countries of residence and the fanatic Orthodox, who await the advent of the Messiah.

Katznelson was definitely right about the Diasporist ideology of the Bund, as the chapters of this study have noted, but the critical tenor of his comments attests not to negation-of-the-Diaspora but to the opposite. His parenthetical statement about the tragic results of the Bund's opposition to Jewish emigration to the United States, even if historically inaccurate,[63] signal a change in his attitude toward the Diaspora. As stated above, in the 1930s, in view of the distress of central European Jewry, he changed his mind about the proper relationship between the Yishuv and the Diaspora. From then on, he no longer considered them two warring national entities but rather complementary participants in the effort to maintain Jewish nationhood.

In 1942, about two years before his death, he stated near the end of a eulogy for Eliezer Yaffe, his friend and rival since the Second Aliya era,

> Some will say that Eliezer was a "new Jew" [and] that "there hadn't been a Jew like him in the past two thousand years." I tend to reject statements like these, even when they relate to people born in the Yishuv, the "sabras," and all the more to people who would not have been what they were had it not been for their "exilic" heritage.[64]

Katznelson's attempt to underscore the positive heritage of the Diaspora, including the Bund, may have been politically motivated as well. Katznelson, an opponent of the partitioning of Palestine, came out in favor of the Biltmore program even though he knew that it would lead to partitioning and that the resulting Jewish state would be unable to accommodate or contain a majority of the Jewish people. His reasons was that the Biltmore program constituted a basis on which most Jews could unite.[65] Therefore, his main concern for the future was how to maintain the integrity of Klal Yisrael by strengthening relations between Palestine and the Diaspora. This reading of events may, however, be a mere conjecture that Katznelson took to his grave prematurely.

About a year later, May 13, 1945, Ben-Gurion mentioned the Bund in a debate in the small Executive Committee about the Biltmore program and the likelihood that the Western powers, foremost the United States, would favor the establishment of a Jewish state. He took issue with the pessimistic views of Itzhak Gruenbaum and Rabbi Fishman, who had expressed doubt about the willingness of powers that had abandoned the Jews of Europe as they were being murdered by the millions to finance the establishment of a state for such Jews as survived. Ben-Gurion began his response by saying, "I understand why you feel that way." Then, with the typical glint that always managed to signal the intensity of Ben-Gurion's feelings about various issues, the Mapai leader took up the case of Arthur Zygielboim. "It was something of a symbolic act that a Bundist committed suicide. By doing it, he elevated the Bund." However, these "glints" expressed not only feelings but also ideological or political stances. Therefore, Ben-Gurion went on directly to state that Zygielboim's noble self-sacrifice "was an act of Bundist escapism. Anyone who does not believe in Zionism should go crazy or commit suicide. But we have Zionist faith. We believe in the Zionist solution."[66]

This remark, made en passant, gives clear evidence of the ambivalence of the Labor Movement leaders toward the Bund throughout their parallel careers: appreciation and admiration on the one hand, and staunch ideological and political opposition on the other.

SUMMARY

The main question in this part of the study was how severely the Klal Yisrael outlooks of the Bund and the Zionist Labor were affected by the emergency that befell European Jewry from the early 1930s to the end of World War II. The two chapters that discussed this period seem to have shown that as the situation worsened, each movement responded to the political plight of the Jewish people in different if not opposing ways. Thus, the separatism of the Bund vis-à-vis Klal Yisrael as an undivided national organism gathered momentum, precisely as the party displayed rising concern for the survival of the Jewish masses, which initially faced persecution and subsequently confronted death in the ghettos and murder in the extermination camps. Here lie the roots of the tragic contradiction in the Bund between Arthur Zygielboim's suicide, on the one hand, and the vacillations about whether to join the Zionists in the Jewish Fighting Organization in the Warsaw ghetto and the anti-Zionist positions taken by the party's representatives in the United States during the war, on the other hand.

In contrast, in the Labor Movement and especially in its largest party, Mapai, a process of rapprochement with the "Zionist klal" and, thence, to the "Jewish klal" ensued at the beginning of the decade and continued up to the beginning of World War II. It was a difficult road for the Labor Movement to follow; it entailed a great deal of ideological vacillation and political doubts. However, by the time the war began, the Labor Movement had positioned itself squarely in the midst of Klal Yisrael. It is here, in the principle of ab initio affiliation with Klal Yisrael, that the main difference between the Bund and the Labor Movement lies. This is also the root of the difference in the movements' regard for each other after the results of the Holocaust became known during the war. The respect that the Bund received from the leaders of the Zionist Labor Movement, due to their historical stance on behalf of Jewish national dignity, originated in their recognition of the Bund, notwithstanding the uncompromising dispute between the movements, as part of Klal Yisrael. The Bund leaders at the time had not yet found a way to reciprocate.

CHAPTER 7

FROM BUND TO BUNDISM, 1947–1985

There is no doubt about the existence of community of fate with regard to the Jewish people.

—E. Szerer

In the fourth period in Bund history, between the end of World War II and the late 1980s, the Bund made a slow and gradual rapprochement with Klal Yisrael. Its move in that direction took place in a "political desert" and lasted forty years, approximately as long as the Bund had existed from its birth until the beginning of World War II. It attests, more than anything else in Bund history, to the power of ideological zealotry, adherence to the political culture of a minority group, and the need for a sense of togetherness that emerges when people are isolated—all of which were put to the test just as the Bund ceased to be a party of political influence among the East European Jews that had ceased to exist. All that remained of the party were tattered remnants of the Polish Bund that clustered in the United States, Argentina, France, and Israel.

Thus, the Bund found itself in a tragic situation that was imposed on it but that it also chose. Along with the rest of Jewry, it mourned the annihilation of one-third of the Jewish people and its lost social and political base among the Jews of Poland. Nevertheless, it chose to maintain its separatism, which became even more conspicuous and intense in view of the triumph of Zionism in establishing the Jewish state and the general Jewish support that Israel received in its first decade—all of which in a Western Jewish society that practiced a lifestyle and culture that were totally different from those that had existed in the Bund's East European cradle. The Bund, which had inscribed war on Jewish poverty on its standard, now confronted a middle-class society that was economically strong and became even stronger after the war, a society that was rapidly integrating into the cultures of its European countries of residence and, in particular, the United

207

States. What is more, the civil equality that these masses enjoyed deprived the Bund of one of its most important concerns and causes in Poland.

The leaders of the Bund were aware of all three dimensions of their special tragedy—the annihilation of the Jews; the destruction of the party in eastern Europe, and the new reality in Western society—and they expressed this awareness boldly and overtly in their newspapers and conventions. The main question for them was to what extent, in view of the new situation, should the Bund rupture the cycle of separatism that it had built around itself up to World War II. This central problem fissured into subsidiary questions: Did the Bund, in its global dimension, need a new form of organization that would be compatible with reality? What political stance should it take vis-à-vis Zionism and the newly founded State of Israel? What essence and contents would Jewish nationhood acquire in Western society? What would be the substance of Jewishness in its new bipolar configuration of Israel and Diaspora? Finally, what does Democratic Socialism mean in terms of the national worldview of the Bund?

These questions relate directly and indirectly to the historical attitude of the Bund toward Klal Yisrael. They retained some of their ideological content but, in the aftermath of the Holocaust, had lost their political importance. Consequently, the national element in the Bund doctrine gained ideological weight at the expense of the Socialist element. As the question of collective Jewish cultural existence became more acute in the eyes of its leaders, the importance of the Bund's class consciousness weakened. As a result, paradoxically, the Bund came around to an Ahad-Ha'amic view of Jewish nationhood. However, it stationed Yiddish culture in the place of Hebrew culture and offered the new global political organization of Bund parties in lieu of the territorial "spiritual" center in Palestine and the political center in Israel. From then on, the Bund consciously adopted Simon Dubnow's national ideology as one might put on a piece of second-hand clothing. Thus, by choice and in full awareness, it became the quixotic defender of a Yiddish culture that was swiftly vanishing as the Jews integrated into the cultures of their countries of residence with ever-rising celerity—both as beneficiaries of these cultures and as contributions to their development. The Bund, however feeble it had become, wished to stanch and resist this trend of assimilation, be it deliberate or inadvertent, by dint of its belief in a renaissance of Yiddish as the language of culture of the Western Jewish masses. By so behaving, it steered itself into yet another "lofty paradox," if not the loftiest of all. In the past, the Bund's struggle for the status of national autonomy within the Russian Social Democratic Party and its conviction that Poland actually did belong to all its citizens and not only to the Poles were rooted in the social and political realities of their time. In contrast, the belief in a renaissance of Yiddish as a vehicle of national culture in the Western Diaspora was utterly unrealistic. Even though the leaders of the Bund viewed the situation soberly, they impaled themselves on their idealistic faith. Thus, the realists of the past became the Utopianists of the present. What is more, their cultural idealism escalated in inverse proportion to their political strength in society.

To carry out its mission in the field of Jewish national culture, the Bund had to find a political way to distinguish itself from other players. In the past, it had accomplished this with the help of the Communists, against whom it struggled; the Polish Socialists, with whom it debated; the anti-Jewish policies of the Polish government and the anti-Semitic movements, which it fought on behalf of the beleaguered Jewish masses; the Jewish clerics, whom it held in contempt; and the Zionists, toward whom it harbored uncompromising enmity. Of all of them, only Zionism was left, and Zionism, ironically, had come away with its greatest achievement—the establishment of the State of the Jews—after the disaster that befell the Jewish people. Thus, the attitude toward Zionism, with its various meanings, became an elixir of life for the vestigial Bund movement. It stimulated a prickly debate between the movement's two segments: the majority, which continued to reject Zionism radically, and the minority, which sought to coexist with Zionism on the basis of a partial compromise. Furthermore, the victory of Zionism presented the Bund with a reverse dialectical challenge, so to speak. From now on, from the Bund's standpoint, the national roles of both movements were reversed. For the Bund leaders and intellectuals, it was their own party that represented the idea and politics of Klal Yisrael and it was Zionism that was thwarting them. This intellectually fascinating flip-flop is the cardinal issue of concern in this chapter.

THE DISPUTE ABOUT ACCEPTING THE JEWISH STATE

The Bund held three world conventions during the first postwar decade: in Brussels in 1947, in New York in 1948, and in Montreal in 1955. All three debated the Klal Yisrael question continually in three concentric circles. The question in the innermost circle had to do with reorganizing the Bund on a global footing. In the middle circle, there was a political debate over the party's stance on the Palestine problem. The outer circle was reserved for the ideological problem, in which there were two matters of concern: the attitude toward Zionism and estimations and aims related to the future of the Diaspora. The debate over the establishment of a global organization of Bund parties in various countries began in late 1946. Until then, these parties interrelated on the basis of personal friendships and an ideological solidarity that had no institutional basis. In this matter, opponents and proponents of the idea engaged each other in a dispute of principle. The opponents argued that by establishing a worldwide organization, irrespective of its nature, the Bund would swerve from the historical ideological outlook that it had evinced since it had been founded, that is, that every "Bundist" Party belongs solely to its own nation-state. Deviation from this principle, if only by establishing a loose world organization, would vindicate the ideology of the Bund's great rival, Poʻaley Tsiyyon, which assumed that the Jewish proletariat, like the Jewish people, is nationally unique in a supraterritorial or global sense. Were the Bundists to go ahead with the global organization plan, the opponents charged, they would redefine the national affiliation of the globally dispersed Jews from civil-territorial-national to supraterritorial-national.

Most Bund leaders did not accept the opponents' reasoning. Foremost among them was Emanuel Szerer, undoubtedly the leading Bund intellectual in the thirty years following the war. As stated (in chapter 5) in regard to his activity in London, Szerer was inclined to political pragmatism that tailored itself to the new situation. Szerer's point of departure was that the destruction of Polish Jewry meant not only the loss of three million Jews, but also a risk to the very national existence of the Jewish people. Now that the natural and unquestioned Jewish cultural and national reality in Poland has tragically disappeared, he argued, a deliberate and focused mobilization for the rescue of the Jewish people from the menace of assimilation is needed, and to fight assimilation all forces loyal to Jewish nationhood should join ranks. Confronting the opponents of the idea, who argued that the Jewish worker did not need his own international organization since the class-based Socialist International existed, Szerer explained that the intention was not to establish a "Bundist International" but to found a Jewish national organization. After all, the International accepted labor parties of various nationalities as members, whereas Jewish workers who belonged to one people were at issue here. (*"Der internatsional nemt arum parteyn fun farshidene lender un felker, mir dakegn gehern takeh tsu farshidene lender ober tsu ayn folk."*) [1]

This was quite an ideological leap; it marked a change in direction relative to the national outlook that the Bund had entertained until the Holocaust.

The principled importance of the debate was reflected in the cautious compromise resolution that bridged the gap between the two outlooks. The convention agreed to establish a coordinating committee of Bund parties around the world but not a world organization of the Zionist sort. One doubts that the Bund parties in the various countries considered the coordinating committee politically important; they usually went about their public affairs independently of it. [2] In ideological terms and relative to its historical tradition, however, this was the Bund's last stop on its way to the "Jewish proletarian klal." The road began in the mid–1890s with recognition of the existence of Jewish masses that had particular social and linguistic indicators; this led to the establishment of the Bund in 1897. It continued with the coalescence of the party's attitude toward national cultural autonomy in 1901–1903 and its attempt to establish a broad-based Jewish labor organization in the 1930s.

These three "stops" were all territorial in nature, situated on east European (Russian and Polish) soil. The decision in Brussels, in contrast, was to establish a "Jewish proletarian klal" on a global basis. This time, however, the emphasis was pointed not at the Jewish workers' social class but at their national affiliation, since if the criterion was their class affiliation the Jewish workers already had a global organization, the Socialist International, as the opponents of the world organization of the Bund argued. Furthermore, the goal that the coordinating committee set for itself, as expressed by those who spoke for the majority, was not to defend workers' rights but to save Jews from assimilation. Thus, the Bund was transformed. Originally the self-appointed champion of the objective nationhood of the east European Jewish masses, it now became the defender of the subjective wish of those segments of the Jewish people that, in its opinion, wished to maintain their Jewish identity.

By implication, the Bund revised its prewar views on the question of Jewish nationhood. Before the war, it denied the existence of an undivided Jewish nation that embraced Jews of different cultures and countries. Now it recognized such nationhood at the level of principle. From the organizational standpoint, however, the party continued to adhere to class separatism, albeit not as a collection of territorial parties but as a world organization.

This change in the scope of the Bundists' national vision did not change their attitude toward Zionism. In fact, they actually stiffened their anti-Zionism in view of the disaster that had befallen the Jewish people and the grassroots passion for the idea of establishing Jewish statehood. Here again, however, in keeping with the historical tradition of the Bund, there were majority and minority views. At two of the Bund conventions—in Brussels in 1947 and in New York in 1948—the majority repudiated the UN resolution in favor of the establishment of a Jewish state in part of Palestine. It did recognize the right of the Jews in Palestine to exist as a national collective but opposed their Zionist pretense of being a national center for world Jewry. The anti-Zionists argued that the establishment of a state was meant to serve the political imperialistic interests of the Western powers. Instead of partitioning the country, they claimed, it would be better to establish a binational state that would assure the Jews in Palestine cultural autonomy.

The minority, led by the veteran activist Jacob Pat, wished to differentiate between Zionism, which it opposed, and Jewish statehood in Palestine, which it favored. These Bundists also distinguished between an aggressive Zionism that ruled out "exilic" (*galuti*) Jewish existence in the Diaspora and a moderate Zionism that accepted this condition. For the sake of Jewish unity, they even agreed to work toward the establishment of an alliance between the Bund and moderate Zionist elements, since both shared a common national basis.[3]

Szerer, taking the opposing view, continued to argue that any differentiation between Zionism and the Jewish state was unsustainable. Acquiescence in and acceptance of Jewish statehood as a crucial and favorable national phenomenon, even when accompanied by the negation of a "Bundist" ideology.[4]

Szerer was definitely right about the prevailing trend of thought in Zionist leadership circles in 1946–1949, during and after the struggle for statehood. Throughout that time and until 1955, Szerer did not ease his rigid anti-Zionism even though he knew that there was no monolithic and unequivocal Zionist outlook. This reinforces the hypothesis, expressed above, that the Bund's uncompromising struggle against Zionism reflected its need to redefine itself and served as a vital "supplement" to the cultural Utopia of struggle for the Yiddish language in the free Western countries. Generally speaking, it was a paradoxical repetition of the struggle between the "universalists" and the "nationalists" in 1903–1906. This time, however, the struggle was played out entirely within the ambit of the national issue. The anti-Zionists espoused a Klal Yisrael without Zionism; their opponents wished to sustain Klal Yisrael and acquiesced to moderate Zionism. The dispute ended with a de facto compromise between majority and minority, in the manner of the political culture of the Bund since the disputes over national autonomy in 1903, joining the Comintern in 1920, and joining the Second International in 1930. Now, too, after eight years of debate starting at the Brussels convention, the World Convention of the Bund in Montreal in 1955 adopted a positive resolution toward the State of Israel: "The State of Israel is an important event [*a vikhtike geshe'enish*] in the life of the Jewish people." Thus, henceforth the Bund would view the State of Israel, in itself, as a favorable occurrence in Jewish history.

This statement definitely clashed with the resolution taken by the conference in New York in 1948: "The State of Israel was established as a result of an artificial partitioning of 'Palestine,' in a violent struggle that endangered the important achievements of the Jewish Yishuv there and threatened its physical existence." By so resolving, the majority in the Bund continued to express its belief in a federative solution to the Palestine problem even after the State of Israel was formed. However, this was the victory of the minority, which upheld the Yishuv's right to national self-determination in the form of a state and asserted the importance of this Jewish entity as part of the worldwide Klal Yisrael.[5] This interpretation, which was widely held in party circles, was obviously not to the liking of the doctrinaire leadership. Therefore, Szerer hurriedly explained that the Bund related to the State of Israel solely as a historical fact and not as a national value. Even as such, however, it was important. Apart from this, there had been a heated dispute among members of the Bund, ever since Israel was founded, about the country's essence and actions. The debate concerned two matters: Middle East policy and the Jewish national outlook. In the first respect, the reference was to the ordaining of peace with the Arab countries, the treatment of Palestinian refugees, and civil equality for Israel's own Arab minority. The Bund's attitudes toward these topics were not novel. Shortly before and for several years after the establishment of Israeli statehood, the Bund identified totally with the political worldview of Brit Shalom in regard to the binational state idea, acceptance of the repatriation of a considerable number of Arab refugees, and acquiescence in certain border adjustments between Israel and the Arab countries. Nevertheless, even Szerer admitted that the Bund had changed its mind about the role that Israel could play in the national struggle for the existence of the global Klal Yisrael. It now believed that Israel should adopt policies subordinate (*untergevorfn*) to the interests of the Jewish people at large, the "world people" (*velt-folk*). This meant first of all, and as a sine qua non, equal rights for Yiddish vis-à-vis Hebrew and dissociation from the ideology of the State of Israel as the sole home of the entire Jewish people. In Szerer's principled opinion, the interests of world Jewry and Jewish society in Israel have but one national and ethical yardstick, equal and shared.[6]

Thus, even though Szerer remained a consistent and uncompromising opponent of the Zionist ideology, his party's new outlook on Klal Yisrael drove him to make a partial and conditional compromise with the State of Israel. The change was preceded by a protracted ideological debate that resembled a historical reckoning without an element of soul-searching about the correctness of the overall doctrine—an element that might have undermined some of the party's basic premises. This approach, a matter of general consensus in the Bund, was logical in several respects. In regard to the general worldview, the Bund remained faithful to its Social-Democratic outlook, which opposed Communist governance but remained critical of the moderate path of social compromise that most Western Social Democrats had taken. From this standpoint, the Bundists championed the "third way," halfway between capitalism and Communism, that the leftist intellectual Harold Laski articulated in the British Labour Party[7] in an attempt to integrate Marxism and democracy into a humane and egalitarian form of governance. Everything that had happened in the Soviet Union from the end of the war to the death of Stalin, and everything that followed this event, made the Bund even more aware that the criticism of the Soviet regime since the early 1920s was on target.

The Holocaust did not weaken the Bund's fundamental conviction, based on its belief that historical development was indeed leading toward egalitarian social democratic governance, that the Jewish problem could be solved only in the Jews' places of residence. This premise contained a tragic paradox. In eastern and Central Europe, the death of millions of Jews had caused the "Jewish question" in those countries to disappear, while in the Western countries, due to the relative paucity of Jews and the practice of liberal democracy, the Jewish question had never been as acute as it had been in the countries whence the Bund had arisen. Therefore, the claim that the Jews were inseparably rooted (*eingevortselt*) in their countries of residence, as Szerer expressed it, was correct after all, even though it no longer pertained to the place where it was first formulated, Poland. This outlook had grave implications for the national-culture worldview of the Bund.

The Bund's basic argument against Zionism—that it offers no solution to the distress of the Jewish masses—also held firm even after the State of Israel was established. Here again, one might say, in a paradox that was both tragic and favorable, that the Jewish state was not a solution. Those who had been murdered could no longer be saved and those living in the free Western countries did not need salvation. The Bund's only acknowledgment of the need for change at the level of principle, in response to the turn of history, was in its attitude toward Klal Yisrael. In this case, the historical reckoning also verged slightly into ideological soul-searching due to the need to justify the Bund's previous outlook on this issue. Szerer, applying his penchant and his skill, expressed the turnaround in intellectual terms. He addressed his few surviving comrades in the name of "Bundism" and not "the Bund," as though Bundism were an ideology in itself, like Socialism. In his opinion, "Bundism" as an idea had always carried the fundamentals of democratic universalism even though the Bund, as a party immersed in practical work, was particularistic, that is, territorial, at all times and in all places. Here Szerer put his finger on the erstwhile determining contrast between Zionism and the Bund: the former was a world-spanning movement that based itself on one country, Palestine, and the latter was a movement of one country, foremost Poland, that stood for the idea of a universal ideology (*velt-ideologie*). Szerer admitted that there had once been a contradiction between the Socialist territorial-nationalist makeup of the Bund and its Socialist-universalistic outlook. Future changes in the global social regime would resolve this contradiction. This prognosis, however, did nothing to clear up the contradiction that existed in the present. Nevertheless, the contradiction was appropriate during the period at issue, the interwar era. The Polish Bund, as a fighting labor party, could help the universalistic Socialist idea to be fulfilled. After the Holocaust, however, the Bund's situation had changed so radically that it had to seek new organizational modalities to align its ideological theory with its political configuration. In Szerer's opinion, the Bund should expand organizationally to accommodate all Bundist parties in the world. In other words, the general universalistic idea of the Bund should henceforth expand to embrace Bund parties in all countries, and a form of cooperation among them (*universaler bundisher velt ko-operatsie*) should be elaborated.[8] Thus, by implication, Szerer broached the idea of a "world Bund" as a basis for a "world people."

Indeed, pursuant to these remarks, Szerer stressed that the Jews were essentially an "exilic people" (*a galus folk*), a timeless minority, wherever they lived. As an exilic people, they were also a "world people." This concept, according to Szerer, had two meanings: the Jews are dispersed around the entire globe and, by extension, their fate is linked with that of the other peoples. This historical fact, he said, expresses the objective relationship between the particularistic-national and the universalistic-Socialist elements of the Jews' makeup. If so, in what way could the "world Bund" Socialists contribute to the national "world people"? In Szerer's opinion, their main potential contribution was their rootedness among, loyalty to, and action on behalf of the Jews—or, in a paraphrase of Abraham Lincoln's famous aphorism—"of the Jews, with the Jews, and for the Jews" (*fun yidn, durkh yidn, far yidn*).[9]

Szerer's remarks were novel in the culture of political debate in the Polish Bund. As its political leaders and intelligentsia attested, practical politics was the party's main concern; intellectual questions about the essence of the Jews as a "world people" were secondary if not marginal. Now the tables were turned: since the Bund had lost its political strength and influence, the theoretical debate over the national issue became more important. In this sense, the party reverted to its Russian period. At that time, too, the party had engaged in drawn-out political debate about the national issue in a reflection, among other things, of its paucity of political influence. However, Szerer's remarks and those of his colleagues in the leadership did not amount to a party wide ideological "soul-searching." Instead, they were an exercise in justifying the party's historical path. The historical reckoning after the disaster that befell

Jewry and the destruction of the Bund was much more complex among the political "intellectuals" in the party membership than among intellectually inclined politicians such as Szerer.

Professor Pesach Liebman Hersch of Geneva University and Y. Y. Trunk, the author and essayist who had exiled himself to New York, made their party's historical reckoning with intellectual honesty without mitigating their absolute allegiance to it as a result. Liebman Hersch was the first to do so. In 1947, ahead of the convention in Brussels, he published a comprehensive essay titled "The Ideological Evolution of the Bund."[10] The purpose of the essay, he said, was to track the development of the Bund's national outlook in order to understand how the party perceived the concept of a Jewish people (*yidishe natsie*) and envisaged the solution to the Jewish problem. The first long section of the essay described the development of the Bund's national thinking from the time the party was founded up to World War I. In the second section, Liebman Hersch subjected the national worldview of the Bund to a critical and intellectually honest examination in view of the reality that had once existed and, especially, the reality that had changed after World War II and the Holocaust. He noted a series of contradictions between the Bund's ideology and its political praxis and explained them in rising order of importance.

The first contradiction was between the process of the worldwide Jewish dispersion and the consolidation of the Bund's national territorial awareness in interwar Poland. To what extent had it been the Bund that expressed the aspirations of the Jewish working class around the world? Liebman Hersch asked. In his opinion, only the Polish Bund had fulfilled the ideas and aspirations of the Jewish proletariat, since only in Poland was there a Bundist party that had practical social and political influence.

The second contradiction, a more substantial one, flowed from the use of cultural criteria, foremost the Yiddish language, to define the Jewish people. Liebman Hersch resolved this contribution much as he had cleared up the first one. He noted the difficulty in defining it from its outset and, especially, as the Diaspora spread geographically and diversified culturally. In the resulting reality, millions of Jews abandoned Yiddish in favor of the vernaculars of their countries of residence but retained their national consciousness—except, of course, for the minority of willful assimilationists. However, this contradiction, like the previous one, did not shake the national worldview of the Bund. Even when linguistic and cultural assimilation gathered momentum in the interwar era, eastern Europe—Poland and its neighboring countries—had a "hard core" of millions of Yiddish-speaking Jews. As long as this situation was assured, the Bund avoided thorough intellectual investigation of this contradiction. However, the party was clearly aware, and had been so ever since it was founded, that the main indicator of nationhood, and especially Jewish nationhood, is national culture. Practically, then, the Bund immersed itself in struggle for the Jewish national culture in interwar Poland and, for all practical purposes, turned a blind eye to events related to Jewish cultural existence in other countries such as Soviet Russia and the United States.

This brought Liebman Hersch to the third and the most substantive contradiction, one that flowed from the fact that the Bund was not an association for the promotion of Yiddish culture but a political party of the Jewish working class—a party for which national culture was not only an expression of a particular spirituality, but also the result of the historical process and political reality of a people that was a minority wherever it dwelled. If so, in his opinion, both Zionism and the Bund, as ideas and as movements, were outgrowths of Jewish history and the social conditions in which the Jewish masses lived. This merely proves that one social reality can give rise not only to different cultures, but also to contrasting political movements. In other words, in the heat of the uncompromising political battle against Zionism, the Bund, with its Marxist worldview, overlooked the contradiction between objective historical development, of which Zionism was an inseparable part, and the subjective rejection of Zionism in accordance with the Bund worldview.

Having exposed the internal contradictions in the worldview and cultural reality of the Bund in the past, Liebman Hersch now confronted the new reality that the Holocaust had occasioned and resurrected two historical theories of the Bund. First, it had been a basic contention of the Bund, since its founding day, that the solution to all aspects of the Jewish problem was territorial-local. Under the new circumstances, Liebman Hersch argued, Jewish centers of major importance in the sense of national culture no longer exist. From now on, all of Jewry is a "world people." By implication, the almost complete tautology between Yiddish language and culture and Jewish nationhood has vanished. Most Jews in the world do not live this culture. Furthermore, from the pan-Jewish standpoint, Liebman Hersch continued, the important historical change is the transformation of the fate and future of the Hebrew-speaking Yishuv in Palestine into the foremost political and national concern of Jews worldwide and an important issue in international policy.

Here Liebman Hersch got to the root of the problem, the national attitude of the Bund toward Zionism and the Yishuv. Here, he believed, lay the key to resolving most of the contradictions in the Bund's past and present worldview. He proposed that his party recognize the legitimacy of the Zionist movement, provided that the movement renounce the principle of negation-of-the-Diaspora and admit that the large majority of Jews would remain in the

Diaspora even after the Holocaust. In return, he urged his party to support the struggle for national territorial autonomy in Palestine. This, as stated, would resolve all three internal contradictions: the interests of a "world people" versus the territorial national reality; the Yiddish language versus other languages that Jews spoke, foremost Hebrew; and Zionism as an objective historical movement versus the Bund's total rejection of Zionism in the past.

Liebman Hersch's predecessor in the ideological soul-searching was Y. Y. Trunk. To his comrades' surprise, Trunk maintained that Zionism and the Bund had been two paths throughout Jewish history, interlocked in struggle. In early 1943, in response to reports about the systematic annihilation of Jews in occupied Europe and in view of his familiarity with the American Jewish reality, which was so different from that in interwar Poland in the national sense, Trunk came to the conclusion that Bundist and Zionist activity in the United States was utterly pointless. All that remained was to engage in metaphysical reflections in an attempt to discover processes in Jewish history that would give the Jews the strength to endure the tragic test of reality and would offer hope for the future.

Prompted by these musings, Trunk drew a historiosophic distinction between two threads in Jewish history from its dawn up to, and perhaps including, the present day: global decentralization and territorial centralization. The first thread (*velt ekspantsie*) was represented by "the Biblical prophets, the first Jewish Christians, the kabbalists, the hasidic movement, and, in the modern era, the Bund." The second thread (*yidishe kontsentratsie*) traced from false prophets who "failed to understand that the God of the Jews intends to be the God of all humankind. Later on, this thread was grasped by the Pharisees and the halakhic sages, the mitnaggedim, the maskilim, and in modern times, the Zionists."[11]

One doubts whether this dichotomous historiosophy can pass the test of historical truth; even Trunk was not totally confident about it. Still, it led him to an optimistic conclusion: since the two threads in this struggle had alternated in primacy in the course of history, so they would in the future. Therefore, if reality had catapulted Zionism to primacy at the present time, changes in conditions might elevate the Bund to primacy in the near or distant future.

After the war, in view of the devastating blow that the Jews had suffered, Trunk reached the conclusion that Jewish existence along both threads, "as the Zionists perceive it and as the Bund perceives it," was but a vision of one aspect of the historical idea in respect to the ideal future. The Zionists considered the indistinguishability of Jews from other nations—territorial ingathering on the national soil—as the ideal, whereas "we see it at the levels of universal social justice."[12] This article, which invested Zionism with such sweeping historical legitimacy, was not amenable to the party leadership even though Trunk repeatedly emphasized his objections to the main provisions of the Zionist creed. Therefore, the editorial board noted that his remarks reflected the views of their author only.

Trunk was not deterred by this sign of disapproval. In 1949, after the second world convention of the Bund, he published an article under a title that left no doubt about the contents: "The Historical Roots of the Bund and Zionism." By this time, Trunk's musings in 1943 had evolved into a well-crafted theory. Pursuant to his previous article, Trunk defined both trends—decentralization and centralization—as historical antitheses that held shares, as it were, in the constructivist Jewish historical thesis (*oyf-boyendiker teze*). Both the tension and clash between the small nation-state, or the aspiration to establish one, and the universal idea of a "world people" enabled the Jewish nation to surmount the difficult ordeals in its life (*das hot oysgekemft ir shvern lebn*). Accordingly, the Bund and Zionism should not be perceived as movements born in the past fifty years and as artificial phenomena in Jewish history that seek to impose their will on the Jewish masses in order to change the course of that history. Instead, Trunk explained,

> These are two central movements [*hoypt-bavegungen*] in Jewish history, on which, dialectically, this history has been based from its outset. It is but an expression of the vital force in Jewish history that is reflected in these two trends, which take on and shed forms in accordance with the time of their advent; which emanate from the depths of the national spirit [*natsionale tifenishn*] into the air of the present; and which influence the development of society in accordance with the conditions of the time.[13]

This prompted Trunk, in a manner that was exceptional for most political leaders of the Bund, to undertake a historical soul-searching in respect to his party's assessment of Zionism in the distant and recent past. He asserted:

> We in the Bund made a mistake [*gemakht a toyes*] by assuming that Zionism, that is, the centralization idea, had already played itself out or completed its task in the progression of Jewish history toward the future and [by believing, in contrast, that] the modern conception of exile [*moderne "galus" kontseptsie*] has taken up a commanding position in regard to the Jews' future. It is not so, since "psychic processes"

[*psikhishe protsesn*] in history, like Zionism, do not liquidate
themselves easily. They have roots and origins [*kvaln*] in the
depths of the nation, and they have made no small contribution to the shaping of [the nation's] character and structure.[14]

Just as the Bund was wrong in the past, Trunk continued, so are the
Zionists wrong in the present, in their conviction that the Bund has suffered
its final historical defeat and that Zionism is the only surviving national
movement on the Jewish scene. It is true, Trunk admitted, that Zionism has
registered an amazing, unbelievable achievement. However, it has not fulfilled its wish of capturing the hearts of the majority of Jews. Therefore, it
is surely heading for a severe disappointment in the future, just as the Bund
was tragically disappointed in the past when it disparaged the historical
trend of territorial centralization. The Diaspora is not on the verge of liquidation, notwithstanding the Zionists' expectations. If Zionism persists in its
all-out negation-of-the-Diaspora, it may create an irreparable schism
among the Jews, between normal existence in the manner of all other nations—"Jewish gentile-ism" (*yidisher goyishkayt*)—and a singular Diasporic existence that carries the finest of the universalistic human values of
the "decentralization" trend in Jewish history. As long as that kind of Diaspora continues to exist, "Bundism" will continue to play a historical role as
the most reliable vehicle of the universalistic Jewish values.

In contrast to his statement of belief in the universalistic Jewish moral
vision—in words almost identical to the phrasings of the nineteenth-century
Reform Movement—Trunk was on the brink of despair as he contemplated
the future of Jewish national culture in the two largest Jewish concentrations,
those in Israel and the United States. In a personal letter in the 1950s, he expressed the assumption that Israel would be overtaken by "Canaanism," because the logic of history said as much, and that a cheap and historically
rootless Jewish culture would take shape in the United States.[15]

The views of the two leading critical "house intellectuals," Liebman
Hersch and Y. Y. Trunk, diverged on this point. Both legitimized Zionism as a
historical phenomenon but vehemently opposed the negation-of-the-Diaspora
ideology. Both welcomed the national "miracle" that was embodied in the establishment of the State of Israel but were very critical of Israel's cultural ideology and Middle East policies. However, they differed in the extent of their
favor of this novelty in Jewish national life. At the second Bund convention
(New York, 1948), these differences came to the surface. Liebman Hersch
welcomed the establishment of the State of Israel and, therefore, proposed that
the resolution taken by the Brussels conference a year earlier, in favor of establishing a binational state in Palestine, be repealed. In his benevolent

regard for the State of Israel, he went so far as to view it, as many Zionists did, as the representative of the entire Jewish people when the United Nations accepted it as a full-fledged member. What is more, he verged on treachery against the cultural tradition of the Bund by proposing that the Bund schools teach Hebrew as well as Yiddish in order to train the young generation in the full spectrum of Jewish national culture. Generally speaking, from Liebman Hersch's perspective, the "world people" concept likened the Jewish people to a living organism with biologically related organs that, when injured, inflict pain on the entire body. Trunk, in contrast—by the same yardstick of biological simile—regarded Israel as a wild growth that might menace the health of the entire body—a small state, in which only a negligible fraction of the Jews could congregate, that wanted to usurp the place of a "world people" (*velt-folk*) as a political and cultural reality and a socionational ideal.[16]

Several months after Trunk's article appeared, Liebman Hersch published a series of articles titled "Our Historical Dispute with Zionism."[17] Unlike Trunk, Liebman Hersch sought a leveling synthesis that would allow "here" (*do*) in the Diaspora and "there" (*dortn*) in Israel to coexist. Unlike his colleagues in the political leadership of the Bund, he proposed a differentiation between the State of Israel and radical Zionism. Thus, after surveying the history of relations between the movements in their fifty years of existence, he tackled the current anti-Israel arguments of his comrades in the Bund leadership and attempted to ease their sting by interpreting them optimistically and constructively. Recognition of the Yiddish language, Liebman Hersch claimed, was a question of cultural policy and not a problem that touched upon the essence of the State of Israel. Therefore, the current derogatory attitude toward Yiddish might turn around in the future. He admitted that Israel was in existential danger but blamed this on the Arab countries that refused to make peace with it. For this reason, Israel's situation was unlike that of other states that had been formed in the midst of war with other nations. In his opinion, the menace to Israel actually required the Jewish people to support it politically and economically. Admittedly, Liebman Hersch, like his comrades, was convinced that statehood would not solve the problem of the dispersed Jewish people. However, he argued emphatically in view of the Klal Yisrael principle that the state of dispersion must not be allowed to drive a wedge between the Diasporic "here" and the Israeli "there." Such a wedge, he said, would cost the Jews a crucial basis for their existence in the Diaspora (*Shtits punkt far unzer kiyum do*). He did agree with those who perceived a material difference between the abnormal Jewish existence in Diaspora and the normality of the Israeli reality. This difference, he said, should be treated with ordinary critical tools. The criticism that he favored, however, should flow from a sense of national solidarity that is based not on an anti-Israel posture but on loyal opposition to Israel, in the vein of His Majesty's opposition (*a loyale opozitsie fun ir mayestet*).[18] Accordingly, the Bund should not merely acquiesce in Jewish statehood but should be an active participant in sustaining the state and in struggle for the social changes that it needs.

Even though the majority at the third convention softened its stance toward Israel, Liebman Hersch's remarks broke new ground. Therefore, the leadership hurriedly clutched the horns of the principled positions that it had adopted. The editorial board of *Unzer Tsayt* attached a comment to the last article in the series—a piece as long as programmatic article, which, if one may judge by its style and vehemence, was evidently written by Emanuel Szerer.[19] The writer of the comment categorically rejected the "here-and-there" outlook and offered in its stead one and only one object worthy of recognition: "here." According to this view, the Jews are a nation in exile even though they have established a small state. Thus, there is nothing dualistic about Jewish existence. The State of Israel is in no way equivalent to the Diaspora; it is an inseparable part of a "world people," that is, a nation that is abnormal because its territory is the entire world. Paradoxically, the writer regarded Liebman Hersch's views not as a reflection of a Jewish unity of "here" and "there" but as the opposite, a sanctification of two Jewish national entities. [*"In etsem iz zayn 'da un dortn' a sanktsianirung fun tsvey yidishe veltn, a kontseptsie fun yidishn natsionaln dualizm."*]

On the basis of this premise, the writer rejected Liebman Hersch's view that at the present time, after the Holocaust, the state was important to the Jewish people. His question was to whom the state belongs—to the Jews at large or only to those who lived there. If Israel is the state of the Jewish people, then the Jews are no longer a "world people." Otherwise, a logical contradiction and a political problem of dual loyalty arise. Both circumstances—the contradiction and the problem—can be solved in one of two ways: recognition of the centrality of Israel in the Jewish reality and main loyalty to it, or an explicit stipulation to the effect that neither modality of Jewish existence is nationally preferable. By implication, the equality of national status is all-embracing and omnipresent.

Paradoxically, this anti-dualistic outlook in favor of the single and collective "here" reinforced the belief in Klal Yisrael. In contrast to the Zionist approach at the time, which sought to build Klal Yisrael around the focal point of the State of Israel, it proposed a Klal Yisrael with many focal points. In this sense, the majority of Bund members at that time outdid even Simon Rawidowicz, the Diasporic Zionist thinker who considered Eretz Israel and the Diaspora "*two* that are *one*."[20] For the Bund, there was only one, not two. Thus, in response to Liebman Hersch's question about why the Bund was willing to cooperate with the French Social-Democratic Party or the British Labour Party but not with Po'aley Tsiyyon, the writer stated that the two situations were materially different. Po'aley Tsiyyon and the Bund belong to the same people and are embroiled in daily struggle for the soul of "our people" (*far der neshome fun unzer folk*). Therefore, national partnership, unlike class partnership, actually aggravates the dispute and rules out the kind of cooperation the Bund practices with other nations' Socialist parties. This led the writer to the extreme, almost Orwellian, dialectic paradox that *unity is disunity,* that is, deviation from the traditional national ideology of the Bund, from its inception to World War II, amidst upholding and continuing its political praxis.

This method allowed the Bund concurrently to broaden and deepen the Klal Yisrael national outlook and to escalate its criticism of the State of Israel.

At its third world convention (1955), the Bund took a resolution that defined Klal Yisrael in the most inclusive and sweeping manner in its serpentine history on this question: "The Jews are a 'world people.' The separate Jewish communities, scattered around the globe, are interrelated by a *shared history and culture* that they inherited due to their awareness of being members of one people. Language and tradition, repression and anti-Semitism, all collectively constitute and build the 'world people.'"[21] It is every community's mission and duty to strengthen and consolidate its national life where it is settled. It is noteworthy that the resolution makes no explicit mention of the Yiddish language as a shaping factor in Jewish nationhood. This omission strengthened the Klal Yisrael outlook even more. However, according to the "Szerer doctrine," the more important the Klal Yisrael idea becomes, the greater the danger that Israel and, especially, Zionism pose to it and the more severely they threaten the national and cultural continuity of Diaspora Jewry. The threat is manifested in Israel's propaganda campaign for the teaching of Hebrew instead of Yiddish in Diaspora communities and in the pledging of most revenues of the United Jewish Appeal to Israel's needs, to the severe detriment of the Diaspora communities' ability to sustain their cultural endeavors. All of this attests—no less!—to the Zionist intention of transforming the Diaspora into a colonial hinterland of the Israeli metropolis [*Der tsiyoynizm vil farvondlen di yidishe yishuvim in kolonies, in a hinterland far der Yisroel melukha*]. By so behaving, in fact, Zionism is deliberately trying to evaporate the economic wellsprings of the Jewish communities' vitality, with all the dire implications of such a development for the national culture. Notably, American Jewish intellectual circles that were unrelated to the Bund had begun to express similar views.[22]

Nevertheless, the "Szerer doctrine" did not "own" the entire Bund. Liebman Hersch's outlook gained ground as well. At this convention, the Bund recognized Israel in principle by defining it as an important event in Jewish history and a sovereign national Jewish entity (*zelbs farvaltndiker yidishe yishuv*). Admittedly, this recognition came with many strings attached. For example, Israel was to waive its goal of becoming the center of the Jewish people, to recognize Yiddish as its second national language along with Hebrew, to renounce the negation-of-the-Diaspora ideology, and to assure the country's Arab minority civil equality.[23] However, one could hear the affirmation in the negation: Israel could play an important role in the existence of the "world people." Even when Szerer hurriedly circumscribed the definition of the Jewish state as an important event by explicating it as a historical fact and nothing more, he admitted that an Israel that jettisoned its Zionist aims, as he demanded, might be of value in the struggle for national continuity. Thus, Israel was important not for its intrinsic value as a sovereign Jewish entity but for its potential as an important auxiliary in fulfilling the existential destiny of the "Jewish klal." Notwithstanding Szerer's admirable intellectual hairsplitting, the minority, under the ideological leadership of Liebman Hersch, definitely registered an important achievement by securing the majority's principled consent to the differentiation of Israel from Zionism. This consent denoted a new three-tiered national outlook: the "world people" as the highest tier in importance, followed by the "State of Israel"—culturally and politically repaired as prescribed by the Bund's worldview—and, at the bottom, a minimalistic Zionism that repudiated the negation of the Diaspora.

Zionism made inroads in the Bund's national outlook in two ways, indirectly and directly. The indirect incursion was effected in the change that occurred in the Bund's attitude toward Jews in the Islamic countries—the erstwhile "Arabs of the Mosaic faith," according to Wiktor Alter, or the "dried branch" of the Jewish people, as Trunk defined them. These Jews, who actually no longer belonged to the Jewish people because they did not speak Yiddish, became an inseparable part of the Jewish people in the 1950s. The Bundists began to take an interest in the matter due to the resumption of aliya from Morocco in the mid–1950s, which the Bund, of course, opposed just as it opposed aliya from Romania in the early 1960s and had urged the vestiges of Polish Jewry not to abandon that country after the Kielce pogrom in 1946.[24] Even though this was a pronouncedly anti-Zionist stance, the inclusion of the Eastern Jews in Klal Yisrael spelled the acceptance of the first and determining principle of Zionism, one that the Bund still rejected vehemently and had, in the past, rejected contemptuously. This, however, led the Bund again into one of those contradictions that had typified its national outlook from its inception. On the one hand, it recognized Eastern and Sephardi Jews as inseparable members of the Jewish people; on the other hand, it demanded the status of a national language for Yiddish in the Diaspora and in Israel. In regard to the Diaspora, one could explain away the contradiction by noting the Ashkenazi extraction of most Jews who lived there. This could not be said about the Jews in Israel, since half of the seven hundred thousand immigrants who had flooded the country were from Eastern countries. The root of the contradiction undoubtedly lay in the Bund's "Ashkenazi-centric" worldview, which the movement was unable to cast off even after the Holocaust. Szerer expressed this worldview with characteristic pungency in his reflections about Bundism in his own time. His remarks on the topic stressed the basic difference between Jewishness in the Diaspora and that in Israel—security and prosperity in the former, insecurity and economic hardship in the latter. Furthermore, he asked his readers to bear in mind that Israel was in Asia and drove the point home by repeating it. (*Yisroel ligt in Azie! Yisroel ligt in Azie!*) "There's lots of Bundism and 100 percent of the truth in these four words," he concluded. [*A groyser shtik bundizm ligt in di dozike dray verter. Un gevis—a fuler 100 prazentiker emes.*][25] After all, the Bund, as an Ashkenazi-centric movement, was also Western-centric.

Emanuel Szerer's remarks also attest to the change in the Bund's attitude toward Zionism. After the third convention, Szerer made a special effort to explain his stance on Zionism for his critics in the non-Zionist Yiddish press. In view of criticism from circles and personalities that were close to the Bund in many senses—especially in their Yiddishist cultural worldview—Szerer had to back down from his dogmatic anti-Zionist outlook. His argument was that the Bund had no objection to moderate Zionism such as the American version, which affirmed Jewishness in the Diaspora—an assertion that was factually correct in the 1950s and was debated in Zionist Movement circles.[26] However, he categorically opposed the Israeli version of Zionism, which urged negation of the Diaspora and ingathering of the exiles. Therefore, the Bund would serve as a Jewish national opposition (*Der bund iz di opozitsie in yidishn natsionaln lebn*), complementing the American neo-Zionism and fighting the Israeli "hyper-Zionism."[27]

Thus, by implication, Szerer considered the Jewish people a "community of fate,"[28] a people shaped by its special history and not necessarily by the Yiddish language, as Y. Y. Trunk, for example, thought. This was clear, since Yiddish as a vernacular disappeared after the Holocaust. As for the historical fate, Szerer, of course, followed his mentor, Otto Bauer, to a certain point. Unlike Bauer, however, he believed in the timelessness of the Jews' singular existence and dismissed the possibility of assimilation into the surrounding society. Paradoxically, this belief was quite similar to the perception of "Jewish fate" in Zionism. By applying associative thinking, one might say that Szerer's "community of fate" phrase unwittingly included two terms coined by Rabbi Joseph Dov Soloveitchik, "covenant of fate" and "covenant of destiny," although Szerer, of course, construed them in a secular national manner.[29] Thus, Szerer, the political leader, accepted the stance of his party's intellectuals—Y. Y. Trunk, who regarded Zionism, like the Bund, as a historically rooted movement, and especially Liebman Hersch, who on the basis of similar premises sought to strike a political compromise of sorts with Zionism. This change, which took place at the third convention of the World Alliance of Bund Parties found meaningful expression ten years later in the resolutions of the Fourth Convention in New York (1965), marking the twentieth anniversary of the end of World War II.[30]

The resolutions that pertained to the condition of the Jewish people, unlike those concerning the international situation and the Cold War, were adopted by acclaim. They underscored with special vehemence the intellectual and cultural task of the Bund vis-à-vis the Jews and expressed concern about the future of Jewish autonomy in this respect. What is more, they lacked the harsh polemic tone toward the State of Israel that had typified previous conventions' resolutions. The more concerned the Bund became about the Jews' intellectual future, the more it seized upon the Yiddish language as a prime defining factor of Jews as members of a nation. Therefore, the Bund considered it the principal task of Diaspora Jews in all free countries to organize in ethnic-culture settings. The opposite tendency, which we defined above as "Ahad Ha'amic," seemed realistic to the Bund leadership in view of the civil liberty and economic well-being that Western Jews enjoyed. The State of Israel had a special role to play in this cultural construct of Klal Yisrael. Therefore, the resolution stated that "The Jews in Israel, who constitute the majority there, have acquired additional intellectual opportunities for national development. Whether they will wish to use this potential . . . to strengthen their Jewishness depends on their own wishes and behavior in several important regards."[31]

The authors of this resolution had been raised in a political culture that demanded the utmost care in the phrasing of ideological statements, even those that were ambiguous. Therefore, they must have been aware of the far-reaching significance of this clause. After all, it admits that a Jewish majority in a Jewish state has a material advantage over the minority status of Jews in the Diaspora in respect to Jewish nationhood and its continuity in the Diaspora countries.

This tendency to invest Israel with rising importance in the lives of Jews as a "world people" persisted in subsequent years. The fifth convention (1972) described Israel as an important event (*geshe'enish*) in Jewish national life, the sixth convention termed it an important factor (*vikhtiker faktor*) in Jewish national life, and the seventh convention stressed the explicit dependency of Jewish continuity on the State of Israel.[32]

THE CULTURAL YIDDISHIST "UTOPIA"

The Bund's forty-year return to Klal Yisrael in the political sense culminated at the seventh convention (1985). The convention resolved that the Bund should take part in all Jewish institutions—not only those associated with the Jewish labor movement—in which it was a member. The reference was to community organizations and international Jewish organizations such as the World Jewish Congress. The resolution urged "Bundist organizations everywhere [to] participate actively in the field of Yiddish culture and in all general Jewish institutions."[33]

As the Bund eased its political attitude toward Israel, it entertained a growing sense of Utopian mission—a view of itself as a movement that struggled to save Jewry from the cultural extinction that threatened it in exile and in Israel. The concept of "Utopia" in the context of the Bund's postwar thinking is different from the "realistic Utopia" concept, explained in the introduction, that applied to the Bund's thinking and politics in two preceding periods, from its founding to World War I in Russia and in interwar Poland. Both outlooks, as Karl Mannheim explained, were outgrowths of incongruence with reality,[34] the Russian and the Polish, respectively. However, the "realistic Utopian" thinking stemmed from a general and Jewish reality in which the Bund's Utopian solutions, in both the national and the social respects, were quite logical. The Bund's post-Holocaust Utopianism, in contrast, was divorced from reality. Therefore, its failure to adjust to this reality was both objective and subjective. In the objective sense, the society and culture of Jews in the West, foremost the United States, were altogether different from those of pre-Holocaust east European Jewry. The Bund intellectuals realized this when they began to discuss the question of nationhood and the status of the Yiddish language and culture in post-Holocaust Jewish existence. However, the remnants of the Bund in the West, in a manifestation of indefatigable if not heroic "subjective" faith, refused to accept reality and chose to rebel against it for the sake of a Yiddishist and also a Socialist Utopia, by sole virtue of which, they argued, the Jewish people might continue to sustain its national culture, even in its diminished state.

The Bund's first Utopian war cry after the Holocaust, sounded immediately after the tragedy, was its call for war on assimilation. In 1944, while artillery still thundered on the fronts of Europe, the Bund Party's newspaper in

France, *Unzer Shtime,* began to reappear in recently liberated Paris. In the lead article of its début edition, the editor, Alexander Stein, discussed the menace of assimilation that the Jews of France, and especially its young people, faced.[35] His remarks, written in the traditional bellicose style of the Bund, which always bucked the odds, were followed up in two forms: organizational plans for the development of Jewish culture, and the floating of universalistic political schemes.

In 1948, ahead of the second convention of the Bund, the essayist and cultural activist H. S. Kazdan, who had headed the CYSHO school system in Poland in the second half of the 1930s, published an article that created a linkage between Jewish Socialism and the Jewish problem in the United States.[36] In the manner of the Utopian bombast that never settles for trivialities but aims for greatness even if it starts out modestly, Kazdan concerns himself with a great problem (*groyse probleme*), the war on assimilation and the centralization of the Bund's "labor of the present," that is, its cultural efforts. The crux of Kazdan's idea was the establishment of a central world organization of Jewish communities (*a veltlekhe yidishe kehile*) that would carry out a mutually agreed program. The world community organization should not play a political role in the sense of representing the Jews' interests vis-à-vis the authorities or serving the cause of the Jewish state; instead, it should deal with day-to-day Jewish life in the widely scattered communities. It should be the cultural organization of a Klal Yisrael that is made up of diverse segments and parties. Only a person such as Kazdan, a Utopianist despite his political experience, could believe in the possibility of separating political disputes in the Jewish street from cooperation in culture. Indeed, Kazdan asked rhetorically whether a united Jewish community in New York were an unattainable Utopia. His answer was no less Utopian: "No, it's just a question of dogged work and organization."

The proposed World Organization of Communities was envisaged as an instrument in the war on assimilation. Kazdan proposed that Yiddish be made its official language, that is, the language of all its official publications and gatherings. Kazdan tasked this pioneering mission, the struggle for worldwide Yiddish cultural autonomy, to the American Jewish labor organizations. After all, labor organizations had been the vanguard of the national struggle in Russia and Poland, too.

Of course, he believed that this national mission should be spearheaded by the World Coordinating Committee of Bund Organizations, the coordinating body of the World Alliance of Bund Parties. The Yiddish-Jewish "labor of the present" should be centralized in all senses, not only fundraising and organizational initiatives in the field of culture. It should be driven by one central ideology (*tsentralizatsie in der ideologie, tsentrale kultur-ideʿen un lozungen*) in broad domains such as schools, theater, literature, and music. Seven years later, Mordecai Kaplan, the founder of Jewish Reconstructionism in the United States and an important Zionist thinker after World War II, published his book *A New Zionism*,[37] in which he unveiled a similar plan for the establishment of a Diaspora Jewish organization based on the Zionist idea. Kaplan's proposed organization would coexist with the State of Israel and maintain strong and inseparable relations with it but would be autonomous. Thus, the Bundists and the Zionists had similar Utopian ideas in regard to the Klal Yisrael question. However, not only the Bund's intellectuals entertained Utopian thoughts; political functionaries with years of experience also toyed with them. In 1955, Emanuel Nowogrodzki, a political personality of the highest order in the New York Bund leadership and secretary of the World Coordinating Committee of Bund Organizations, published a pamphlet titled, "A New Approach to Old Truths."[38] Its main message was an attack on the Zionist national pretensions of the State of Israel, which, Nowogrodzki claimed, cannot solve the problem of the Jewish people. Therefore, he ruled, the Jewish future in this respect will be no different from the Jewish past. However, at the end of the tract Nowogrodzki presented a fundamentally anti-Zionist Utopian vision.

As an antithesis to Ben-Gurion's "corporeal state-people" vision, Nowogrodzki posited the Utopia of a "spiritual world-people." The Jews, in his opinion, are a "world people" for a reason other than their geographical dispersion. They had managed to survive in history, unlike other ancient peoples, not by organizing themselves as a state in the material world but by adhering to a worldview (*velt banem*) that is fundamentally and materially universal and, for this reason, assumes responsibility for both global and national society. Therefore, just as a state is foremost a political and geographical concept, the Jewish people is foremost a cultural and historical entity. Nowogrodzki presented this argument, which of course takes issue with Zionism and the concept of Jewish statehood, as a preface to his universalistic Utopian vision, the establishment of a world federation of peoples, as opposed to states[39] (*in kegenzatz tsu melukhes*). Finally, Nowogrodzki assigned the duty of disseminating the idea of the Socialist Utopia to the Jewish intelligentsia (*yidisher inteligents*), which had been carrying the torch of the social and national redemption of humankind since the Bund had been founded sixty years earlier.

The "Bundist tragedy" was expressed in its most ardent Utopian form by the Bund Party's main ideologue and its spokesman in all its world conventions, Emanuel Szerer. Szerer defined the national historical role of the Bund as an uprising against destruction (*vidershtand kegn khurbn*). He admitted, however, that the Jewish masses in the Diaspora were unwilling to rise up (*viln nisht aza vidershtand*). They had mired themselves in a psychological ambience of opportunistic pursuit of material comforts, reflected in a manner of living that derived its justification from the premise that one must adjust to the new conditions.

To counter this tendency, the Bund called for a *spiritual uprising* (*tsum gaystikn vidershtand*) against the opportunistic and self-satisfied trend in Jewish thinking (*zelbst gezetikayt un zelbst tsufridenkayt* [italics in the original]. From this point of view, Szerer thought, the Jewish people needed the Bund more than ever. The Bund's exhortation to the Jewish people for a national awakening would be a difficult task for the messengers. However, it was basically a struggle of quality versus quantity (*a kamf fun kvalitet kegn kvantitet* [italics in the original]. The quantity resists and negates the Bund's entreaty. The masses do not wish to rise up. However, the lofty goals (*groyse tsiln*) outweigh the large numbers (*groyse tsoln*) in world history and, in particular, in Jewish history. And it is those grand, lofty goals, at the national and universal-Socialist levels, that constitute the Bund's special mission at the present time. As for Szerer's remarks about quantity and quality, one may say—following the Marxist adage about how quality is born of quantity—that the fewer Bundists there were among the Jews, the greater their quality would be.[40] Szerer's turns of phrase exude the aggrieved tone of someone who has been defeated but has not surrendered, almost akin to the spirit of the sixteenth-century French Huguenots: "Even if it is hopeless, the mission should be accepted; even if we do not succeed, we should persist at it." Since Szerer, like most of his colleagues, was graced with pronounced Utopian optimism, he found consolation by adopting a Utopian outlook toward the future, based on predictions of great technological innovations and sweeping social changes that would lead to the establishment of a democratic Socialist society by the year 2000.[41]

However, the more clearly "problematic" the role that the Bund had undertaken would be—to bring the light of the extinct Yiddish culture to the Jewish masses, which were mired in a rapid cultural assimilation—the stronger Szerer's Utopian tendencies became.

In 1967, in two articles about basic problems in world and Jewish Socialism, Szerer advocated a rebirth of moral social "idealism" as an antidote to the socioeconomic "realism" that had overtaken general and Jewish society after the World War II. He defined "realism" as the practical propensity to deal with current social affairs and "idealism" as "the ideas and ideals that human beings harbor and aspire to realize."[42] According to this definition, "ideal" and "Utopia" are identical concepts both as propensities and as mentalities.[43] However, Szerer, as a saliently political person and thinker, also thought in organizational political Utopian concepts. He entertained the hope that at some future time, as social conditions matured, a "Socialist klal" of sorts would come into being and unite all the Socialist parties, including Communist parties. The purpose of such a klal would be to fight for the establishment of a free Socialist society that would be needed as an antithesis of capitalist society in its advanced stages. The transition from the new capitalism to the future Socialism would be powered solely by a maximalist Socialist idealistic impetus. In the aftermath of the social reforms that traditional, conservative Social Democracy had brought about, the time had come when "Socialist maximalism can be both idealistic and realistic."

This belief was a conspicuous manifestation of realistic Utopian thinking, that is, the premise that processes of social development in economics, science, and politics would make it possible to realize exalted social ideals.

In another article, Szerer used these standards of measurement, "realism" and "idealism," to evaluate the trends at work in Jewish society and to determine what this society might expect of them in the future.[44] In his opinion, the Jews evinced both clashing phenomena, "realism" and "idealism," and did so more blatantly than other peoples. Jewish existence over the generations was strongly dependent on a religious idealism that was becoming increasingly impractical, that is, increasingly far from the changing reality. In the Jews' present situation, they were in dire need of the sort of "idealism" that bears the characteristics and messages of a spiritual uprising against a reality that is dominated by practical realism, that is, one that leads to assimilation. Consequently, all anti-assimilationist Jewish forces are driven by the spirit of idealism.

Szerer considered the imperative of idealism so important that he cited the ideological enemy, Zionism, to prove his point. "In our era of Jewish life," he wrote, "a paradox exists. Those who were unrealistic for decades—the Zionists—have attained their political ideal."[45] Although this happened as a consequence of various political developments and of the greatest tragedy of the Jewish people, in their absence the State of Israel would not have come into being. That, however, does not negate the historical achievement of Zionist idealism. However, now that Israel has become a reality, Szerer noted dialectically, the greatest fanatics and Utopianists (*fanatistim un utopistim*) among the Jews have become the greatest "realists," the torchbearers of the idea that he called "statist realism" (*melukhe realizm*). This approach came with political power, he said, but it also carried intellectual weakness that resulted in the sacrifice of political, social, and national values on the altar of state power interests. Examples, he stated, were the unequal treatment of the Arab minority, the existence of social gaps between immigrants and nonimmigrants, and the

attempt to "dominate" Diaspora Jewry, among others. Zionism itself had
been compromised, in his opinion, by the realistic interests that had supplanted the movement's idealistic aspirations.

This critique of the accommodationist bourgeois pragmatism of Diaspora Jews and the statist power fixation of the State of Israel prompted
Szerer to pronounce an "Ahad Ha'amic" diagnosis: the Jewish condition
had become one of "slavery amidst freedom." In his opinion, the more inconsequential the existential "Jewish problem" became in the Jews' eyes,
the more serious the "Jewishness problem" (*yidishkayt-frage*) became.
This, of course, was related to the "Yiddish problem" (*di yidish frage*), the
question of the status of the Yiddish language.

In this situation, the Bund should become the Prometheus of Jewish
culture, carrying the torch of idealism and illuminating with it the "dark-
ness" of crude, self-serving materialistic realism. Szerer did not delude
himself into believing that the Yiddish culture renaissance movement would
be a mass movement. On the contrary, at its outset it would surely be small,
composed of groups of individuals in dispersed Jewish communities
around the world. However, Szerer, inspired by upside-down Marxist optimism, argued that just as quality is born of quantity, so might the Yiddish
language undergo the opposite process—quality compensating for the loss
of quantity. The Bund should realize its idealism in Yiddishist activity
wherever Jews lived and, by so doing, should create the basis for an integration of realism and idealism (*a reale grunt baseh fun unzer idealizm is
di yidishe doyikayt*). Szerer's adherence to belief in the possibility of a Jewish national-culture rebirth in the free Western Diaspora drove him to an almost mystical optimism about the future. Just as developments in science
proved that imagination could become reality, so in regard to the Jewish rebirth was there reason to hope and believe that today's Bundist idealism
would become tomorrow's reality (*Der bundisher idealizm fun haynt ken
vern a realizm fun morgn*).

As the strength and influence of Israeli statehood gathered momentum in the Jewish street after the Six-Day War, Szerer tried even harder to
invest the Yiddish language with an important if not a determining status
in the struggle for the national existence of the "world people." "I admit,"
he wrote, "that Yiddish is not the only bulwark against the tide of assimilation, but it is the highest and therefore the most important of them." Therefore, he stated, the Jewish people needed the Bund more than ever
(*Faktish—nukh noytiker vi amal un nisht vayniker gerekht*).[46] Paradoxically,
Szerer's very adherence to the Bund's historical truths under present-day
circumstances, which were totally different from those of the interwar past,
prompted him, as stated, to adopt a markedly Ahad Ha'amic approach but

in reverse and in a much more idealistic way. It was Ahad Ha'am, after all, who had fathered the idea of the Jewish center in Palestine not as an existential alternative to exile but as a sociospiritual hub that, by projecting its influence, would safeguard the Jewish centers that were in jeopardy of becoming separated. In Szerer's rendering, it was Yiddish culture, propagated by the world organization of the Bund, that would become a unifying framework for all segments of Jewry, including Israel. Therefore, in a mirror image of Zionism, which had ingrained the State of Israel as the center of Jewish existence in the Diaspora, the Bund turned the Diasporic Yiddish culture into the center of Jewish life as the life of a world people. By the time it did so, the Jewish existential state of Diaspora, denoting the lack of equal rights, had ceased to exist in the democratic West. Aware that ramparts of foreignness that had separated the Jews from their surroundings had collapsed, Szerer reached a conclusion similar to that expressed by Simon Dubnow and Ahad Ha'am, each in his own way. Both of these thinkers, and the Bund as well, fought against assimilation. Dubnow wished to build a rampart in the form of an autonomous Jewish community organization; Ahad Ha'am sought to do the same by establishing the center in Palestine—ad the post-Holocaust Bund proposed to attain the same goal by fighting for the Yiddish language. Apart from this, the Bund had nothing left to offer that was related directly to Jewish life. Szerer did not regard the Jewish organization in the Western countries as enough of a barrier to the Jews' sweeping use of the vernacular and acceptance of local culture as their sole culture. In the Zionist State of Israel, of course, he observed assimilation trends that, although "of a different kind," were leading to the same result—the undermining of Klal Yisrael. Even the Bund, as a political organization, could not possibly counteract these trends, he believed. All that remained, then, was the idea and the ideal of "Bundism," which Szerer likened to a branch that was inseparable from the trunk (*shtem*) of the national tree. As long as the tree lives, Szerer vowed, "Bundism" would be one of its vital forces.

The more Szerer felt the Bund's political strength waning, the stronger his idealistic and Utopian style became. Five years after the aforementioned writings, in 1972, after the fifth world convention of the Bund, he wrote:

> It was a great convention. Without power (*makht*). Its greatness lay in its spirituality only. The convention of a movement immersed in a reality in which quality is supplanting quantity. A convention whose great, perseverant, and unchallengeable (*umtsushterlekher*) strength lies in the idea," that is, in "Bundism."[47]

In another article written pursuant to these remarks, Szerer asked himself what the Bund would offer the Jewish people and, especially its youth. He answered,

> We offer an exalted vision [*a derhoybndiker vizionerishn program*]. We are not approaching [the Jewish people] with masses, but we have to continue marching . . . by the force of belief in the truth of the Bundist idea [*bundisher ide'en*]. We come in the name of the great idea . . . of the Yiddish cultural counterrevolution [*gegenditiker kultur-revolutsie*], the one that illuminated the lives of Polish Jews and the one that all the Jewish Diaspora needs badly today.[48]

Thus, Szerer proposed to integrate the Bund's cultural vision into the "new Utopia"—the revolution of the young in the 1960s and 1970s—just as in the past it had been integrated in the Socialist Utopia. It was in this present-day integration, Szerer believed, that the Bund would derive its strength in the struggle against Zionism for the spiritual leadership of Klal Yisrael.

The editor of the Bund Party journal in Israel, Yitzhak Luden, continued to argue in the same vein some ten years later. In an article whose title speaks for itself: "A New Man in a New Society,"[49] written to mark the eighty-fifth anniversary of the founding of the Bund, Luden applied the Utopian idealistic contents to the entire history of the Bund. The Bund, he claimed, had never intended to take up the reins of political power. The party had been established, he asserted, mainly to change the human being (*kedey ibertsumakhn dem mentsh*), that is, to reeducate the Jew to render him fit for life in tomorrow's free society.

Some, of course, might contemplate this unrealistic Utopian rhetoric with contempt or with its opposite, sympathy. However, it should also be viewed as a sincere trend of thought that was nurtured by this group of Bund survivors, people who were living out their lives in the spirit of the aforementioned motto of the Huguenots: struggle against all odds by the few, a struggle in which their very perseverance was moral even if not all their motives were "pure."

The "Ahad Ha'amic" spirit in its Bundist construction was confirmed publicly in the 1980s by Professor Arthur Lermer of Montreal, who had succeeded Liebman Hersch and Emanuel Szerer as the party's leading intellectual.[50] Lermer articulated an idea that was a synthesis of sorts between Ahad Ha'am and Dubnow, one that would link the Jewish state and the organized Jewish Diaspora. By so proposing, Lermer attempted to retrieve Bundism from Utopia and reposition it in "Utopian realism," with which Zionism, too, had reconciled itself by this time. He also sought a compromise that would produce an accord between the progressive religious streams and the nonreligious. All of which, of course, for the same goal—Klal Yisrael, the cause of Jewish existence.

In sum, one may say that from the mid–1970s to the mid–1980s, the Bund covered the last stretch in its decades-long journey, which began at the end of the war, to a Klal Yisrael that existed as it was and was institutionalized in its own way. From then on, organizational cooperation with bourgeois and even Zionist institutions, both moderate and progressive, carried the party's sanction.

Indeed, the resolutions of the seventh convention (1985) admitted frankly, for the first time, that "the theoretical statement that the Bund accepts the principle that the Jews, dispersed around the globe, are one people with a shared fate, marks a new turning point [*vend-punkt*] in Bund thinking."[51] By implication, the Bund would henceforth play an active role in responsibility for the spiritual existence of the Jewish people around the world and the well-being of the State of Israel by adopting a critical attitude toward the policies of the Jewish political establishment "here" and "there." The Bund also manifested its integration into the worldwide Klal Yisrael symbolically by replacing the concept of exile (*galut*), in its various renditions, with the term customarily used by Western Jews, Diaspora (*tefutsa*). Influenced by the liberal consciousness in Western culture, the Bund acknowledged a principle that most of its members in the interwar years had rejected: that religion is the individual's personal concern and that one needed only to separate it from the state.

In a contrasting resolution, the Bund accepted the basic Zionist premise that the Jewish majority and Jewish sovereignty in the State of Israel were of special and extra meaning in the sustaining of Klal Yisrael, relative to the Diaspora, even if Israel's policies and actions, in the Bundists' opinion, were inconsistent with the interests of Klal Yisrael.

If so, what remained of the traditional Bund ideology? Two things remained: the war on assimilation, which became increasingly quixotic, and opposition to "Zionist colonialism," in which the Bund found increasingly numerous allies in various circles.

Comparing the Polish period in Bund history with the American, one may say that in Poland, from the political standpoint, there was much justice in the Bund's position that Polish Jewry could not solve its problems by means of emigration. The party was wrong in the domain of ideological principle, that is, its total negation of the Jewish national aspiration to establish a national home in Palestine. In the United States after the Holocaust, in contrast, the party's error was political and tragic, since it no longer had Jewish masses that it could lead. However, the Bund was right in the ideological sense of Klal Yisrael and in respect to relations between the State and People of Israel.

In regard to the continuity of the Jewish Diaspora, a special kind of cultural rebirth had taken place. Admittedly, it was not a Bundist rebirth, but an attempt was definitely being made to establish an equilibrium between Israel and the Diaspora in this respect. Thus, by way of the historical paradox, the mission of principle that the Bund had taken upon itself was being carried out by others who used different contents.

Furthermore, in the late 1980s and the early 1990s, after the Bund held its eighth convention, the party's anti-Zionism also took on a quixotic turn. While the party's Utopian, romantic, and idealistic nature stood out in its war on assimilation, its staunch opposition to Zionism became increasingly ridiculous in the political sense because, during this time, Zionism as a movement had practically ceased to exist in the Diaspora. By contrast, in ideological and idealistic terms, just as the Bundists were convinced that the Jewish people needed Bundism more than ever under the new post-Holocaust conditions, one might also say that Bundism was equally in need of Zionism as a sweepingly comprehensive ideology of Klal Yisrael.

CHAPTER 8

FROM ZIONIST KLAL TO JEWISH KLAL

We want a national home for all the Jews . . . for all who wish it.
—David Ben-Gurion, 1948

At the end of World War II, as the disaster of the Holocaust was followed by the achievement of the establishment of Jewish statehood, the Zionist Labor Movement found itself in disequilibrium. As a pioneering movement, it had lost its main source of vitality, its youth movement in Poland, but as a party it became the largest political force in Israel.[1] From then on, for more than the generation, it not only spearheaded the building and shaping of Israeli society, but also had a powerful influence on relations between the State of Israel and Klal Yisrael in the Diaspora, by means of the leading party, Mapai. Thus, by enacting the Law of Return (1950), the State of Israel presented Klal Yisrael with a basic constitutional statute that transformed the historical status of the Jewish people by giving Jews all over the world, in addition to civil status in their countries of residence, the additional and unrestricted option of citizenship in their national homeland. By so doing, Israel not only put an end to the "wandering Jew" phenomenon but also gave and vested the Jews with a special privilege: the right to choose between two homelands. This principle, implemented in the immigration policies of the Government of Israel for Zionist ideological reasons and political interest, eliminated, in theory and in practice, the focal points of Jewish political and economic distress in Europe, Asia, and Africa. Israel's actions in this regard made it the only Jewish political force that could offer comprehensive solutions to the problems of Klal Yisrael.

However, there was something paradoxical about this new phenomenon, in which Jewish sovereignty in Israel affected the status and condition of Klal Yisrael (or, as we call it, the "Jewish klal"). Most of the immigrants, Holocaust survivors from Europe and traditional-minded Jews from Islamic countries, arrived without Zionist education and awareness as the Labor Movement construed these terms. What is more, since the Zionist Movement had failed to sink deep roots among Western Jews, especially the young, aliya from the West, particularly of young people, was scanty and would so remain. Consequently, the transition from "Zionist klal" to "Jewish klal," which began back in the 1930s, accelerated powerfully in the 1950s and the 1960s in view of the rising awareness that as the existential danger to the Jews as individuals receded, concern for their existence as a Jewish people escalated.

The Bund shared this concern, as the previous chapter showed. However, whereas the Bund treated the matter mainly as an intellectual and Utopian issue because of the party's marginal status in Jewish public life, the Zionist Organization seemingly built it into a central political question. Now, however, for the first time in its history, the Zionist Movement had to confront free Western Jewry without its eastern European Jewish hinterland. Eastern European Jewry had had a profound and ramified national consciousness, in which the national interests of the Jewish people were paramount. In contrast, the Western Jewish tradition, including the Zionist tradition, was noted for its attempt to integrate the Jewish interest with civil rights, which were its main concern.

It was hard for the leaders of the Zionist Labor Movement to adjust to this new historical phenomenon, just as the leaders of the Bund never managed to understand it. Both movements, after all, were products of the national and political culture of eastern Europe. Therefore, the Bundists adhered to the Utopian vision of a Yiddish cultural renaissance while the latter advocated the strengthening of the halutsic movement as a leading force among the Jews of the West. Here again, however, there was a salient difference between the Bund's absolute Utopia and the Labor Movement's "Utopian realism." Therefore, the Bund dissociated itself from reality as it was and the Labor Zionists sought ways to adjust to it without relinquishing their less absolute Utopian vision.

One may define the relationship in the Labor Movement between these two fundamentals—realism and Utopian faith—as a traditional dialectic because it has accompanied the movement throughout its history and led to the synthetic political approach that I term "progressive compromise"—the kind of compromise through which the compromiser makes progress toward its goals even if it falls short of full attainment.

In Israel's first decade, it was mainly two people—David Ben-Gurion, the national leader, and the philosopher and professor Nathan Rotenstreich—who attempted, each in his own way, to develop and articulate this "progressive compromise." The former did so in the language of political ideology; the latter adopted a perspective that was both ideological and political. Rotenstreich, in his approach, was in several respects a successor to Berl Katznelson in his thinking, whereas Ben-Gurion, in the twists and spurts of his thinking, remained true to himself.[2]

Obviously, these two personalities were not the only participants in the debate. Even after the state had come into being, the Labor Movement continued to sustain both of its traditional outlooks—the one that Ben-Gurion defined as "from class to people" and the one that I call "from people to class." Importantly, the movement and its leader, Ben-Gurion, adhered to both views. This was especially evident in the two large kibbutz movements, Hakibbutz Hame'uhad and Hakibbutz Ha'artzi, which jointly had established Mapam, a left-wing opposition to Mapai. Both movements concurrently favored large-scale, unrestricted immigration but pinned their main Zionist hopes on halutsic aliya.[3] However, the "Jewish klal" issue was definitely of marginal concern in the debates of the labor parties, especially the larger of them, Mapai. At the seventh Mapai convention (1950), the veteran Zionist functionary Berl Locker, in a sarcastic expression of gratitude, noted that only two speakers in the debates addressed themselves to the problem of Israel-Diaspora relations. All the others concentrated on Israel's pressing existential issues.[4] Only eight years later, at the eighth Mapai convention (1958), did Moshe Sharett initiate a discussion about the state of the Diaspora. Even this, however, amounted to the receipt of reports from various countries; there was no comprehensive debate.[5]

Comparing these discussions with similar debates in the 1920s and 1930s, we see that, in view of Israel's social and economic problems, the Israel-centrism in the 1950s surpassed the Palestino-centrism of the past in its intensity. This illustrates with greater emphasis the importance that Ben-Gurion and Rotenstreich attributed to the topic and underscores their contribution, unusual for its time, to the "public thought" that dealt with it.

The public debate over Israel's relations with the "Jewish klal" had two phases and two facets. The first phase and facet concerned the political dispute over the basis of relations between the Israeli state and the World Zionist Organization; the second was typified by ideological debate about the essence of the relationship between the Jewish state and the Jewish people in Diaspora. The main protagonists in the political dispute were the charismatic American Zionist leader, Abba Hillel Silver, and his right hand man, Emanuel Neumann, on the Diaspora side, and Prime Minister David Ben-Gurion and the erstwhile Polish Zionist leader and Ben-Gurion's rival, Itzhak Gruenbaum, on the Israeli side.[6]

The confrontation focused on three issues: the place of the Zionist Movement in the Diaspora alongside the Jewish state; the status of the WZO in Israel relative to that of other Jewish organizations; and how, in essence, to differentiate between a Zionist and a non-Zionist when neither "makes aliya" (moves to Israel). The debate over these questions was both ideological and political, and it is difficult to determine which of these aspects came first. There is no doubt, however, that both mingled inseparably in the minds of members of that generation. What is more, the issues were of intrinsic material importance for the very existence of Zionism as the Jewish national movement. Accordingly, the root factor in the polemics was the contrast between two historical approaches in Zionism: Palestino-centrism, which had evolved into Israel-centrism, and exile-centrism, which had become Diaspora-centrism. Both outlooks had been strengthened by the Holocaust, in which most of the European Diaspora had been annihilated, and by the establishment of the Jewish state. According to those of the Israel-centric mind-set, the state belongs to the Jewish people at large and, for this reason, is the political center of the Jewish people. By implication, Israel is responsible for the continued existence of Diaspora Jewry. According to the Diaspora-centric view, precisely due to Israel's nature as a Jewish state, Diaspora Jews should take special care to be loyal citizens of their countries of residence above all. Behind this political argument, which carried a large measure of truth if considered mainly from a psychological perspective, was a historiosophic outlook. It derived its ideas from the historical past, that is, the Second Temple era, in which the Jewish Judea coexisted and interacted closely with an autonomous Jewish Diaspora. In view of their political concerns and historical awareness, the leading WZO personalities in the United States, Silver and Neumann, expressed three demands. First, they insisted on keeping Israel and the WZO totally separate; thus, only Zionists in the Diaspora were to operate under the WZO umbrella. Second, the functions of the Government of Israel were to be separate from those of the Zionist Executive, which was to be seated in New York, not Jerusalem. Third, Jewish culture in the Diaspora should be encouraged by the diasporic WZO and not by the Government of Israel.

Across the divide stood the Zionist leaders of eastern European origin, who, for political and ideological reasons, objected to this triple separation and, in particular, to the relocation of the Zionist Executive from Jerusalem to New York. The most outspoken member of this group was the erstwhile leader of the no longer extant Polish Jewry, Itzhak Gruenbaum. Gruenbaum, following the eastern European tradition, considered nationality an organic historical phenomenon and not a civil designation, as it was conventionally viewed in the West. According to this principled outlook, the Zionist Movement should be headquartered in the Jewish national home, should make that home its focal point, and should treat the state and the worldwide Zionist Movement as a single national entity.

BEN-GURION BETWEEN NEGATION AND ACCEPTANCE OF THE DIASPORA

Although Ben-Gurion agreed with Gruenbaum in principle, his political thinking was different. His twenty-five years of experience had acquainted him with
psychological leanings of American Jews in general and American Zionists in
particular. He knew the "dual loyalty" issue not only as a political problem, but
also as a question of principle. Therefore, he sought to set this special and new
relationship between the Jewish state and the Jewish Diaspora within a broader
and more flexible conceptual framework. To accomplish this, he resurrected an
"artful" formula that he had invoked in his testimony to the Peel Commission
in 1937. According to the wording that he had used there, world Jewry should
prefer a "national home" over a "Jewish state" in Palestine. A "home" would
be a manifestation of Jewish national sovereignty; a state would reflect the
sovereignty of its Jewish citizens only. The establishment of a Jewish state
might create tension between these two segments of the Jewish people. The
citizens of a Jewish state, for example, would be free to shut the gates of aliya
whereas the inhabitants of a Jewish "home" would not. Now that the sovereign
Jewish state had been established, Ben-Gurion's phrasing was mainly theoretical and forward-looking. "The state is not yet tantamount to the fulfillment of
Zionism," he said, "because it still lacks something that, just to say it nicely, I
will define by using the concept 'Jewish national home'—a home for the Jewish people." The state, in his opinion, belongs to its Jewish citizens, whereas
"we want a national home for all the Jews." Then, to be prudent, he immediately circumscribed himself: "for all who wish it." This, he said, would em-
body "the true partnership between the state and the Jewish people." Having
thereby created a constitutional distinction between the Jewish state and the
Jewish people, he was convinced that he had resolved the dual-loyalty issue.[7]
From then on, Jews who so desired could be citizens of their countries of residence and members of their "national home" in the State of Israel. Even the
United States Senate, Ben-Gurion noted, had favored the establishment of a
national home for the Jewish people in Palestine.

By saying this, Ben-Gurion seemingly attached a coherent definition
to the concept of the "Jewish klal" as used in this study. The "Zionist klal"
had been ideologically defined and so remained; "Klal Yisrael" was mainly
a matter of political intent. The term "Jewish klal," in contrast, articulates
the novelty of Jewish existence in the global sense: a state that has a diaspora and a diaspora that is linked to a state. Ben-Gurion's idea of the establishment of a shared framework for both components of the "Jewish
klal"—the State of Israel and the Jewish people—evolved in his thinking
into an outlook that negated establishment Zionism, as I show below. It was
this outlook that led Ben-Gurion to relate to the problem in two different

and clashing ways: covertly and overtly. Back in December 1948, at a debate in the Zionist Executive, Ben-Gurion had sent Itzhak Gruenbaum a note that expressed the gist of the worldview that had led him from the "Zionist klal" to the "Jewish klal":

> . . . It is clear that the Zionists have become Zionistically bankrupt. (The reason is obvious: the annihilation of Eastern European Jewry.) At this great hour—possibly the greatest in Jewish history—Jewry in exile does not have a leadership that is suited to the time. At the very moment when Zionism has triumphed, the Zionists have failed.[8]

Then, however, he mitigated this pessimistic assessment with optimistic remarks: "The Jews in exile have not become bankrupt and they sense the greatness of the hour. The Zionists do not know how to guide the Jews and are not fit to do so. On the contrary: they have become an obstacle between the state and the Jews."[9]

We may determine Ben-Gurion's opinion about the personalities of these "failed" leaders, foremost Silver and Neumann, from the contemptuous labels he applied to them in an internal debate at the Mapai Secretariat. He termed them "swindlers" (*shvindlerim*) and a leadership that had generated a climate of "bluff."[10]

The contents of Ben-Gurion's note to Gruenbaum were not slips of the pen. A year and a half later, in June 1950, he convened a group of Mapai activists at the Defense Ministry to discuss the situation of the WZO in the United States.[11] In his remarks, he accused the WZO of being a buffer between the state and the Jewish masses. To circumvent the WZO in the United States, he proposed the establishment of a Mapai action center that would develop a plan for direct activity among American Jews and, especially, the young.

In the aftermath of this initiative, Ben-Gurion signed the well-known agreement between himself, as the Prime Minister of Israel, and Jacob Blaustein, the president of the non-Zionist American Jewish Committee. According to the agreement, American Jews owed their first loyalty as American citizens to the United States and, as such, had no political commitment to the State of Israel. The Government of Israel undertook not to intervene in the internal affairs of American Jewry; American Jewry promised to give Israel economic aid and to facilitate halutsic aliya. The two leaders repeated these undertakings in their correspondence in 1956 and again in 1961.[12]

The agreement gave the impression of having been signed on behalf of all of American Jewry, an altogether unrealistic scenario in view of the political and spiritual realities of this Jewish community. However, it did attest to the political path that Ben-Gurion had adopted, a path that led him consistently from the Zionist movement to the Jewish people.

As an extension of that political and ideological line that Ben-Gurion had taken against establishment Zionism, a dispute erupted between him and a majority of the movement leadership over the question of the legal status for the WZO in Israel. At the XXIII Zionist Congress (Jerusalem, 1951), the following resolution was passed with the consent of all parties:

> The Congress believes it necessary for the State of Israel to bestow, by passing appropriate legislation, a recognized status upon the World Zionist Organization as *the representative of the Jewish people* in all matters related to the *organized participation* of Diaspora Jewry in the development and building of the country and in the rapid absorption of the immigrants.

In view of our remarks above, it is obvious that Ben-Gurion could not accept the WZO as the "representative of the Jewish people" for the "organized participation" of the people in assisting the State of Israel. Therefore, when about a year later the government presented the Knesset with a bill to regulate the WZOs status and defined the WZO as "the competent agency that will continue to operate in Israel for the development and settlement of the country," Ben-Gurion spoke out against it. As he explained from the Knesset rostrum, the WZO could not be recognized as the representative of the Jewish people in Israel since the state lacks the authority to determine this on behalf of a Jewish people that, in greater part, lives outside its borders. Behind the legalistic logic of this statement, however, lurked Ben-Gurion's disillusionment with Zionism and his frustration over the ineptitude of the WZO, on the one hand, and his great passion for the Jewish people—which would also prove short-lived—on the other. Ben-Gurion's negation of the Zionist establishment was so strong that he even rejected a compromise motion, prepared by Mapai members of the Knesset, that defined the WZO as the *organized* representative of the Jewish people. Ultimately the motion was defeated on a parliamentary technicality.

At the end of our survey of this debate over the relationship between the WZO and the Jewish state, it is hard to avoid a paradoxical reflection: there was something "Bundist" about the discussants' attitudes. At that very time, as we have seen, the Bund, after severe internal disputes and struggles, came around to a view that distinguished between the Jewish state and the Zionist Movement. In regard to the former, the Bund agreed that the establishment of statehood was an important event in Jewish history and that, therefore, Israel should be supported and strengthened. In regard to the latter, the movement stuck to its historical guns and continued to depict Israel as a menace to the integrity of the "Jewish klal."

In the first phase of the WZO debate, Silver and Neumann, each for a totally different reason, adopted a "Bundist" stance on the issue of separating the Jewish state from the Zionist Movement. In the second phase, Ben-Gurion, who had objected to the separation at first—thereby proving the point of the extreme wing of the Bund—became a zealous and consistent advocate of separation. His motives and rationales were totally different from theirs, of course. He considered Israel the center of the world Jewish reality; they deemed it to be only one of several Jewish realities in the far-flung Diaspora.

The debates over the status of the WZO in Israel and the nature of the "Zionist klal" ended in 1953–1954. Ben-Gurion temporarily retired to his ostensible "political desert" in Sede Boqer and demonstratively quit the WZO because, in his opinion, it had ceased to fulfill its Zionist missions. In 1954, his successor, Moshe Sharett, shepherded through the Knesset the covenant between the State of Israel and the WZO, which demarcated the spheres of activity of the latter in Israel and defined its status there.

From then until his final resignation in 1963, Ben-Gurion instigated thoroughgoing debates about the essence of Zionism after the establishment of the State of Israel. In this sense, he had reached the third stage in the development of his national thought. In the Second Aliya era, he had been one of the most extreme champions of the "halutsic klal"; in the 1930s, he had led the transition from the "halutsic klal" to the "Zionist klal"; and after the State of Israel came into being he spearheaded the changeover to the "Jewish klal." His transitions from phase to phase were dialectical in nature, composed of contrasts based on continuity and unity. Therefore, each new phase rested on the ideological foundations of the previous phase. In his thinking, this process was always conditioned on historical developments and influenced by his Utopian leanings. He began it by "seeking the way," continued by "leaping" in the new direction, and finished by "shaping" the new path that he had chosen.[13]

The first leap belonged to the era of the Second and Third aliyot. The second belonged to the 1930s, the establishment of the State of Israel, and the mass immigration in 1949–1952; the national watershed was crossed at this time. The third leap took place in subsequent years, after it had become clear that the appropriate shaping of Israel's new society would entail a special effort. Ben-Gurion construed the leap from the "Zionist klal" to the "Jewish klal" as a vehicle to use in this shaping. His thinking rested on two basic premises. First, the mass immigration, foremost that from the

Islamic countries, was dissimilar to the preceding waves of Zionist immigration from eastern Europe because it was more Jewish than Zionist. Second, the American Diaspora was neither Zionist in the traditional eastern European sense nor on the verge of liquidation.

The shift in Ben-Gurion's thinking occurred gradually. As early as 1950, he proclaimed, "The entire state [of Israel] is a Zionist enterprise and the property of the Zionist Movement and the Jewish people." To wit, unlike the past, a national triangle of sorts has come into being: state, movement, and people. This outlook, which elevates the Jewish people to equal status vis-à-vis Israel and the Zionist movement, would steadily gather strength over the years, but even then it was no longer pure theory. Ben-Gurion's new attitude, which, as stated, was influenced by his political struggle with Abba Hillel Silver over the extent of independence that the Zionist Organization of America should be allowed to exercise, would be applied in later years to the World Zionist Organization. Ben-Gurion felt that he would be addressing a different Jewish people than the one that Zionism had known before the Holocaust. In eastern Europe, he said, Zionism had been an "egoistic" interest of a Jewish public that was struggling for its political and economic status, whereas now, among Western Jews, Zionism was mainly an expression of altruistic national identity. On the basis of this distinction, he shifted at this time toward acquiescence in the differentiation between *gola,* exile, and *tefutsa,* diaspora. He agreed with those who claimed that diaspora preceded exile in Jewish history, and even if he limited his consent by contending that the dichotomy was neither absolute nor permanent and that a diaspora might become an exile if conditions changed for the worse, he basically accepted the philosophy of the American Jewish Committee, according to which American Jewishness is different from all its precursors in Jewish history.[14]

In 1951, while visiting United States, he stressed that while he considered the "ingathering-of-exiles" idea possible he doubted that it was actually a historical imperative.[15] Therefore, he asked of American Jewry only to participate actively in the newly evolved national triangle: by relating personally to the State of Israel, by studying of the Hebrew language, and by sending halutsim, pioneers, on aliya. Already then, however, he stated with deliberate emphasis that under the new conditions, "The Zionist message of the present day depends on two [factors]—the state and the [Jewish] people at large." Consequently, the more he valued the Jewish people, the more he devalued the WZO. Indeed, Ben-Gurion's critics noticed this trend from its very outset. In 1952, when Ben-Gurion presented the Knesset with the aforementioned bill to regulate the status of the WZO in Israel, he noted in his speech the historical importance of the WZO, its actions at the present time, and its role in the future.[16] He took the same opportunity to shower the Jewish people with praise for its contribution to the establishment of the State of Israel. In the debate that his speech set in motion, his critics claimed that he had overstated the importance of the Jewish people's contribution and, by so doing, was weakening the status of the Zionist Movement. Ben-Gurion replied, "I admit to having committed a greater sin: my Zionism is merely a part and an expression of my Judaism, and not the other way around. I am a Zionist only because I am Jewish, and not because there is anti-Semitism in the world." By saying this, he acknowledged the possibility of a different kind of Zionism, such as the Herzlian variety, and conceded that he would not rule it out. "However, many of us who are of Russian Jewish origin—and I include myself in that multitude—were born Zionists because we were born Jewish; we inherited our Zionist aspirations and our ties with the homeland of our ancient Jewish forebears."[17]

These remarks marked the beginning of the additional turning point in Ben-Gurion's Zionist Weltanschauung. Just as he made a leap in the early 1930s from a working class to a working nation, so now he wished to leap from the Zionist Organization to the Jewish nation. Back then, the practical meaning of the idea was to shift the center of national action from the Histadrut, the Federation of Labor, to the *Histadrut Tsiyyonit,* the Zionist Organization. Now, similarly, the idea was to shift the emphasis of action from the Zionist Organization to the Jewish people. Moreover, just as Ben-Gurion had once been convinced that class values could help to shape the Jewish people, now he believed it possible to "infect" the nation with the Zionist idea. In the 1930s, Ben-Gurion realized that the price of turning to the people was a temporary diminution of social Utopianism and political activism. In the 1950s, he quickly deduced that an appeal to Western Jewry would also come at a price: limiting the Zionist vision to the small groups of Jews who would fulfill it. Therefore, even as he labored to pass the bill that would regularize the status of the WZO in Israel, he already believed that the WZO had lost its vitality and had become superfluous. In a personal letter in early 1953, he proclaimed, ". . . Zionism means living in Eretz Israel and not belonging to the Zionist Organization," adding that life in Eretz Israel is Zionist only if it is a life of service. Therefore, he stressed, "In my opinion and according to the belief . . . by which I live, a person is a Zionist if he lives in Israel, raises his children there, and devotes his life to the cause of Israel, the development of the Hebrew culture, and the absorption of new immigrants."[18] He addressed these remarks to the fulfillers of Zionism and its potential servants in Israel and the Diaspora. The next stage of his transition occurred in late 1953, when in a blunt and provocative public statement in a letter to the Zionist Executive Council, he ruled that Zionism means one thing only: aliya.

Thus, Ben-Gurion marked his passage from the "Zionist klal" to the "Jewish klal" by returning to the "halutsic klal."

The stronger his Utopian urge became and the more firmly he became connected with young people, the more pungent his attitude toward establishmentarian Zionism became and the more his criticism evolved into attacks. What is more, his conciliatory attitude toward Diaspora Jews changed. In 1954, he still asked the WZO, "Does Zionism also have consideration for de facto assimilation . . . into the non-Jewish culture?"[19] By so asking, he wished to say that his demand for the aliya of Zionists was meant primarily to resist assimilation in the Diaspora. However, at the First World Ideological Conference (Jerusalem, 1957), he exclaimed passionately: "The name 'Jew' not only preceded the name 'Zionist,' it is much more than the name 'Zionist.' *Judaism is more than Zionism* [emphasis mine], and the existence of Judaism is inconsistent with assimilation, which is the lot of most of those who call themselves 'Zionists' in exile [gola]."[20]

Although he did not mean to suggest that this assimilation was deliberate, he pointedly stressed his belief that de facto assimilation was equally dangerous if not more so. In his bellicose frame of mind, he went on to state that "The State of Israel is now the Zionist Movement; it is [the state] that carries the vision of redemption to those who dwell there and to the [Jewish] people in exile [gola]."[21]

As stated, the tenor of his remarks about the Diaspora also changed. In this matter, Ben-Gurion found himself trapped between his belief in the process of continual change in history—especially Jewish history—and his adherence to stable values. To wit, he was snared by the sharp distinction that he drew between Jewish existence in eastern Europe, the cradle of the Zionist ideology, and Jewish existence in the West, which needs the Zionist vision for its survival. One may say with confidence that Ben-Gurion had, in fact, made peace with the existence of an exile-Diaspora (*gola-tefutsa*) and negated exile (galut) in theory only. Although he distinguished between Soviet Jewry (which was still living in exile/gola) and American Jewry (which inhabited a diaspora/tefutsa), he found a common denominator in both states of existence. Its gist was the connection with Eretz Israel, the status of minority, tension between the two centers of cultural authority, and the peculiar economic status, exclusive to them, on which their existence was based. In sum, he believed that Jews outside of Israel could be likened to "human dust that attempts to cling together more than other people under the same conditions might."[22] That stinging expression, "human dust," was not really meant pejoratively in this context. It was more like his objective assessment of a collectivity that maintained its national consciousness in the absence of a political framework. Ben-Gurion advised this collectivity to retain its messianic purpose, to learn Hebrew, and to maintain a personal relationship with the State of Israel.

Ben-Gurion's principled attitude toward exile as a historical phenomenon was quite different. In 1957, Ben-Gurion inveighed, in a style reminiscent of his youthful Second Aliya days, against those who engaged in the "glorification" of exile:

> Each of us contemplates in respectful awe and profound admiration the great moral strength that the Jews displayed in their wanderings and suffering in exile. [It was due to this strength that they were able] to withstand enemies and scorners, oppressors, and murderers without relinquishing their Jewishness. However, the exile amidst which the Jews are still living is, in my eyes, a woeful, impoverished, wretched, and dubious experience. It is nothing to take pride in. On the contrary—it deserves categorical negation. I would respect any man who is steeped in illness, suffering, and agonies but struggles for his existence and refuses to succumb to his bitter fate, but I would not consider his situation an ideal one. . . . I do not condemn Shylock for charging interest for a living. He had no choice in his place of exile and in his moral quality he surpassed the grand nobles who humiliated him. But I will not transform Shylock into an ideal and a role model. The Jews in exile [gola] are not Shylocks but it is difficult to equate the glorification of life in exile with the ideal that, seventy years ago, was titled "Zionism," and as a negator of exile I negate the glorification of exile.[23]

It was evidently this outlook, among other factors, that prompted Ben-Gurion in 1960 to take the staunch public stance that he manifested in the issue of having Adolf Eichmann tried before a Jewish court of law in Israel. In the teeth of international public opinion and pressure from some American Jewish leaders—especially the president of the American Jewish Committee, his friend Joseph Proskauer—Ben-Gurion stood his ground, asserting that the State of Israel was entitled to prosecute Eichmann on behalf of the Jewish Holocaust victims who had no other national entity to represent them. He said this even though Proskauer had warned him that such an action might be harmful to Israel's security interests, since at that very time Ben-Gurion was attempting, without notable success, to persuade the American President, Dwight Eisenhower, to provide Israel with various types of advanced arms. To persuade the American administration to change its mind, Proskauer stressed to Ben-Gurion, sympathetic public opinion would be needed. Ben-Gurion undoubtedly intended by his action on Eichmann to strengthen Israel's status as the defender of the national interest of world Jewry[24] and, thereby, as the exemplar of the historical and political watershed that Klal Yisrael had crossed.

There is, of course, a connection between Ben-Gurion's concern for the "Jewish klal" and his reduction of the concept of "Zionism" to the trickle of Jews who immigrated to Israel and lived pioneering lives there. His wish in regard to the halutsim was that they would revive the pioneering aliya spirit that began with the Second Aliya. He demanded that Israel's own young people demonstrate the pioneerism of a "serving elite" and he set a personal example in this regard by retiring to Sede Boqer. By so doing, he returned to his "first leap" in the middle of his "third leap." At that time, contemplating the masses of non-Zionist immigrants, he "discovered" a motive force that, in his opinion, they possessed—messianic yearning. When Nathan Rotenstreich pointed out the contrast between Zionism and messianism—after all, messianism targets the end of history while Zionism is a historical movement and an outgrowth of special historical conditions that aimed to create a different historical reality for the Jewish people— Ben-Gurion retorted in a manner that attests to both his Utopian leanings and his turn to the "Jewish klal": "I construe the messianic goal and vision not metaphysically but *socially, culturally, and morally.* The messianic idea denotes not the end of history but the process of its *redemption*." Moreover, the process corresponds to the nature of the "Jewish klal," as I define the term, because "This belief of mine is based on familiarity with the Jewish people and not on mystical faith. The divine splendor is within us, in our souls, and is not external to us."[25]

In his "leap" from the "Zionist klal" to the "Jewish klal," Ben-Gurion seems to have needed dialectical balances. Thus, in contrast to establishmentarian Zionism, which he deemed to be degenerating, he lauded the young Jews in Israel and the Diaspora who were imbued with pioneering spirit, and in his *acquiescence* in the existence of the Jewish Diaspora (tefutsa) he reemphasized the *negation* of the Jewish exile (galut). By using this balancing dialectical method, even if he did so inadvertently, Ben-Gurion was able to maintain continuity in his worldview despite occasional severe revisions. Therefore, his ideological innovations always had prior foundations. Indeed, it seems that Ben-Gurion had never ceased to be a man of the Second Aliya. It was in that era, too, that he had experienced a "messianic" thrill upon the publication of the Balfour Declaration, which he considered an augury of the Jewish national redemption.

THE CONTROVERSY BETWEEN BEN-GURION AND ROTENSTREICH

The only intellectual in the Zionist Labor Movement who tackled Ben-Gurion's old-new doctrine, directly and indirectly, was Nathan Rotenstreich, then a young academic and original thinker. Ben-Gurion may have been attracted to Rotenstreich's thinking by the balanced and deep Katznelsonian tone that resonated from it and by his continual psychological need for intellectual sparring in matters related to Weltanschauung. The left flank of the Labor Movement—the Mapam leaders Ya'akov Chazan, Yitzhak Tabenkin, and Me'ir Ya'ari, his spiritual comrades and political rivals—met this need in the ideological debate over the essence of Socialism and the attitude to take toward the Soviet Union. In issues of Zionism and Jewish existence, in turn, his partner in dialogue was Nathan Rotenstreich.

In contrast to the messianic craving that Ben-Gurion defined as the motive force in Jewish national existence, Rotenstreich considered the aspiration to "auto-emancipation" a national imperative without which the "Jewish klal" might disintegrate. In other words, he attempted to apply Leo Pinsker's formula in a Jewish reality that had changed. Pinsker had spoken of the auto-emancipation of "pre-emancipation" and "emancipation" Jews, whereas Rotenstreich demanded an "auto-emancipation" effort on the part of "post-emancipation" Jews in the free Western democracies.

Alternatively phrased, Rotenstreich's intention was to insert an additional phase in the dialectical process of the Jewish national liberation—from "emancipation" as a universal principle to "auto emancipation" as a Zionist national imperative and thence to the "auto-post-emancipation," so to speak, of the free Jews.

Paradoxically, one may say that Pinsker's and Rotenstreich's dialectic also corresponds to the phases of the development of the Bund—from Socialist-style "emancipation" to autonomous national "auto-emancipation" in the Socialist society, and thence to the "auto-post-emancipation" of the Jewish national culture in free Western society.

In 1944–1945, as World War II was winding down and the magnitude of the Holocaust had become evident, Rotenstreich realized that Zionism henceforth would be facing a different Diaspora, in terms of its political status and spiritual essence, than that of eastern Europe. He was the first to note that Western Jewry, which had passionately supported the establishment of a Jewish state in Palestine since the Biltmore conference in 1942, differentiated between Jewish sovereignty in Palestine and the ingathering of Jews there. Rotenstreich, unlike Pinsker, did not regard the establishment of a Jewish state as the pinnacle of Jewish "auto-emancipation," as most American Jews did, in his opinion, including the political Zionists and, of course, non-Zionists who favored the idea of statehood.[26]

In contrast to both outlooks, Rotenstreich proposed a third: the "Jewish klal" auto-emancipation viewpoint. Its crux is liberation in three senses: from political subjugation by means of the restoration of national sovereignty; from the menace of disintegration and dispersion by ingathering large segments of the Jewish people in its historical homeland; and from the danger of assimilation into the surrounding culture. Therefore, until this reality changes fundamentally, Jews outside of Eretz Israel are mired in exile (galut) even if those in the enlightened countries term it a "diaspora" (tefutsa).

Thus, "exilic" awareness, a state dependent of time, place, and conditions, became for Rotenstreich a crucial element in the existence of the globally dispersed "Jewish klal." As mass immigration to Israel liquidated the exile (gola) in various parts of the world, the *state* of exile (galut) continued to exist. Rotenstreich, unlike many Zionists, admitted that the Jewish emancipation in the West and, particularly, in the United States, had been successful. However, he wished to point Zionist education in the direction of the fear that flowed from this success, that is, the danger of the eradication of Jewry by means of cultural assimilation. Accordingly, in his opinion, only by challenging the premise that emancipation had solved the Jewish problem in exile might one create a dialogue between the two segments of the nation—that in the homeland and that in exile. The dialogue, he continued, would be based on recognition of the existence of parallel forms of Jewish life, in the United States and in Israel, as a historical phenomenon that must be accepted but not as a national reality to be lauded. Hence, struggle against it is necessary.[27] In Rotenstreich's judgment, this educational path, intended solely for a minority, corresponds to an interim phase in the history of the Zionist Movement that will last until the vision of ingathering the exiles would become a reality. In this sense, his outlook meshed perfectly with the beliefs and aspirations of Ben-Gurion and the kibbutz movements on the activist Left.[28]

It was on the basis of this "unifying pioneerism" theory that its developer, Rotenstreich, took a stance in the debate about the status of the WZO in Israel.[29] Rotenstreich decried the inclination of some American Zionists to give the WZO an autonomous status, because this notion flowed from, and was nourished on, an ideology of exile that accepts the fragmentation and dispersion of the Jewish people. However, Rotenstreich, unlike Ben-Gurion, believed that the State of Israel could not replace the WZO because its sovereign domain did not extend to a majority of Jews.

As for Israel-Diaspora relations, Rotenstreich differentiated between two types of state power, the power to decide and the power to act. The former is principled and absolute, the latter is practical and relative. In matters pertaining to the State of Israel and its citizens, the state reserves the supreme right to decide. This is not the case in regard to the power of world Jewry to act or take initiatives vis-à-vis the state. Here, Israel–Diaspora cooperation is possible and necessary, provided of course that here, too, the right to decide remain in the state's hands. To encourage this cooperation, Rotenstreich proposed in the establishment of a "supreme chamber," in which both the Diaspora and the State of Israel would be represented. Even if the Diaspora Jews turn down this proposal lest they be accused of dual loyalty, it is Israel's duty to offer it to them.

Pursuant to this line of reasoning, which proposes to gather the many forms of Jewish life under one umbrella, Rotenstreich advocated a restructuring of the WZO. The WZO, he said, should be an alliance between Israel and Diaspora Jewry in which the former is represented not by voluntary political parties but by its legislature. "Thus, the key difference between Zionists in Israel, who are Zionists within a political bloc, and other Zionists, will be expressed." This union of the institutions of state and of Zionism would emphasize the Zionist complexion of the state. Rotenstreich realized that such an alliance between the state and the WZO would be no simple matter in many respects, for both sides. "It cannot possibly be an easy alliance, because the reality that it reflects is not simple but multifaceted and strewn with difficulties." Therefore, the "norm" of seeking convenience should be supplanted by the norm of recognizing the social and political multifacetedness of the Jewish condition. Accordingly, "The constitution should reflect Jewish sociology and not disregard it." Thus, although he was a member of Mapai, Rotenstreich swerved from his party's stance and, in particular, from Ben-Gurion's, in respect to relations between Israel and the WZO. Unlike Ben-Gurion's "Israel-centric" approach, which lurked behind legalistic and formalistic rationales, Rotenstreich wished to give the representative organ of the Jewish people a special status in Israel. The very existence of the "supreme chamber" that he proposed to establish might deprive the state of some of its sovereign authority even if its powers were limited to Israel–Diaspora relations. Ben-Gurion objected to this on political grounds; Rotenstreich disputed Ben-Gurion's viewpoint on the status of the WZO for the same reason. Ben-Gurion, as stated, agreed to give the Zionist organ a limited official status in Israel, whereas Rotenstreich tried to find a formula for the creation of a setting that would create an organic union between Israel, on one hand, and the WZO and other Jewish organizations, on the other. This explains Rotenstreich's proposal to create a link between the Knesset, representing the Jewish collective will in Israel, and the Zionist Movement in the Diaspora, reflecting the will of the Jews as individuals, within the unifying framework of the restructured WZO. This proposal vaguely resembled Ben-Gurion's attitude, immediately after the state was established, toward the ideological and political identity of the State of Israel and the Zionist Movement and, in particular, the Zionist Executive. For Rotenstreich, the idea stemmed from recognition of multifacetedness, whereas for Ben-Gurion it flowed from the wish to attain oneness. Rotenstreich's intention, then, was not to impose the will of the state on the movement but to create conditions for cooperation within one setting.

In Rotenstreich's opinion, the WZO would deserve the status of the unifier of Jewish and Israeli life only if it admitted "that the Jewish question has not been solved, that the Jewish question is a question for all Jews, and [that] there is no discrimination among Jews."

Rotenstreich's outlook prompted him to take issue with Simon Rawidowicz, who had developed a theory of absolute equality and balance between the center in Eretz Israel and the Diaspora as a material historical phenomenon of Jewish existence. According to this outlook, the Jews' timeless existence depends not on one center but on multiple centers. In the new reality that followed the establishment of the State of Israel, Jewry resembled not a circle with Israel in its center but an ellipse with Israel at one end and the Diaspora at the other, the two combining into "two that are one."[30] Rotenstreich and Rawidowicz did agree about several basic premises. First, the Jews' dispersion endangers their national existence; this is the current meaning of the state of exile. In the opinion of both thinkers, the Jewish problem is one in all locations and there is no meaningful difference between one form of existence and another. Both accepted the relative equivalency of all segments of the Jewish people, an acknowledgment that was related to their disapproval of, if not opposition to, Ahad Ha'am's spiritual-center theory. However, they differed on one crucial point: the distinction between relative and absolute equality and, in regard to this, the difference between the autonomous status of the Diaspora and that of Israel as the epicenter of the all-inclusive Jewish reality.

Rotenstreich agreed with Rawidowicz that "No segment of the Jewish people is valuable in itself [except as part of Klal Yisrael]." In this sense, the segments are equivalent in a way. However, where the Jewish state is at issue, this particular segment of the Jewish people, the one that has gathered in the State of Israel, has an advantage over all other segments due to its comprehensive national status, "since the entire Jewish fate depends on the achievements and success of the operation that this segment has been asked to perform." This led Rotenstreich to the important dialectic premise that "Jewish unity is such that is not only consistent with preference of the State of Israel and matters related to it over any other interest in Jewish life, but also necessitates this priority." Although this expresses some degree of equivalence, it is not a total equivalence in terms of the overall national interest. Therefore, "As long as it is the overall national meaning of diverse Jewish life that counts in our calculus, we may take the Diaspora into consideration but must not grant of equal status in overall national terms." For this reason, Rotenstreich categorically rejected Rawidowicz's claim that recognizing the equivalence would solve the Jews' existential problems. "Equality itself," he said, "is the most problematic aspect of the whole matter." By saying this, Rotenstreich took a swipe at the most beloved goal in the Diasporist ideology.[31]

In the first Israeli–American dialogue of Jewish intellectuals, which took place almost ten years later (1962), Rotenstreich explained why equality is problematic in a way that sparked controversy.[32] Israel, he said, is a fact that was created by a spiritual aspiration. Any other form of Jewish life, however important and influential it may be, is merely a fact, albeit a "fortunate fact." This led him to argue that Israel is the only form of Jewish life that is shaped by the Jewish collectivity as such. American Jewry, in contrast, is a collection of Jewish individuals who come together to maintain collective life. Beyond this distinction, he outraged his American interlocutors by stating that the goal of Diaspora Jewry is Jewish survival whereas that of Israeli society is creative life.

By expressing himself in this fashion, Rotenstreich did not mean to dismiss Jewish existence in Diaspora on moral grounds. On the contrary: "There is no doubt"—he stated in the mid–1950s—"that the Jews of the Western exile [gola] have a powerful and dynamic wish to exist as Jews, and [this] inspires them to act in various ways and withstand various tests that their environment and its development present."[33] Objectively, however, this will is all that these Jews retain; they have long since shed the other attributes of nationhood, such as distinctive language, spatial concentration, an inclusive set of institutions, and even a standard religious pattern. Moreover, Rotenstreich had no doubt that objective reality would prevail in its confrontation with the Jewish subjective will. In contrast, "The very act of the Jewish ingathering in the State of Israel, objectively and by necessity, re-positions the Jews of Israel in Jewish history and [requires them] to live within the Jewish historical horizon." Diaspora Jews, who participate in the history of their countries of residence, have no influence on the overall collective Jewish history as Jews in Israel have. Therefore, they consider their support of Israel an expression of their contribution to an overall Jewish history in which they have no active personal role. The result, paradoxically, is the strengthening of Israel's status in the Jewish reality for a reason that is undesirable in the overall national sense. The desired goal, after all, is unity within the idea. The idea at issue, first of all, recognizes Jewish nationhood at large and, in this sense, gives the State of Israel an objectively preferred status within it. The idea flows from an inclusive historical consciousness that links the past to the present and both to the future. By expressing this demand, Rotenstreich attempted to create an awakening for the national ideal in a "post-emancipation" Jewish society that, in its objective essence, in terms of its status in its milieu, no longer needed it with the exception of the subjective wishes of several segments that were steadily dwindling even as Rotenstreich penned his words. Therefore, like the Bundists at the time, the Labor Zionists became increasingly Utopian.

SUMMATION

To sum up the direct and indirect debate between Ben-Gurion and Rotenstreich, one may say that the controversy revealed a difference, although not a clash, between two outlooks on the "Jewish klal." Ben-Gurion, having despaired of the "Zionist klal," turned to the "Jewish klal" in the Utopian belief that it would engineer a rebirth of the "halutsic klal," without which he could not imagine the building of Jewish statehood in the qualitative sense.

It is difficult at this point to avoid the urge to liken Ben-Gurion's Utopian idealistic frame of mind to the similar mind-set of Emanuel Szerer, the intellectual leader of the vestigial Bund in the United States, whom we discussed in the previous chapter. I do not consider the similarity a coincidence. Both men had become disillusioned with reality and, therefore, increasingly resorted to dreams. Yet there was a difference between them. Szerer yearned for Utopia while standing on the shattered fragments of his dream, whereas Ben-Gurion headed a creative endeavor that had not yet become worthy of his dream. For this reason, both of them pinned their Utopian hopes on a can-do elite—Szerer on the zealous and devoted perpetuators of Yiddish culture and Ben-Gurion on the Zionist-fulfillment halutsim. Both also entertained Utopian attitudes toward scientific development and revolutionary technology.

After having made this comparison, one should also compare the outlooks of the two "house intellectuals," Y. Y. Trunk and Nathan Rotenstreich, from their clashing points of departure, the Bundist-national-ideological and the Zionist-national. In the 1950s, both men constituted one-man intellectual oppositions, so to speak, within their respective parties. They remained loyal to their movements' ideas but distanced themselves from, and even criticized, the party politics that the movements practiced. Their Socialist and national Weltanschauung was based not only on rational analysis of the social and political reality but also on Kantian ethical idealism. Thus, both vehemently rejected the dogmatic materialism of Marxism, chiefly but not exclusively in its political manifestations. Trunk indirectly, and Rotenstreich directly, criticized monistic materialism as an explanation of the march of history and the essence of society. Taking issue with Marxism, they stressed spiritual and psychological elements as the motive forces of individual and group actions. From this standpoint, both thinkers also predicated their worldview on Utopianism, but with one basic difference: Trunk was a realistic Utopian in the social and national sense in interwar Poland and became a national-culture Utopian after the Holocaust. Rotenstreich, in turn, started out as a Utopian realist and so remained, both as the Zionist and as a "house intellectual" in the Labor Movement. As the years passed after the establishment of the State of Israel, his view of Klal Yisrael became increasingly realistic.

Against this background of Trunk's Utopianism and Rotenstreich's Utopian realism, they came to agree on several basic premises. Both advocated the national auto-emancipation of post-emancipation Jewry as a condition for the continued existence of Klal Yisrael. Neither considered the state the be-all and end-all of Jewish nationhood; both judged the dispersed segments of the Jewish people to be equivalent. Rotenstreich even retreated from his assertion of the exclusive centrality of the State of Israel vis-à-vis the Diaspora, as I showed above. By so positing, he, like Trunk, recognized the historical legitimacy of the existence of the Diaspora.

The difference between them, as stated, was the difference between a Utopianist and a Utopian realist. Trunk's Utopianism was mainly ideological and spiritual; it addressed itself to collective nationhood and culture. Rotenstreich's Utopian realism, in contrast, was associated with society and with the national consolidation of a state and a movement. This is why he championed the establishment of a world Jewish parliament, so to speak, in which Israel and the Diaspora would be represented. This is also why he strove to elevate the Zionist Movement in Israel over other Jewish organizations and regarded pioneering aliya, above all, as the strand that would forever bind Israel and the Diaspora together.

At day's end, both men experienced a similar denouement within their parties: a lack of ideological influence. This seems to be the fate of the "house intellectual" in his or her political milieu. Viewed in retrospect, the intellectuals sometimes do prove to have been right. In the case at hand, both Trunk and Rotenstreich were right. In our era of globalization, multiculturalism, and border-crossing diasporism, Klal Yisrael cannot exist without the "supreme idea" of a "world people" that struggles continually for its national and intellectual auto-emancipation.

Nevertheless, there was and remains a basic difference between them. Trunk started out as a Utopian realist and became a Utopianist; Rotenstreich remained a Utopian realist throughout. Therefore, the former found refuge for the dying Yiddish culture in idealistic ideation while the latter

stopped trying to develop a principled ideological framework within which
the political Klal Yisrael could exist. Basically, their approaches were differentiated by the "total constructivist" outlook of the Zionist Labor Movement, which, by attaining its goals only in part, generated unending
disappointment but also steadily regenerating hope. This is why, notwithstanding the dispute between them, Rotenstreich and Ben-Gurion were
close in a very real way.

According to Ben-Gurion's thinking, the reinstatement of Jewish
statehood would eventually solve the Jewish problem primarily by means
of aliya; this failing, the unshakable bond between Diaspora Jews and the
State of Israel would accomplish the same. Rotenstreich, in contrast, did
not regard the achievement of statehood as a national solution. Thus, countering the "statist emancipation" that Israel had ostensibly given Diaspora
Jewry, he posited a Jewish auto-emancipation that transforms the Israel-
linked "Jewish klal" into a equal partner in the effort to sustain its integrity
and unity. This klal is equal in status but not equal in value, as Ben-
Gurion's polemic with Simon Rawidowicz shows. After all, Ben-Gurion
argued, the unity of the "Jewish klal" depends more on the national center
in Israel than on any Diaspora center or all Diaspora centers combined. In
other words, the "Jewish klal" outlook itself entails the preference of the
Jewish state in this sense. Here and there one finds a minute but important
difference in the way the two leaders viewed the centrality of the State of
Israel in the reality of the "Jewish klal." Ben-Gurion had been Palestinocentric before the state had been founded and remained "Israel-centric" afterwards. Rotenstreich was "Jewish-centric" above all; he gave the State of
Israel a preferential status due to his wish to sustain world Jewish national
unity. Therefore, Rotenstreich recommended the establishment of a single
institution in which both Diaspora Jewry and Israel would be represented
and could pursue their shared interests. Ben-Gurion opposed this because,
in his opinion, the State of Israel was the sole representative of the Jewish
collective will. From Ben-Gurion's standpoint, this debate was a reincar-
nation of his dispute with Berl Katznelson in the 1920s about participating
in the Zionist Organization.

The public importance of the discourse between the two has diminished
over time, but on its way to oblivion it made two "stopovers" that proved the
correctness of both thinkers' arguments. The first was the eruption of solidarity and national identification on the part of Diaspora Jewry, especially in
the United States, during the Six-Day War—a "Jewish klal" demonstration of
support of Israel according to the Ben-Gurionic worldview and an auto-
emancipationist awakening of American Jews, the sort for which Rotenstreich had hoped. In the years immediately after the war, halutsic aliya from

the United States surpassed all previously known levels. Even though half of the thousands who arrived (nearly 9,000) returned to their prior homes within a few years, the residues of that auto-post-emancipation awakening, which included aliya, are still visible in American Jewry.

At the time of the Yom Kippur War (1973), concern for Israel's survival became a problem of the "Jewish klal" in the Diaspora. This concern, like its predecessor—the auto-emancipationist awakening—further strengthened the feeling of "Jewish klal" at the expense of the "Zionist klal." This meant that Zionism, embroiled in the complications and contradictions that flowed from its historical achievements, made its peace with the "Jewish klal" as it was instead of energizing the "Jewish klal" and serving it as a source of ferment.

On this point, Nathan Rotenstreich was unquestionably right in that, paradoxically, the strong centripetal forces at work in the "Jewish klal," in the absence of a shared guiding and unifying ideal, endangered the integrity of this collective. Evidence of this is the transformation of Holocaust remembrance into a central ethos in the Jewish collective reality and the dislodging of Israel from its position at the epicenter of the Jewish klal's collective identity.[34] From this standpoint, in view of the polar trends among the Jews, it is worth redebating Zionism as an idea that, in the existing historical reality, captures the concept of Jewish peoplehood in the most comprehensive way. Zionism, after all, has incorporated parts of the ideological and value fundamentals of each of its components: the religious, the secular, the nationalist, the political, the democratic, and the liberal. Therefore, only in Zionism, among the diverse worldviews that one encounters among the Jewish people, is there at least an intellectual and ideological element and a historical tradition that gives expression to Klal Yisrael.

CHAPTER 9

CONCLUSION

*Even the Bund who fought against Klal Yisrael politics was in fact
serving Klal Yisrael.*

—Yaʿacov Lestschinsky, 1940

CONVERGING ALTERNATIVES

At the end of an era, at the terminus of a journey down the twentieth century in the intricacies of the public thought of the Bund and the Zionist
Labor Movement, with its serpentine references to Klal Yisrael, we return to
that Reform center in New York and the event that took place there, an event
pregnant with historical symbolism, and ask one question: Has the music
faded, leaving behind only the lyrics and the separation that they create?

They have not, I would say. That music articulates the collective ethos
and the lyrics express the collective myth, as the members of that generation
perceived and construed their aspirations, struggles, and realities in both the
past and the present. The "musical notation" of the ethos was related to values: rebellion against the present-day state of exile and total rejection—
political, economic, and cultural—of this condition, and the nurturing of
collective pride by means of uncompromising effort to normalize the Jews'
individual and national status in modern society; the "Utopian" goal of rein-
venting the Jew—a brave, proud, and quiet person, devoted to the public interest—all of which as part of an optimistic universal amalgam, a future
society in which the national, economic, and civil contradictions and dis-
tresses of today's society are cleared away. In the course of that century,
some of these ethoses came to pass and others were shattered amidst tragedy.
Thus, the Soviet Union and interwar Poland denied the Jews the recognition
that they craved as an equally privileged nationality, but the Jewish state
came into being. The Emancipation failed horrifically in the Holocaust but
the Jews' civil status has changed in crucial ways in the half-century that has

259

lapsed since the Second World War. The ethoses that both movements share played a perceptible role in these political accomplishments, foremost in the spirit of struggle and rebellion against a reality that they instilled in that portion of Jewry that had embraced modernity and, especially, in youth movements and organizations that appealed to young adults. This rebellion, although aimed in different if not contrary directions, had a common denominator: the ethos of national resurrection, be it in the Diaspora or in Eretz Israel. It was this commonality that led the postwar remnants of the Bund, after a lengthy journey, to the ideological and political setting of Klal Yisrael.

As for the lyrics that expressed the "collective myth," that is, the shared conceptual awareness and political experience, the historical perspective leads us by necessity to a different conclusion. The radicalism of the Bund and the Labor Movement was a manifestation of two modern Utopianisms— the "Utopian realism" of the former, with the emphasis on "Utopian," and the "realistic Utopianism" of the latter, with the emphasis on the "realistic." Both movements were outgrowths of the Jewish reality in Imperial Russia. Both carried a practical logic from the moment they appeared in the Jewish public scene, at the beginning of the twentieth century, to World War II. The logic of the Bund stemmed from the Jewish national reality in eastern Europe; that of the Labor Movement, influenced by the general national reality in that area, found that the Jewish people would not survive as a nationality unless at least part of the nation returned to its historical territory. Both movements were Utopian and realistic, and it is the historian's inescapable duty to determine which was more so. The question should be first explored in respect to the initial and main period in the lives of these movements, from the time they were founded to the beginning of World War II. From then on, the fate of European Jewry would be determined mainly by objective external forces.

The main question that preoccupied both movements in the first period of their history was not the Jews' physical existence but their collective national continuity. From this standpoint, the unavoidable conclusion is that the theories and predictions of the Bund, based on its ideological concepts and social analyses, were fundamentally mistaken. First, the Bund denied the Dubnowist and the Zionist assumption that a world Jewish people exists. Its main observation here was that, in cultural and linguistic terms, large segments of Jewry, especially in the Western democracies to which Jews were emigrating, were rapidly disengaging from their nation. The Bund's mistake was its premise that linguistic assimilation and national assimilation are one and the same. They are not. After all, groups of Jews who spoke languages other than Yiddish and Hebrew belonged to the Zionist Movement. Furthermore, as the Bund admitted, the rapid integration of Soviet Jews into general

Socialist society was having far-reaching effects on the assimilation tendency of Jews as individuals, a fortiori when the new regime directed the tendency at the entire Jewish collectivity. What, then, was the real underlying logic of the Bundist belief that such a process of assimilation would not recur in Poland when, in the near future, Polish society would undergo democratization and the Jewish masses' standard of living would improve? What is more, the Bund believed that the future Polish society would be Socialist in nature. The Bund did rule out politically induced assimilation and believed that, under Social Democratic governance that adhered to the principles of freedom and equality, every national minority should be allowed and assisted to maintain its culture. However, there were circles on the left flank of the party that did not negate the possibility of *volitional* assimilation. Moreover, all Bundists realized that in the democracies Jewish culture was waning continually even in the absence of coercion. All that remained, then, was their blatantly Utopian belief that the future worldwide Socialist regime would be predicated on a range of national cultures that are not necessarily linked to specific territories. Even at the present time, Western countries that are affected by multicultural processes with ethnic implications, public education systems do not recognize national languages equally, as the Bund had hoped to accomplish in its futile struggle for official recognition and state support of its Yiddish-language school system.

Furthermore, the Bund was unwilling to draw the correct conclusion from the natural tendency of modern Jewish parents under any progressive regime, Communist or democratic, to enroll their children in public schools as a way to assure their future in the society that they inhabit.

Thus, when we examine the national outlook of the Bund on the basis of its most treasured object, the Yiddish language, we cannot but conclude that this party, which was highly realistic in its reading of the Jewish condition in the present, was utterly Utopian about the Jews' national future according to its own concepts, that is, the future of Yiddish in an equal and open civil society.

Consequently, the historical defeat of the Bund's national philosophy should not be blamed solely on the Holocaust and the disappearance of eastern European Jewry. Even had the Holocaust not occurred, the Bundist outlook would have been doomed to failure by its own concepts, that is, integration into a modern and specifically Socialist society in which, in the absence of territorial concentration, cultural and national autonomy could not possibly endure. Such a concentration had not come to pass in the Soviet Union, even partly, and it certainly had no chance in Poland, as the Bund leaders themselves conceded.

In contrast to the Bund's realistic national outlook in the present, which evolved into a Utopian faith in regard to the future, the Zionist Labor

Movement considered the present a Utopia and became increasingly realistic over the years. This was because Zionism, under the leadership of the
Labor Movement, managed even before World War II and the Holocaust to
establish in Palestine a territorial national autonomy that wielded powers
that transcended the cultural and linguistic domains. In fact, the Zionists'
achievement was the most successful fulfillment of the idea of assuring autonomous existence for national minorities, as expressed in the Versailles
treaty that followed World War I. Thus, the Utopian vision of American
President Woodrow Wilson came true above all in the new Jewish national
society in Palestine. Hence, in a historical paradox, the irrational became
rational and vice versa.

The question to ask here is where the Utopian realism of the Labor
Movement and the realistic Utopianism of the Bund crossed paths. The intersection, I would say, is located in the movements' different attitudes toward the Klal Yisrael idea—in the ab initio decision of each movement
about whether to be "in" or "out."

This brings another paradoxical phenomenon to light. At first glance,
objectively, the Labor Movement was outside of Klal Yisrael due to its
Palestino-centrism, its negation of the Diaspora, its zealous advocacy of the
Hebrew language, its pioneering-elitist complexion, and its condescending
attitude, prompted by its sense of historical destiny. Furthermore, it ostensibly existed outside its milieu, although headquartered in Palestine, by developing youth organizations in the Diaspora. The Bund, in contrast,
objectively belonged to Klal Yisrael as a party of the impoverished Jewish
masses in eastern Europe, a zealous promoter of the Yiddish language and
culture, and a believer in the perpetuity of exilic Jewish society. Subjec-
tively, ideologically, and politically, however, the opposite occurred. Due to
its constructivist nature, the Labor Movement was an inseparable part of the
world Klal Yisrael sphere despite its separatism and its elitist pioneerism,
whereas the class separatism of the Bund ruled out ab initio any attempt at
inclusion in, or at least cooperation with, Klal Yisrael. Therefore, the worse
the situation of European Jewry became, the more supportive Klal Yisrael
became of the national enterprise in Palestine. Concurrently, the Bund dissociated itself from this enterprise even though throughout his history, and
especially in the interwar period, it was increasingly involved in pan-Jewish
affairs in Poland—organizing community administrations, establishing
trade unions, and, in the main, waging war on anti-Semitism. Another background factor was the inability of the Zionist alternative to offer a solution
to the steadily escalating Jewish distress in the second half of the 1930s.
The Bund was politically blindsided by this success, and therefore on the
eve of the war its leadership rejected dismissively, condescendingly, and

vehemently the appeals of personalities whose worldviews resembled their own—A. Cahan, A. Lessin, and, especially, Simon Dubnow—to join Klal Yisrael and cooperate with Zionism on behalf of the nationally beleaguered Jewish people. They so behaved even though, unlike the Russian Bund, which involved itself in general Russian affairs, the Polish Bund was concerned mainly with the problems of Polish Jewry.

Was there an ideological, political, and cultural inevitability to all this—a response to some immutable specific social reality? There was not. Notwithstanding the deterministic power of experience and the constraints of the time, personalities and movements are able to rebel against them and change the direction of their thinking and conduct. After all, the entire history of the Bund was a tale of rebellion!

The right way to reflect about the matter, I propose, is by comparing the attitudes of Bund and the Reform Movement toward Klal Yisrael and Zionism at the same period of time, the late 1930s. Of course, there was a basic difference between the Reform as a religious movement and the Bund as a political party that, since the late nineteenth century, had been struggling with Zionism and the Jewish bourgeoisie for control of the Jewish street. Nevertheless, it is instructive to note that the respective movements' ideas on the Jewish national question were tenuously related. Both movements, despite their diametrically opposed ideological points of origin, rejected the Klal Yisrael concept in its principled national sense. Reform was an outgrowth of the culture and Weltanschauung of Central and Western European liberalism as subsequently augmented by American universalism; the Bund grew in the Marxist class culture of eastern Europe. The Reform parted ways with halakhic Judaism; the Bund parted ways with Jewish national unity. Both movements were intrinsically reformist: the former vis-à-vis religious culture and the latter vis-à-vis Socialist culture. Both were radical in their reformist outlook: Reform in its corrective religious prescriptions and the Bund in its Socialist Democratic activism on the Left wing of the Second International. On this conceptual basis, both ruled out Jewish national territorialism, regarding the very dispersion of the Jews as an advantage, an assurance of Jewish continuity, and a mission among the non-Jewish peoples. This mission came with an ethical idea that carried credic or Socialist versions. Both movements hitched the cart of Jewish continuity, religious or national, to the engine of progress—that of universalistic liberalism or that of world Socialism. Therefore, both rejected Zionism categorically. From this standpoint, in view of the totality of their values and the society in which they operated—liberal and democratic in the West, national and undemocratic in eastern Europe—both movements had realistic Utopian worldviews. In the late 1930s, however, in view of the ascendancy of Nazism and anti-Semitism, the Reform Movement took a realistic-Utopian turn and the Bund became simply Utopian. At its convention in Columbus, Ohio, in 1937, after protracted debates, the Reform Movement amended its ideological platform and adjusted its national outlook to the changing reality without relinquishing its main traditional tenets. This was reflected, of course, in the dramatic turnabout in its attitude toward Zionism. The clause pertaining to the matter is worth quoting in full:

> . . . In all lands where our people live, they assume and seek to share loyally the full duties and responsibilities of citizenship and to create seats of Jewish knowledge and religion. In the rehabilitation of Palestine, the land hallowed by memories and hopes, we behold the promise of renewed life for many of our brethren. We affirm the obligation of all Jewry to aid in its upbuilding as a Jewish homeland by endeavoring to make it not only a haven of refuge for the oppressed but also a center of Jewish culture and spiritual life. . . .[1]

In this classical phrasing of the Klal Yisrael perspective, the Reform Movement accepted the essence of Zionist ideology without foregoing its key traditional universalistic principles. This wording, if one replaces the religious and spiritual terminology with Socialist-materialist expressions, could also of course correspond to the ideology of the Bund, were not for the political zealotry of the latter movement's leaders. I say this even though the Bund deviated from this idea in important ways, such as its attempt to the station itself at the forefront of a "pan-Jewish" front in Poland for war on anti-Semitism and its joining, after severe vacillation, the Jewish Fighting Organization in the Warsaw ghetto, which was headed by the Zionist youth movements. However, those were national emergency measures only, not instances of national policy. Indeed, immediately after the Holocaust, some important members of the intellectual leadership of the Bund realized that their party had been mistaken and proposed to change the ideology accordingly. That it took nearly forty years for this outlook to triumph attests to the intensity of the Bundists' ideological zealotry even when it was bereft of political, social, and cultural logic.

In the Zionist Labor Movement, the process was different. What began in the Bund after World War II as a four-decade process of return to Klal Yisrael began in the Labor Movement forty years earlier, at the time of the Second Aliya, as a process of growing involvement in Klal Yisrael. It was then that the Labor Movement, by placing itself at the forefront of the building of Jewish national autonomy, changed the meaning of Jewish history. Of course, the movement could not have acquired this status in Jewish history had it not been an inseparable part of Klal Yisrael from the outset. Obviously, even if the Bund had overcome its craving for ideological and political separatism, the fate of European Jewry would have been no less tragic. However, the party could have affected the nature of Jewish society in Palestine by encouraging the emigration to Palestine of thousands of Bund members while it was still possible. The establishment of a national but non-Zionist "Bundist" society does not transcend the limits of the imagination. After all, an anti-Zionist ultraorthodox Jewish society has come into being in Israel.

Here is the place to perform another paradoxical comparison on the Klal Yisrael question between two hostile and totally uncompromising rivals, the Bund and Agudath Israel, Zionism's great adversaries of Zionism among Polish Jewry. The Zionist national outlook, be it in its Socialist or its religious sense, was the absolute negation of both parties' worldview and beliefs. Both were active political movements that acknowledged their inability to effect an absolute and complete solution to the Jewish problem at the present time. The Bund linked such a solution to the triumph of world Socialism; Agudath Israel hinged it on the advent of the Messiah. Consequently, according to both, the Jewish people would remain in a state of exile until "redemption," either at the hand of God or by men through the Socialist revolution. Both directed their messages at a culturally specific population. For the Bund, the main target population was Jewish "workers" in Jewish workshops; Agudath Israel aimed its appeal at the folk religious strata that was confused by the dynamic development of modern secular society. Neither movement had an ideologically or theologically innovative leadership. Agudath Israel's goal was to solve contemporary problems in the spirit of the Torah and the Jewish tradition; the Bund proposed to tackle them in the spirit of the Marxist "Torah" and the radical revolutionary tradition. Agudath Israel placed the supreme decision-making prerogative in the hands of the wisest and most incisive rabbis whom it designated as the sole interpreters of the *halakha* (rabbinical law). These rabbis ruled on the basis of what they, and they alone, determined to be *da'at Torah* (the opinion of Torah).[2] Similarly, no one in the Bund broke new doctrinal ground Socialism or even on the national question. Their "halakhic arbiters," who ruled on the basis of the Marxist "da'at Torah," were—after Marx and Engels—the mentors of Western social democracy. The entire contribution of the Bund's master intellectuals boiled down to an attempt to align the Socialist "da'at Torah" with the national reality of the Jewish working class. Both movements had two ideological rivals in their conceptual fields. The Bund was embroiled in unremitting strife with the Russian Social Democratic Party and Bolshevik

Communism; Agudath Israel was attacked by the leaders of extreme *haredi* (ultraorthodox) circles, which furiously criticized its religious complexion on the grounds of modernistic leanings. Paradoxically and with a measure of humor, one may state that just as the Russian Social Democratic leaders pointedly ridiculed the Bund for being "Zionists who are afraid of getting seasick," so did the Munkaczer Rebbe in the early 1920s accuse the leaders of Agudath Israel of posing as and mimicking the behavior of Zionists. Both, after all, were striving for the physical development of Palestine, in contravention of the hallowed tradition that reserved the Holy Land for religious study and prayer only.[3]

These absurd comparisons between the Bund and Agudath Israel make one wonder about these movements' attitude toward the Klal Yisrael perspective. In this matter, we should distinguish between Jewish politics and the "Jewish klal" Weltanschauung. In the sphere of Jewish politics, the movements took different positions toward de facto cooperation with rival parties in several settings: community administrations, representation in the Polish parliament, and the nonpartisan organization of Polish Jewry. The Bund confined itself to the community administrations; Agudath Israel occasionally extended its cooperation to the parliamentary domain as well.[4]

In the second sense, however, the principled one, the movements were far, far apart. Agudath Israel believed in the existence of an undivided Klal Yisrael that included even "sinners," whereas the Bund wrote off various groups within the Jewish people that had seceded from the Klal either by changing their language and culture or by having assimilated deliberately. Furthermore, there was, of course, a basic difference in the movements' assessments of the standing of Eretz Israel in the Klal Yisrael consciousness. Eretz Israel was marginal and neglected in the Bund consciousness but central in the creed of Agudath Israel. This explains the cautious but very significant difference in the two movements' attitudes toward the idea of establishing a Jewish state in part of Palestine in 1937. Although both agreed that Zionism was dangerous—to the Jewish people according to the Bund and to Judaism according to Agudath Israel—some in Agudath Israel, including important rabbis (such as Dr. Isaac Breuer), favored Jewish statehood due to the worsening plight of the Jewish masses.[5] The Bund, in contrast, remained staunchly opposed to the idea. This principled difference had no effect on reality. Both movements consistently, albeit for different reasons, ruled out aliya and both lost their communities in eastern Europe in the Holocaust. However, Agudath Israel, while rejecting Zionism, remained true to Eretz Israel and therefore established a cultural toehold there. The Bund, dismissing both Zionism and Eretz Israel, did not establish a cultural proletariat stronghold of its own in Palestine that could influence the social development of the Yishuv. However, in another paradoxical reversal, the Bund made a de facto peace with the State in Israel after the state was founded. Initially it acknowledged Israel as the nation-state of the Jewish people; later, it also accepted moderate Zionism, that is, the kind that did not "negate exile." Agudath Israel also came to terms with Israel as a state that had a Jewish majority but continued to oppose Zionism with indefatigable passion. All of this happened because the Bund accepted Simon Dubnow's national urgings fifty years after the fact while Agudath Israel remained true to its anti-Zionist and antinational (as Dubnow angrily described them at the time) principles. This difference further validates the importance of the national principle, which, unlike a fanatic religious outlook, may engender a rapprochement among old rivals if the historical conditions change.

One may contend, of course, that the Bund acquiesced in the Zionist state partly due to its weakness. However, Agudath Israel also emerged battered from the Holocaust, its popular base in Central and eastern Europe annihilated. Nevertheless, it was unwilling to lend the State of Israel the same principled recognition that the Bund gave it after severe internal irresolution.

This leads us to a summarizing thought about the attitudes of the Bund and the Labor Movement toward the Klal Yisrael concept. In regard to the Bund, one may say that the attitude progressed in two rounds. The first round began at the dawn of the twentieth century and ended on the eve of World War II. It included several "stops" that brought the Bund nearer to Klal Yisrael at the de facto level—the national-autonomy idea, self-defense, participation in community-administration elections, an appeal to the Jewish masses, and the war on anti-Semitism, to name a few. However, the Bund's separatist tendency returned in 1938 in Henryk Erlich's correspondence with Simon Dubnow. The second round began in 1947, after the Holocaust, with the establishment of the World Alliance of Bund parties and gradual recognition of the Zionist state of the Jews. It ended with the closing of a circle in the late 1980s, as the Bund returned to the institutional Klal Yisrael, that is, to the array of national and international Jewish organizations.

Thus, an unanswerable question is suspended in the void of history: If many hundreds of thousands of Jews had survived in Poland and attempted to reestablish themselves there, and if the Communist regime had accepted the Bund party, would the world Bund then, too, have continued to make its slow journey toward integration into Klal Yisrael and recognition of the State of Israel as the nation-state of the Jewish people? Since this is obviously a theoretical question that has no historical basis, only a speculative answer may be broached: on the basis of the ideological scuffling that the Bund experienced in regard to these issues during the first forty years after the end of the war, there is no doubt that both trends—the centrifugal ("separatist") and the centripetal (pro-unity)— would have collided within the party much more intensively than they actually did.

This leads to another question: what caused those ninety years of "separatism" in the Bund, from the late 1890s, when the party was founded, until the late 1980s? This question becomes more pointed if we ask, in puzzlement, what prompted the Bund to stay in the desert of Jewish politics for forty years *after* the Holocaust. One may, of course, explain this phenomenon in several different and complementary ways. One may point to the organizational dynamics of "a party that dwells alone"; the political inclinations of its leaders, who were unwilling to subordinate themselves to the leadership of a large movement; and perhaps, too, their political mistake, which was such a common and human one in political life. Additionally, there is no doubt that the party's volitional isolation flowed from the cultural and psychological ethos, the sense of "family," of the party's hard core—those hundreds or thousands of members who had formed an unbreakable bond characterized by the sense of intimacy and conscious devotion that typifies any minority that is fighting for its views. Even if each of these explanations contains some truth, one cannot understand the behavior of the Bund in each of its three historical periods without understanding its Weltanschauung in all the ideological controversies and political struggles that it experienced in the Socialist movement generally and in Jewish society particularly. The "ideology trap" was particularly blatant in regard to the Klal Yisrael question. Here the Bund tumbled into the contradiction between ideological and political negation of Klal Yisrael and spearheading the defense of the beleaguered Klal Yisrael; between the materialistic creed of nullifying national unity and replacing it with class struggle and the idealistic belief that the basis of any nation is the language and its culture. Therefore, the Bund was in the throes of an ongoing national drama that manifested itself in tension between political opposition to Klal Yisrael and social identification with the Jews' agonies.

Here we should return to the Bund's leading theoretician on the national issue at the time, Vladimir Medem. In 1919, after the Balfour Declaration and the Versailles Treaty had kindled hopes for Jewish national action at two levels—in Palestine and in Eastern Europe—Medem returned to the ineradicable line that separated the two movements. He defined the two as enemies (*faynd*) who were fighting each other to the finish and depicted them as proletariat versus bourgeoisie—the former as a *party of class* and the latter as *Klal Yisrael* (*a klal-yisroel bevegung*). Both movements, he stated, wish to change the Jews' living conditions. The difference is between those who are aware of the existing reality and those who dream of an imaginary one.[6]

Indeed, the Bund's championing of the struggle for the eastern European Jewish masses, some of which were impoverished and most of which faced civil political discrimination, indirectly justified its war on Zionism, which, according to its philosophy, could not solve the problem by prescribing mass emigration to Palestine. This allegation was groundless; after all, as I have shown in this study, no Zionist leader in the interwar era thought that emigration to Palestine would eradicate the Diaspora. However, since various Jewish public circles shared the Bund's view, one may say that, paradoxically, in its principled and political opposition to Zionism the Bund had allies in Klal Yisrael, even though it refused to cooperate with them politically.

In contrast, the attitude of the Zionist Labor Movement toward Klal Yisrael, throughout the period discussed in this study, may be likened to an unbroken line that ran, amidst unending tension, from the "halutsic klal" to the "Zionist klal" and thence to the "Jewish klal." It happened neither merely for ideological reasons nor due to practical political and economic needs that flowed from the ideological principles. Thus, on this point the movements parted ways in their attitude toward Klal Yisrael, the Bund choosing self-segregation and the Labor Movement integration.

These choices do not lend themselves to any class, sociological, or cultural explanation. Both movements were outgrowths of the same society with the same atmosphere and the same set of class cleavages. Thus, the choice was ideological and subjective. Over time, it was augmented by general political factors and personal motives that differentiated between the movements and acted to keep them apart.

Nevertheless, despite the ideological distance and the political contrast between them, the Bund and the Zionist Labor Movement were close in their modern national outlook. Therefore, the melodies sung at that event in New York belonged to both. Although today's post-national and, of course, non-Zionist academic climate treats the Bund, which was defeated by history, with understanding if not "affection" and subjects the Labor Movement, which defeated history, to merciless criticism. Such seems to be the fate of the "defeated," who fail the test of making their Utopias into reality, and of the "victors," who fulfill them in part only.

Thus, at the end of their political road, both movements—one with its partial but feasible victory and the other in its tragic, inevitable failure, ultimately made de facto peace with each other.

From here on, from the standpoint of both movements, the State of Israel and the Jewish Diaspora together constitute Klal Yisrael—admittedly not the Klal Yisrael that they had hoped for, neither overwhelmingly Zionist nor largely Yiddishist, but nevertheless a "world people."

Here, at the end of the study, the questions we should ask are two: What may this unique concept add to the importance of national ideology in the march of history in general? and does it point to possibilities in the development of ethnic consciousness among Jews in particular? The litmus test for these questions, especially in Jewish history during the past century, is the Jewish labor movement in its two streams, the Bund and the Zionist Labor Movement.

Theoretical discussion about of the nature of Zionism as a national movement has been taking place for decades in academia in Israel and elsewhere. Most of the leading scholars in this field, each in his/her own way, came to the conclusion that every national movement has its own uniqueness and, therefore, little in common. This is a fortiori the case in Zionism, an objectively special specimen among national movements. Furthermore, both scholars add, Jewish existence in history is able both to reinforce and to negate several theories of leading scholars in the research of nationalism.

Pursuant to this argument, I wish here to examine briefly how well the national ideologies of the movements at issue may be explained by the theories of scholars of nationalism such as Hans Kohn, Eli Kedourie, Ernest Gellner, Benedict Anderson, and Anthony Smith, who did not rule out Jewish nationhood as did the dogmatic Marxist Erich Hobsbawm.

The combination of Socialism and Jewish nationalism is problematic ab initio. The proof is that the founders of the Socialist movement in its various streams, from Otto Bauer to Lenin, did not recognize the existence of Jewish nationhood. Therefore, as this study has shown, the leaders of the Bund viewed them as targets for ideological polemics and political struggle. The Zionist Labor Movement waged a similar ideological and political struggle with the heads of the British Labour Party. Thus, while Zionism at large struggled for international recognition as the national movement of a people entitled to political self-determination, Jewish Socialism, in both of its branches, also entered into an ideological struggle over this question with the world Socialist movement.

I wish to examine the application of the theories that I noted above on the basis of this double dilemma. The pairing of Socialism and Jewish nationalism is undoubtedly a product of the thinking and action of intellectuals, or of a "*polu-intelligentsia*," as Jonathan Frankel indicates it. One doubts, however, if this pairing was established by frustrated intellectuals who wished manipulatively to attain leading social positions for themselves, as Kedourie and his current successors believe. Since the 1880s, after all, Jews had been able to take part in Western and Eastern European Socialist movements and had climbed to the front ranks of leadership in them, as they had not in any other modern liberal movement at the time. It suffices to mention L. Martov, Leon Trotsky, Rosa Luxemburg, Eduard Bernstein, and Léon Blum. Thus, the path to the leading ranks in the Socialist movements was open to the intelligentsia that stationed itself at the head of the Bund and the Zionist Labor Movement. If so, the reason for their choice of Jewish nationalism should be sought elsewhere—a place that I return to at the end of my remarks.

Furthermore, we must not ignore Ernest Gellner's theory about the relationship between statist modernization and nationalism. After all, the Jewish labor movement, in both of its rivaling flanks, was the most modern phenomenon in Jewish society at the time. However, this nationalism has nothing to do with the modern state. Not only were the Jews a minority in the modern states, but the majority in these states did not accept Jewish national determination. This was so both in the West, due to the liberal civic outlook that prevailed there, and in the East, due to the anti-Semitic policy, and the rejection of Jewish nationalism by the Social Democrats. Therefore, the Jewish labor movement related to the state in three ways. Communists attempted to achieve total integration; Bundists sought to be an integral part of the state as an autonomous national organization; and Zionists aspired to build an independent Jewish political entity in their historical homeland.

One element in the explanation of the Jewish Socialism phenomenon may be found in the worldview of Hans Kohn, who observed the messianic and moral drive of nationalism at its outset, as we stressed in this study by noting the Utopian leanings of the leaders of both movements discussed. More than this, however, it seems to me that, paradoxically, Anderson's postmodern theory, which defines the national group as an "imagined community," is well suited to both modern Jewish movements. Indeed, the Bund and the Zionist Labor Movement created, in their consciousness and before it came into being, an "imagined community" of a Jewish proletariat that shoulders the historical task of establishing the most modern national and social revolution that the Jewish people would ever perform. They did so while their objective weight in Jewish society was minuscule. Were it not for this sense of virtual consciousness and priorness, one doubts whether either movement would have played so important a role in twentieth-century Jewish history. Additional to this is the importance that Anderson ascribes to written language in the shaping of nationhood. Both movements nurtured a national language in literature—Yiddish for the Bund and Hebrew for the Zionist Labor Movement. Thus, there is no doubt the national consciousness in both movements was enhanced by the principle of their historical role and political action taken on its basis.

These theories aside, it seems to me that Anthony Smith's primordialist approach goes the farthest in explaining the national trend in Jewish

Socialism. His premise that modern nationalism is the result of a process of historical development from the ancient "ethnic community" to the modern nation-state is compatible with the ideologies of both movements. The Bund ideology recognized the historical development of Jewish nationhood as a primordially religious and territorial phenomenon from the biblical or patriarchal era, as Smith believed, to a modern exterritorial modern national phenomenon. The Zionist Labor Movement, in contrast, wished to return the Jewish nation as it existed to its primordial historical territory. This explains the centrality of the "cult" of the Bible in the Zionist Labor educational outlook. Perhaps it is not by chance that the Vladimir Medem's return "home," to his people, was influenced initially by the biblical stories that he had read as a boy. David Ben-Gurion and the Second Aliya people, in turn, considered themselves the successors of the tradition of their biblical heroes.

Furthermore, both movements sought to establish a broadly empowered Jewish national autonomy—the Bund for the Jewish minority in eastern Europe and the Zionist Labor movement—until the mid-1930s—for the Yishuv in Palestine. This autonomism was not far from Smith's "ethnic community" concept.

At day's end, paradoxically, I have reached the conclusion that the theories of postmodernism, of all things, do much to explain the nationalism of both Jewish Socialist movements, which were fundamentally modern. The nationalism of both movements was "virtual," if to borrow Yehoshua Arieli's term, that is, representative by force of intrinsic authority, without official recognition, of the nationhood of the Jewish people as a "world people."

In this study, then, I believe that I have done justice to both, not only in regard to their past. After all, if we look ahead and exchange past tense for present tense, nationhood for ethnicity, and revolutionary Socialism for liberal Socialism, as accepted in progressive streams in the West, we will find that the ideologies of both movements are still valid in their belief, with its Utopian-realistic hue, that the Jewish people exists despite all arguments to the contrary and that, therefore, it is concurrently an "imagined community" and a real-life one.

NOTES

INTRODUCTION

1. See Yosef Gorny, *The British Labour Movement and Zionism* 1917–1948, (London: Frank Cass, 1983).

2. Joseph Marcus, *Social and Political History of the Jews in Poland 1919–1939,* (Berlin: Mouton, 1983), pp. 427–429; and Daniel Blatman, *For Our Freedom and Yours, The Jewish Labour Bund in Poland 1939–1949,* (London: Vallentine Mitchell, 2003), pp. 26–30 and (Jerusalem: Yad Vashem and Hebrew University, [Hebrew], 1996).

3. Dan Horowitz, Moshe Lissak, *mi-yishuv li-medina* [From Yishuv to State: The Origins of Israeli Polity: The Political System of the Jewish Community in Palestine Under the Mandate] (Tel Aviv: Am Oved, [Hebrew], 1977), Appendices A, B.

4. Levi Arie Sarid, *The Pioneers – "Hechalutz" and the Youth Movements in Poland 1917–1939* (Tel Aviv: Am Oved, [Hebrew], 1979), pp. 476–479.

5. Horowitz-Lissak, *From Yishuv to State,* p. 114.

6. Jonathan Frankel, *Prophecy and Politics: Socialism, Nationalism and the Russian Jews, 1862–1917* (Tel Aviv: Am Oved, [Hebrew] 1989), and English (Cambridge: Cambridge University Press, 1981).

7. Michael Confino, "On Intellectuals and Intellectual Traditions in Eighteenth and Nineteenth Century Russia", *Daedalus*, (spring 1972).

8. "Nisht hobn keyn galusike neshomo"—E. Szerer, "Bundism un der hayntiker tsayt," *Unzer Ttsayt,* November 1974.

CHAPTER 1. BETWEEN CLASS AND NATION

1. See Moshe Mishkinsky, *Reshit tenuᶜat ha-poᶜalim ha-yehudit be-Rusia* [The beginning of the Jewish labor movement in Russia] (Tel Aviv: Hakibbutz Hameʾuhad [Hebrew], 1981), chs. 8, 9, pp. 177–213; and Frankel, *Prophecy and Politics,* pp. 202–262.

2. See "Fun der redaktsie," *Der Idisher Arbeiter* 1 (1896).

3. See Frankel, *Prophecy and Politics,* "Hayyim Zhitlovsky populist rusi ve-sotsialist yehudi 1887–1907" [Hayyim Zhitlovsky, Russian populist and Jewish populist 1887–1907], ch. 5: 295–327.

4. Ben-Ehud (Hayyim Zhitlovsky), "Tsiyoynizm oder sotsializm?" *Der Idisher Arbeiter* 6 (March 1899).

5. Ibid., pp. 6, 9, 14.

6. Ibid., p. 14.

7. See (a) N. Keifman, "Di tsiyonizmus," *Der Idisher Asrbeiter*, pp. 72–86; (b) Rabi Karov, "Di natsionale frage," pp. 87–94; (c) Ish Tikva, "Natsionalizmus un natsional rekht," pp. 94–100, in *Der Idisher Arbeiter*, 11 (1901); (d) Max Tset-terbaum, "Di Opgabn fun der idisher arbayter bevengung," *Der Idisher Arbeiter*, 12 (1901), and "Di Tsiyonistishe demokratishe fraktsie," ibid., 14 (1902); (e) "Natsionalitet un asimilatsie," *Der Idisher Arbeiter* 15 (June 1904; (f) Vinitsky, "Di sotsial democratie un di natsionale frage," *Der Idisher Arbeiter 17* (1904).

8. See Ish Tikva, "Natsionalizmus," p. 96.

9. See Vinitsky, "Di sotsial democratie," pp. 30, 33–34.

10. See Tsetterbaum, "Di opgabn," pp. 55–58.

11. See Frankel, *Prophecy and Politics*, pp. 290–292.

12. Report [Minutes] of the Fourth Bund Convention (1901) (Jerusalem: Hebrew University [Hebrew], 1971), p. 23.

13. Ibid., p. 19.

14. Vladimir Kossovski, *Otonomie oder federatsie?* (London: Bund publi-cation, June 1903), pp. 21, 25–27.

15. "Di diskusie vegn der natsionaler frage oyfn tsuzomenfer fun 'Bund,' June 1903, Zurich," *Unzer Tsayt,* December 1927, pp. 85–87.

16. "V. Kossovski un V. Medem un di natsionale frage," in *Vladimir Medem, tsum tsvontsiksten yartsayt,* 131 (New York: Bund publication, 1943).

17. V. Kossowski,"Deriber gefinen di tsiyoynistn a bodn in der mase," *Unzer Tsayt,* 1, January 1928, p. 84.

18. Ibid., pp. 85–86.

19. Mark Lieber, *Unzer tsayt*, 2, November 1927, p. 91–92.

20. See Bund Archives, YIVO Institute, New York, Second Convention, London, 1903, Fifth Session (translation into Yiddish): [*Der tsvayter tsuzomenfar fun di rusishe sotsial demokratishe arbayt partey],* MEI—13.15. For the entire de-bate, see Frankel, *Prophecy and Politics*, pp. 277–280.

21. A. Littwak, *Ma she-haya: zikhronot ʿal tenuʿat ha-poʿalim, mivhar maʾamarim* [What was: memories of the labor movement, selection of articles] (Tel Aviv: Y.L. Peretz [Hebrew], 1945).

22. See Moshe Mishkinsky, Introduction to *Vladimir Medem—zikhronot* [Vladimir Medem—memoirs] (Tel Aviv: Y.L. Peretz [Hebrew], 1984), pp. 7–15.

23. Tsviya Horowitz, *Unzer Tsayt,* 1, January 1928, p. 88.

24. See Frankel, *Prophecy and Politics,* pp. 276–277.

25. Ibid., pp. 291–292.

26. See Simon Dubnow, *Mikhtavim ʿal ha-yahadut he-yeshana ve-ha-hadasha* [Letters on old and new Judaism], Letter 10: "Musar haskel shel yemey ha-zaʿam" [The moral of the days of rage], (Tel Aviv: Devir [Hebrew], 1937), pp. 112–137.

27. Dubnow, *mikhtavim*, pp. 124–127.

28. B. Babsky, "Di klasn politik funʿm 'Bund,'" *Der Verker,* January 1906,16–17, 13–15. See also A. Id, "Dubnow vegn khatayim fun 'Bund,'" *Der Verker,* December 25, 1905.

29. See (a) Elgin, "Vos veln yetst ton di liberaln," Der Verker, January 6, 1906; (b) A. Littwak, "Kuntsnmakher," *Der Verker*, January 30, 1906 [a dispute with Ze'ev Jabotinsky concerning the latter's proposal for the establishment of a Jewish Sejm]; (c) R. "Der idisher sejm," *Der Verker*, January 6, 1906.

30. M. N., "Natsionale kultur fun proletarishn shtandpunkt," *Der Verker*, January 5, 1906.

31. Moshe Mishkinsky, "Vladimir Medem, Ha'ish Bi-tenuʿato" [Vladimir Medem, the man in his movement], in *Yehudim bi-tenuʿot mahapkhaniot: Kovetz Ma'amarim* [Jews in revolutionary movements: A Collection of Essays], edited by Eli Shaltiel, (Jerusalem: Zalman Shazar Center, 1983), pp. 67–74.

32. Vladimir Medem, *Zikhronot* [Memoirs], (Tel Aviv: Y. L. Peretz [Hebrew], 1984), p. 135.

33. Ibid., p. 254.

34. Ibid. pp. 162, 188.

35. Chaim Weizmann, *Kitvey Chaim Weizmann, igrot* (Writings of Chaim Weizmann, letters], vol. A (Jerusalem: Mossad Bialik [Hebrew], vol. 1, 1970), pp. 41–42.

36. Vladimir Medem, *Zikhronot* [Memoirs], pp. 206–207.

37. Vladimir Medem, "Yaʿakov Dineson, *Vladimir Medem tsum tsvontsikstn yartsayt,"* (New York: Bund publication [Yiddish], 1943), pp. 346–348. The full statement follows: "*S'iz do a daytsh vort 'pietat'.... S'iz nisht stam derekh-erets. S'iz a derekh-erets far a haylikayt, faraynikt mit a lib-shaft un mit a shtiln zorgfuln op'haytn.*"

38. V. Medem, "A klayn forvort," V. Medem, *Zikhronot un artikeln,* (Warsaw: Verlag Yiddish, 1917), pp. 67–68.

39. Ibid.

40. Otto Bauer, *Die Nationalitatenfrage und die Sozialdemokratie,* [The National Question and Social Democracy] (Wien: Verlag der wiener volksbuchhand-lung, 1907, 1924).

41. V. Kossovski, *K voprosu o natsionalnoi avtonomii* [On National Autonomy] (London: Bund publication, 1902).

42. See also Frankel, *Prophecy and Politics*, pp. 269–270; and V. Kossovski, "V. Medem un di natsionale frage," in *Vladimir Medem, tsum tsvontsiksten yartsayt,* p. 131.

43. The minutes were translated from Russian into Yiddish, reconstructed by Kurski on the basis of a manuscript, and published in three installments in

Unzer Tsayt 2, November 1927; *Unzer Tsayt* 3, December 1927; and *Unzer Tsayt* 1, January 1928.

44. "Di SD hot a pozitivn tsil—bashitsn di natsie fun unterdrikung, fun kinstlerer gevaltsamer asimilatsie," *Unzer Tsayt* 2, November 1927, p. 93.

45. Vladimir Medem,"Di sotsial-demokratie un di natsionale frage (1904)," in *Vladimir Medem, tsum tsvontsiksten yartsayt,* p. 177.

46. Ibid., p. 189.

47. Ibid., pp. 189–190.

48. Ibid., "ot der anderer bagrif di natsie, vy asome fun ale yekhidim, velkhe gehern tsu a bashtimter historish-kultureler grupe, umfahendik derfun vos zey vaynen oyf farshidene territories," p. 219.

49. V. Kossovsky, in *Vladimir medem tsum Tsvontsikstn,* p. 135.

50. V. Medem, "Natsionalizm oder 'naytralizm,'" in *V. Medem zikhronot un artikeln* (Warsaw: Bund publication), pp. 112–135.

51. Ibid., pp. 118–119.

52. Ibid., p. 132.

53. V. Medem, "Di Alveltlikhe yudishe natsie (1911)," *Vladimir Medem, Zikhronot un artikeln,* pp. 60–112.

54. See Professor Liebman Hersch, "Di ideologishe evolutsie fun bund," *Di Zukunft* (May–June 1947). See also H. S. Kazdan, "Der 'bund' un di ideal vegn alveltlekhkeit fun der yidisher natsie un qiyum ha-ʾuma," *Unzer Tsayt,* November–December 1947.

55. *Zikhronot un artikeln,* pp. 85–86.

56. Ibid., pp. 87–88.

57. Ibid., p. 99.

58. Ibid., p. 94.

59. Ibid., p. 104.

60. Sofie Dubnow-Erlich, "Das lebn fun Vladimir Medem," in *Vladimir Medem, tsum tsvontsiksten yartsayt,* p. 109.

61. V. Medem, *Zikhronot un artikeln,* pp. 135–160.

62. V. Medem, *Zikhronot un artikeln,* p. 150. "Gevis rekhenen mir zikh alayn oyf far eyner fun di dazige kreftn un aza oyfn iz oykh der goyral fun der natsie obgehangn fun dem, vas mir troen."

63. V. Medem, *Zikhronot un artikeln,* pp. 154–156.

64. Ibid., p. 160.

65. V. Medem, "Nakhamal 'mir un unzer natsionalizm,'" *Zikhronot.un artikeln,* pp. 161–164.

66. "Vayl aza poshut antkegenshteln fun tsvey zakhn—di toyva fun der natsie un di toyva fun'm arbayter-klas hot aygentlikh kayn zin nisht," *Zikhronot.,* p. 161.

67. V. Medem, "Nar meysim vern ferglivert, lebedige mentshn pasn zikh tsu tsu di faderungen fun'm lebn. Der shtandpunkt blaybt der alter, di oysfihrungen kenen zayn naye," *Zikhronot un artikeln,* p. 164.

68. V. Medem, "Der natsionaler separatizm," *Unzer Shtime,* October 1918; See also "Fun mayn notits-bukh," *Lebens Fragn,* September 27, 1916, October 11, 1916, December 11, 1916, December 15, 1916, December 23, 1916, January 18, 1917, February 18, 1917.

69. C. S. Kazdan, "V. Medem un di yidishe-veltlekhe shul," *Medem, tsum tsvontsiksten yartsayt,* pp. 160–169.

70. V. Medem, "Yiddish," *Lebens Fragn,* 11.2.1916.

71. CZA, 96/VIII/15A, quoted from Marcus Zilber, *She-Polin ha-hadasha tihiye em tova le-khol yeladeha; ha-ma'amats be-merkaz eiropa le-hasagat otonomiya le'umit li-yehudei polin ha-kongresa'it be-milhemet ha-'olam ha-rishona* [May the new Poland be a good mother to all her children: the effort in Cetnral Europe to attain national autonomy for the Jews of Congress Poland in World War I] (Ph.D. dis., Tel Aviv University, 2001), p. 174.

72. See *Ha-bund ha-russi bi-shnat ha-mahapekhot 1917, te'udot vehahlatot* [The Russian Bund in the year of revolutions 1917, documents and resolutions], edited, annotated, and with preface by Arye Gelbard (Tel Aviv: Tel Aviv University, 1984), p. 46. See also other resolutions on the same issue, ibid., pp. 73–82, 117–121.

73. See Mordechai Altshuler, "Ha-nisayon le'argen kinus klal-yehudi be-Russia aharei ha-mahapekha" [The attempt to organize a pan-Jewish conference in Russia after the revolution], *He-'avar* [Hebrew], 12 (1968): 75–89.

74. C. S. Kazdan, "V. Medem, Un di yidishe-veltlekhe shul," in V. Medem, *Tsum tsvontsiksten yartsayt,* pp. 160–169.

75. In this sense, his fate resembled that of his contemporary and ideological rival, Ze'ev Jabotinsky, who died in the United States in 1940.

76. See n. 34 above.

77. B. Borochov, "Ha-platforma shelanu" [Our platform], *Ketavim* A (Tel Aviv: Hakibbutz hame'uhad, 1955), p. 222.

CHAPTER 2. BETWEEN ERETZ ISRAEL AND THE DIASPORA

1. See "To All Young Zionists in Exile," *Ha-po'el ha-Tsa'ir* 2 (1908).

2. Y. A. [Yosef Aharonowitz], "A Voice from the Outside (On the Question of the Workers)," *Ha-po'el ha-Tsa'ir* 13 (May 24,1909).

3. Y. A., "[Remarks] about the 'Bottom Line,'" *Ha-po'el ha-Tsa'ir* 13 (May 19, 1912).

4. 'Ahad Ha'Am, "The Bottom Line," *Writings,* (Tel Aviv: Devir [Hebrew], 2nd edition, 1949), p. 601.

5. Y. A., "The Spirit and the Substance," *Ha-po'el ha-Tsa'ir* 38–39 (July 18, 1913).

6. Y.A., "Old Allegations," *Ha-po'el ha-Tsa'ir* 40 (July 17, 1914).

7. Ya'akov Rabinowitz, "Negating the Diaspora," *Ha-po'el ha-Tsa'ir* 39 (June 16, 1914).

8. B. Katznelson, *Darki le'Eretz Israel* [My Way to Palestine] (Tel Aviv: Ayanot [Hebrew], 1945), p. 45.

9. See Yosef Gorny, "The Hope and the Despair: Remarks on the Zionist Outlook of Yosef Hayyim Brenner," *Asupot* 2 (November 1971): 5–29 [Hebrew].

10. D. Ben-Gurion, *Letters,* vol. 1 (Tel Aviv: Am Oved [Hebrew], 1972), p. 112.

11. Y. Zerubavel, "Patience," *Ha'Ahdut* 35, July 7, 1911.

12. Avner [Y. Ben-Zvi],"The Jews and the Political Act," *Ha'Ahdut* 11–12, December 23, 1912.

13. B. Borochov, "The Confederation of the Opponents of Zion," *Writings, B* (Tel Aviv: Hakibbutz Hame'uhad [Hebrew], 1958), p. 389.

14. D. Ben-Gurion, "Di ge'ula," *Der Idisher Kemfer* 39 (New York, November 16, 1917).

15. Bar-Yohai (Y. H. Brenner), "Trivialities and Great Matters Too," *Ha-po'el ha-Tsa'ir* 15 (1913).

16. Aharon Reuveni, "Trivialities and Inaccuracies," *Ha'Ahdut* 17, February 7, 1913.

17. A-LR. [A. Heshin], "Why Did They Rage?" *Ha'Ahdut* 37, July 10, 1914.

18. See B. Borochov, "On the question of Zion and Territory", *Writings, A* (1955), p. 153.

19. See B. Borochov, "Our Attitude toward the Zionist Congress," *Writings, B*, p. 205.

20. See B. Borochov, "Regulation of Jewish Emigration and the Emigration Congress," *Writings, B*, pp. 321–373.

21. B. Borochov, "Why are we striving for unity?", *Writings, B*, p. 199.

22. B. Borochov, "Remarks on Raging Criticism and Juristic Rationales," *Writings, B*, p. 224. Heshin took a similar stance in his article, "Etlikhe verter ibern Helzingfors," *Proletarisher gedank* 2 (January 31, 1907). In this matter see also Katriel, "Our Work in the Diaspora Countries, *Ha'Ahdut* 44/45, September 26, 1913.

23. B. Borochov, "Pan-Jewish Problems and Socialism (1913)," *Writings, C* (Tel Aviv: Hakibbutz ha-me'uhad [Hebrew],1966), pp. 381–387. For discussion of Medem's articles, see chapter 1 above. I thank my friend M. Mintz, who called this article to my attention.

24. The reference is to his speech at the Po'aley Tsiyyon convention in Kiev, "Eretz Israel in Our Program and Tactics." The speech is quoted in Shmuel Bar, "Upon His Return to Russia," *Kuntres* 322 (1928): 28–29.

25. See N. T., "The Opposition and Its Reasons," *Ha-po'el ha-Tsa'ir* 24 (September 2, 1912).

26. See Y. Zerubavel, *'Aley Hayyim* [Leaves of Life], (Tel Aviv: Y.L. Peretz [Hebrew], 1960), p. 344.

27. Ibid.

28. Ibid.

29. Y. Zerubavel, "In the Wake of Reality," *Ha'Ahdut* 10, January 15, 1912.

30. A. LR., "Why Did They Rage?" *Ha'Ahdut* 37, July 10, 1914, p. 392, quoted as in *Yalqut Ha'ahdut*, pp. 391–394.

31. Y. Zerubavel, "Oyfn shvel fun yudishn sotsializm," *Der idisher arbayter* (March 21, 1912): 1–2.

32. Avner, "The Jews and the Political Act." The article is quoted as in *Yalqut Ha'ahdut*, pp. 343–348.

33. H. Zhitlovsky, "On the Question of Culture," Ha-'*Ahdut* 38/39, July 24, 1914.

34. Heshin, "Heavenly Renaissance, Earthly Renaissance," *Ha'Ahdut* 40/41, August 7, 1914.

35. D. Ben-Gurion, "Vos un vy azoy," *Der Idisher Kemfer* 41, Novmber 30, 1917, pp. 1–2.

36. I. Ben-Zvi, "Unzer arbayt in Eretz Yisrael," *Der Idisher Arbayter* 19, June 4, 1908, pp. 1–3.

37. "Tsu unzere khaverim," *Der Idisher Arbayter* 56, October 6, 1909, pp. 1–2.

38. Labor Movement Archives, minutes of the sixth convention, file 403/4, provisional number 3, Po'aley Tsiyyon.

39. Rachel Yanna'it, "The World Convention of Po'aley Tsiyyon," *Ha'Ahdut* 37, July 24, 1911. Quoted from *Yalqut Ha'ahdut*, pp. 407–408.

40. D. Ben-Gurion, "An ofener brief," *Der Idisher arbayter* 6, February 10, 1911, pp. 2–3.

41. Katriel [Leon Hazanovich], "Our Work in the Diaspora Countries," *Ha'Ahdut* 44/45, September 26, 1913.

42. Ibid.

43. Yosef Aharonowitz, "Old Allegations," *Ha-po'el ha-Tsa'ir* 38 (July 1914).

44. I. Ben-Zvi, *Po'aley Tsiyyon in the Second Aliyya* (Tel Aviv: Mapai Publishing [Hebrew], 1951), pp. 53–54.

45. See memoirs of Y. Shohat, Po'aley Tsiyyon file 403/2, Labor Party Archives, Tel Aviv.

46. I. Ben-Zvi, *Po'aley Tsiyyon in the Second Aliyya.*

47. Third Convention, Po'aley Tsiyyon File 403/9, Labor Party Archives, Beit Berl.

48. Third Convention, ibid.

49. Report of the Sixth Convention, April 23–24, 1910.

50. Report of the Party Council, September 1911, *Ha'Ahdut* 1–2, November 11, 1910.

51. Alexander [A. Heshin], "Heavenly Renaissance, Earthly Renaissance," *Ha'Ahdut* 40–41, August 7, 1914.

52. Y. Israeli, [Y. Zerubavel], "A Local Perspective," *Ha'Ahdut* 41–42, August 18, 1913.

53. Circular C (Central Committee), *Ha'Ahdut* 9, December 12, 1913.

54. Ibid.

55. Report of the Fourteenth Convention of Po'aley Tsiyyon, February 21, 1919, *Yalqut Ha'ahdut*, pp. 574–604.

56. See remarks by Schmid, ibid., p. 585.

57. Ibid., p. 574,

58. Ibid., p. 595.

59. Ibid., p. 599.

60. Yosef Gorny, "The Strengths and Weaknesses of 'Constructive Paternalism': The Second Aliyah Leaders' Image of the Yemenite Jews," *Cathedra* 108 (July 2003): 131-162.

61. Yosef Aharonowitz, "Replacing Ashkenazi Workers with Yemenites," *Ha-po'el ha-Tsa'ir*, 1910, *Writings* A (Tel Aviv: Am Oved [Hebrew], 1950).

62. Eliezer Yaffe, Assembly of farm workers in Galilee, *Ha'Ahdut* 16, January 26, 1912.

63. Ibid.

64. Rachel Yanna'it, Report of the Party Council, October 20, 1910, Jaffa, *Ha'Ahdut* 102, November 11, 1910.

65. Ya'akov Zerubavel, Ha'Ahdut 102.

66. D. Ben-Gurion, " Hukka 'Ahat" [One Set of Rules], *Ha'Ahdut* 25–26, April 1, 1912.

67. Ibid.

68. Ibid.

69. See Ben-Gurion, "One set of Rules," ibid.

70. For discussion of this affair, see Yehuda Nini, *Were You There or Was I Dreaming?—The Yemenites of Kinneret* (Tel Aviv: Am Oved [Hebrew], 1996).

71. Letter from worker in Petah Tiqva, *Ha'Ahdut* 14–15, Jerusalem, February 4, 1912.

72. Editorial, "A New Factor," *Ha'Ahdut* 31, June 13, 1912.

73. *Ha'Ahdut* 27–28, May 13, 1913.

74. Editorial, "After the Convention," *Ha'Ahdut* 11, December 1913.

75. Ibid.

76. D. Ben-Gurion to S. Fuchs, Tel Aviv, 2 January 1907, *Letters* A (Tel Aviv: Am Oved [Hebrew], 1972), p. 94.

77. D. Ben-Gurion, "Our Social Labor," *Ha'Ahdut* 2–3, September 1911.

78. See also D. Ben-Gurionn's article, "Elucidating our Political Situation," *Ha'Ahdut* 3 (August 1910).

79. See Report of the Seventh Conference, *Ha'Ahdut* 27, May 19, 1911.

CHAPTER 3. FROM CLASS TO PEOPLEHOOD

1. See Mario Kessler, "The Bund and the Labour and Socialist International," in *Jewish Politics in Eastern Europe, The Bund at 100*, edited by Jack Jacobs (New York: New York University Press, 2001), pp. 183–196.

2. Gertrud Pickhan, "Kossovsky, Portnoy and Others: the Role of Members of the Bund's Founding Generation in the Interwar Polish Bund," in *Jewish Politics in Eastern Europe*, 69–80.

3. *Di konferents fun di bundishe organizatsies in Poyln* [Minutes of the first conference of the Polish Bund] (Warsaw: Bund publication, 1918), pp. 8–16.

4. Ibid., p. 13.

5. W. Alter, "Tsu unzer natsionaln program," *Lebens Fragn* (September 7, 1919, September 12, 1919, and September 19, 1919); V. Medem, "Fun mayn notits-bukh", *Lebens Fragn* (September 24, 1919), (October 3, 1919). See also Emanuel Nowogrodzki, *The Jewish Labor Bund in Poland 1915–1939,* (Rockville, MD: Shengold, 2001), ch. 16: 329–334.

6. H. Erlich, "Men muz zikh anshlisn ('tsu der diskusie vegn anteyl in di kehilla valn')," *Folks Tsaytung,* March 1923.

7. H. Erlich, "Kampf far der yisidher shul," *Folks Tsaytung,* February 1923.

8. H. Erlich, "Der kampf far der shul," *Shul un lebn,* March 20, 1921, pp. 12–16. See also Piotr Wrobel, "From Conflict to Cooperation: the Bund and the Polish Socialist Party, 1897–1939," in *Jewish Politics in Eastern Europe,* pp. 155–171.

9. See note 5 above.

10. Nathan Cohen, "The Bund's Contribution to Yiddish Culture in Poland between the Two World Wars," in *Jewish Politics in Eastern Europe,* pp. 112–132.

11. See C. S. Kazdan, "Der 'Bund' un di ideien vegn alvetlikhkeit fun der yidisher natsie un kiyum ha-umma," *Unzer Tsayt* (November–December 1947): 32–36.

12. B. Mikhalevich, "Neytralizm oder kiyum ha-ʾumma," *Di Tsukunft* (December 1910).

13. B. Mikhalevich, "Kol yisroel khalomot oder realpolitik?" *Unzer Shtime* (August 1918 [a pamphlet published by the Bund Central Committee]). For discussion of the Bund's idealogical vacillations on this issue that the comproise that it accepted at the end of the debates, see Mordechai Altshuler, "Ha-nisayon le'argen kinus klal-yehudi be-Russia aharey ha-mahapekha" [The attempt to organize a pan-Jewish conference in post-Revolution Russia], *Heʿavar,* quarterly on the history of Jews and Judaism in Russia, 12 (Autumn 1964): 75–89 (Tel Aviv).

14. See B. M. [Mikhalevich], "Aktive asimilatsie," *Folks Tsaytung,* February 10, 1922; B. B., "Der klerikalizm," *Folks Tsaytung,* March 17, 1922; B. M., "Der emeser zin," *Folks Tsaytung,* August 25, 1922; B. M., "Klasn kamf un folkizm," *Folks Tsaytung,* October 6, 1922.

15. See B. M., [Mikhalevich], "Tsvey natsies," *Folks Tsaytung,* April 3, 1925.

16. B. Mikhalevich, "Unzer nationale program in likht fun der praktik," *Unzer Tsayt* (February 1927, January 1928).

17. Below is the full wording of the definition in its original language. After he explained what the Bund did *not* believe in, Mikhalevich wrote, "*Dos iz geven a geshikhtlekh-gezelshaftlekhe oyffusung, vos batrakht natsies als poyel-yoytse fun geshikhtlekh-geshofene gezelshaftlekhe umshtendn, voz habn dorkhgemakht a gemeynzamen shikzal un zenen geformet gevern dorkh gemeynzamer kultur.*" *Unzer Tsayt* (February 1927): 15.

18. B. Mikhalevich, "Unzer Natsyonale Program in Licht fun der Practic," *Unzer Tsayt* (February 1927, January 1928).

19. See discussion elsewhere in this study.

20. B. Mikhalevich, "Natsionale otonomie," in *Sotsialistishe etyudn un politishe skitsn* (Warsaw: Bund publication [n.d.]), pp. 135–136.

21. B. Mikhalevich, "Der utopisher sotsializm," ibid., p. 64. This article was first printed in the 1918 pamphlet in which Mikhalevich published his "Utopian" social program. B. Mikhalevich, *Unzer program,* (Warsaw: Bund publication, 1918).

22. V. L. Kossovski, "Di natsionale frage un di sotsial demokratie," *Di Tsukunft* (March 1925): 171.

23. B. Mikhalevich, "Der utopisher sotsializm," in *Socialistishe Etyudn,* pp. 135–136.

24. See Wiktor Alter, "Oyf Bundishe temes, der Bund in der 'yidisher sevivo,'" *Unzer Tsayt* (February 1928).

25. Ibid., p. 48.

26. Ibid., pp. 49–50.

27. Ibid., p. 53.

28. Ibid., p. 55.

29. Noah [Portnoy], "Zelbsanaliz oder pilpul," *Unzer Tsayt* (November 1927).

30. E. Moss, "Religie—a privat zakh?" *Unzer Tsayt* (December 1927).

31. David Einhorn, "Sotsializm un religie," *Naye Folks Tsaytung,* February. 22, 1929, and March 1, 1929.

32. B. Mikhalevich, "Kamf oder oyfklerung, sekte oder masn-partey? Tsu der diskusie: partey un religie," *Unzer Tsayt,* February 1928.

33. In the matter of the "ideological pathology," it is noteworthy that in advance of the Zionist Congress in 1925, the paper published a cartoon showing a Jew with his hand extended to receive money. The pronouncedly anti-Semitic style of the drawing preceded the illustrations in the Nazi *Sturmer* by several years. See *Folks Tsaytung,* February 13, 1925.

34. See *Naye Folks Tsaytung*: (a) Shtand, "Gerikht in Yerushalayim un Tsfas," September 2, 1929; (b) I. Berman, "Blutiker anhoyb in Palestine"; (c) Continuation of the riots, September 3, 1929; (d) Prof. Liebman Hersch, "Araber," September 6, 1929; (e) W. Alter, "Yidish blut," September 27, 1929: the bloodshed in Palestine is like grease on the wheels of Jewish reactionism; (f) H. Erlich, "Unzer idea," October 25, 1929: "The Correctness of the Bund's Path in Its Struggle against Zionism."

35. See also: (a) Tsivion [Dr. Benzion Hofman], "Megen un kenen" (conversations about Zionism), November 8, 1929. The overall ideological and political reckoning with Zionism in the aftermath of the violent incidents in 1929 was drawn up by the leader of the left flank of the Bund, Yosef Khmorner (Leshchinski), in a special pamphlet: Y. Khmorner, *Vos lernen uns di gesheenishn in Palestine?* (Warsaw: Bund publication, 1929), pp. 52–58; (b) Tsivion, "Vos zoln yidn ton?" November 22, 1929: "Zionism should have been done away with; since it is unrealistic, one should hope that political Zionism will be vanish and that only cultural Zionism will survive."

36. H. E. [Erlich], "A nayer tsiyonistisher manifest," *Naye Folks Tsaytung,* September 7, 1931.

37. H. E., "Rothschild un Hitler," *Naye Folks Tsaytung,* October 19, 1931; see also his article on the same topic and in the same vein, "A zifts nakh di alte gute tsaytn," *Folks Tsaytung,* July 4, 1932.

38. H. E., "An arbeter kongres," *Naye Folks Tsaytung,* December 23, 1932.

39. W. Alter, "Morgn vet das zayn unzer shtolts," *Naye Folks Tsaytung,* December 16, 1932.

40. See H. Erlich, "Der iker fun Bundism (1934)" in *Gedenk Buch, edited by H. Erlich and W. Alter* (Buenos Aires: Bund publication, 1945), p. 78.

41. A. Liessin, "Eretz Yisroel un galus," *Di Tsukunft* (July 1926); A. Liessin, "Tsum draysig-yaringen yuveleum fun Bund un fun Tsiyonism," *Di Tsukunft* (October 1927). In this article, Liessin went out of his way to note that, back in 1903, he had "predicted" the possibility of the formation of a Socialist Jewish society in Palestine that would set an example for the world. He had apparently done this pursuant to Herzl's *The Jewish State* and his Utopian novel, *Altneuland.* See also A. Liessin, "Der Idisher univerzitet oyfn Har Hatsofim," *Di Tsukunft* (April 1925).

42. W. Alter, *Rayzn briv—der emes vegn Palestine* (Warsaw: Bund publication, 1925).

43. See Ya'acov N. Goldstein, *Jewish Socialists in the United States: the Cahan Debate 1925–1926* (Portland, OR: Sussex Academic Press, 1998).

44. See H. Erlich, "A. B. Cahan in Palestine," *Folks Tsaytung,* November 6, 1925, November 8, 1925.

45. See H. Erlich, *A. B. Cahan un der Bund in Poyln* (Warsaw: 1932), pp. 39–59 (collection of exchanges of remarks between Cahan and Liessin—no editor cited).

46. Ibid., p. 42.

47. Ibid., pp. 43–44.

48. Ibid., pp. 58–59.

49. Dr. Liebman Hersch, "Fun statistik tsu politik—tsu der debate vegn tsiyonizm," *Di Tsukunft* (August, September, October 1927).

50. See H. Erlich, "Politishe perespektivn," *Unzer Tsayt,* January. 2, 1932; W. Alter, "Rekhts un links," *Unzer Tsayt;* V. Kossovski, "Yidishkeit un interes," *Naye Folks Tsaytung,* September 8,1933; and lead articles in the last-mentioned newspaper carrying the initials V. K., *Unzer Tsayt,* September 10 and September 15, 1933.

CHAPTER 4. BETWEEN THE "ZIONIST KLAL" AND THE "HALUTSIC KLAL"

1. Editorial, "For the National Assembly," *Kuntres* 14 (October 13, 1919).

2. I. Ben-Zvi, "The Palestine Council," *Kuntres* 58 (October 1921).

3. D. Ben-Gurion, "To Find Our Way," *Kuntres* 118 (December 7, 1922).

4. See remarks by Ben-Gurion in report of the Histadrut Executive Council, vol. C, 1923, meeting of November 26, 1923.

5. See Yosef Gorny, *Ahdut ha-ʿAvoda* (Tel Aviv: Hakibbutz Hameʾuhad, [Hebrew], 1973), p. 119.

6. Ibid., p. 121.

7. B. Katznelson, "On the Eve of the Congress," *Kuntres* 128 (May 18, 1923).

8. For discussion of this controversy and its origins, progression, and results, see Yigal Elam, *The Jewish Agency, First Years 1919–1931* (Jerusalem: Zionist Library [Hebrew], 1990).

9. B. Katznelson "[Remarks] on the Jewish Agency Issue," *Writings,* B, pp. 58–59.

10. M. Ben-Kedem (M. Shertok), "From the 13th Congress," *Kuntres* 142 (September 7), 1923.

11. Yosef Gorny, *Partnership and Conflict: Chaim Weizmann and the Jewish Labor Movement in Palestine* (Tel Aviv: Hakibbutz Hameʾuchad [Hebrew], 1976), especially chapter 1.

12. Ahdut ha-ʿAvoda Council, February 16, 1924, Ahdut ha-ʿAvoda Archive, [Hebrew], 404/IV, file 5.

13. For discussion of Beilinson's Socialist-Zionist outlook, see Yosef Gorny, "Moshe Beilinson as an Elite Social Democrat," *Zionism* 19 (1995): 347–368 [Hebrew].

14. M. Beilinson, "The Jewish Agency," *Kuntres* 188 (September 26, 1924).

15. M. Beilinson, "The Zionist Movement and the Federation of Labor," *Kuntres* 192 (November 1924).

16. See Golomb's remarks at the Ahdut ha-ʿAvoda Council, which convened to discuss the conclusions of the Jewish Agency committee, *Kuntres* 243 (June 1928).

17. See D. Ben-Gurion, Seventeenth Histadrut Council, February 1927, p. 52.

18. See note 17 above.

19. D. Ben-Gurion, "Our Move to the Jewish Agency," *Davar,* July 7, 1929.

20. See Yosef Gorny, *Ahdut ha-ʿAvoda,* pp. 68–71.

21. Third Convention of Ahdut ha-ʿAvoda, Haifa, 1922, *Kuntres* 119 (February 1923): 56–57.

22. B. Katznelson, "On the Question of Where Halutsism is Heading— 1927/28," *Writings,* C, p. 372.

23. See Yosef Gorny, *Ahdut ha-ʿAvoda,* p. 64.

24. B. Katznelson, "The London Convention," *Writings, A,* pp. 229–230.

25. M. Beilinson, "The Dictatorship and Democracy Crisis," *Kuntres* (January 16, 1925).

26. M. Beilinson, "Movements and Their Crises," *Davar*, February 16, 1927.

27. B. Katznelson, "On the Eve of the Congress," *Kuntres* 310 (July 29, 1927).

28. B. Katznelson, *Letters,* A, p. 124.

29. See Gorny, *Ahdut ha-ʿAvoda,* pp. 305–311, for the progression of the dispute until it was resolved.

30. Ibid., pp. 306–307.

31. Quoted from Yosef Shapira, *Ha-poʿel ha-Tsaʿir*, (Tel Aviv: Am Oved [Hebrew], 1967), pp. 348–349.

32. Yisrael Oppenheim, *The He-haluts Movement in Poland 1917–1929* (Jerusalem: The Magnes Press [Hebrew], 1982).

33. As quoted in ibid., pp. 173–179.

34. See Yosef Gorny, "The Romantic Element in the Second Aliyya," *Asupot* 10 (1996): 55–74 [Hebrew].

CHAPTER 5. THE TRAGIC ILLUSION

1. The debate is discussed below in this chapter.

2. See W. Alter, *Naye Folks Tsaytung,* July 3 and July 6, 1935; and V. Kossovsky, *Naye Folks Tsaytung*, January 4, 1935.

3. W. Alter, *Naye Folks Tsaytung,* July 26, 1935; August 4, 1935; Aug. 3, 1936; March 19, 1936; H. Erlich, *Naye Folks Tsaytung,* August 7, 1935, and May 24, 1936.

4. Editorials, *Naye Folks Tsaytung,* March 31, April 17, and June 11, 1936; and W. Alter, January 7, 1938.

5. H. E. [H. Erlich], *Naye Folks Tsaytung,* September 7, 1935; November 8, 1935; February 18, 1938; May 28, 1938. See also V. Kossovsky, *Naye Folks Tsaytung,* August 9, 1935; W. Alter, *Naye Folks Tsaytung,* November 8, 1938.

6. *Naye Folks Tsaytung,* April 19, 1936.

7. Ibid., July 3, 1938.

8. Ibid., July 12, 1938.

9. W. A. [W. Alter], *Naye Folks Tsaytung,* July 21, 1938; H. Erlich, October 23, October 28, November 4 and November 12, 1938.

10. W. Alter, "Marx is zikh noykm in Hitler," *Naye Folks Tsaytung*, May 5, 1939.

11. Ibid. August 26, 1939.

12. W. A., *Naye Folks Tsaytung,* April 8, 1939; H. E., *Naye Folks Tsaytung,* April 10, 1939.

13. W. Alter, *Naye Folks Tsaytung,* August 27 and October 7, 1938; H. Erlich, *Naye Folks Tsaytung,* August 18, 1937, and September 6, 1938.

14. H. E., *Naye Folks Tsaytung,* November 25, December 2, December 7, and December 30, 1938; W. Alter, *Naye Folks Tsaytung,* November 25 and December 3, 1938.

15. L. H. [L. Hades], *Naye Folks Tsaytung*, March 17, 1939; and V. Kossovsky, *Naye Folks Tsaytung*. August 17, 1939.

16. S. Mendelsohn, *Naye Folks Tsaytung*, February 7, 1939.

17. Mendelsohn, *Naye Folks Tsaytung*. August 3, 1939.

18. See J. M. Borski, "Sprawa zydowska a socjalizm; Polemika z Bundem," (Warsaw 1937), in Blatman, *For Our Freedom and Yours*, p. 23.

19. See Y. Y. Trunk, *Yidishe kultur-fragn un der sotsializm* (Warsaw: Kultur Lige, 1935). See also *Sotsialistishe impresies* (Warsaw: [publisher unknown], 1939).

20. Y. Y. Trunk, *Yidishe Kultur-fragn*, p.12.

21. Ibid, p.13.

22. Ibid., p. 9.

23. Ibid., p. 31.

24. Ibid., pp. 40–41.

25. Y. Y. Trunk, *Sotsialistishe Impresies*, p. 29.

26. Ibid, p. 31.

27. Ibid, p. 36.

28. For statistics, see Zvi Barzilai, *The Bund Movement in Interwar Poland* (Jerusalem: Carmel [Hebrew], 1994), p. 87. In regard to the paltry enrollment in the CYSHO schools, it is interesting to read a passionate appeal in 1938 from the organization's management to Jewish parents to enroll their children in these Yiddish language schools: "A ruf tsu di yidishe tates un mames," in *Eltern—tribune khoydeshrift for haym un shul* (Warsaw: CYSHO, June 1938), year 2, no. 7.

29. Emanuel Ringelblum, *Diary and Notes from the Warsaw Ghetto, September 1939–December 1942* (Jerusalem: Yad Va-shem [Hebrew] 1993), p. 376.

30. "Geshikhte konferents, tsvayter shultsuzamenfahr," Vilna, YIVO, File 24—CYSHO.

31. *Land konferents fun geshikhte-lerer in di shuln fun CYSHO, January 7–8, 1939* (Warsaw: CYSHO, 1939).

32. "Program—proyekt fun limud fun geshikhte," *Land Konferenz*, pp. 44–56.

33. W. Alter, "Unzere tsiln," *Unzer Tsayt*, January 1932.

34. W. Alter, "Demokratie un diktatur," *Unzer Tsayt* (May 1932). See also W. Alter, "Vegn proletarishe demokratie," *Naye Folks Tsaytung*, January 17, 1936.

35. W. Alter, *Tsu der yidn-frage in Poyln* (Warsaw: Monografia, Bund publication, 1937), p. 24.

36. Ibid., p. 29.

37. Ibid., p. 40.

38. Ibid., p. 111.

39. See W. Alter, "Nakh dem kongres," *Naye Folks Tsaytung*, January 18, 1937.

40. See W. Alter, *Tsu der yidn frage*, pp. 114–117.

41. See H. Erlich, "Der iker fun bundism (1934)," in *Henryk Erlich un Wiktor Alter gedenk bukh* (New York: Bund publication, 1943), pp. 75–86.

42. *Manifest 1937*, ibid., p. 272.

43. S. Dubnow, "Vegn der izolatsie fun 'bund' un der tsiyonistisher folks-bavegung (a briv tsu a bundistishn fraynd)," *Di Tsukunft* (June 1938): 329.

44. See *Di Tsayt* (London), August 18, 1939.

45. H. Erlich, "Tsi is der tsiyonizm a befrayende demokratishe bavegung? An entfer prof. S. Dubnow," *Di Tsukunft* (October 1938): 566–572. See also *Naye Folks Tsaytung,* July 29–31, 1938.

46. A. Liessin, "Tsum 40 yahringn yuvileum fun 'bund,'" *Di Tsukunft* (October 1937).

47. See Daniel Blatman, *For Our Freedom and Yours,* pp. 159–162

48. Ibid., p. 230.

49. L. Hades, "Unzer separatizm," *Unzer Tsayt,* August 1941.

50. E. Nowogrodzki, "Bundism un mistifikatsie," *Di Tsukunft* (May 1940).

51. See Shlomo Netzer, "'Labor of the Present'—Its Fundamentals and Its Application by the Polish Zionists," *Milet,* Studies of the Open University in Jewish History and Culture, A (1983) [Hebrew].

52. See Daniel Blatman, "The National Ideology of the Bund in the Test of Anti-Semitism and the Holocaust, 1933–1947," in *Jewish Politics in Eastern Europe,* edited by Jack Jacobs, pp. 197–212.

53. Shimon Redlich, *War, Holocaust and Stalinism, A Documented History of the Jewish Anti-Fascist Committee in the USSR* (Luxemburg: Harwood Academic Publishers, 1995), pp. 9–19.

54. See *Henryk Erlich and Victor Alter: Two Heroes and Martyrs for Jewish Socialism,* trans. from theYiddish by Samuel A. Portnoy (Hoboken, New Jersey: Ktav Publishing House, 1990), pp. 183–190.

CHAPTER 6. BETWEEN PIONEERHOOD AND PEOPLEHOOD

1. See David Ben-Gurion, "The National Destiny of the Working Class," 1925, in *Mi-maʿamad laʿam* [From Class to People] (Tel Aviv: Devir [Hebrew], 1933), pp. 231–234. See also Yosef Gorny, *Ahdut ha-ʿAvoda,* p. 63.

2. Ahdut ha-ʿAvoda - Ha-poʿel ha-Tsaʿir union conference, January 5–7, 1930, Tel Aviv, address by David Ben-Gurion, pp. 4–5, 6, 13, 15, Labor Party Archives, Beit Berl [Hebrew], 2-21-1930-6.

3. Ahdut ha-ʿAvoda - Ha-poʿel ha-Tsaʿir union Conference, speech by Yosef Sprinzak, pp. 5, 6.

4. Party Council, at Kefar Yehezkel, 1932, Labor Party Archives, Beit Berl, 2–22–1932–8 [Hebrew], p. 15.

5. David Ben-Gurion, "The Crisis in Zionism and the Labor Movement," *From Class to People* (Tel Aviv: Devir [Hebrew], 1933), p. 184.

6. Ibid., p. 186.

7. Ibid., p. 178.

8. Ibid., p. 195.

9. See Party Council, at Kefar Yehezkel, 1932; Shai Lavie, p. 13; Y. Merminski, pp. 30–31; E. Golomb, pp. 31–32; S. Yavne'eli, Y. Tabenkin, p. 35–36; S. Dayan, p. 37; Gurfinkel, p. 38. [Beit Berl Archive [Hebrew], 2-22-1932-8.

10. D. Ben-Gurion, Second Mapai Convention, First Session, October 30, 1932, Beit Berl Archive, 2-21-1932, p.100.

11. Ibid., p. 102.

12. B. Katznelson, *Writings,* vol. I (Tel Aviv: Labor Party [Hebrew], 1950, 3rd. edition), pp. 60–86.

13. Second Session of the Second Mapai Convention, December 3, 1932, pp. 1–8. The speakers were Bar-Yehuda, Yavne'eli, Ben-Eli, Loewenstein, and Arlosoroff. Beit Berl Archive, 2-21-1932.

14. Ibid., p. 92.

15. Ibid., pp. 3–4.

16. All the foregoing quotations are from the First Session of the Second Mapai Convention, pp. 1–16.

17. Ibid., ibid.

18. The matter was debated at length at the Party and Zionist Organization levels. See Aviva Halamish, "Zionist Immigration Policy in the 1930's: From 'Redemption' to 'Survival,'" *Zmanim* 58 (Spring 1997), pp. 86–98.

19. Yosef Aharonowitz, Second Mapai Council, January 19, 1933, p. 22. Beit Berl Archive [Hebrew], 2-22-1933.

20. At the end of the debate, a compromise motion by Ben-Gurion and Sprinzak with an amendment by Pinchas Lavon was adopted: "certificates" would be given to skilled workers who had some relationship with the Hehaluts assocation and to middle-class individuals who are suited to labor in Palestine; however, the majority of "certificates" would be reserved for pioneers. For discussion of the Zionist Executive policy on this matter, see Aviva Halamish, "Was 1933 a Turning Point in the Zionist Immigration Policy?" in I*yunim Bitkumat Israel, Studies in Zionism, the Yishuv and the State of Israel,* 3 (Sede Boqer: Ben-Gurion University of the Negev Press [Hebrew], 1993), pp. 98–113.

21. Second Mapai Council, January 19, 1933, pp. 24–25. Beit Berl Archive, 2-22-1933.

22. B. Katznelson, "A Voyage to the Diaspora," *Writings,* vol. 7 (Tel Aviv: Labor Party [Hebrew], 1948), pp. 369–382.

23. B. Katznelson, "In the Footsteps of Diaspora Youth" (at the Ha-no'ar ha-'Oved Council, January 1934), *Writings,* vol. 6 (Tel Aviv: Labor Party [Hebrew], 1947), pp. 354–360.

24. Ibid. p. 359.

25. B. Katznelson, "Destruction and Uprooting" *Writings*, vol. 6, pp. 365–367. On the significance of the Ninth of Av mourning in Katznelson's Jewish and national outlook, see Avraham Tsiviyon, *A Jewish Portrait of Berl Katznelson* (Tel Aviv: Siffriat Po'alim [Hebrew], 1984), pp. 254–259. See also Anita Shapira, *Berl,* (Tel Aviv: Am Oved, vol. B [Hebrew], 1980), pp. 547–548.

26. Ibid., pp. 365–366.

27. B. Katznelson, "Everlasting Origins," *Writings,* vol. 6, pp. 385–393.

28. Ibid., pp. 392–393.

29. See Yosef Gorny, "On Social 'Etiquette' and National Interest, [Remarks] on the Question of Coexistence between the Nonreligious and the Religious

in the Zionist Movement," in *Priesthood and Monarchy, Studies in the Historical Relations of Religion and State,* Edited by Isaiah Gafni and Gabriel Motzkin, (Jerusalem: Zalman Shazar Center [Hebrew], 1987) pp. 269–276.

30. In the background of these results was an increase in the strength of the Labor Movement in the Zionist Organization. At the XVII Zionist Congress in 1931, the Labor faction received 29 percent of the votes, the Revisionists 21 percent, the General Zionists 36 percent, and the Mizrachi movement 14 percent. At the XVIII Congress in 1933, the breakdown was Labor 44 percent, Revisionists 14 percent, General Zionists 35 percent, and Mizrachi 12 percent. At the XIX Congress (1935), the results were Labor 45 percent, General Zionists 28 percent, Mizrachi 24 percent, and other political groups 11 percent. The plebiscite among Histadrut members took place on March 24, 1935. Among 29,024 out of 60,000 eligible voters who participated, 16,474 opposed the agreement and 11,522 favored it. See Ya'akov Goldstein and Ya'acov Shavit, *The Agreement between D. Ben-Gurion and V. Jabotinski and Its Failure, 1934–1935* (Tel Aviv:Yariv-Hadar [Hebrew] 1979), p. 134.

31. Third Mapai Convention, March 17–18, 1935, at Hadera [Hebrew], p. 36, Beit Berl Archive, 2-21-1935-18.

32. D. Ben-Gurion, Party Council, London Agreements Debate, January 4–5, 1935 [Hebrew], Beit Berl Archive, 2-22-1935, pp. 7–8.

33. Ibid., pp. 9–10.

34. Ibid., p. 9.

35. Ibid., p. 11.

36. B. Katznelson, "On the Labor Agreement with the Revisionists" (at the Party Council), Aug. 24, 1934, *Writings,* vol. 7, pp. 367–368.

37. B. Katznelson, Third Mapai Convention, 1935, March 18, 1935 [Hebrew], Beit Berl Archive, 2-21-1935-18.

38. Ibid., p. 13.

39. Ibid., p. 14.

40. See *Studies in the Palestine Partition Plans 1937–1947,* Edited by: Me'ir Avizohar and Isaiah Friedman (Sede Boqer: Ben-Gurion University of the Negev [Hebrew], 1984): (a) Anita Shapira, "The Perception of Time in the 1937 Partition Debate," pp. 21–39; and (b) Yisrael Kolatt, "The Partition Debate in the Labor Movement," pp. 40–54. See also Yosef Gorny, *The Arab Question and the Jewish Problem* (Tel Aviv: Am Oved [Hebrew], 1985), pp. 248–314.

41. See Dina Porat, *Leadership in a Trap* (Tel Aviv: Am Oved [Hebrew] 1986); Chava Eshkoli (Wegman), *Mapai in View of the Holocaust 1939–1942* (Jerusalem: Yad Izhak Ben Zvi [Hebrew], 1994); Yehiam Weitz, *Aware but Helpless, Mapai and the Holocaust 1943–1945,* (Jerusalem: Yad Izhak Ben-Zvi [Hebrew], 1994); Tuvia Friling, *Arrow in the Dark: David Ben-Gurion, the Yishuv Leadership, and Rescue Attempts during the Holocaust,* vols. A-B (Sede Boqer: The Hebrew University of Jerusalem and Ben-Gurion University of the Negev Press [Hebrew], 1998).

42. See Dina Porat, "The Question of Rescue in the Holocaust Era in View of 'Negation of the Diaspora' in the Yishuv," *Zionism,* 23 (2001) [Hebrew], pp. 175–194.

43. Fifth Mapai Convention, Third Session, October 25, 1942, at Kefar Vitkin [Hebrew], Beit Berl Archive, 2-21-1942-18, pp. 10–12

44. Ibid., p. 10.

45. Ibid., p. 12.

46. Ibid., ibid.

47. Y. Tabenkin, *Devarim*, vol. 4 (1943–1949) (Tel Aviv: Hakibbutz Hame'uchad [Hebrew], 1976), p. 33.

48. Ibid., p. 36.

49. Mapai Council 1940, Beit Berl, 2-22-1940-30 [Hebrew], pp. 14–16.

50. B. Katznelson, "In the Aftermath of a Conversation about the Diaspora," June 6, 1944, *Writings*, vol. 12 (Tel Aviv: Labor Party [Hebrew], [n.d.]), pp. 217–226.

51. Ibid., p. 219.

52. Ibid., p. 225.

53. B. Katznelson, "Chapters in the History of the [Zionist] Labor Movement," *Writings*, vol. 11 (Tel Aviv: Labor Party [Hebrew], 1953, 3rd edition), pp. 48-50.

54. Ibid., p. 55.

55. Ibid., p. 46. As for the Bund's stance on emigration, see note 53 below.

56. Ibid., p. 66.

57. Ibid., p. 37.

58. Ibid., p. 64.

59. Ibid., p. 50.

60. Ibid., p. 54.

61. B. Borochov, *Writings*, Vol.1 (Tel Aviv: Hakibbutz Hame'uhad [Hebrew], 1955), note 167, p. 484.

62. B. Katznelson, "Chapters in the History of the [Zionist] Labor Movement," *Writings*, vol. 11, p. 93.

63. The Bund ruled out emigration as a solution to the Jewish problem but did not oppose it as a way of alleviating unemployment and destitution among the Jews. See, for example, our discussion in chapter 5 about the settlement enterprise in Birobidjan. The Bund did not even oppose the emigration of some of its leaders to the United States, most notably in the case of Vladimir Medem. This was true *a fortiori* in the interwar era from the mid-1920s on, when the Western countries no longer offered refuge for masses of Jewish emigrants. Therefore, Katznelson must have been referring to the Bund's attitude before World War I.

64. B. Katznelson, "In the Birth Pangs of Man," *Writings*, vol. 5 (Tel Aviv: Labor Party [Hebrew], 2nd edition, 1953), p. 264.

65. Anita Shapira, *Berl*, vol. B, pp. 694–695.

66. Quoted from Yosef Heller, *The Struggle for the Jewish State: Zionist Policy 1936–1948* (Jerusalem: Zalman Shazar Center [Hebrew], 1985), p. 379.

CHAPTER 7. FROM BUND TO BUNDISM, 1947–1985

1. Emanuel Szerer, "Zin un gayst fun Brisel," *Unzer Tsayt*, September 1947.

2. When formed, the coordinating committee of Bund parties had twenty-nine representatives: eight from Poland, seven from the Americas, six

from France, three from Belgium, two from Great Britain, two from the DP camps, and one at large. Its budget was $90,000: $30,000 contributed by the Bund parties ($15,000 from New York) and $60,000 contributed by Jewish labor organizations. In the 1950s, the committee was downscaled to seventeen members (Bund ME 18/File 50, Kordinir-Komitet).

3. See debate between Emanuel Nowogrodzki and Jacob Pat, *Unzer Tsayt,* December 1946; see also Jacob Pat, *Unzer Tsayt,* September 1948; and Yosef Brumberg, *Unzer Tsayt,* December 1946.

4. E. Szerer, "Zin un gayst fun Brisel."

5. See Resolutions of the Second Convention, *Unzer Tsayt,* October–November 1948, and Resolutions of the Third Convention, *Unzer Tsayt,* May 1955.

6. E. Szerer, "Mit akhrayut farn haynt un morgn," *Unzer Tsayt,* May 1955.

7. Michael Newman, *Harold Laski, A Political Biography* (London: Macmillan, 1993), pp. 284–309.

8. E. Szerer, "Bundishe velt-kooperatsie," *Unzer Tsayt,* May 1946.

9. E. Szerer, "Di tekufa fun yidisher revolutsie," *Unzer Tsayt,* November–December 1947.

10. Liebman Hersch, "Di ideologishe evolutsie fun Bund," *Di Tsukunft* (May–June 1947).

11. Y. Y. Trunk, "Dialogn vegn yidishe kiyum frage," *Di Tsukunft* (January 1945). See also Trunk, "Problemn fun yidishn kiyum," *Unzer Tsayt,* November 1943.

12. Y. Y. Trunk, "Velt Bund," *Unzer Tsayt,* June 1946.

13. Y. Y. Trunk, "The Historical Roots of the Bund and Zionism" [Di historishe vortslen fun Bund un Tsiyonizm], *Unzer Tsayt,* February 1949.

14. Y. Y. Trunk, "The Historical Roots," *Unzer Tsayt,* March 1949.

15. Letter to M. B. Stein, YIVO, 1453–5B-File 11. See also I. I. Trunk,"Vos maynt yudisher sotsializm," February 28, 1954, YIVO, 114/1453.

16. See Y. Y. Trunk, discussion in "Di tsvayte velt konferents fun Bund," *Unzer Tsayt,* October–November 1948.

17. Professor L. Hersch, "Our Historical Dispute with Zionism" [Unzer historisher shtrayt mit tsiyonizm], *Unzer Tsayt,* August–September 1949.

18. Ibid., October 1949.

19. "Entfer fun der redaktsie," comment of the editorial board to this article of Professor L. Hersch, ibid.

20. Simon Rawidowicz, *Israel, the Ever-Dying People* (London/Toronto: Associated University Press, 1986), pp. 147–182.

21. "Di drite velt konferents fun Bund" [The proceedings of the third World Convention of the Bund], *Unzer Tsayt,* May 1955.

22. See Yosef Gorny, *The State of Israel in Jewish Public Thought: The Quest for Collective Identity* (New York/London: New York University Press and Macmillan, 1994), ch. 5.

23. Resolutions of the Third Convention.of the Bund (see note 21 above).

24. See (a) editorial, "Exodus from Poland," *Unzer Tsayt,* August–September 1946; (b) resolution of the Central Committee of the American Bund,

"Di lage fun yidn in Morocco," *Unzer Tsayt,* October 1955; (c) S. Milman, "Di yidn in Morocco," *Unzer Tsayt;* (d) C. S. Kazdan, "Exodus from Africa," *Unzer Tsayt,* November 1955.

25. E. Szerer, "Gedanken vegn bundizm," *Unzer Tsayt,* April–May 1957.
26. See Yosef Gorny, *The State of Israel in Jewish Public Thought,* ch. 2, pp. 41–53.
27. E. Szerer, "Neo-tsiyonizm un hiper-tsiyonizm," *Unzer Tsayt,* June 1955.
28. The expression is quoted from an article by E. Szerer in English on the history of the Bund, published evidently in the mid-1950s in a book about various phenomena in modern Jewish society. I do not know its name; a photocopy of Szerer's chapter in the book is in my possession.
29. See Joseph Dov Halevi Soloveichik, *'Ish Ha'emuna* [The Lonely Man of Faith] (Jerusalem: Mossad Harav Kook [Hebrew], 1978), pp. 86–95.
30. The lengthening of time between conventions was undoubtedly a reflection of the Bund's financial and organizational difficulties. The intervals were only one year between the first convention and the second, seven years between the second and the third, and ten years between the third and the fourth.
31. "Di ferte velt-konferents fun bund" [the proceedings of the Fourth World Convention of the Bund], *Unzer Tsayt,* June–July 1965.
32. See "Fifth Convention," *Unzer Tsayt,* June–July 1972; "Sixth Convention," *Unzer Tsayt,* November–December 1972; "Seventh Convention," *Unzer Tsayt,* November–December 1985.
33. "Resolutions of the Seventh Convention," *Unzer Tsayt* November–December 1985.
34. Karl Mannheim, *Ideology and Utopia* (New York: A Harvest Book, Harcourt, Brace and Company, 1936), p. 192.
35. See Alexander [Stein], "Unzer sotsialistisher kamf—kegn asimilatsie tendentsn in yidishn yishuv," *Unzer Shtime* (October 1, 1944); Alexander, "Asimilatsie un di yugent," *Unzer Shtime* (December 6, 1944).
36. C. S. Kazdan, "Der yidishe sotsializm un di yidishe problemn do in land," *Unzer Tsayt,* April–May 1948.
37. M. Kaplan, *A New Zionism* (Jerusalem: Me'orot, 1959). See also Gorny, *The State of Israel in Jewish Public Thought,* pp. 89–99.
38. Emanuel Nowogrodzki, *A nayer tsugang tsu alte emesn* (Buenos Aires: Bund publication, 1955).
39. Nowogrodzki, *A Nayer Tsugang,* p. 44.
40. E. Szerer, "Tifeh iberlebungen un groyse tsiln," *Unzer Tsayt,* May 1965.
41. E. Szerer, "A blik in yar 2000," *Unzer Tsayt,* December 1965. The article also appeared in the Bund newspaper in Paris, *Unzer Shtime,* on October 9, 1968, slightly amended and titled "*In dem yar 2000.*"
42. E. Szerer, "Sotsialistishe grunt fragn," *Unzer Tsayt,* April–May 1967.
43. See K. Mannheim, *Ideology and Utopia,* chapter 4 ("The Utopian Mentality"), and introduction to F. and F. Manuel, *Utopian Thought in the Western World,* (Cambridge, MA: The Belknap Press of Harvard University Press, 1979).
44. E. Szerer, "Yudishe grunt-fragn," *Unzer Tsayt,* June 1967.

45. E. Szerer," In Gayst fun Bundism," *Unzer Tsayt*, April–May 1972.

46. E. Szerer, "Nekhtn—haynt—morgn," *Unzer Tsayt*, November–December 1967.

47. E. Szerer, "In gayst fun bundizm," *Unzer Tsayt*, April–May 1972.

48. E. Szerer, "75 yar—un vayter—der historisher veg fun bund," *Unzer Tsayt*, October–December 1972.

49. Yitzhak Luden, "A nayer mentsh in a nayer gezelshaft," *Lebns Fragn* (November–December 1982).

50. Professor Arthur Lermer,"Fun Ahad Ha'am biz Dr. Goldmann—tsum anti-Herzlianer alternativn fun tsiyonizm," *Lebns Fragn* (November–December 1983). Over a four-year period, 1983–1987, Lermer published a series of articles in this journal, discussing the history of the national idea in the Bund, current cultural issues, and Israel–Diaspora relations.

51. Seventh Convention, *Unzer Tsayt*, November–December 1985.

CHAPTER 8. FROM ZIONIST KLAL TO JEWISH KLAL

1. The reference is to both parties—Mapai (Palestine Labor Party) and Mapam (United Labor Party)—which accounted for half or more of the Knesset (Parliament) in Israel's first decade.

2. See D. Ben-Gurion's meetings with intellectuals: *Meetings with Intellectuals—First Meeting, March 27, 1949; Second Meeting, October 11, 1949*; Ben-Gurion Archives, Ministry of Defense, Z.A. File 470. These discussions explored the question of the contribution of intellectuals to the absorption of two groups of immigrants, those from DP camps in Europe and those from Islamic countries.

3. See remarks by Mapam delegates to the XXIII Zionist Congress, held in Jerusalem in 1951: Ya'akov Hazan (p. 61) and Yisrael Bar Yehuda (p. 110), *Book of the Zionist Congress*, (Jerusalem: The Jewish Agency [Hebrew], 1952). See also debate in Mapai Secretariat ahead of meeting of Zionist Executive Council, Labor Party Archives, 2–24-1949–22.

4. Labor Party Archives, 2-21-1950-36.

5. Ibid., 2-21-1958-48.

6. In this matter see Gorny, *The State of Israel in Jewish Public Thought*, chapter 1, "The Tangle of Normalization 1942–1950," pp. 9–35, in which the concepts are discussed: "general normalization," "specific normalization," and "Jewish normalization." The last two mentioned belong to the differences in approach between Ben-Gurion and Silver.

7. See meeting of Zionist Executive Council, August 24, 1948, CZA 55/323.

8. See *The War of Independence, Ben-Gurion's Diary 1948–1949,* edited by G. Rivlin and Dr. E. Oren (Tel Aviv: Ministry of Defense Press [Hebrew], 1983), vol. 3, p. 892.

9. Ibid.

10. See Mapai Secretariat meeting, April 24, 1949, Labor Party Archives at Beit Berl, 24-1949–2-2.

11. The Zionist Movement and American Jewry 1948–1963, Ministry of Defense 62/161, File 656.

12. See Naomi W. Cohen, *Not Free to Desist, A History of The American Jewish Committee 1906–1966* (Philadelphia: The Jewish Publication Society of America, 1972), pp. 311–315.

13. See Yosef Gorny, "The 'Utopian Leap' in David Ben-Gurion's Social Thought 1920–1958," In *Israel—The First Decade of Independence,* edited by Ilan S. Troen and Noah Lucas (Albany: State University of New York Press, 1995), pp. 125–142.

14. See Naomi W. Cohen, *Not Free to Desist.*

15. David Ben-Gurion, "American Jewry and the State of Israel (1951)," in *Vision and Path C* (Tel Aviv: Labor Party [Hebrew], 1953), p. 150ff.

16. D. Ben-Gurion, "The Status of the Zionist Organization in Israel (May 5, 1952)," in *Vision and Path C*, pp. 13–22.

17. D. Ben-Gurion, "Remarks in Response," *Vision and Path,* pp. 23–24.

18. D. Ben-Gurion, "Letter to Shimon Diglin," Ministry of Defense, Ben-Gurion Archives, 62/161, File 656.

19. D. Ben-Gurion, "An Attachment to the Eternity of Israel," *Vision and Path E*, p. 62.

20. D. Ben-Gurion, "Files for Study of Issues in Zionism, Nation, and State," *Hazut D* (1958): 167.

21. David Ben-Gurion, "An Exemplary State, Goal and Means," *Vision and Path E*, p. 81.

22. D. Ben-Gurion, "Between Israel and Exile," *Vision and Path E*, p. 87.

23. Ben-Gurion, *Hazut D* (1958): 167.

24. See correspondence between Proskauer and Ben-Gurion, May 31, 1960, July 7, 1960, Ben-Gurion Archives 13/804. See also Hannah Yablonka, *The State of Israel* vs. *Adolf Eichmann* (Jerusalem: Yad Izhak Ben-Zvi [Hebrew] 2001), ch. 2, pp. 59–67.

25. "To Explore an Issue—Exchange of Letters between D. Ben-Gurion and N. Rotenstreich," *Hazut C* (1957), p. 29. See also Hannah Yablonka, *The State of Israel.*

26. N. Rotenstreich, "Conceptual Exploration of the Essence of the Jewish Exile," in *Al Ha-temura, Perakim bi-she'elot Ha'am ve-hamedina* [On the Change, Chapters on Issues of People and State] (Tel Aviv: Am Oved [Hebrew], 1953).

27. N. Rotenstreich, "Parallel Tracks," in *On the Change*, pp. 91–94.

28. N. Rotenstreich, "Putting the Spiritual Center Idea to the Test," in *On the Change*, pp. 85–108.

29. N. Rotenstreich, "Between a People and Its State," in *On the Change*, pp. 109–118.

30. See also Simon Rawidowicz, *Israel The Ever-Dying People.*

31. See Simon Rawidowicz, "Between Israel and Israel," *Hazut A* (1953), and N. Rotenstreich's response, "A Unity with Substance Attached," *Hazut A* (1953).

32. See Yosef Gorny, *The Quest for Collective Identity*.

8-33. Nathan Rothenstreich, "Israel and World Jewry 1962," *Congress Biweekly*, 1962.

33. Nathan Rotenstreich, "Temurot ba-yehasim she-beyn medinat Israel ve-golat Israel," in *'Iyunim ba-zionut ba-zeman ha-ze* [Examining Zionism Today] (Jerusalem: Hassifria Hatsionit, 1977), pp. 38–43.

34. See Yosef Gorny, *Between Auschwitz and Jerusalem* (London and Portland, OR: Vallentine Mitchell, 2003), ch. 4.

CONCLUSION

1. "The Guiding Principles of Reform Judaism—Columbus 1937," Central Conference of American Rabbis, 1999. See also Michael Meyer, *Between Tradition and Progress: History of the Jewish Reform Movement* (Jerusalem: Zalman Shazar Center [Hebrew], 1980), pp. 374, 384, and 450.

2. In regard to da'at Torah, see Gershon Bacon, "Da'at Torah and the Pangs of the Messiah: on the Question of the Ideology of Agudath Israel in Poland," in *Between Authority and Autonomy in Jewish Tradition*, edited by Ze'ev Safray and Avi Sagi (Tel Aviv: Hakibbutz Hame'uhad [Hebrew], 1997), pp. 84–94, and Jacob Katz, "Da'at ha-Torah—the Claiming of Unlimited Powers by the Halakhic Masters," in *Between Authority and Autonomy*, pp. 95–104.

3. See Avi'ezer Ravitzky, *Messianism, Zionism, and Jewish Religious Radicalism*, (Tel Aviv: Am Oved, [Hebrew] 1993), pp. 63–66.

4. See Shlomo Netzer, *The Struggle of Polish Jewry for Civil and National Minority Rights 1918–1922*, p. 150; Emanuel Melzer, *Political Strife in a Blind Alley, The Jews in Poland 1935–1939*, p. 261.

5. See Shmuel Dotan, *The Partition Dispute in the Mandate Era* (Jerusalem: Yad Izhak Ben-Zvi [Hebrew], 1980), ch. 3; and Shulamit Eliash, "The Zionist and non-Zionist Religious Attitude toward the 1937–1938 Palestine Partition Plan," in *Studies on Partition Plans 1937–1947* (Be'ersheva: Ben-Gurion University of the Negev [Hebrew] 1984). See also Yosef Pound, "Zionist Symbolism in the Symbols of Agudath Israel," *Zionism* 23 (2001 [Hebrew]), pp. 35–48.

6. A. Nerezshin, *Bundizm un tsiyonizm* (with introduction by V. Medem), (Warsaw: Lebens Fragn Press, 1918).

SELECTED BIBLIOGRAPHY

A. ARCHIVES

1. YIVO, New York
   Bund 1897–1939, MG 1, MG 2, MG 4, MG 6, MG9, MG10, MG 12
   I. I. Trunk—private collection
2. The Labor Party Archive, Beit Berl, Israel
3. Ahdut ha-ʿAvoda Archive, Lavon Institute, Tel Aviv, Israel

B. NEWSPAPERS AND PERIODICALS

In Hebrew

Davar—1925–1957 (newspaper)
Ha-ʾahdut—1910–1914 (journal)
Ha-poʿel ha-Tsaʿir—1906–1914 (journal)
Kuntres—1920–1930 (journal)

In Yiddish

Der Anfang (journal)
Di Tsayt (journal)
Di Tsukunft—1920–1985, New York (journal)
Folks Tsaytung—1922–1925, Warsaw (newspaper)
Naye FolksTsaytung—1926–1939, Warsaw (newspaper)
Lebens Fragn—1912–1920, Warsaw (journal)
Lebens Fragn—1951–1983, Tel Aviv (journal)
Shul un Leben—1921–1925, Warsaw (journal)
Unzer Shtime—1944–1995, Paris (newspaper)
Unzer Tsayt—1927–1932, Warsaw (journal)
Unzer Tsayt—1947–1990, New York (journal)

C. BOOKS ABOUT THE BUND

In Hebrew

Barzilai, Zvi. *The Bund Movement in Poland between the World Wars,* Jerusalem: Carmel, 1994.

Blatman, Daniel. *For Our Freedom and Yours: The Bund in Poland 1939–1949,* Jerusalem: Yad Vashem & The Hebrew University, 1996. [And in English, London: Vallentine Mitchell, 2003].

Edelman, Marek. *The Ghetto Fights: Young Members of the Bund in the Warsaw Ghetto,* ed. and introduction by Daniel Blatman, Tel Aviv, Hakibbutz Hame'uhad, 2001.

Frankel, Jonathan. *Prophecy and Politics: Socialism, Nationalism, and Russian Jewry 1862–1917,* Tel Aviv: Am Oved, 1989. [And in English: *Prophecy and Politics: Socialism, Nationalism, and the Russian Jews, 1862–1917,* Cambridge University Press, 1981].

Gelbard, Arye. Editor, *The Russian Bund in the Year of Revolutions, 1917, Documents and Decisions,* Tel Aviv, Tel Aviv University, 1984.

Medem, Vladimir. *Vladimir Medem, The legend of the Jewish workers movement, Memoirs,* Tel Aviv: Y.L. Peretz, 1984.

Mishkinski, Moshe. *The Inception of the Labor Movement in Russia—Basic Trends,* Tel Aviv: Hakibbutz Hame'uhad, 1981.

Peled, Yoav. *Cultural Autonomy and Class Struggle: Development of the National Platform of the Bund 1893–1903,* Tel Aviv: Hakibbutz Hame'uhad, 1997.

In Other Languages

Getzler, Israel. "The Jewish Bund and the Dignity of Man", In *Religion, Ideology and Nationalism in Europe and America, Essays Presented in Honor of Yehoshua Arieli,* 547–577, Jerusalem: The Historical Society of Israel, 1986, pp.

Goldstein, Ya'acov N. *Jewish Socialists in the United States: The Cahan Debate 1925–1926,* Brighton UK & Portland, Oregon: Sussex Academic Press, 1988.

Jacobs, Jack L. Editor. *Jewish Politics in Eastern Europe: The Bund at 100,* New York: New York University Press, 2001.

Jacobs, Jack. "Bundist Anti-Zionism in Interwar Poland", In *Antisemitismus, Antizionismus Israelkritik, Tel Aviv: Wallstein Verlag, Tel Aviver Jahrbuch für deutsche Geschichte,* 2005, pp. 239–259.

Johnpoll, Bernard K. *The Politics of Futility: The General Jewish Workers Bund of Poland 1917–1943,* Ithaca, N.Y.: Cornell University Press, 1967.

Marcus, Joseph. *Social and Political History of the Jews in Poland 1919–1939,* Berlin: Mouton, 1983.

Mendelsohn, Ezra. *Jewish Politics in East Central Europe Between The World Wars,* Cambridge: Harvard University Press, 1984.

Minczeles, Henri. *Histoire Ge'ne'rale du Bund: Un mouvement revolutionaire Juif,* Paris: Austral, 1995.

Nowogrodzki, Emanuel. *The Jewish Labor Bund in Poland 1915–1939,* New York: Shengold Books, 2001.

Pickhan, Gertrud. *"Gegen den Strom": Der Allgemeine Judische Arbeiterbund "Bund" in Polen 1918–1939,* Deutsche Verlags-Anstalt Stuttgart Munich: Schriften des Simon-Dubnow-Instituts Leipzig, 2001.

Polonsky, Antony. "The Bund in Polish Political Life 1935–1939." In *Jewish History: Essays in Honor of Chimen Abramsky,* 547–577. Edited by Ada Rapoport-Albert and Steven Zipperstein, London: P. Halban, 1988.

Tobias, Henry J. *The Jewish Bund in Russia from Its Origins to 1905,* Stanford, California: Stanford University Press, 1972.

D. BOOKS ABOUT THE LABOR MOVEMENT IN POLAND AND PALESTINE (ALL IN HEBREW)

Avizohar, Me'ir. *In a Cracked Mirror: Social and National Ideals and Their Reflection in the World of Mapai,* Tel Aviv: Am Oved, 1990.

Ahad Ha'am. *Ketavim* [Writings], Tel Aviv: Devir, 1950.

Aharonovich, Yosef. *Ketavim,* Writings, Tel Aviv: Am Oved, 1941.

Ben-Gurion, David. *Igrot* [Letters], vol. I, Tel Aviv: Am Oved, 1972.

Ben-Gurion, David. *Mi-ma'amad La'am* [From Class to People], Tel Aviv: Davar, 1933.

Ben-Gurion, David. *Hazon Va-Derech* [Vision and Path], vol. III, vol. IV, vol. V, Tel Aviv: Labor Party, 1951–1953.

Ben-Zvi, Yitzhak. *Po'alei Zion ba'Aliya ha-Shniya,* Tel Aviv: Labor Party, 1951.

Borochov, Dov Ber. *Writings,* Tel Aviv: Hakibbutz Hame'uhad, vol. I, 1955; vol. II, 1958; vol. III, 1966.

Gorny, Yosef. *Achdut ha-'Avoda 1919–1930—The Ideological principles and the Political System,* Tel Aviv: Ha-kibbutz Ha-me'uchad, 1973.

Gorny, Yosef. *Ha-hipus ahar ha-zehut ha-le'umit,* [The Quest for Collective Identity], Tel Aviv: Am Oved, 1986. [*The State of Israel in Jewish Public Thought,* New York: New York University Press, 1994.]

Katznelson, Berl. *Igrot* [letters], Tel Aviv: Am Oved, vol. II, 1974.

Katznelson, Berl. *Ketavim* [Writings], Tel Aviv: Labor Party, vol. I, 3rd edition, 1950; vol V, 2nd edition, 1953, vol. VI, 1947; vol. VII. 1948; vol. XI. 3rd edition, 1953; vol. XII, 2nd edition, [n.d.].

Katznelson, Berl. *Darki le-'Eretz Israel* [My Way to Eretz Israel], Tel Aviv: Ayanot, 1945, 1965 (revised edition).

Mintz, Matityahu. *Pangs of Youth 'Hashomer Haza'ir' 1911–1921,* Jerusalem: Hassifria Hazionit, 1995.

Oppenheim, Yisrael. *The "Hehalutz" Movement in Poland 1917–1929*, Jerusalem: The Magnes Press, 1982.

Oppenheim, Yisrael. *The Hehalutz Movement in Poland 1929–1939,* Sede Boqer: Ben-Gurion University of the Negev Press, 1993.

Rawidowicz, Simon. *Israel, The Ever-Dying People,* Rutherford: Fairleigh Dickinson University Press, 1984; London and Toronto: Associated University Presses, 1986 [English].

Rotenstreich, Nathan. *Al ha-Temura: Perakim Bi-Sheʾelot Haʿam ve-hamedina* [On the Change: Chapters on Issues of People and State], Tel Aviv: Am Oved, 1953.

Rotenstreich, Nathan. *Iyunim ba-Tsiyonut ba-Zeman ha-ze* [Examining Zionism Today], Jerusalem: Hassifria Hazionit, 1977.

Sarid, Levi. *The Pioneers – "Hechalutz" and the Youth Movements in Poland, 1917–1939,* Tel Aviv: Am Oved, 1979.

Shapira, Anita. *Berl,* Tel Aviv: Am Oved, 1980.

Shapira, Yosef. *Ha-poʿel Ha-Tzaʿir,* Tel Aviv: Ayanot, 1967.

Yalkut Ha-ʾAhdut, Edited by Yaʿakov Zerubavel, Tel Aviv: Am Oved, 1962.

Zerubavel, Yaʿakov. *Alei Hayim* Leafs of Life], Tel Aviv: Y.L. Peretz, 1966.

E. BOOKS ABOUT THE POLITICAL SITUATION OF POLISH JEWRY (ALL IN HEBREW)

Melzer, Emanuel. *Political Strife in a Blind Alley: The Jews in Poland 1935–1939,* Tel Aviv: The Diaspora Research Institute, 1982.

Mendelsohn, Ezra. *The Zionism in Poland: The Formative Years, 1915–1926,* Jerusalem: Hassifria Hazionit, 1986. [And in English, New Haven:Yale University Press, 1981].

Netzer, Shlomo. *The Struggle of Polish Jewry for Civil and National Minority Rights (1918–1922),* Tel Aviv: Tel Aviv University, 1980.

F. THEORETICAL LITERATURE

Anderson, Benedict. *Imagined Communities,* London: Verso, New Left Books, 1983, 1991.

Ben-Israel, Hedva. *In the Name of the Nation: Studies in Nationalism and Zionism,* Sede Boqer: Ben-Gurion University of the Negev, 2004 [Hebrew].

Ben-Israel, Hedva. "Theories of Nationalism and their Application to Zionism," *Zionism: A Contemporary Controversy,* Ben-Gurion and Tel Aviv Universities, 1996, pp. 203–222 [Hebrew].

Dubnow, Simon. *Mikhtavim al ha-yahadut ha-yeshana ve-ha-hadasha* [Letters on the Old and and New Jewry], Tel Aviv: Devir, [Hebrew], 1937.

Gellner, Ernest. *Nations and Nationalism,* Oxford: Basil Blackwell, 1983.

Hobsbawm, E. J. *Nations and Nationalism Since 1780,* Cambridge: Cambridge University Press, 1990.

Jacoby, Danny. Editor. *From National Movement to State,* Jerusalem: The Magnes Press, 2002 [Hebrew].

Kedourie, Elie. *Nationalism,* London: Hutchinson, 1985 (3rd edition).

Kohn, Hans. *Nationalism: Its Meaning and History,* Princeton, NJ: Van Nostrand Company, 1955.

Seton-Watson, Hugh. *Nations and States,* London: Methuen, 1977.

Shimoni, Gideon. *The Zionist Ideology,* Waltham, MA: Brandeis University Press, 1995.

Smith, Anthony D. *Nations and Nationalism in a Global Era,* Cambridge and Oxford: Polity Press, 1995,1996, 1998, 2000.

Smith, Anthony D. *The Nation in History,* MA: University Press of New England, 2000.

INDEX

Made in the USA
Las Vegas, NV
02 September 2021